SEASONS UNDER THE JUNIPER TREE

A Daily Devotional

Tricia Kirchmeyer

CLAY BRIDGES
P R E S S

Seasons under the Juniper Tree
A Daily Devotional

Copyright © 2020 by Tricia Kirchmeyer
Illustrated by Jenny Shute

Published by Clay Bridges in Houston, TX
www.claybridgespress.com

All rights reserved. No part of this publication may be reproduced, stored in a retrieval system, or transmitted in any form by any means, electronic, mechanical, photocopy, recording, or otherwise, without the prior permission of the publisher, except as provided for by USA copyright law.

Unless otherwise indicated, all Scripture quotations are taken from the New American Standard Bible® (NASB), Copyright © 1960, 1962, 1963, 1968, 1971, 1972, 1973, 1975, 1977, 1995 by The Lockman Foundation. Used by permission. www.Lockman.org.

Scripture quotations marked (MSG) are taken from THE MESSAGE, copyright © 1993, 1994, 1995, 1996, 2000, 2001, 2002 by Eugene H. Peterson. Used by permission of NavPress. All rights reserved. Represented by Tyndale House Publishers, Inc.

Scripture quotations marked (NIV) are taken from the Holy Bible, New International Version®, NIV®. Copyright ©1973, 1978, 1984, 2011 by Biblica, Inc.™ Used by permission of Zondervan. All rights reserved worldwide. www.zondervan.com The "NIV" and "New International Version" are trademarks registered in the United States Patent and Trademark Office by Biblica, Inc.™

Scripture quotations marked (NLT) are taken from the Holy Bible, New Living Translation, copyright ©1996, 2004, 2007, 2013, 2015 by Tyndale House Foundation. Used by permission of Tyndale House Publishers, Inc., Carol Stream, Illinois 60188. All rights reserved.

Some verses have been paraphrased in the author's wording.

ISBN: 978-1-68488-003-4 (paperback)
ISBN 978-1-68488-002-7 (ebook)

Special Sales: Most Clay Bridges titles are available in special quantity discounts. Custom imprinting or excerpting can also be done to fit special needs. For standard bulk orders, go to www.claybridgesbulk.com. For specialty press or large orders, contact Clay Bridges at info@claybridgespress.com.

THANK YOU

Tom Jr., Tom 3, Kristy, and Kyle
Also Brianne, Carson, Brady, and Cameron
You are the loves of my life.

Thank you, Valerie and Michael

DEDICATION

To Cathy, Deanne, Jenny, Karen, Marlene, and my sister Valerie—special, gutsy ladies who have taught me so much through the lives they live and their beautiful hearts.

To Terrie. There are no words. We've cried, we've sat stunned, we've eaten, we've laughed, we've become the Green Berets of prayer warriors, and we've stood strong.

To all kids in the foster system, to all families in the family court system, and to those of us who've royally blown it—there is hope.

To Casey and Ellie—warriors and thrivers.

Most importantly, I dedicate this devotional to my Savior, Jesus Christ. Be magnified and glorified through these words.

CONTENTS

A Note from the Author   1

Autumn

Introduction		5
Week 1	Elijah	6
Week 2	Esther	15
Week 3	Esther	24
Week 4	Life of Jesus	33
Week 5	Moses	42
Week 6	Israelites	52
Week 7	Israelites	61
Week 8	David	71
Week 9	Jonathan	81
Week 10	Joseph	91
Week 11	Jesus's Arrest	100
Week 12	Thanksgiving	109
Week 13	Isaiah 40	117

Winter

Introduction		129
Week 1	David the Shepherd	130
Week 2	David the Shepherd	139
Week 3	Adam and Eve	148
Week 4	Christmas	157
Week 5	Micah	166
Week 6	Paul	175
Week 7	Paul	184
Week 8	Luke 15	193
Week 9	Isaiah 43	202
Week 10	1 John	212
Week 11	1 John	221
Week 12	Love	231
Week 13	Love	240

Spring

Introduction		251
Week 1	David and Bathsheba	252
Week 2	David and Bathsheba	262
Week 3	Job	272
Week 4	Job	282
Week 5	Peter	292
Week 6	Easter	303
Week 7	Easter	313
Week 8	Daniel	323
Week 9	Hebrews	333
Week 10	Acts	343
Week 11	Kings	353
Week 12	Jonah	363
Week 13	Jonah	373
Special	Mother's Day	383
Holiday	Father's Day	385

Summer

Introduction		389
Week 1	Jesus	390
Week 2	Noah	400
Week 3	Noah	410
Week 4	Isaiah 11	420
Week 5	Touched by Jesus	430
Week 6	Elisha	441
Week 7	Elisha	451
Week 8	The Church	461
Week 9	Joshua	471
Week 10	Fruit of the Spirit	482
Week 11	Revelation 20–22	492
Week 12	Armor of God	502
Week 13	Isaiah 53–55	512

Salvation	523
Author Bio	525
Notes	527

A NOTE FROM THE AUTHOR

Originally, I wrote *Seasons under the Juniper Tree* as a devotional for kids in a private foster organization. It took me a couple months talking with these children to realize that all of us—adults and children, in the system or in single-family homes—experience different degrees of the same things throughout life. They are the hard times, the brokenness, the injustice, the gut-wrenching events, the insecurities—the smiles, the victories, the healing, and the confidence.

Then this devotional—this walk with God through His living, loving words in the Bible—transformed into a book for all people.

At the first writing, I was a wife, a mom of three, a daughter, and a sister. I had worked in the K–12 public school system, been a mentor and Bible study teacher, and worked as a nanny for multiple families. As of this publishing, I can add grandma of three, volunteer in the juvenile justice system, volunteer for a crisis pregnancy center, and friend to parents of thriving children and kids struggling with substance addictions. I walk beside friends who have experienced sexual assault, family rejection, betrayal, manipulative relationships, and more.

Do you know what I know to be true? God's Word, the Bible, covers every part of our lives. God loves us, incredibly so. He has given us tools, wisdom, courage, and strength to get through this tough life. He gives do-overs, lots of them. He accepts us, never leaves us, shelters us, and saves us. And have I mentioned that He loves us?

Come. Join me under the shelter of a juniper tree. It's a scrappy, durable evergreen that can protect us through every season of life. It's the perfect picture of God.

Instead of the thornbush will grow the juniper, and instead of the briers, the myrtle will grow. This will be for the Lord's renown, for an everlasting sign that will endure forever (Isa. 55:3).

AUTUMN

AUTUMN

INTRODUCTION

I love fall. The air is cool and crisp, sweeping through trees while their leaves change colors. Thoughts turn to school and seeing friends, and teachers who've been absent from our lives all summer long. Outside, flowers, vegetables, and leaves are giving us their last beauty and taste of life. Yet the hearts and minds of most people are budding with the newness of the start of the school year, sports, and new school clothes.

That's the picture we see on advertisements, isn't it? For some people, that is their autumn reality. Others find the season outside mirrored in their everyday living. The cool breeze coming from cold or absent family members isn't refreshing. A bone-deep chill stiffens their hearts and minds as they try once again to succeed in school and work while surviving family life.

Instead of savoring the last fresh fruits and vegetables or the beauty of the falling leaves, some see the whole experience as a time of dying. Hope, confidence, and courage have withered and blown away. The air is full of fear . . . of the unknown and the authority of those who can change lives in just a few words. It tastes bitter to think of the trust that was betrayed yet again.

Grab a sweater, and let's go together into this autumn season and see how God[1] through His Son, Jesus, and in the power of His Holy Spirit walks with us. We will experience being in His presence through all the phases of this changing season. And we will gain His perspective, learn to see through His eyes, and finally understand the truth of how autumn's ending and dying season leads to new life.

---

1. God is the Trinity. This is hard to completely understand, but a good picture is an egg. One egg is made up of three components—shell, white (albumen), and yolk. In the Bible, God tells us He is one God but triune—three in one—Father, Son (Jesus), and Spirit.

Week 1

ELIJAH

Day 1

Life has changed yet again. What are we doing here, back in a routine we hate or fear, away from everything familiar? The start of school or a new job feels like the start of a broken treadmill. We jump on and start running, but it leads to nowhere. We try to keep up and please someone—anyone—but in the end, our efforts seem to fail. Our families are still broken, our hearts are still frozen and wounded, and we still have no control.

Worse than anything, though, is the feeling of being completely alone—alone in hating this time of year, alone in fighting to survive more change, alone in the middle of a group of people we don't know and can't risk trusting. Alone.

Elijah was a man in the Old Testament of the Bible who felt very alone and completely defeated too. He loved and obeyed God when most of the people and all the leaders did not. Bravely, Elijah confronted 450 prophets of the idol Baal and the people of Israel with God's truth. God showed that He is real and powerful by sending fire from heaven to consume Elijah's sacrifice and altar after Baal's prophets failed in their attempts.

The fight and success Elijah experienced turned to fear when he heard the queen wanted to kill him. Without thinking about what God had just done, he took off running for his life into the wilderness. Elijah threw himself under a juniper tree and said, "I have had enough, Lord. Take my life, for I am as good as dead anyway." And he fell asleep.

Listen to how God responds to Elijah and to you and me in the dying, defeating, fearful, exhausting times of our lives. An angel touched Elijah and told him, "Get up and eat!" Elijah looked around and saw some bread baked on hot stones and a jar of water. So he ate and drank and lay down again. The angel of the Lord came back a second time and touched him and said, "Arise, eat because the journey is too great for you" (1 Kings 19:7).

Isn't that an amazing kind of love? God didn't chew Elijah out. God didn't give him a good pep talk and push him back into the fight. Our loving God lets you, me, and Elijah sleep. He took care of the most basic needs we have—food, water, and rest. Patiently God allowed Elijah to take in his new place under the juniper tree, eat, and heal. But God let Elijah know that he would indeed keep on living and traveling through life. "Eat, for the journey is too much for you." Sometimes you and I can't go on another step until we let God fill us up.

"Come to Me, all who are weary and heavy-laden," Jesus said, "and I will give you rest" (Matt. 11:28). Jesus taught, "I am the bread of life; he who comes to Me will not hunger, and he who believes in Me will never thirst" (John 6:35).

Tell Jesus how you feel in this time of your life. Give Him your hurts and problems, even your anger with Him. And ask Him to give you His rest. Read His Word, the Bible, and be fed with His promise, strength, and wisdom. He will give you His eyes to see that this autumn of dying wishes and cold change will begin the process of new life and lasting beauty.

Bible Reading: **1 Kings 18:1–19:8 (The NIV, NLT, and NKJV call the juniper tree a broom tree.)**

Day 2

How is it we can feel alone in the midst of a crowd—alone even though friends and family are right next to us and talking with us? People may tell us we are not the only ones who have experienced certain hurts and injustices, and others may share that they think and feel the same way we do. Yet still . . . we feel alone.

Remember, Elijah felt that same way. When he met Obadiah in 1 Kings 18, Obadiah told him that he loved God and was faithful to Him. In fact, at great risk to himself, Obadiah had hidden 100 of God's prophets in caves to protect them from death.

Fast forward to 1 Kings 19:8–18. After taking in the rest and food God had provided, Elijah started back on his journey through life. He traveled

40 days and ended up in a cave where God finally asked, "What are you doing here, Elijah?" Twice Elijah answered, "I have been very zealous [passionate] for the Lord, the God of hosts; for the sons of Israel have forsaken Your covenant, torn down Your altars and killed Your prophets with the sword. And I alone am left; and they seek my life, to take it away" (verses 10 and 14).

Perspective is the key to all our feelings. The truth was that Elijah was not alone. We just read that at least 100 other people in Israel loved God. And God had given Elijah that encounter as a reassurance that others were with him. But Elijah, like you and me, was human. The events he lived through and stood strong in were huge. In the midst of it, Elijah's eyes were fixed on God. That was survival. He was so far out of his range of ability and comfort that God was the only choice. Once it was over, once the adrenaline rush faded and the enormity of where he was and what had happened settled in, he caved in.

I'm alone, God! Abandoned, isolated, and cut off. We start to look in, only seeing ourselves, our pain, our efforts, and our failures. Our head goes down, our eyes tear up, and all we see is us—barely able to stand, alone.

King David found in God the same thing Elijah did. David said in Psalm 3:3, "But You, O Lord, are a shield about me, my glory, and the One who lifts my head." God our Father puts His fingers under our chins and gently lifts our heads. "You are not alone. I am always with you," He says. Then He shows us others in our world who are with us too.

God told Elijah in 1 Kings 19:18 that there were 7,000 people who had never bowed to Baal, the false god. They were just like Elijah who knew what it felt like to fight for rightness and justice. God says the same thing to you and me. We are not alone. Most people may not understand what we are going through, but a lot do. They understand and care. They fight the same fight we do.

God is always with us—always. Sometimes He slips his hand into the "glove" of a person in our lives, and that person gently lifts our head, helps us fight our fight, and loves us where we are. As Jesus prepared to go back to heaven after His death and resurrection, He said, "And lo, I am with you always, even to the end of the age" (Matt. 28:20).

We may feel alone, but that does not make it a fact. The truth—the glorious, reassuring truth—is that God stands with us and has brought other people to stand with us too.

***Bible Reading*: 1 Kings 19, Psalm 3**

Day 3

Elijah started his journey with an experience some of us may have had. Everyone around Elijah was making bad choices. A long line of kings had disobeyed God and started worshipping idols, and most of the people followed without objection. So Elijah, who was just a regular man, went and told the king that as the Lord God of Israel lives, there would be no rain or dew for years, except by His word (1 Kings 17:1).

Do you know how God rewarded him for his brave obedience? He warned Elijah to go away from there and hide himself. God allowed His faithful servant to be on the run for his life. Chapter 17 shows us that God did protect Elijah and provide for his needs, but let's take this personally. Would we be happy with that?

Some of us have stood alone in our fight for justice, safety, and fairness. We've seen neglect, substance, and power abuse go unnoticed by people who should care and help. Finally, we speak of the truth to someone, and *WHAM*, the bottom drops out of our world. Our honorable and courageous stance hits us in the face. With fear and anger we think, "I've done everything properly! I stood for the right thing, and now I have no control. Where is God in this?"

Look back to Elijah. Eventually he ended up staying with a poor widow and her son, and God miraculously kept her flour and oil jars full. Then her son died, and listen to Elijah's words to God. "O Lord my God, have You also brought calamity to the widow with whom I am staying, by causing her son to die?" (1 Kings 17:20).

What telling words! "Have You *also* brought calamity to the widow?" Do you think Elijah was feeling as if God had already brought calamity or disaster into his own life? None of his past years looked like he thought they would. He would do the hard and right thing and be the hero—at least to God. God would allow him to stay in his home and not be affected by the drought, right? Wrong! Elijah had to leave everything and everyone at his home and go to a different, new place. God provided for all his needs, but with just enough. There was no luxury or abundance.

The word *perspective* comes to mind here. From our perspective (point of view, angle), living with a strange family, having just enough to eat, and death are bad. From God's perspective, it looks different. He sees the big picture—years down the road as well as this very moment. God sees all the people touched by our circumstance. We see ourselves and the obvious ones in our immediate life. What is God's lesson to us? Just because it hurts doesn't make it bad. Just because it feels good doesn't make it right. The truth is that God does allow us to experience pain and injustice for a time, maybe a long time. But we were created for eternal life, and this life here is like a vapor, just a short time (James 4:14).

David finally reached God's point of view after many victories, mistakes, and much pain in his life. In Psalm 145 he praised God's goodness through it all. The Lord is gracious and merciful, slow to anger and great in lovingkindness. The Lord is good to all, and His mercies are over all His works. The Lord sustains all who fall and raises up all who are bowed down. God will hear our cry and save us because He sees, He cares, and He is good.

Bible Reading: **1 Kings 17, Psalm 145**

Day 4

Fear. Every person has felt it. Imagine the strongest, most dominant soldier; the wisest, most powerful leader; the godliest, most faithful believer. Picture a small child, an old grandparent . . . you. One of the things that puts all these people on common ground is fear.

To those of us on the outside, Elijah looked indestructible. He was a G.I. Joe for God. He faced off thousands with God as his only backup. God asked Elijah to trust Him to do impossible things, and Elijah did. Elijah asked God to do unbelievable things in front of a watching nation, and God did. Then the queen threatened to kill Elijah . . . and he slammed into the wall of fear.

Being afraid causes us to think and do things that make no sense. Even animals become crazed with fear and put themselves in harm's way in their attempt to get safe. Frightened horses run into a barn to get to their stalls when it catches on fire. When they are scared witless, they run to a familiar yet dangerous place trying to find a feeling of security.

So what is the thread that ties Elijah, horses, you, and me together in our fear? It is our perspective. We stand frozen, staring at what is causing our fear. The flames leap higher, and the threat grows bigger until all we see and know are the danger and the fear.

Psalm 112 gives us a guideline, a lifeline, on how to get through our fear. Verse 1 says how blessed is the one who fears the Lord. Now this fear is different from terror. This word means being in awe of the Lord, respecting the Lord so much that we are careful and reverent with Him. When we know God very personally and deeply, we can't help but be amazed by Him, in awe of His power and abilities, and completely aware of His authority over the universe and our life's details.

Verse 6 says a person who looks at God this way will never be shaken, crazed, or overcome by fear. Verses 7 and 8 go on to say we will have no fear of evil news, and our heart will be fixed, trusting in the Lord. Our heart will be secure, and we will have no fear. In the end, we will look in triumph on our enemies.

Elijah looked his fear straight in the eye and got trapped in it. Horses fix their eyes and brains on the fire and let it overcome them. I've done the same thing. How about you? We put the object of our fear in God's place. We start to think it is all-powerful, in control of everything, even mightier than God. If we dare look away from the fear, it is only to look at ourselves and then quickly back at our circumstances.

Stop! If we can't look away at first, we can cry out to God and ask Him to pull our minds to Him. We can ask Him to give us the strength to flick our eyes from our problem to His face, from ourselves to His Word. He will do it. He has in the past, He is right now, and He always will be there for us to focus on and lean on. In another version of the Bible, verse 8 says the heart of a person who fears the Lord will be *upheld* (instead of the word *secure*). God will hold our heart close to Him and up high—too high for the snarling dogs to jump and bite, too high for the flames to reach. We may still be in a dangerous or scary situation, but our minds, hearts, and focus are not. They are centered and stuck on our solution—God.

Bible Reading: 1 Kings 19:1-3, Psalm 112, John 16:32-33

Day 5

There are few emotions as crippling as grief. It is so much more than sorrow and deeper than sadness. Grief can cause an ache in our bones and a despair in our hearts that words cannot tell. The dying of a loved one brings an obvious grief, but we are sometimes blindsided when it hits us from another area.

Elijah's grief caused him to cry out, question God, and want to curl up and sleep until it all went away. The first time we see it is when the widow, wracked with her own grief, tells Elijah her son is dead. "What do I have to do with you, O man of God? You have come to me to bring my iniquity to remembrance and to put my son to death!" (1 Kings 17:18). Sometimes when we grieve, we, like this widow, think it must be our fault and that we are being punished for something bad we've done.

Elijah took the boy and cried out his own questions to God. Remember, he had to flee for his life after he told the king that God was going to punish the land for their sins. First, God fed him by ravens in the desert, and then He brought him to this poor widow's home to live day to day. The boy's death was the last straw. It was just too much. "God, have You also brought tragedy to this family that helped me?"

Then, after God used Elijah to raise the boy from the dead and show Israel that God was real and Baal was a powerless false god, after God answered Elijah's prayer and sent rain to end the three-year drought, fear and grief kicked Elijah in the gut.

We've looked at Elijah's words before, but let's listen to them once more. "I have been very zealous for the Lord, the God of hosts; for the sons of Israel have forsaken Your covenant, torn down Your altars and killed Your prophets with the sword. And I alone am left; and they seek my life, to take it away" (1 Kings 19:10). Do you hear Elijah's grief? It destroys him to see the injustice, crime, and ugliness of the people of his country. He is heartsick at their betrayal. Anger and hopelessness mingle in his stomach until it burns. Heaviness and embarrassment press on his heart until he wants to drop and just stop the world. He is done. The hurt is huge. He is grieved.

There is a benefit to grief. Job, a man with his own deep pain, said to God at the end of it all, "I have heard of You by the hearing of the ear; but now my eye sees You" (Job 42:5). Being at the end of ourselves, completely spent without any strength or ideas left, allows us to intimately live God—to thoroughly experience Him and know that we know Him, to take the words we've been taught and have them become real and alive inside us.

In Psalm 30:5 David writes, "For His anger is but for a moment, His favor is for a lifetime; weeping may last for the night, but a shout of joy *comes* in the morning."

We are not alone in our grief. The pain is guaranteed to knock our wind out, bring us to our knees, and wring our hearts. But as we're learning, we must focus on God. Look to Him. Cry out to Him. Yell that it hurts, it stinks, and we can't do it. Ask God to hold us and get us through it. Take Him up on His promise that we will know Him and see Him with our own eyes. We are also guaranteed that there will be joy in the morning.

Bible Reading: Psalm 30, 2 Corinthians 1:2–7

Day 6

We have faced change, loneliness, broken expectations, fear, and grief this week. That would knock some people out for the count. Yet here we are, still standing. I am so proud of all of you. You have been in my heart and my prayers as I have written this, and I love you without ever having met you. That may not seem possible to you, but throughout this year, you will learn that God's love is like that. He pours it into us until it overflows, and we swell with tenderness and caring for those God has placed in our lives. I thank Him for including you in my life.

We've looked only briefly at God's response to Elijah throughout his difficult and triumphant life. So let's step closer and listen in on their relationship. God protected Elijah throughout the years of this story—not the way we may want to be protected, wrapped carefully in a soft blanket and kept out of the reach of danger or hurt. God's protection keeps us on the edge of our seats and vitally alive, yet ultimately safe.

Elijah went from confronting a king, running when his life was threatened, showing himself to this same king and an entire angry nation, running for his life again, collapsing in utter despair, and standing in the presence of God. God didn't protect Elijah *from* apprehension of the unknown or physical hunger. God didn't protect Elijah *from* the pain of death or fatigue. God protected Elijah *in the midst* of all that. Elijah's heart faltered, but God lifted him up. His courage ran dry, but God stepped into the gap. His stomach was empty and his mouth was dry, and God fed him through the ravens and the angel of the Lord. In all things, in all ways, God protected Elijah.

God said, "It shall be that you will drink of the brook, and I have commanded the ravens to provide for you there" (1 Kings 17:4). At the widow's house, Elijah said, "For thus says the Lord God of Israel, 'The bowl of flour shall not be exhausted, nor shall the jar of oil be empty, until the day that the Lord sends rain on the face of the earth'" (1 Kings 17:14). God provided the fire as well as the rain when Elijah prayed. The angel of the Lord provided water, freshly baked bread, and time to rest. And at the end of chapter 19, God provided closure to Elijah's ministry. The Lord recognized that he was tired and had done well. He told Elijah, "Jehu the son of Nimshi you shall anoint king over Israel; and Elisha the son of Shaphat of Abel-meholah you shall anoint as prophet in your place" (1 Kings 19:16). God loved and respected Elijah so much that He let him be part of finding his replacement.

We've seen more than once that Elijah was just a normal man. He was great because he trusted God and obeyed Him, but he was just like you and me. Whatever your situation is right now, God will protect you and provide for you. Hebrews 13:8 says, "Jesus Christ *is* the same yesterday and today and forever." What God did for Elijah He will do for us. How God protected Elijah, He will protect us. (Are you ready for the ride of your life?) The way God provided for Elijah He will provide for us. (Okay, maybe not being fed by ravens, but fed by a miracle? Yes!)

"But the Lord is faithful, and He will strengthen and protect you from the evil *one*" (2 Thess. 3:3). "Do not worry then, saying, 'What will we eat?' or 'What will we drink?' or 'What will we wear for clothing?' But seek first His kingdom and His righteousness, and all these things will be added to you" (Matt. 6:31, 33).

How does God respond? He loves, protects, and provides.

Bible Reading: **Matthew 6:25–34**

Week 2

ESTHER

Day 1

There was a little girl whose mom and dad died. Her older cousin took her into his house to live with him, and he was good to her. Because they were living in a different country from their home, he taught his little cousin about their homeland. Most importantly, he taught her about God, the one true God, not all the various made-up gods of the land they were in.

Mordecai, the girl's cousin, loved her so much that he adopted her to be his daughter. She grew up to be beautiful in every way, and her name, Esther, which meant "star," fit her perfectly. Esther loved Mordecai and followed all his teachings and directions.

Now, while the king was a powerful man because he was king, he was a weak man in every other way. He drank too much, reacted in anger instead of thinking first, and surrounded himself with selfish, lazy, evil men. After listening to the advice of these men at a party, the king divorced his queen.

Four years later, after losing a war with Greece, the king came home and was lonely without his queen. So the kingdom had a beauty contest. However, the beautiful young women did not have a choice in the matter. If their appearance fit the stated guidelines, they were brought to the palace to prepare to meet the king. So Esther found herself taken from her home once again and thrust into a world she had never even imagined.

Mordecai and Esther were Jews whose families had been taken from Israel years before. But Mordecai knew many people did not like the Jews, so he had told Esther not to tell anyone at the palace who her people were.

Finally, it was Esther's turn to go before the king. Everyone from the palace guards to the other beautiful girls loved Esther. Soon the king did too. He was captivated by her beauty and her peaceful and kind ways. The announcement came that the king had chosen his new queen, and a party was given in honor of Queen Esther.

During this time, Mordecai sat at the king's gate and overheard two men plotting to kill the king. Quickly he told Queen Esther. The men were arrested, and the king's life was saved. This was written in the record books and then forgotten. And still, nobody knew Mordecai was Queen Esther's adoptive father and that they were from Israel.

At every point during Esther's and Mordecai's early lives, they could have wondered where God was in all of this. There was so much loss and change for both of them. Eventually it became normal for them, with no thought of God working out His plan in and through their lives; that is, until Esther was taken to the palace. The questions started again. Where was God in that? Fear and uncertainty would be natural emotions, trying to imagine how this could possibly work for good.

I challenge all of us to look at our lives in a different way—with a new perspective. Instead of seeing the circumstances and all the emotions that go with them, let's look for God's fingerprints. He's moving, working, and setting up events to do an amazing thing. Let's choose to be part of it instead of fighting it. Let's ask God to show us how to trust Him for the next step.

Bible Reading: **Esther 1–2, Psalm 33:11**

Day 2

Have you ever done the right thing and gotten no credit for it? Have you seen other people be praised and promoted when you knew they were lying? If you have, you know how Mordecai must have felt. He had saved the king's life, and it barely caused a stir in the palace. Haman, however, bragged, strutted, and loudly put others down and bossed them around. So the king promoted him to second in command.

Mordecai sat by the king's gate every day, which indicated that he was one of the decision-makers and men of influence in the kingdom. Each day when Haman came by, everyone was supposed to bow and worship him. But Mordecai loved God and would not worship anyone but Him.

Remember, we are looking at these events with a different perspective or point of view. Put yourself in Mordecai's shoes. You are in a place where a group of people tell you to do something you know you shouldn't do. The easy thing would be to go along and get out of there as safely as possible. But you know it's wrong, and it may not end there. How do you feel? What are you thinking? Who do you trust?

Mordecai refused to bow, and Haman was furious. He could have legally killed Mordecai for disobeying the king's order to bow to him. But that wasn't enough for his enraged pride. Haman told the king it would be in his best interest to kill all the Jews throughout the kingdom. And the king, a weak, uninterested leader, said okay.

The threads of God's plans are starting to show a picture, aren't they? All the Jews were to be killed on one day, 11 months from that time. Yet no one knew the queen was a Jew.

Soon the sound of wailing and crying came from every city in the kingdom as the Jews received the news. Someone told Queen Esther, and she sent a servant to Mordecai to find out what was going on. He gave a copy of Haman's law to the servant and told Esther to go into the king and try to save her people.

Here's the problem. If the king did not call you and you went to see him, you would be killed unless he raised his scepter. Esther relayed a message to Mordecai that the king had not called her for a month. We know Mordecai loved Esther. How his heart must have slammed in his chest. But there was no other choice. "Do not imagine that you in the king's palace can escape any more than all the Jews. For if you remain silent at this time, relief and deliverance will arise for the Jews from another place and you and your father's house will perish. And who knows whether you have not attained royalty for such a time as this?" (Esther 4:13–14).

Mordecai understood that God had been working all along. The plan was his orphaned cousin, Esther. Little, lonely, sad—Esther was all grown up, beautiful and strong. Mordecai's daughter had been ripped from his home and thrust into the palace of selfish, wicked men. His Jewish queen and his sovereign God were working together to save his people.

From where they both were standing, this was scary—impossible, insurmountable. From God's perspective, He had everyone just where He wanted them.

***Bible Reading*: Esther 3–4, Isaiah 55:8–9, Jeremiah 29:11**

Day 3

Esther listened to Mordecai's words. She was queen, and he was a relatively minor statesman, but she listened. Then she reached down into the deepest part of her and gathered all the courage and strength God had been slowly building into her life. A shift, slight but significant, took place, and the adopted daughter became Mordecai's queen in every way.

"Go, assemble all the Jews who are found in Susa, and fast for me," Esther said. "Do not eat or drink for three days, night or day. I and my maidens also will fast in the same way. And thus I will go in to the king, which is not according to the law; and if I perish, I perish" (Esther 4:16). Mordecai did just as Esther had commanded him.

Let's slip into Mordecai's and Esther's places for a moment. They don't know the end of this story. They can't see past the "right now." Pride mingled with apprehension in Mordecai's heart. His little girl amazed him! He had made so many mistakes raising her. Some things he had gotten right and had seemed easy, but bringing up kids was hard. They had each put on a brave face when Esther was taken to the palace, but he had been troubled for her. There were things she would encounter that he had not prepared her for.

More than that was the fact that he had not been able to see Esther or talk to her for a long time. His arms and heart ached to hug her and tell her he loved her. Instead, he had to put on tough love and press her to take her responsibility as queen to the point of death. This was hard. This one pushed him to the breaking point. Mordecai thought he had given Esther to God, that he had trusted the Lord to care for her. God was showing him yet another level of this. It was as if God was saying, "You trust Me when it's easy; you trust Me when it's a little hard—a little different. Does your confidence in Me go all the way to the danger of death, to the place where you realize you have no control?"

Esther knew for the first time that she was on her own. She had always had Mordecai's strength to lean on. Even during the past year in the palace, she had formed friendships with people who advised her and offered encouragement. She stood alone now, a young woman whose only power seemed to be in her looks. Her father had taught her differently, that their power came from God. And now they both were pushing her.

Her heart pounded, and her stomach churned as she considered her father's words. If she didn't do this, God would use someone else. Swallowing, Esther made her decision. If she died, she died. She did believe God was in control. This was bigger than her, and a thrill of excitement mingled with fear shot through her. "Fast and pray for three days," she ordered her father and all her people. It was through God's strength and wisdom that the Jews would be saved.

That was the plan. Fast and pray. We would want to know—then what? At this point, the answer was "I don't know." This can't work. It sounds good in a religious way, but let's be real. People's lives were at stake. Someone needed to kill Haman, arm the Jews, and change the law. Doesn't God help those who help themselves? Do something!

"It is He who sits above the circle of the earth . . . He *it is* who reduces rulers to nothing, who makes the judges of the earth meaningless" (Isa. 40:22–23). Perspective.

***Bible Reading*: Esther 4:13–17, Isaiah 40:12–26**

Day 4

Dressed in her royal robes, Esther went into the king's throne room. She waited, he looked up, everyone held their breath . . . and the king raised his scepter. "What is *troubling* you, Queen Esther? And what is your request? Even to half of the kingdom it shall be given to you" (Esther 5:3).

A year ago, or even three days ago, that may have seemed like the ultimate answer. Time in God's presence had revealed the difference between the power and wealth of her king's kingdom and God's. Her husband thought he was being generous offering half of all he had. Esther knew God offered all His kingdom to her. The choice was easy. She was not even tempted to take the king's offer.

"If it pleases the king, may the king and Haman come this day to the banquet that I have prepared for him" (Esther 5:4). That was it? That was the great plan God had given her?

The king and Haman hurried to her banquet, and still Esther did not answer the king's curiosity. Esther replied a second time, "If I have found favor in the sight of the king, and if it pleases the king to grant my petition and do what I request, may the king and Haman come to the banquet which I will prepare for them, and tomorrow I will do as the king says" (Esther 5:8).

Let's jump back into Mordecai's and Esther's skin for a moment. Mordecai had no idea what was going on. There were no obvious signs from the palace of God's great plan. He sat and waited—and prayed, and waited.

Esther was pleased with the events of the day, but still tomorrow was uncertain. She could see God's wisdom in rebuilding her relationship with the king. How clearly she now saw Haman's fawning and kissing up, his ego, and his selfish ambitions. But would the king? Would this plan work as she envisioned it, or did God have another twist she was unaware of?

Whose place are you in? Are you waiting to see what happens in someone else's life with no power or control over the matter? Are you in the dark, affected by the outcome, but powerless in the process?

Have you stepped up and put yourself on the line to keep you and others in a safe and good place? Are you willing to do what it takes but not sure exactly what that is or how effective you really could be?

Looking in doesn't give the answers. Looking around shows us the problem but can trap us in the enormity of it all. Looking up reveals the solution—perhaps not all the details but all the power and wisdom.

We can go to bed and rest along with Mordecai and Esther, not knowing the future but knowing the God who holds it in His hands. We stepped up and did the hard thing. We knelt down and waited and prayed. God is more faithful than we are, and He has done His part too. So rest. Tomorrow the plan unfurls.

Bible Reading: **Esther 5:1–8, Isaiah 40:12–26**

Day 5

Sometimes not knowing everything is a blessing. It's enough to get through our day and handle the load we've been given. Esther's and Mordecai's heads were full of the tragedy and injustice they were trying to avert, as well as listening for God's direction in the plan in which they were key players.

Haman's head was full of Haman. He swaggered out from the banquet. But when he saw Mordecai at the king's gate and observed that he neither rose nor showed fear in his presence, he was filled with rage against Mordecai (Esther 5:9). Haman called his wife and friends to his home and bragged about all the kids he had, how great he was to the king, and how he went to Queen Esther's banquet. Yet all of that did not satisfy him when he thought of Mordecai. His wife and friends told him to build a high gallows and have the king hang Mordecai on it in the morning. And Haman smiled for the first time since passing the king's gate.

We are starting to juggle a lot of balls in the air now. Esther is planning her next banquet and words to the king. Mordecai is waiting and listening and praying. Haman is plotting and building a gallows. And the king is having a hard time getting to sleep but is otherwise oblivious. It makes you glad that God is the One doing the juggling and not you, right?

"Read me the book of records," the king said. "That should put me to sleep." In those records, he discovered the account of how Mordecai had exposed the plot to kill the king. When they realized Mordecai had never been rewarded, the king asked Haman, who was in the courtyard, what should be done to reward a man whom the king wanted to honor. Haman, of course, figured he was the man and said this:

> *Let them bring a royal robe which the king has worn, and the horse on which the king has ridden, and on whose head a royal crown has been placed; and let the robe and the horse be handed over to one of the king's most noble princes and let them array the man whom the king desires to honor and lead him on horseback through the city square, and proclaim before him, "Thus it shall be done to the man whom the king desires to honor."*
>
> —Esther 6:8-9

"Great," said the king. "Go do all of that for Mordecai, and you be the prince who leads his horse and shouts his praise." Can you picture Haman's face? To anyone looking on, Haman was a powerful man in control of his own destiny. He had it all—wealth, fame, power, women, friends. No one could stop him.

Haman went home, humiliated, after obeying the king. He told his wife and friends, and they told him he was in big trouble. While they were still talking with him, the king's eunuchs arrived and hurried Haman away to the banquet Esther had prepared.

From where we sit now, we can see God's fingerprints all over the people and events taking place. But again, let's make this personal. Look at everything going on in your life, the people you know, the changes, the problems, the hurt and anger, the injustice, the successes. Imagine for a moment what could be going on in the courts, at home, or in school about which you have no idea. Do you see God's involvement? Is He as clear to you in your life as He is in the lives of Esther, Mordecai, the king, and Haman?

"God is our refuge and strength, a very present help in trouble. Therefore we will not fear, though the earth should change and though the mountains slip into the heart of the sea; Cease *striving* [stop struggling] and know that I am God; I will be exalted among the nations, I will be exalted in the earth" (Ps. 46:1–2, 10).

Bible Reading: Esther 5:9–14, Esther 6, Psalm 46

Day 6

We've left Esther and Mordecai dangling from a cliff, haven't we? God's full plan will be revealed next week, but for now, let's look at God's words to us through this amazing book.

The book of Esther is the only book in the Bible where God's name in not uttered at all. The word *prayer* is not mentioned either. We've talked of Esther and the Jewish nation praying when they fasted because that was their custom. Throughout the Bible, fasting is connected with time spent talking and listening to God in prayer.

To me, this is a very special gift from God. Esther and Mordecai were in the same position we are in. At no time did God speak with a voice from heaven to them. He did not provide for them in a sensational, miraculous way. Jesus did not walk with Esther or Mordecai and teach them God's Word. God was there, present, active, and aware, but He could not be found in a physical way.

As we saw with Elijah, God can show Himself anyway He pleases, and there are times when He shouts at us to get our attention. But on the whole, our Lord seems to like to come to us in a gentle breeze, in a still, small voice. He wants us to stop our working, trying, and struggling, and listen to Him.

Hebrew and Aramaic are the original languages of the Old Testament. The word *listen* in Hebrew means "to hear with attention or interest, to agree with." The New Testament was written in Greek, and the word *listen* there means "to consider what is or has been said, to get by hearing, to learn."

One of the reasons God talks softly to us is so we will quiet down in order to hear Him. He wants us to be interested in what He has to say and consider or think about it. Then, after listening intently, we say, "Oh, I get it. I understand where you are going with this, God." Or if we don't get what He's saying, we at least "get" Him. "No, God, I don't understand your plan.

It doesn't seem good or right to me, but I do get You. You have always been faithful and good to me and to others. You have protected me and provided for me. So I will agree with Your will and plan because of that."

Today God's primary way of speaking to us is through His Word, the Bible. But if we believe Jesus is the Son of God who died on the cross for our sins and rose from the dead three days later to live in heaven, Jesus will live in our hearts. The Holy Spirit will fill us and help us hear and remember all Jesus has taught us in the Bible. That is when we can start to hear Him in our hearts.

That quiet voice that tells us, "Yes, you're doing well; keep going" or "Stop. You're wrong. Don't do this."

How great a love our Lord has for us to want to talk with us instead of treat us like puppets or slaves. Even more amazing to me is that He listens to us with the same rapt attention He wants from us.

Our lives are complicated. Stuff is going on that we don't understand. Let's be like Esther and Mordecai and stop and listen. Let's cry out to God and tell Him what we need help with. He loves us. He'll listen. Will you?

***Bible Reading*: John 3:16–18, Romans 10:9–10**

Week 3

ESTHER

Day 1

Esther had been completely unaware of Haman's other plans and Mordecai's public honor. The banquet and mission took all her focus. Finally, the king and Haman arrived, and Esther took a deep breath. There was no turning back.

The servants filled wine goblets and plates as Esther watched Haman. He didn't seem as arrogant as before. Something had changed. Her eyes flicked to her husband, and the king asked, "What is your petition, Queen Esther? It shall be granted you. And what is your request? Even to half of the kingdom it shall be done" (Esther 7:2).

Queen Esther said, "If I have found favor in your sight, O king, and if it pleases the king, let my life be given me as my petition, and my people as my request; for we have been sold, I and my people, to be destroyed, to be killed and to be annihilated. Now if we had only been sold as slaves, men and women, I would have remained silent, for the trouble would not be commensurate with the annoyance to the king" (Esther 7:3–4).

Stunned seconds ticked by, and then the king asked, "'Who is he, and where is he, who would presume to do this?' Esther said, 'A foe and an enemy is this wicked Haman!' Then Haman became terrified before the king and queen" (Esther 7:5–6).

The palace guards arrested Haman and hanged him on the gallows he had made for Mordecai. Haman knew in the end that Someone was more powerful than he or the king.

Let's stop and look at the end to Haman's life. There are mean, bad people in this world. Some of them are in a position of power, and there seems to be no justice for their victims. If you look at your life or watch the news, it would be easy to wonder where God was in all of this. Does He know? Does He care? People like Haman seem to be above the law.

Galatians 6:7-9 says, "Do not be deceived, God is not mocked; for whatever a man sows, this he will also reap. For the one who sows to his own flesh will from the flesh reap corruption, but the one who sows to the Spirit will from the Spirit reap eternal life. Let us not lose heart in doing good, for in due time we will reap if we do not grow weary."

Those last words remind us of where our perspective needs to be. Life is not all about us. It's not about our comfort and getting our own way. We were created to be eternal, so pain and injustice here is not the end. Look up. In the proper time—from God's view—we will reap what we sow, either life and death without God or continuous and eternal life with God. Haman hurt a lot of people, and while his death did not take away the damage of his actions, it did give a sense of closure and rightness to those he hurt. Esther saw justice served that day through God's hand. And God will see justice served again at the end of this age.

Our decision is this: What will we sow? Will we plant the seeds of Jesus's complete and final payment for our sins—of grace, fairness, kindness, morality, and justice? Will we sow the seeds of God's truth in our hearts and others' hearts? God says, "I, the LORD, search the heart, I test the mind, even to give to each man according to his ways, according to the results of his deeds" (Jer. 17:10).

Bible Reading: **Esther 7, Galatians 6:6-9**

Day 2

Can you imagine how Esther felt when she heard for the first time that Haman had made his gallows to hang her father? The day just kept getting more dramatic, and it wasn't over. Esther told the king of her relation to Mordecai, and the king gave Mordecai Haman's position in the government.

With new boldness, Queen Esther approached the king later that day, fell at his feet, and begged him to stop Haman's evil decree.

> *So King Ahasuerus said to Queen Esther and to Mordecai the Jew, "Behold, I have given the house of Haman to Esther, and him they have hanged on the gallows because he had stretched out his hands against the Jews. Now you write to the Jews as you see fit, in the king's name, and seal it with the king's signet ring; for a decree which is written in the name of the king and sealed with the king's signet ring may not be revoked."*
>
> —Esther 8:7–8

So Mordecai wrote that the Jews could fight and annihilate all their enemies who might attack them, taking all their possessions. And there was great rejoicing in all the cities (Esther 8).

One of the first things to notice is the change in Esther. She transformed from beauty queen to warrior. She had steel in her backbone, and nothing would stop her from finishing her mission. For all she knew, the king could have tired of the unpleasant drama and had enough of his queen for a while. Risking her life once again, she approached her husband without being summoned, fell at his feet, and begged for her people. The king lifted his scepter and reached a solution.

When we dare to do what God has called us to do, we grow stronger. We still see the danger. The risk is understood. But our perspective has changed. Quitting in fear is no longer an attractive option. God's courage and strength surge through our hearts, and we can't wait to see what He will do next. When fatigue hits, we look to God to lift us up because giving up is just not going to happen.

Mordecai's integrity shone in bright contrast to Haman's treachery. Vengeance was not on his agenda. He wrote a decree that would keep his people safe for a long time but did not allow them to act in hatred and attack without cause.

God honored Mordecai's humbleness and integrity. The man who sought glory and power was brought to his knees, and the man who sought justice with no thought for himself was elevated.

Life's circumstances are never about just one thing. The big picture was about saving a nation, saving a man, and bringing a man to justice. Just as important to God was building a woman of strength, beauty, and character, and teaching a man to let go of his daughter and trust the God of the universe with her life and his.

ESTHER

Can you see the big picture in your life? Do you know the small things God wants to grow in you? Look up. Ask Him. Listen.

Bible Reading: **Esther 8, Isaiah 40:26, 28–31**

Day 3

Take in the scene 11 months later. Every enemy of the Jews who wanted to destroy them took up their weapons to act according to Haman's irrevocable decree, and the Jews took up their weapons to defend themselves as the new order allowed. Many people were killed on that day, yet still some enemies remained. Once again the king asked his queen what she desired concerning this, and she asked that the Jews be given another day to fight and rid the land of all who were a threat to their lives. In the end, the Jews were victorious.

This is a great story, but what does it mean for us today? Charles Swindoll says in his book on Esther, "Think of it this way: Not only did the Jews gain mastery over their enemies, they gained mastery over themselves."[1]

Esther 9:15–16 says this:

> *The Jews who were in Susa assembled also on the fourteenth day of the month Adar and killed three hundred men in Susa, but they did not lay their hands on the plunder. Now the rest of the Jews who were* in the king's provinces assembled, to defend their lives and rid themselves of their enemies, and kill 75,000 of those who hated them; but they did not lay their hands on the plunder.

The enemies who carried out Haman's decree were not defending themselves or their families. It was hatred and greed that formed the ruling and motivated their violence. The Jews took up arms in self-defense and had the right, according to the king's new decree, to take all the property of the men they killed. But they drew a line. They wouldn't go there—to retaliation, getting even, or revenge.

There is a sick cycle people can fall into when they are victimized. Someone attacks physically, verbally, or emotionally, and the other person is hurt. The wound starts bleeding, and the victim grabs it in pain. Over time the victim can start to want that pain. They think it gives them strength and causes them to never forget and never allow it to happen again. Soon, the wound (emotional, spiritual, or physical) begins to fester with infection. The poison of bitterness and unforgiveness spreads through the victim's heart and mind. Vengeance seethes behind their eyes, and all possibility of happiness or peace eludes them. After a time, anyone who crosses their path risks being contaminated or hurt.

The Jews did not want that. Their focus was not on the enemy or on the injustice and fear that enemy stirred up. Their focus was on the big picture, on their God, on life after the war, on having to look in the mirror in the morning. Ultimately they chose to give the enemy no power over them. They would not let the enemy change their character and turn them into replicas of their evil, greedy selves. The victims displayed self-control and dignity in their fight for safety and justice.

There are few things sadder than seeing a person who has won a war but has lost themselves. Because God wants to protect us from that, He tells us, "Never pay back evil for evil to anyone. Respect what is right in the sight of all men. Do not be overcome by evil, but overcome evil with good" (Rom. 12:17, 21).

Bible Reading: **Esther 9:1–19, Romans 12:17–21**

Day 4

Let's look back at Esther chapter 3.

> *But he disdained to lay hands on Mordecai alone, for they had told him who* the people of Mordecai *were; therefore Haman sought to destroy all the Jews, the people of Mordecai, who were* throughout the whole kingdom of Ahasuerus. In the first month, which is the month Nisan, in the twelfth year of King Ahasuerus, *Pur, that is the lot, was cast before Haman from day to day and from month to month, until the twelfth month, that is the month Adar.*
>
> —Esther 3:6–7

Haman decided the day and month on which the Jews would be slaughtered by casting lots or dice, which in Persian is called "pur" (*purim* is the plural). It is amazing how random and impulsive some people are when they are playing with other people's lives, isn't it?

Haman's plans had been thwarted. So what happened now that the crisis was over? How should we handle a major battle being won? We've defeated our enemy, but the price was high. Our whole life was centered on surviving mentally and emotionally. It may not show, but we're bleeding and barely standing on the inside. Physical scars may even mar our bodies, and we're almost glad. We feel the need for evidence of the damage that was done to us. Do we do a victory dance for a day and then try to get back to normal?

Part of God's care of the Jews was providing Queen Esther and Mordecai as their leaders. "Then Mordecai recorded these events, and he sent letters to all the Jews who were in all the provinces of King Ahasuerus, both near and far, obliging them to celebrate the fourteenth day of the month Adar, and the fifteenth day of the same month, annually" (Esther 9:20–21).

Two days of celebration were declared to honor the memory of God's remarkable deliverance, and it was called the Feast of Purim. The very thing that was used to determine the date of their enemies' evil intent was turned into the title of their celebration.

Life's tragedies have a way of hitting hard . . . and then we move on. Divorce rips through a family, physical abuse hits like a tornado, rejection, neglect . . . and then life rushes on. We are left with wounds that never heal properly, blurred memories and nightmares, and no lessons learned, no lasting perspective.

As with the 9/11 memorial in New York City, like the war memorials in Washington, DC, and just like the Feast of Purim—we need to build a memorial to our tragedies, a time or a place we can go to and remember the heartbreak and how it turned to victory, something solid that reminds us of the lessons learned. We need a place where we can look back and view the terror and anger and fatigue with eyes that have seen more of the picture—eyes that have a perspective gained by time and the event we now commemorate.

Let's be careful not to build a shrine where we place our heartbreak or victimization. Wallowing in blame, bitterness, and resentful hatred is not the purpose of a memorial. Making sure those very things are dealt with, cleaned out, and healed is why we celebrate. Seeing our bleeding, festering wounds healed to healthy and fading scars is why we're here. We need a memorial we can take our children and grandchildren to so the lessons will be passed on.

"So these days were to be remembered and celebrated throughout every generation, every family, every province and every city; and these days of Purim were not to fail from among the Jews, or their memory fade from their descendants" (Esther 9:28).

Bible Reading: Esther 9:20–32, Luke 22:15–20

Day 5

Esther's and Mordecai's lives are a reflection of autumn. Change flowed through their years bringing death, fear, immense sorrow, aloneness, small comforts, betrayal, growth, victory, and honor. Yet the changes we have witnessed have served a purpose. On a very personal level, we have seen despair turn to joy, pain give way to healing, and fear transform to confidence. On a much larger scale, we have seen the same things—a nation gripped by small-minded, selfish men reformed by a few people of courage and integrity.

This last chapter of Esther shows us again the power of perspective. Every skirmish in our lives has the ability to swallow us whole and drown us in the moment. The possibility is also there for those same battles to strengthen and embolden us—for our world to be bettered because we have been part of it and have chosen well.

Esther 10:3 says, "For Mordecai the Jew was second *only* to King Ahasuerus [Xerxes], and great among the Jews and in favor with his many kinsmen, one who sought the good of his people and one who spoke for the welfare of his whole nation."

Life is *never* just about us. We all have a story, and that does make us special. In order to be great, though, to be more than a statistic of "those who have survived the foster system, or those who've endured injustice or brokenness," we need to be a Mordecai. He chose to think beyond his circumstances. His love for God drew his focus from the heat of his situation to the plight of others. He would not bow to a man, a system, or political correctness to save his skin in that moment. Instant gratification marked the men of the day, but not him. There was a future. God always had a plan, and it always worked for the good of all. Like Esther, Mordecai believed that if he died in his fight, he died. And that would count. He would live with God in heaven, and others would have an example to follow. But if he lived through his battles, then he lived for honor. He lived to do good for his whole nation; he lived for God.

I will tell you right now that God is on the throne just as He was throughout Esther's and Mordecai's lifetimes. Some of us have lived through difficult situations that not all people could handle. God has allowed it. "'For I know the plans that I have for you,' declares the Lord, 'plans for welfare and not for calamity to give you a future and a hope'" (Jer. 29:11).

You already know you can get pretty beat up in the middle of God's plans. Some even die in the working of God's plans. But in the eyes of God, that is not harm. Those who have believed in Jesus will be in heaven forever when they die. That is our hope. History has proven that we are capable of standing stronger, with integrity and valor and authority after weathering the storms in life. Read the stories of courageous, everyday people such as Corrie ten Boom, Brother Yun, Sojourner Truth, and Jesus Christ, to name a few, to see that you are in very good company. God is growing you because He understands that you have inner strength and courage you don't know about yet. There is a special place for each of you in our world, and you have the possibility to be great.

Get the perspective of Esther and Mordecai. Look to God and at others, and surround yourselves with people of principle and integrity. You are kings and queens in the making. You are right in the middle of God's good and perfect plan. You have a future.

Bible Reading**: Esther 10, John 15:9–17**

Day 6

In a book where God is invisible, we've seen He is not absent. In a book where God is silent, we've heard His actions speak louder than His words. In a book where the odds are against truth and justice, we've experienced victory over tyranny. Esther has taught us much.

We learned that humility and brokenness are useful. God does not throw us out when we break; He builds us back up, fills us, and uses us. A little orphaned foreigner proved that point.

We also saw the power of one. One person can make a difference. No one liked or admired Haman, yet only Mordecai said he wouldn't be bullied by him. It was not an army that brought evil down; it was one woman who was brave enough to put her life on the line and patient enough to wait for the perfect moment. And in the end, one woman and one man showed a nation of potential victims how to win with dignity and honor.

We observed that when no one else sees or acknowledges the good we do, God does. Hebrews 6:10 says, "For God is not unjust so as to forget your work and the love which you have shown toward His name, in having ministered and in still ministering to the saints." Mordecai saved the king's life because it was the right thing to do, and it was forgotten. The eventual reward he received from people was ridiculous compared to the reward he received from God.

Next, we learned that God uses anyone He wants to accomplish His purposes. No king intimidates God, no heart is too evil or hard, and no one is more powerful than God. Proverbs 21:1 tells us, "The king's heart is *like* channels of water in the hand of the LORD; He turns it wherever He wishes." God is sovereign, on His throne, and in control.

We saw that there will always be people who hate and resent our love of God or honorable lifestyle. Knowing that will keep us safe and ready for the unjust attacks that will come our way.

Calling *wrong* wrong, saying a person who is evil is evil, and stating the ugly facts truthfully are appropriate. Esther did not mince her words to the king when it was time for her to tell him her problem. The quickest way to reach a solution is to state the truth. On that note, however, we learned the power of discretion—praying and waiting for the right time and words to solve the problem and stating the truth and stopping before spraying the room with name-calling and ugly gossip.

Following that we saw the honor of restraint. Just because we have permission to strike back does not mean we have to. It may be our right to say something or take something, but that doesn't mean it is the best thing for us to do. The responsibility of taking care of our safety and the safety of others is important. We need to prayerfully leave the punishment to God's leading.

Finally, we learned the joy of celebrating our victories over tragedy—remembering while forgiving, teaching future generations from our lives, embracing our scars that are healed and clean instead of our festering wounds.

Esther has some power for an orphaned beauty queen, doesn't she? The same God who worked through her can work through you and me. Tell Him you want that, and ask Him to fill you with His courage and purpose.

Bible Reading: Esther 4:13–16, Psalm 1

Week 4

LIFE OF JESUS

Day 1

Jesus promised change. He said He came to set His people free, yet He did not take up weapons to fight the Romans. Instead, He said the reform would start in hearts. Love was what He taught, as well as forgiveness and respect. This revolution didn't look as many had imagined, yet for the disciples it didn't feel all wrong either. Most of Israel, under Roman rule, longed for a revolution that would free them politically. God's plan was to free Israel and the entire world spiritually now and in a way that would last for eternity.

We want social and political change. That would solve our problems, make us happy, and bring us justice. We want to fight. We want our rights. We want our God to do things our way.

Sit on the side of the mountain with the disciples and a large crowd, and drink in the words of Jesus. Allow His words to stir a new vision of freedom in your heart. The passion for revolution will not die, but the process will change.

> *You have heard that the ancients were told, "You shall not commit murder" and "Whoever commits murder shall be liable to the court." But I say to you that everyone who is angry with his brother shall be guilty before the court; and whoever says to his brother, "You good-for-nothing," shall be guilty before the supreme court; and whoever says, "You fool," shall be guilty enough to go into the fiery hell.*
>
> —Matt. 5:21–22

So often we focus on the outside. Don't murder—that's tangible, people can see it, and it's obvious. Jesus said don't let your anger kill someone's reputation or feelings. He was taking this from our actions to our heart, changing how we thought, how we talked, and who we were.

How does that play out in our lives today? Sometimes we angrily reject people as fools if they don't agree with our vision of social justice, religion, or politics. Disdain and contempt color our words, and we feel justified dismissing these people as worthless and stupid. How easily we can step on someone and push them aside when they are insignificant to us. Showing contempt for a person's character and intelligence also reveals our lack of respect for them as humans. We can claim to value the lives of others, to respect them and believe we are all equal, but our words and actions will tell the truth of our hearts.

How do we feel about the homeless, the incarcerated, or police officers? If people disagree with our views and methods of problem-solving, what is our response? Do we lump people into groups of gender and race and make judgments about them? Bring this closer to home. Are we respectful of our parents and siblings, even the ones who fail more than they succeed?

Jesus continued to speak. "Therefore if you are presenting your offering at the altar, and there remember that your brother has something against you, leave your offering there before the altar and go; first be reconciled to your brother, and then come and present your offering" (Matt. 5:23–24). Jesus taught that before the absolute grace of the cross was in place. But what He was teaching is applicable and true. It is not beneficial for us to serve God while holding on to hate and strife with others. Those who believe Jesus is God are loved and forgiven forever, but if we choose to be in conflict with others, our service and sacrifice will leave us empty and be ineffectual to us.

Revolutionizing—transforming—our world starts with each one of our hearts.

Bible Reading: Matthew 5:21–24, 1 John 4:7–21

Day 2

While He was in one of the cities, behold, there was a man covered with leprosy; and when he saw Jesus, he fell on his face and implored Him, saying, "Lord, if You are willing, You can

make me clean." And He stretched out His hand and touched him, saying, "I am willing; be cleansed." And immediately the leprosy left him. And He ordered him to tell no one, "But go and show yourself to the priest and make an offering for your cleansing, just as Moses commanded, as a testimony to them."
—Luke 5:12–14

One of the most dreaded diseases of Bible times was leprosy. This disease deadened the nerves, starting in the fingers, toes, and nose. Because the person could no longer feel, injuries went unnoticed until infection set in and the person lost their fingers, toes, or nose.

Leprosy was likened to sin in the Bible. First, it deadened the person's conscience, and then it ate at them little by little until they could barely recognize themselves when they looked in the mirror. Sin and leprosy increased and corrupted until the person was basically dead while still alive.

It's interesting that this man did not ask to be healed but to be cleaned. Honestly, we can relate to him. Sin makes us feel dirty. There are days when we can't scrub enough to get the stench and filth of our choices washed off. Being clean would mean that the reeking infection caused by our sin—sin's personal results—would be purified and cleansed.

In Bible times, leprosy was thought to be contagious, yet Jesus was willing to reach out and touch the man. Instead of disgust and fear, Jesus showed compassion. He saw the man and not the disease, just as He sees you and me and not only our sin. When we look at ourselves, sometimes all we see are our mistakes, and other people's sins stand out to us as the biggest thing in their lives. Jesus sees the person, our potential to be whole and clean. Without a second thought, He reaches out His hand and touches us when we ask Him to clean us of all unrighteousness.

More important to Jesus than telling people we've been healed by Him is proving it. Live clean. We are to let our clean hearts and minds change our actions and words. Our behavior and motives will prove the condition of our hearts. Psalm 24:3–4 says, "Who may ascend into the hill of the Lord? And who may stand in His holy place? He who has clean hands and a pure heart, who has not lifted up his soul to falsehood and has not sworn deceitfully." Our hearts and actions will validate each other.

Let's check ourselves right now. We may have made excuses or felt justified in our bad choices; but we knew they were wrong. We did it to survive, to feed our family, to stay safe, to make the pain go away. But in the end, doing the wrong thing proved to only give relief for a moment. The problem didn't go away, but our self-esteem and reputation did.

Lasting change comes from Christ Jesus. The solution is in His hands. He speaks to us through His Bible with answers and forgiveness. When we believe He died and rose to live eternally, He cleans us to be white as snow forever. We'll blow it and sin even after that, but when we turn back to Him (repent), Jesus meets us and leads us back into a close relationship with Him, wiped clean from our fall.

Bible Reading: Luke 5:12–14, John 13:5–12, Hebrews 10:4–12, 1 John 1:9

Day 3

On that day, when evening came, He said to them, "Let us go over to the other side." Leaving the crowd, they took Him along with them in the boat, just as He was; and other boats were with Him. And there arose a fierce gale of wind, and the waves were breaking over the boat so much that the boat was already filling up. Jesus Himself was in the stern, asleep on the cushion; and they woke Him and said to Him, "Teacher, do You not care that we are perishing?" And He got up and rebuked the wind and said to the sea, "Hush, be still." And the wind died down and it became perfectly calm. And He said to them, "Why are you afraid? Do you still have no faith?" They became very much afraid and said to one another, "Who then is this, that even the wind and the sea obey Him?"

—Mark 4:35–41

As fishermen, most of the disciples were well aware of how dangerous sudden squalls could be. The fear they felt was natural. Experienced seamen were on all the boats that night, and they had worked the oars and sails hard before finally waking Jesus. The wild fear in each man's gut was precisely because they knew boats overturned in such fierce winds, and the results were deadly.

When we're not in the storm, it can be easy to recite Jesus's words and directions. Jesus had said they would go to the other side, so they would get to the other side. He had never set them up or misled them before. Let's put ourselves in the disciples' place. Jesus has promised to always be with us and to grow our strength and wisdom as we need it. But in the midst of a raging storm—being taken from our home and family, being betrayed by someone, people lying about us, losing our job, a loved one dying—don't we feel like yelling the same thing at Jesus? *Don't you even care that we are going to drown? We thought if we did things God's way, we'd be safe.*

So often we believe God will not allow storms in our lives if we're with Jesus, that He'll keep us above harm when we obey Him and work with Him. God cleared up that misconception in one stormy night. Storm clouds were evident before the group left shore, but because Jesus said to go, perhaps they believed the storm would not touch them.

Clearly, Jesus was trying to teach them to trust Him *in* the storm. Sometimes God wants His children to go though hard or even scary things, and He also wants them to trust Him while they are being tossed around by the waves. They were upset because Jesus had allowed the storm and hadn't acted as panicked or concerned as they wanted. He had not validated their fear and frantic work at all, so the men fought back with anger and accusations.

Looking at this from Jesus's perspective, we see things differently. Jesus was not angry that they awakened Him. He had said before that they could always ask Him for help; in fact, that should be the first thing they did. His frustration was that the disciples had not trusted Him to protect them and didn't think He cared. Mainly, Jesus was determined to make them strong enough to get through any hard time they would come across in life. Jesus wanted them to trust Him more than they feared the circumstance. Their faith in Him needed to be the biggest part of them so they would run to Him first instead of trying to bail themselves out.

This lesson is for us. Jesus is bigger than our problems. Run to Him first with confidence.

***Bible Reading*: Luke 8:22–25, Proverbs 3:5–8, Philippians 4:4–7**

Day 4

The messages about God that stormy night apply to us. Like in the book of Esther, we see again that God's silence did not mean He was unaware. Being slow to act did not indicate that God was uninterested. As Jesus slept in exhaustion, the Father watched His plan unfold.

The disciples woke Jesus and said to Him, "Teacher, do You not care that we are perishing?" And He got up and rebuked the wind and said to the sea, 'Hush, be still.' And the wind died down and it became perfectly calm" (Mark 4:38–39).

After Jesus told the wind to be quiet and the waves to stop, every man from every boat was stunned. They had awakened Him because they wanted Him to save them, and when He did, they were shocked. What did they expect? Anything would have been a miracle. But what manner of man could tell the wind to be quiet and be effective? Who talked to nature and controlled it?

The One who spoke that sea into existence and the world and stars into being is the only One who could calm the storm with a few words. God does not fit into a box that people can understand. He is just too big. And honestly, this is a comfort. If any person could explain God or completely figure Him out, then He wouldn't be God. And if He were just a powerful form of man, which all the false gods are, if God did things based on human emotions and motives, if He could be totally explained, He wouldn't be worth following.

Jesus truly is the Son of God. Because of that, He has the right to lead us anywhere, even into a storm. We need to really understand this. Jesus is God, and He is good and completely trustworthy. If trouble and pain hit us as we live for Him, we can trust Him to take care of us. Through danger and fearful situations, Jesus is faithful and dependable. We can cry through it; we can shout in fear or even anger. But when our shattered emotions tell us that God doesn't see or care, we must remember the truth. He will never, *ever* leave us or forsake us (Heb. 13:5). He loves us more than anyone ever has (John 15:13).

The heart of God is for His children to grow up, be strong, and know Him in every way. He sees our storms, and He sees them as a gift. Those who do not choose to follow God are hit with hardships too. There is no getting away from that. But those who turn to Him are refined from the process. The powerful force of the waves washes away all our false securities. The constant pounding surge of hurt and injustice smooth the rough layers of God's children like sandpaper smooths a board of wood.

We will not get the answers to all our questions, but we can know more of God through our difficulties. The disciples grew up that stormy night. Their faith matured. Job said after going through many sorrows and hardships, "I know that You can do all things, and that no purpose of Yours can be thwarted. I have heard of You by the hearing of the ear; but now my eye sees You" (Job 42:2, 5). The storm had grown Job up in his faith, and it had matured the disciples. Your storm can do the same for you. God's perspective is that the storm is a gift, a time of strengthening, growing, and knowing Him in a deeper and more personal way.

Cry out to Him, and know that He sees you. He cares, and He is capable of rescuing you. Keep your eyes fixed on God.

Bible Reading: **Romans 11:33–36, 1 Peter 1:3–9**

Day 5

After three years of traveling with each other, Jesus and His disciples had experienced miracles, hardships, joy, laughter, and sorrow together. Finally, the disciples knew and understood that Jesus was truly the Son of the living God, the Messiah.

"From that time Jesus began to show His disciples that He must go to Jerusalem, and suffer many things from the elders and chief priests and scribes, and be killed, and be raised up on the third day. Peter took Him aside and began to rebuke Him, saying, 'God forbid *it*, Lord! This shall never happen to You,'" (Matt. 16:21–22). There was no way that could be the plan. Peter thought they could do more good with Jesus alive; it couldn't possibly be right for Him to die. However, Jesus rebuked him.

Jesus turned to all the disciples and said, "For whoever wishes to save his life will lose it; but whoever loses his life for My sake will find it. For what will it profit a man if he gains the whole world and forfeits his soul? Or what will a man give in exchange for his soul?" (Matt. 16:25–26).

That was always the message of Jesus. The first will be last; the least will be the greatest. Try to save your life, and you'll lose it; give up your life, and you'll find it. He saw things so differently than anyone else. So what did He mean this time?

We should be willing to be mocked for our belief in Jesus. If a group of people say many roads lead to God, do we keep quiet or agree with them? Do we speak the truth that Jesus said He is the only way to the Father? What if someone else is being ridiculed because of their faith in Christ? Are we willing to lose our comfort and cool reputation to stand up for God?

Many people loved Jesus, but a lot hated Him. Soon the disciples would be faced with either standing for Christ or hiding. They had to be willing to be hated for His sake—prepared for life to be tough, for words to be harsh. The choice is to lay down the comfort and safety of this physical life because as believers we'll gain the eternal comfort and safety of heavenly life.

Denying Jesus may save us for a short time, but the cost is huge. We deaden a piece of our souls to try to keep our popularity or comfort alive. Jesus wants us to choose to keep the abundantly full, peaceful life by giving up a safe, comfortable moment in today's life.

As far as gaining the world and losing your soul, how many people have done that? How many have sold themselves for money and power? They're suspicious and never happy or satisfied, trusting no one because they know they have not been trustworthy. They gained in the world's way but lost who they were—empty shells trying to be filled with more money, more people, more control. And when they died, nobody cared. There was probably more relief than grief. They had gained the world and lost their soul.

A person who compromises for any reason is never finished. Other people keep pushing them to give in again, to back off their beliefs just a little more. The pressure doesn't stop when we try to save face or act like one of the crowd. Another piece of who we are is just chipped away. We can't lose our salvation, but our reputation, peace, and hope can erode.

Jesus loves us enough to prepare us for this difficult truth. We will face the tough choice of dying to our selfish desires and comforts or compromising and having a piece of our integrity die. What does it profit a man to gain the world and lose his soul? Count the cost.

Bible Reading: Matthew 16:21–25, Joshua 24:14–18, Philippians 4:13

Day 6

Jesus's three-year ministry with His disciples was short but packed with a lifetime of memories and lessons. The disciples were like you and me, regular folks. Young and passionate, some educated and some not, these men were far from perfect. Yet they lived extraordinary lives because they looked to God for wisdom, strength, and perspective. Their ideas and motives died in order for God's to grow in them—and that's as hard as it sounds.

The mountain sermon was spoken in an atmosphere of violence with revenge running just under the surface. Roman rule was oppressive and cruel, and some Jews felt betrayed by others. Jesus opened the hearts of people and exposed their motives. Murdering a person's reputation with angry words, contempt, and disdain was more about revenge than solving a problem. In order to be unified with God, we need to forgive and restore relationships.

He will free us and enable us to fight in His strength. Jesus revolutionized hearts and minds.

Leprosy and sin plagued society. Like leprosy, sin's effect was easy for all to see. We saw firsthand that Jesus was willing to reach out and touch a leper in his filth, to clean him and make him whole. The offer of wholeness and cleanness is for us today. If we are willing to ask Jesus, He is willing to make us new and right. Then our clean hands, our actions, will prove our pure heart. We can have purpose and vitality even after a life of wrong choices.

The storm that almost killed the disciples instead made them stronger and more mature men of God. We learn that working with God does not mean we'll never get beat up by a storm. God sometimes wants us to go through the hard times in order to grow stronger and trust in Him. And we can trust God because He is God who is bigger and more powerful, wise, and good than any person we can imagine. God has proven that He is capable of solving problems no person can. The smart choice is to run to Him first in trouble instead of trying to bail ourselves out.

We also learned that God does care how frightened we are. He does want us to call on Him. Our Father doesn't even mind our anger. But our anger and fear should never be an excuse for accusing Jesus of not caring. We call Him, believing in His ability, and let Him handle our trial His way. Trusting in Jesus will enable us to hang on to Him in the midst of the longest and roughest storms.

Peter and the disciples learned that God's plan was good and must happen His way. Trying to keep our life by compromising will end with losing our soul. When we believe in Jesus, we are sealed by the Holy Spirit forever. Living for God means dying to self. If we give up our rights and comforts for Christ, we will gain rich life now and into eternity. Jesus said that people who sell their soul to gain the world end up with no profit. Those who walk away from the world's view of "making it" and walk toward God gain everything that lasts.

Jesus looks at our hearts. It starts there. Why did we do something? Why were we angry, afraid, and complaining? Who were we trusting? Our hearts show in our actions. Our actions show what is in our hearts.

Living with Jesus is not easy, but it's never boring. Jesus gives an abundant and eternal life. He cleans us inside and out so we can look in the mirror, like what we see, and then go out and live fully and victoriously.

***Bible Reading*: John 10:10-11, Matthew 19:16-30**

Week 5

MOSES

Day 1

Moses was born at a time when the people of Israel lived in the land of Egypt. Though they had come years before of their own free will to escape a famine, they were held as slaves to the new Egyptian king. This king, or Pharaoh, became afraid because the Israelites were growing in number, so he made a law that all baby boys born to the Israelites be killed at birth.

Moses's mother hid him for three months; then she made a special basket and hid him in the rushes in the Nile River. Soon the daughter of Pharaoh, the princess, heard a baby crying and found Moses. Moses's older sister had been watching and offered to find an Israeli mom to feed and care for the child. The princess agreed, and Moses's mom was paid to feed and care for her son. Later, the princess took the baby to the palace to raise him and named him Moses.

Before we go into the story any further, let's stop for a moment and consider Moses's view from the basket to the palace. Though in a place of luxury and ease, Moses actually spent his childhood in a foster home.

There are many reasons for being placed in a foster home, and Moses's mom had the noblest reason. She knew she could not protect him or provide for him. At some point, however, most children wonder if that is the whole truth. Could the natural parents have done more, fought harder, not given up? Feelings of rejection and abandonment could easily weasel their way into a person's mind no matter what the facts show.

As Moses grew up in the home of the princess, he knew she was not his natural mother. Intellectually, Moses probably understood he was better off physically and financially. He also knew he did not fit in. Neither Egyptian nor Israelite, Moses was a boy without a nation, a young man without a true family or a true connection. He stood separate from all others.

Rejection and abandonment lie to us. *I'm not lovable. My parent rejected me because I did something wrong.* Someone needs to be blamed for our pain, so we start to attack ourselves. We also look at the people in our lives with suspicion. They can't be trusted to not leave us or to love us. These feelings turn into thoughts, which influence how we live our lives.

Many destructive behaviors are connected to the actual feelings of abandonment and rejection or the fear of them. Anorexia, bulimia, cutting, and all kinds of addictions are the outcry of people who are overwhelmed with these damaging feelings and thoughts. Doctors now say that anxiety or fear of abandonment and rejection are thought to be one of the causes of some breathing problems, various skin diseases, heart and stomach problems, and depression.

God does not leave us in this desolate place. Psalm 139:23-24 says, "Search me, O God, and know my heart; try me and know my anxious thoughts; and see if there be any hurtful way in me, and lead me in the everlasting way." Philippians 4:6-9 tells us:

> *Be anxious for nothing, but in everything by prayer and supplication with thanksgiving let your requests be made known to God. And the peace of God, which surpasses all comprehension, will guard your hearts and your minds in Christ Jesus. Finally, brethren, whatever is true, whatever is honorable, whatever is right, whatever is pure, whatever is lovely, whatever is of good repute, if there is any excellence and if anything worthy of praise, dwell on these things . . . and the God of peace will be with you.*

Choosing our focus directs our life.

Bible Reading: Exodus 2:1-10, Philippians 4:4-9

Day 2

Let's take a moment to look at Moses's mother today. In our short time of study, we have discussed the importance of perspective. Looking at things from God's eyes or a higher view, or seeing a bigger picture than before gives us a truer evaluation of our lives. Sometimes the truth is that a person was bad and wanted to hurt us. Sometimes a person made bad choices and was selfish, but they never intended to hurt us; they just didn't have the tools to live right. Then there are times when a person had to do a very hard thing because it was best. It was sacrificial love, knowing the person they loved most may never understand.

Moses's mom fell into the last category. Her choices caused the same pain as if she had done it for the wrong reasons, but she did the right thing. We are going to look at this because Jesus said in John 8:32, "And you will know the truth, and the truth will make you free."

Placing her three-month-old baby in a basket in the Nile River had to be the hardest thing she had ever done. How could that be the only option? Moses's mom asked her little daughter to watch the basket from a safe distance because she couldn't leave him there all alone. Then Pharaoh's daughter offered to pay Moses's mother to feed and care for her son. When Moses was old enough, probably between one and three years old, his mom took him to Pharaoh's palace and gave him to the princess. Again, can you imagine her fear? The second-hardest day of her life was when she walked away and left her little boy forever in the arms of another mother.

Moses would never be whipped by the slave drivers like all the other Israelite men. He would never know the pangs of hunger. He would be alive and educated. With great love in her heart and tears in her eyes, Moses's mom left the palace with empty arms.

You may never know the truth about your family situation. Or you may find it to be hurtful. As we unfold Moses's story, we will see that there are choices we all have for how we handle our life. First is that we do not allow other people or circumstances to dictate what we know to be true of ourselves. Psalm 139 tells us that God was there with us in our mother's womb, forming us and knitting us together just the way He wanted us. Even if our mothers didn't plan on us, even if they didn't want us or took drugs while pregnant with us, the truth that will set you free is that God knew about you before you were born. He wants you. He loves you. He made you to look and think and be the only you ever to be made. Ephesians 2:10 says to believers that we are God's masterpiece, created for a good work that God planned beforehand.

The second truth is that we must forgive. Jesus told us to forgive because we have been forgiven, and if we don't forgive, we will not be forgiven by our Father in heaven. On top of that, we are to forgive over and over again. Luke 6:37 says, "Do not judge, and you will not be judged; and do not condemn, and you will not be condemned; pardon, and you will be pardoned." Our last truth is tied to forgiveness—to not condemn other people—which frees us from being condemned by others. When we show mercy to others, others are more willing to show it to us. We will make mistakes, but we will be so relieved when we are given forgiveness and grace.

Dealing with this type of pain is not something we should do on our own. Ask God to give you wisdom to find a pastor, counselor, or friend who will lead you to Bible truths as well as walk with you along this journey. It is within your power to start the healing now.

Bible Reading: **Psalm 139:1-16, Matthew 6:14-15**

Day 3

> *Now it came about in those days, when Moses had grown up, that he went out to his brethren and looked on their hard labors; and he saw an Egyptian beating a Hebrew, one of his brethren. So he looked this way and that, and when he saw there was no one around, he struck down the Egyptian and hid him in the sand. He went out the next day, and behold, two Hebrews were fighting with each other; and he said to the offender, "Why are you striking your companion?" But he said, "Who made you a prince or a judge over us? Are you intending to kill me as you killed the Egyptian?" Then Moses was afraid and said, "Surely the matter has become known."*
>
> —Exod. 2:11-14

There was Moses—a young man who didn't belong with the Egyptians or the Israelites—walking and watching the world around him. Suddenly he saw one of his kinsmen being beaten, and he reacted—instantly, without thinking. There were thousands of slaves, most of them mistreated, and Moses killed over one man's beating. Talk about not seeing the big picture! How would that solve the overall problem? What were his motives? Guilt? Anger? A desire to help?

Because God wants to protect us from making Moses's mistake and the rest of the world from any of us Moses look-a-likes, He told us in Proverbs 20:22, "Do not say, 'I will repay evil'; Wait for the Lord, and He will save you." Wait. Let your temper cool down. Think, pray . . . trust God to lead you. Know that the problem is probably more complex than just that one incident. And know that it is not your job to get even.

We may try to justify our fighting responses, but when we look at Moses, it is plain to see that he knew what he was about to do was wrong. If you feel the need to look around to see if anyone is watching . . . don't do it! Those few seconds were proof that rational thinking was going on, that the right decision could be made, that logic could win over emotion.

Moses witnessed an injustice. Fighting for those who are weaker or less fortunate is good and something God wants us to do. But it needs to be done correctly. We should be angry over the abuse of others, but we are given a clear way to handle that anger. Ephesians 4:26–27 says, "BE ANGRY, AND YET DO NOT SIN; do not let the sun go down on your anger, and do not give the devil an opportunity." The foothold is easy to see in Moses's life. He killed in his anger and then covered it up. Doing one wrong thing snowballs, as I'm sure we have all experienced.

The situation in Exodus chapter 2 is a little different from what you or I would likely face. If we find ourselves or others in physical danger, we can call 911 to get the immediate help we need, but we all know that the courts don't always get it right in the long-term protection of a person. We can do the same thing Moses should have done—pray in our waiting time. We grasp the fact that God allowed us to see this situation or be part of it for a reason. He wants us to be actively involved in the solution, just as God wanted Moses involved. That could be anything from becoming a police officer, social service worker, lawyer, or leader of a humanitarian organization. As Moses eventually did, we may be here to take the hurting out of the system we are in and lead people to new ways of healing and living.

One Hebrew word for *wait* means "to take a stand, to stand with, to hold one's ground." Waiting on God is not a lazy pose. The enemy knows we're there, standing and alert, but God—not our emotions—tells us what to do.

Bible Reading: **Exodus 2:1–14, Ephesians 4:20–27**

Day 4

Moses learned a few more difficult lessons in his inept handling of the beaten slave. Someone is always watching—always. Someone is always listening. Don't ever think you won't be found out—good or bad. Moses found that out the next day. Ephesians 5:11–15 tells us to be careful how we walk or live out every moment of our day because it will become visible when exposed to light.

We must remember that our actions and words matter. They mean something and have power. Destruction and contempt may be the results of our behavior, or it may be change and healing. There will be an instant reaction and a long-term, ongoing one. By now, I'm sure you know which reaction you should be most concerned with.

The next painful message Moses got was that the very people he tried to protect looked on him with disdain. He was not appreciated, and sticking up for his kinsman was rejected. Motive is important. If we step in to help so we will be accepted or admired, we could fall apart when the situation does.

Wounded people still have pride. They don't want strangers coming in to the rescue and making them feel useless and stupid. Oftentimes they don't even want help from people who are close to them. For many emotional and psychological reasons, the victim often turns on the rescuer. Recognizing that will keep us on our feet when our help is rejected. It will also test our motives. Moses's heart may have been right when he wanted to stop the beating, but he should have done it with a plan. Our motives should be to help in a lasting way and to glorify the God who called us into this plan, not to glorify or comfort ourselves. When our focus is up and then out, we will be able to carry on when we are not appreciated.

The last lesson we come away with is that doing good in our own way and in our own power is ineffective and exhausting. When God wants us to work in a place, He will give us the power and energy to carry on for the long haul. And He will always be successful.

Galatians 6:9 says, "Let us not lose heart in doing good, for in due time we will reap if we do not grow weary." Isaiah encourages us with this:

> *Do you not know? Have you not heard? The Everlasting God, the* Lord, *the Creator of the ends of the earth does not become weary or tired. His understanding is inscrutable [hard to make out]. He gives strength to the weary, and to* him *who lacks might He increases power. Though youths grow weary and tired, and vigorous young men stumble badly, yet those who wait for the Lord will gain new strength; they will mount up* with *wings like eagles, they will run and not get tired, they will walk and not become weary.*
>
> —Isa. 40:28–31

God does not get tired of helping us. Amazingly, we see that Moses needed as much help as the Israelite slaves; he just didn't realize it until he blew it so badly. We are in the same situation. No one gets off without some pain in their lives, yet we are all useful. Our challenge is to look at where we are in life and ask God what He has planned for us. While God has us waiting, we should deal with the emotions and motives in our hearts so when the time for action comes, we will not grow weary. We will run and not get tired. We will walk through God's plans and not become worn out.

Bible Reading: **Ephesians 5:11–15**

Day 5

Moses's worst fears became a reality. When Pharaoh heard of this matter, he tried to kill Moses. But Moses fled from the presence of Pharaoh and settled in the land of Midian. Then he sat down by a well (Exod. 2:15). This verse shows us the family life of Moses a little better. There was no love between Moses and his foster grandfather. With his life at risk, Moses ran from everyone and everything he knew.

Finding himself alone once more, Moses was a man without a country or a family, but he was still a man who had a heart for the downtrodden. The priest of Midian had seven daughters who came to draw water and filled the troughs to water their father's flock. Then the shepherds came and drove them away, but Moses stood up, helped them, and watered their flock (Exod. 2:16–17).

What a beautiful lesson we see in Moses's life. God made him a protector and a leader. Each of us has been made with specific gifts and desires. When we see them crop up over and over again, we should take notice.

Moses was invited to eat with and then live with the family he helped, and he eventually married one of the daughters. They named their firstborn Gershom, which means "I have been a sojourner in a foreign land." God granted Moses a new family and a new place, yet still we see his heart felt out of place. He felt he was just stopping over in a different land. It wasn't permanent, and it wasn't home.

What a time of drastic change for Moses, from a palace to a desert field. Yet God was always present. The Lord's plans and preparations were always moving forward. Looking at people from history allows us to view the training ground of their lives. Every step Moses took, from the basket to the desert, taught him something. None of it was wasted time.

Where are you on your life's journey? You may very well feel as Moses did, that you are in a foreign place for a short time. Our choice is how we deal with the changes. Look around. You are here for a reason. What can you learn, how can you grow, and what potential will you fulfill in your life while you are here? God has placed specific people in your path for this time. Ask Him why. Have you noticed certain gifts or things that matter to you that show up no matter where you are? Our lives are a training ground for God's amazing plan for us and the world around us. Don't waste a moment of it.

While Moses was going on with his life in the desert, things were happening in Egypt.

> *Now it came about* in the course of *those many days that the king of Egypt died. And the sons of Israel sighed because of the bondage, and they cried out; and their cry for help because of their bondage rose up to God. So God heard their groaning; and God remembered His covenant with Abraham, Isaac, and Jacob. God saw the sons of Israel, and God took notice* of them.
> —Exodus 2:23–25

Are you getting excited? We've seen this happen before with Esther and Mordecai, haven't we? God is never sleeping; He is always aware. The Lord may be silent, but He always cares. He sees the big picture, and at just the right time, things start to move.

Bible Reading: Exodus 2:15–25, Jeremiah 29:11–13

Day 6

God has impressed one word on me this week. Forgiveness.

As we discussed on Day 1 this week, Moses probably needed to forgive his mom and dad, people from the king's household, Pharaoh himself, the men Moses tried to help who did not appreciate him, and the list could go on. We all have people we need to forgive. Some of the reasons exist only in our minds, and some are very real.

In the Hebrew language of the Old Testament, there are two words for *forgive*. One meaning is "to lift up, bear, or take away." The other meaning is "to cleanse, make atonement for, make reconciliation, or cover over." The New Testament Greek also has two words for *forgive*—"to send away, let go, give up" and "to be kind, graciously to restore one to another."

What does that mean to us today? First, God forgives us permanently through Jesus's death and then lifts the burden and results of our sin, bearing them with us. He takes away our feeling of guilt when we confess to Him honestly. Jesus paid the death penalty for our sins and brought us together with our Father God. He covered our shame and let go of the righteous anger He had toward us and our wrongdoing. In God's kindness, He restored us to Him.

We should forgive the people in our lives in the same way. Notice that God helps us bear the burdens of the earthly consequences, but He doesn't take them away. Forgiving someone does not release them from the responsibility of their action but from our personal condemnation of them. For us to cover a person's reputation after they've hurt us means we do not keep bringing up the wrong and harm they have caused. We don't tell everyone all the time about that person's mistakes. Jeremiah 31:34 tells us that God says, "I will forgive their iniquity, and their sin I will remember no more." God chooses not to remember our wrong, and we can make that choice too. If we see a physical scar, we can choose to not remember the second-by-second pain, emotional agony, and betrayal that caused it. Instead, we can remember what we've learned. Jesus has scars caused by us, and His choice is to not remember what we did to cause them.

When we let go of the anger and other negative feelings we have toward a person and give up wanting to make them pay, we free ourselves as well as them. In fact, the other person may never know we have forgiven them, but the chains of bitterness, hatred, and anger will be broken in our lives, and we will be free.

When we believe Jesus is the Son of God, that He paid for our sins by dying on the cross, and that He rose three days later to live for us in heaven, we have received forgiveness. That was a debt we all were completely incapable of paying. God paid it for us. And God says to you and me, who do you think you cannot forgive after He has done so much for you? Whatever that person owes you, it will never match the debt you owe God. Let it go.

We need to realize that while we no longer harbor bad feelings for a person, it may not be wise to let them close to us. If that person has not changed, if after praying we see they are still unsafe, we need to release them from our anger and condemnation but realize there never was a good or healthy relationship to begin with—and we can't restore that. We keep a wise and safe distance, making sure our hearts are always free from anger and unforgiveness.

***Bible Reading:* Matthew 18:21–35, Ephesians 2:17–22**

Week 6

ISRAELITES

Day 1

Let's spend some time with the people of Israel who had been enslaved for generations in Egypt. God sent Moses and Aaron to speak and perform miraculous signs to them. So the people believed, and when they heard that the Lord was concerned about the sons of Israel and that He had seen their affliction, they bowed low and worshiped (Exod. 4:29–31).

Just knowing someone heard us breaks through some protective barriers in our hearts. People who have been hurt or traumatized over a period of time tend to build tight walls around certain thoughts and emotions in order to survive. While the worst of the abuse is going on, they "check out" emotionally and mentally. It's as if the empty shell of their body was being attacked and then later standing and moving on, functioning properly.

Hurt people can go for years without crying. They laugh when they see it is appropriate, but they feel no joy or humor. Life is survival, going through the motions.

The Israelite slaves were like every person today. They worked hard, had family responsibilities, knew about God, said what they were supposed to, did what they were expected to do—but they had bottled up hopeless minds and hearts.

Then the God they had cried out to sent a man from the past and his brother who had lived among them, and things started to shift inside. The words *when* and *then* stand out in Exodus 4:31. Aaron spoke; Moses, empowered by God, performed the miraculous signs; and the people believed God had sent them. Yet the people did not bow and worship God.

Exodus 4:31 says that *when* they heard God was concerned about them and had really seen their problems, *then* they bowed low and worshiped. In

Hebrew, the word *concerned* means "to deposit, pay attention to." God told them He looked closely at their lives as a banker would look at his bank accounts, and God decided to make a deposit into their accounts. He was going to invest Himself and others into their lives. Their Lord cared enough to put His best man on the job to make sure His deposit was handled properly.

The people also liked the fact that God had seen them. He had not just glanced their way and recognized them as a possible group to add to His charity list. God intently inspected their lives, and He discerned more than just the outward parts of their problems. When a person or situation is seen this way, the resulting action brings about a long-term solution as opposed to a slapped-on bandage and photo opportunity for the rescuer. So *when* the people understood how deeply God's knowledge and care for them was, *then* they bowed low and worshiped Him.

Do you understand that God sees you in the same way? Do you know that God has already made a very costly deposit into your account and wants to continue to be actively involved in your life? Since Jesus Himself has gone through suffering and temptation, He is able to help us when we are being tempted. And there is no creature hidden from His sight, for we do not have a high priest (Jesus) who cannot sympathize with our weaknesses, but One who has been tempted in all things as we are, yet without sin (Heb. 2:18, 4:13, 15). Jesus deposited His life into ours. He's been abandoned, abused, betrayed, hungry, lonely, afraid . . . and victorious.

Bible Reading: **Exodus 4:21–31, Hebrews 2:18, 4:13–16, 1 Peter 5:7**

Day 2

Listen to this fairy tale. Once upon a time, there was a king who was known for being kind and generous to all in his empire. His love for his children was legendary, even outside his kingdom. One day the young son and daughter of the king were captured by an evil dragon. They were taken to his land and made to work day and night mining jewels from the mountain. The dragon roared loudly and spewed fire at them anytime they looked toward the valley or a path on the mountain. So the children lived in fear and dread and did everything the dragon demanded of them.

One day the children looked up to see sunlight glinting off the armor of two knights riding their mighty horses toward them with their swords drawn and their father's banner unfurled. Fear mingled with excitement as the warriors drew closer. "We have found you at last," said one knight, "and have come to take you home."

The children were uncertain, but the knights told them they would read a decree from the king to the dragon so he would set them free. The dragon, however, breathed fire toward the knights and mocked their king and his decree. Flying swiftly to the children, the angry dragon's chief taskmaster demanded that they now dig the same number of jewels out of the mountain by hand instead of with tools.

The next day, the children ran past their father's knights into the dragon's lair and begged him for mercy and help. Laughing in their faces, the dragon told them they were lazy and ordered them back to the mines.

"Why did you not run to your father's men for help?" asked one of the knights. "We have a plan worked out by your father who has always fought and sacrificed for you."

But the children would not listen and, in fact, hurled insults at the knights. "It is your fault we are being treated so badly—yours and our fathers! Leave us alone to work this out for ourselves."

We probably think how crazy it was for the children to run to their enemy for help. It was obvious that the dragon was bad and evil and wanted to harm them. On top of that, the children treated their rescuers with contempt and had no memory of their father's power, abilities, and love. Solving their own problems was laughable. What twisted logic! Yet we do the same thing. We bellow at God for letting hurt come to us. Any person claiming to know God's Word or wanting to help us will be sliced by our sharp words. And we run to our enemy, the one who tells us that vengeance will rescue us, hatred will kill our dragon, and fear and hiding will give us safety.

The Israelites did the same thing in Exodus 5. When their enemies made life more brutal, they ran to them for relief. That is the mindset our enemy the devil wants us to wallow in. Focus on your circumstance. Spotlight your situation. Concentrate on your enemy. Keep your friends close and your enemies closer. You are weak and dependent, but you are the only one you can count on. It's God's fault, the church's fault, the government's fault. In every way the enemy wants us to believe lies, and when we have been beaten down for a time, that is natural and easy to do, even though our Father and his knights are standing in front of us.

Bible Reading: Exodus 5, 6:1–8

Day 3

Exodus 6:9 says, "So Moses spoke thus to the sons of Israel, but they did not listen to Moses on account of *their* despondency and cruel bondage." Another version of the Bible uses the word *discouragement* for *despondency*.

You will remember that Moses was sent to rescue the Israelites because they were miserable. "And the sons of Israel sighed because of the bondage, and they cried out; and their cry for help because of *their* bondage rose up to God. So God heard their groaning; and God remembered His covenant with Abraham, Isaac, and Jacob" (Exod. 2:23–24).

These people had been mistreated, underfed, physically abused, verbally abused, used, ridiculed, and despised for generations, and they hated their lives. No one wants to live like that. Even if we were born into that, as all of Moses's people were, instinctively we'd know that wasn't right. Humans were created in God's image and for eternity in heaven, and deep within our souls, every person desires dignity and love. So they cried out for help.

Yet when Moses came to them with God's message of the freedom they had asked for, they didn't listen to him for some interesting reasons. Hopelessness gripped their hearts and minds. They felt powerless. Even though the men and women were not fed well, they were still physically strong because of the work they did. Exodus chapter 1 tells us there were more of them than their Egyptian captors, yet they still felt unable to change their situation. Why?

Mental, emotional, and spiritual bondage enslaves people more effectively than physical chains and beatings. Today we see women staying with men who beat them (and vice versa) and children defending parents who neglect and abuse them for the same reasons the Israelite people stayed in slavery in Egypt. Hopelessness. Discouragement. Low spirits. Feeling powerless. Fear of the unknown. Darkness. Lies. Despondency. Suffering. Depression.

I have heard some people criticize others who don't fight back in the way the critics think they should. They say things like, "They must like it, or they'd get out. It's their own fault. They aren't very smart if they can't see all the open doors through which they could leave."

Yet the truth is that every person has been in slavery to something, and even the most critical person has not been able to walk free on their own power. Insecurity rules a lot of us. Fear of rejection stalks us. Addictions—to drugs, alcohol, sex, shopping, food, work, neatness, you name it—are taskmasters that push us relentlessly. Anger, unforgiveness, anxiety, greed, fear of other people's opinions, guilt, and shame are slave drivers that own our hearts, minds, and lives. And when we hear that Jesus came to set us free from all that, we, like the Israelites, don't listen because of our discouragement and cruel bondage.

So as we walk along with the Israelites, we will easily be able to step into their shoes (or sandals). We share their mindset to some degree, but may we be sharp students and learn to trust God sooner than they did. "It was for freedom that Christ set us free; therefore keep standing firm and do not be subject again to a yoke of slavery" (Gal. 5:1). Jesus came to free us from sin and all the strings or chains attached to it. If we have believed in Him as the Son of God and asked Him to have our hearts and lives, He has unlocked the prison door and all the chains that hold us mentally, emotionally, spiritually, and physically. We need to uncurl from our tight ball on the floor, look up into the light and freedom in God, and walk free.

Bible Reading: Exodus 6:1–9, Galatians 4:28, 5:1

Day 4

Chapters 7 through 11 of Exodus describe God's battle with Israel's enemy. Through God's chosen leaders, Moses and Aaron, He performed miracles and sent terrible plagues upon Pharaoh and all of Egypt. Pharaoh made promises he quickly broke and dealt harshly with his slaves. God, however, remained constant and firm.

The people watched and listened, so when Moses said it was time to go, they packed up and went. Their minds were full of God's strength and power, and they readily obeyed all that Moses and Aaron told them to do. On the outside, it looked as if they had finally conquered all their fears and doubts. But God knew that though they were willing and wanting, inside they were still not ready for some things.

> *Now when Pharaoh had let the people go, God did not lead them by the way of the land of the Philistines, even though it was near; for God said, "The people might change their minds when they see war, and return to Egypt." Hence God led the people around by the way of the wilderness to the Red Sea; and the sons of Israel went up in martial array from the land of Egypt.*
>
> —Exod. 13:17–18

Isn't that amazing? They hated the land of bondage and deeply longed for the Promised Land of beauty, rest, and plenty, but they were not quite ready to fight for it. They were dressed for a fight, but they weren't psyched for a fight.

It's hard to criticize that because here we are, all dressed up with no fight inside us. We are sick of living in fear, and we willingly take a giant step of faith out of the relationship or place where we've lived with it, but we aren't ready to fight it to the death. Just the thought of having bitterness and anger burn inside us makes us sick. We don't want to live that way anymore. But we can't let it go. The memories grab us, and we hold on once again to our right to be angry and resentful. Intellectually we know the facts. Deep inside we can't get it, and the only fight we'll wage is with anyone who tells us we can break those chains.

I love the fact that God did not criticize or rebuke them. They wanted out—okay. They weren't ready to fight—He'd wait. He wants us covered with His armor, but He's willing to take us the long way to our Promised Land. But be aware that it is through a wilderness. The only way to be ready for battle is to completely trust God for every moment. That is the wilderness experience. There is no water for as far as the eye can see, but God will supply it. There is no food to hunt or gather, but God will supply it. There is no way to preserve what God supplies, so take just enough for today, and trust for tomorrow—total dependence on God.

Now before we balk, remember back to Egypt. That was total dependence on the enemy. Pharaoh decided how much food they had. He determined what tools they used. And he definitely did not allow anyone to be dressed for battle—no protection, no defense, no security.

God takes us just as we are, tells us to put on our armor, and leads us in the direction we are ready to go. Your path will not look like my path, and that is all right. As long as our leader is God and our destination is the place He has promised us all, we need to trust His direction. He wants us to live in peace. He desires that we have deep joy and contentment. He yearns for us to be free from sin and all its chains. He has promised us a full life here and in heaven. And He has provided us Jesus as our strength and the Holy Spirit as our guide.

Bible Reading: **Exodus 13:17–22, Ephesians 6:10–18**

Day 5

Relief and hope swept through everyone like a refreshing breeze. God would take care of them. Moses and Aaron would quickly get them to their new home where all the desires of their heart would come true. Seeing their men dressed for battle made them feel invincible.

What a stunning surprise to find out God's desire did not match theirs. He did not want them magically set down in their new home with no effort on their part. God had no plans to spoon-feed them and coddle them. He knew they had many problems that needed to be brought into the open, cleaned out, and healed. Their Lord wanted them to grow up and take responsibility for themselves. His desire was for mature men and women to be productive and strong, His children who would reflect His goodness and justice.

So when Pharaoh let the people go, God did not lead them on the road through the Philistine country, although that was shorter. God said, "If they face war, they might change their minds and return to Egypt." So God led the people around by the desert road toward the Red Sea. The Israelites went up out of Egypt armed for battle (Exod. 13:17–18).

That looks and sounds appealing at first, doesn't it—skirting around the big battles in our lives; avoiding conflict; taking the easy way out? The fact is, no matter which way we go, at some point we will face an obstacle that is bigger than we are. In a few short days, the Israelites faced the Red Sea, and when they looked over their shoulders, they saw all the Egyptian army bearing down hard on them.

So what was God talking about when He said they weren't ready for war? It was coming to them, and there was no way out. But God had another plan. You see, God does punish those who oppress and harm His children, and that was something He needed to finish here. However, God's actions always produce more than one outcome. Boot camp had just begun for His people. They weren't ready to fight, but they were going to trust. Which was harder?

They complained and blamed, Moses prayed and listened, and God confused the enemy, gave the orders, and parted the Red Sea. Lesson one was keep your eyes ahead. Watch your leader, obey his instructions, trust God is leading him, and go forward.

Lesson two was trust God when nothing looked like we imagined it should. Huge walls of water lined the path that thousands of people had to take to get to the other side and away from the enemy. Do we question how that possibly happened, or do we accept the reality and move forward? Do we let common sense and fear take over, or do we get it that God is bigger than we are and move forward? Realize that the first war we fight in will be fought within our minds.

When we aren't able to fight and defeat our enemies, God will do it for us, but He always believes we are capable of great things. "Watch Me fight this one," He says, "but to get a good seat you're going to have to trust me to do a God-sized miracle." To ensure that we do take those scary first steps of faith, God sometimes limits our options. Step into the middle of the parted sea or stay on the shore and be killed by the enemy. Trust Him for this step . . . and then the next step . . . and then the next step. Focus on His power, His goodness, His plan. Don't look back. Let God, not your enemy, overwhelm you. Be exhilarated by the desire of God's heart beating in yours.

Bible Reading: Exodus 14, 2 Corinthians 10:3–7

Day 6

If there is one thing we have experienced in life, it is that taking the first steps out of our familiar place of despair is hard. This week's look into history shows us that this has always been true. In fact, any situation we are firmly entrenched in—wrong choices, harmful people or ideas, despair—is very difficult to leave.

There were two events that initiated God's rescue plan for the Israelites. The people cried out to God and asked for His help. Then they looked at the things that happened that were way outside the normal and beyond any person's capabilities and believed God was able to rescue them. They believed in God's power and authority.

From the very beginning, God has been willing to come to us when we are in a mess. That is amazing because God is completely holy, and we are completely *not* holy. *Holy* means "set apart, undefiled (or not dirtied or stained) by sin, free from wickedness, pure."

Let's define sin so we can understand this clearly. Very simply, *sin* means *missing the mark*. If we throw a dart or ball at a target and miss the bull's-eye, we miss the mark. Another definition of sin is *anything that disagrees with God's way of thinking or way of doing something*. So God is our mark, our target. He is pure and undefiled, unpolluted.

Let's start from the outside and work in. If we act violently or cruelly, deceitfully or sexually impure, we're not acting in a way God does. We have missed our target. That is sin. When we believe and live as if we are a loser, a mistake, or someone who is worthless, we disagree with God. Psalm 139:13-16 says God made us wonderfully and just the way He wanted us. We can believe Him and hit our mark or believe a lie (essentially call God a liar) and miss the mark. That is sin.

We can scrub up, work hard, and look pretty clean in our actions. It is harder to do that constantly with our feelings, but we can at least hide them from others. But God sees all of us. And on our own, we cannot make ourselves spotless in every area. Unless our soul is pure like God's, we won't even want to always be clean.

So just like with the Israelites, God came to us when we were a mess. "But God demonstrates His own love toward us, in that while we were yet sinners, Christ died for us" (Rom. 5:8). "For if while we were enemies we were reconciled to God through the death of His Son, much more, having been reconciled [restored, made right], we shall be saved by His life" (Rom. 5:10).

We will be saved through Jesus's life. The Greek word for *save* means "to keep safe and sound; to rescue from danger or destruction; to save a suffering one from disease; to make well, heal, restore to health; to deliver from the penalties of judgment (eternal death, hell)."

The picture God gave us of the broken slaves in Egypt is an illustration to each of us. We cry out for help and resist it when it comes because we are so discouraged. "Nobody's perfect" or "I can't help it because I was born this way" are excuses for our resistance. God doesn't give up on us. His way of complete rescue starts from the inside out. Until we are filled with God's strength and wisdom on the inside, we won't be ready for the fierce war. We may fight in a battle or two on our own, but we can't endure the total brutality of the war in its entirety. Our victorious first steps are in the power of Jesus Christ.

Bible Reading: **Romans 5:1–11**

Week 7

ISRAELITES

Day 1

The first steps out of slavery and hopelessness were highlighted in Israel's exodus from Egypt. Their hearts and minds dictated their physical condition, and we are about to see how that continued to keep them chained even though they were moving forward in a free land.

That is an astounding situation. You and I can be captives in our emotions and thoughts while at the same time we are moving forward with God. We, like the Israelites, can experience great victory by God's miraculous power and still hold on to ideas and desires that are directly against God's Word. The consequence is drastic.

A quick overview of Israel's 40 years of wandering reveals great insight. My prayer is that we all will carefully look into our own lives and expose our attitudes to the light. It is the only way we will reach the abundant life of joy, peace, purpose, and wisdom here on earth. Our exposed hearts and minds will show us if we ever really trusted God and followed Him or if we were merely carried along with the momentum of the crowd and the emotion of leaving a place we hated.

Two and a half months after seeing the Red Sea miracle, the Israelites complained to Moses about their food and water. The following years vibrated with the grumbles of bad water, long waits, impatience, discontent, disbelief, and fear. Throughout this time, Moses pointed out that their complaints about the leadership were actually complaints against God. Doesn't it just seem a little safer to blame our leaders out loud and hide the fact that we are mad at God for not doing things our way?

That's the next step on the path to complete freedom—understanding and accepting that God will do what is best, even if it doesn't look like what we want. "'For My thoughts are not your thoughts, nor are your ways My ways,' declares the Lord. 'For *as* the heavens are higher than the earth, so are My ways higher than your ways and My thoughts than your thoughts'" (Isa. 55:8–9).

There is nothing wrong with having an idea or a dream. We just need to learn to hold on to them loosely and be willing to let them go if they don't match God's plans. Our concepts of success may not match God's. Our ideas of family life and experiences will not always agree with God's. Let me assure you, God thinks outside the box. Push your imagination to the limit for the answer to your problem, and then realize that God can go beyond that. He's bigger than us. He is smarter than we are. And that's reassuring. It's why we can put our trust in Him and relax.

Read the rest of Isaiah 55. Rain and snow come, and we sometimes don't like that. It interferes with our plans. Yet because God has a purpose that not only touches you and me but people all around for far into the future, He lets us get wet and cold. His purpose will be completed, and it will be good. What we think is for bad will turn out for good.

No more grumbling. No more second-guessing God. If we want to get through this wilderness and into complete freedom in our Promised Land, we have to be willing to follow God's plans. And you will go out in joy and be led forth in peace . . . instead of the thornbush there will grow the juniper tree (Isa. 55:12–13). The results are worth the surrender. Let's give God the lead.

Bible Reading: Isaiah 55:6–13

Day 2

Then Moses led Israel from the Red Sea, and they went out into the wilderness of Shur; and they went three days in the wilderness and found no water. When they came to Marah, they could not drink the waters of Marah, for they were bitter; therefore it was named Marah. So the people grumbled at Moses, saying, "What shall we drink?" Then he cried out to the Lord*, and the* Lord *showed him a tree; and he threw it into the waters, and the waters became sweet. There He made for them a statute and* *regulation, and there He tested them. And He said, "If you will give earnest heed to the voice of the LORD your God, and do what is right in His sight, and give ear to His commandments, and keep all His statutes, I will put none of the diseases on you which I have put on the Egyptians; for I, the LORD, am your healer."*

—Exod. 15:22–26

Let's put ourselves in Israel's place. This plan appears to have some holes in it. Didn't Moses think ahead to how much water thousands of people and animals would need? We've said it before, but it bears repeating. Following God blindly and not having supplies or a clear direction sound good in a religious way, but get real. This is life-and-death. There comes a time when you set religion down, roll up your sleeves, and get to work. Engage your brain.

That is what every person would think when they look at this from a purely physical standpoint. However, God thinks differently than we do. He thinks outside the box. He told Moses to throw a tree—a dirty, normal tree— into the bitter water. And the water became sweet. Some scientific reasons have been suggested for this, so at the least it shows God's knowledge of the science of His creation and at the most His miraculous power. Then God said, "If you listen to Me and do what is right in *My* sight, not yours, and if you keep all My laws, I won't put the diseases on you I put on the Egyptians because I, the Lord, am your Healer."

For the first time, this new aspect of God's nature is revealed to us. He is Healer. God said He would like to keep our physical bodies from disease. That is important to Him but not the most important thing. More than that He wants us to listen to Him and follow Him. God is willing to sacrifice our bodies' comfort and health in order to save us spiritually. He is not willing to sacrifice our souls to save our bodies. Amazingly, He cares about each detail of every part of us, but again, God has priorities. And our physical healing, important as it is, comes second to our spiritual healing and growth.

God has placed this idea in my heart, and I am still trying to wrap my brain around it. I believe we are physical beings. I believe we are intellectual, emotional, and spiritual beings too. We tend to think that the biggest part of us is our physical and that it's the strongest part of us. I think God wants our spirits to be the biggest part of us . . . our spirits to be stronger than our bodies or emotions or thoughts. That way when life hits us—our parents reject us, one of them beats us, we're hungry or scared—it hits the smallest part of us. We still feel it and even flinch from the hit, but it hits the least vital part of us—the smallest part of us instead of the largest part of us. And our strong spirit takes us through things that seemed impossible to survive.

Isaiah said his God was his strength (Isa. 49:5). Jeremiah said God was his strength and his stronghold (Jer. 16:19). Paul tells us, "Finally, be strong in the Lord and in the strength of His might" (Eph. 6:10). God in us gives us the strength to move forward in the midst of incredibly painful or hard times.

Bible Reading: **Zechariah 4:6, Psalm 37:39–40**

Day 3

We are still camping by the well of bitterness today. God said, "If you listen to Me, do what I say is right, and obey Me, I will heal you." Then He said, "For I, the Lord, am your healer."

Let's be very honest with each other. Bitterness is something you and I have felt, maybe even nurtured. The ex-slaves are given a pass on that because we feel sorry for them. So many bad things victimized them; how could they not be bitter? Coming from a dysfunctional family or enduring any kind of abuse may make us feel as if our bitterness is justified and also excusable. But we aren't alone. Every person has been wronged to some extent, which leaves a bitter taste in their mouths. Our whole world could be a well of bitterness.

Before God said He wanted to take disease from our bodies, He healed the bitter water. Feel this churning, burning emotion with me. Sour resentment swirls in our stomachs when we think of what happened to us. A person's name causes anger to burn a path through our chest. There are days when we rehash the memories over and over until the acid swells from our stomach into our mouth. The bitterness infects our mind and actions as well as our body.

Hebrews 12:15 says, "See to it that no one comes short of the grace of God; that no root of bitterness springing up causes trouble, and by it many be defiled." A bitter person stains and pollutes the whole atmosphere in a room and causes trouble for everyone.

It is interesting that the first time God revealed Himself as our Healer, our Great Physician, it was not to cure leprosy or cancer or the common cold. He chose something far more contagious, far more menacing, much more common—bitterness. It's a condition that tears apart people, families, friendships, churches, and countries.

God wants to make us healthy and safe to be with. We may be away from the place that hurt and enslaved us, but we can still drink from the deep well of bitterness. We hear our bitter words and think, *Whoa! That sounds terrible.* So we work hard to not voice our thoughts. We take away the obvious bitterness. But the root of bitterness is still there, and it springs up when we least expect it. Suddenly we barf all the ugly words of hostility, resentment, and anger that we thought we had buried. The people closest to us and the room are sprayed with the vile, slimy vomit, and the smell lingers long after the mess is cleaned up. You can see why the Bible says many are defiled by the root of bitterness.

But God can purge bitterness out of us. If you will allow me this analogy, we could say that God threw the tree of the cross into our well of bitterness, and the waters became sweet. He didn't clean out the stuff in the water that made it bitter; He threw the tree into the middle of the contaminated water. He doesn't erase our memories or take away events that have the potential to cause bitterness. Jesus and His death on the cross come into the middle of our polluted lives and turn the bitterness into sweetness.

It is our choice if we participate in this cleansing and healing. Ephesians 4:31-32 says, "Let all bitterness and wrath and anger and clamor and slander be put away from you, along with all malice. Be kind to one another, tenderhearted, forgiving each other, just as God in Christ also has forgiven you." Doing it God's way is sweet.

***Bible Reading*: Exodus 15:22-26, Ephesians 4:23-32**

Day 4

Walking on with the Israelites, we find ourselves reflected in their lives once again. God has taken us this route because He knew we were not ready to face our enemies in a fierce battle. Yet emotionally and intellectually—spiritually too—we feel as if we have been in a war. Trusting God for each bite of food and each drink of water is hard. Letting go of old thinking and bitterness takes an inner strength and self-discipline that pushes us to our limits. And now the time has come. The enemy has ambushed us from behind, and we are going into battle.

> *Then Amalek came and fought against Israel at Rephidim. So Moses said to Joshua, "Choose men for us and go out, fight against Amalek. Tomorrow I will station myself on the top of the hill with the staff of God in my hand." Joshua did as Moses told him, and fought against Amalek; and Moses, Aaron, and Hur went up to the top of the hill. So it came about when Moses held his hand up, that Israel prevailed, and when he let his hand down, Amalek prevailed. But Moses' hands were heavy. Then they took a stone and put it under him, and he sat on it; and Aaron and Hur supported his hands, one on one side and one on the other. Thus his hands were steady until the sun set. So Joshua overwhelmed Amalek and his people with the edge of the sword. Moses built an altar and named it The Lord is My Banner.*
>
> —Exod. 17:8–13, 15

Make this real. War—hand-to-hand combat, swords, knives, and spears. The air was heavy with the smell of fear, blood, and death. War cries mixed with anguished screams of wounded and dying men. There is no glamour in real battles, only the raw hunger to survive and the burning knowledge that you fight for your families' survival as much as your own.

Moses raised his hands toward God while watching, smelling, and hearing this war. His arms cramped, fell asleep, and slowly went down—and the tide turned. The enemy pushed forward. Moses needed help, so they got a rock for him to sit on and placed a man on each side to hold up his arms all day. He had to be in his own kind of agony. What was the purpose?

In his early days, Moses fought first and prayed later. Now he followed God's plan and raised his hands in continual prayer while Joshua led the men into battle. The battle was God's, not man's, and Moses prayed to His Commander in Chief. I believe praise was part of this too. We raise our hands in praise to a God who amazes us with His strength in the midst of life's battles. While we are praying and watching, praying and fighting, we see God working. With our hands raised high, we say *help!* in one breath and *praise You!* in the next.

No matter how prepared we are for war, there is really no way to be ready for the brutality of it. We will never be the same after a battle. Satan ambushes us, and we fight like Israel. His evil intent is to take our families and twist them and break them. He wants us to believe God doesn't care and has forgotten us, and his lies fill our minds. He warps love until we think its sex, until we think strength is brutality, truth is hatred, and money determines a person's value.

We cannot do this alone. If we are the soldier in the combat of our life, we need people praying around us, watching us, and knowing our needs. And if we are the prayer warrior, there are times when we will need other people who love Jesus to come next to us and hold up our arms. A new side of God has been revealed. The Lord is my Banner—my flag that goes before me into battle. The Lord is a warrior; The Lord is His name (Exod. 15:3).

Bible Reading: **Exodus 15:1–11, Psalm 44:1–8, 1 Peter 2:6–7**

Day 5

God came down to a mountaintop to talk with Moses and give him the Ten Commandments. The people trembled as thunder, lightning, the sound of the trumpet, and the mountain smoking convinced them of God's great power and presence. The LORD then told Moses, "Thus you shall say to the sons of Israel, 'You yourselves have seen that I have spoken to you from heaven. You shall not make *other gods* besides Me; gods of silver or gods of gold, you shall not make for yourselves'" (Exod. 20:22–23).

Why would He need to tell these people not to make fake gods after all they had seen, heard, and experienced with the real God? Let's keep an eye on our hearts as we look at them.

God gave Moses detailed rules to help the people, and they told him they were committed to following God. Moses went up to the mountain again to spend time with God and receive the commandments written by God's finger on tablets of stone. Forty days and 40 nights later, the people were at the breaking point. They were tired of waiting for Moses and told Aaron, Moses's brother, to make them some gods to follow. And Aaron did it.

Moses was furious with the people and with his brother. Then Moses said to Aaron, "What did this people do to you that you have brought such great sin upon them?" Aaron's response? "Oh come on, man, don't be mad. You know these guys tend to be pretty bad. I mean, what was I supposed to do? They asked for it (blaming them), and you were gone a long time (blaming Moses), so I told them to give me their gold. We threw it into the fire, and *BAM!* Out comes this calf. Can you believe it? (not my fault)."

People who don't take responsibility for their actions are destined to remain in their mess. They'll wander from getting it right to making huge mistakes, and all the time it will be someone else's fault. Their leader tends to be as weak and indifferent as they are, and the only thing that honestly matters to them is if the consequences of their actions are uncomfortable.

In Exodus chapter 20, God said don't have any gods *before* Him and any gods *besides* Him. Do not put your trust and love in anything but God—not in money, the law, a person—no god *before* (in front of) the real God. Furthermore, He will not share His position. Don't have God plus religious rituals, God and your own way of problem-solving—no god *besides* (in addition to) God. Our need for physical help that we can grab on to and see is huge. We don't always want to leave God out, but at times we feel He is just not enough.

I think it goes deeper than that. God had not done things their way and on their timetable. All of us at some point in our lives have wanted to make God in our image. We want to tell Him what to do and when to do it, and then we want Him to bless our plan with great success. There—we prayed about it. We put money, education, ideas, religious rituals, people, sports, and music before and beside God in our lives. They are what we run to first. But ultimately, we are the little gods who manipulate and control it all. We want to decide what should happen, how it should happen, and when it should happen. Like Israel, we dance around the image of our god feeling good that we did something—anything besides waiting in silence.

"Commit your way to the LORD, trust also in Him, and He will do it. Rest in the LORD and wait patiently for Him" (Ps. 37:5, 7).

Bible Reading: Exodus 20:3, 23, Exodus 32

Day 6

We're finally at the edge of Canaan, the Promised Land. God told Moses to send out 12 spies to see what the land and people were like. They came back with fruit from the area and praise for the land's lushness, just as God had promised. But the people who lived in the land were strong, and the cities were fortified and very large; and their longtime enemies, the Amalekites, lived there. Ten of the spies gave the land a bad report.

Yet Caleb and Joshua believed God would keep His promise. Twelve men went out. Twelve men saw the fertile, watered, beautiful land they had been dreaming about, but only two men believed it was good enough to fight for. Only two men believed God was faithful enough to fulfill His promise and powerful enough to defeat their enemies.

> *All the sons of Israel grumbled against Moses and Aaron; and the whole congregation said to them, "Would that we had died in the land of Egypt! Or would that we had died in this wilderness! Why is the* LORD *bringing us into this land, to fall by the sword? Our wives and our little ones will become plunder; would it not be better for us to return to Egypt?" So they said to one another, "Let us appoint a leader and return to Egypt."*
>
> —Num. 14:2–4

All these years and all these miracles later, and Israel was still not ready to fight. It's bizarre to say that because they had fought many wars by this time. Fighting for survival and fighting for what God has promised us are two different things. When attacked or threatened, we either curl up in a corner or come out swinging. However, when our toes are on the line, separating us from whatever it is God has promised—a restored family, success in school or work, moving into a safe place—our hearts do a double take. We stare at the promise and see that it is so much bigger than we thought, bigger than we are. We don't deserve it; we're not even sure we want it at all. It dawns on us that there is great responsibility with this promise, and we inch a step back. The promise is there but not on a silver platter. We'll have to work, probably even fight a little, before it is completely ours. So what do we do?

Every time things looked dismal or hard, Israel wished for the "good old days"—you know, the days in Egypt as slaves when they were beaten and starved. "Do not say, 'Why is it that the former days were better than these?' For it is not from wisdom that you ask about this" (Eccles. 7:10). Their perspective was faulty. They were looking at the wrong thing.

Truthfully, it is easier to look back on what we've already survived or accomplished. It is done, and we made it. Of course, anticipation and suspense will beat together in our hearts at the thought of a new challenge. But that is life! Don't retreat. Don't doubt God. Move forward into His promise. Perspective again. Look up to our great God and forward to His promise.

When we are God's children, the enemies who hate us are God's enemies too. The very first battle Israel fought was against the Amalekites, and God swore to completely defeat them. Again, Israel rejected God's promise and feared their enemy instead. Do we do the same thing—stare at our longtime enemy and forget that God is our Banner, our Warrior?

Caleb and Joshua were the only two of that generation who eventually made it to the Promised Land. The people didn't want it, so God didn't give it to them. His promise is there for us, too, but we have to step forward—trusting Him—and take it.

Bible Reading: **Numbers 13:25–33, Numbers 14:1–38**

Week 8

DAVID

Day 1

A father presided over his busy house and family. The oldest was a handsome, strong son. The father looked proudly at all his strapping boys—well, all but one. The youngest was tending the sheep, but someday that teenage boy would grow into a fine man too.

News reached the house that the prophet Samuel was in town and wanted to worship God with Jesse and his sons. That was not the full purpose, however. Samuel had been sent by God to anoint the second king of Israel. With King Saul still on the throne, that was quite a mission, for Saul had rejected God, and God had rejected Saul as king.

When Samuel entered the house, he looked at the oldest son and thought surely that was God's chosen man. All honor, inheritance, and prestige went to the oldest son in that society. Combine that with the physical presence of the man, and the choice was easy.

"But the LORD said to Samuel, 'Do not look at his appearance or at the height of his stature, because I have rejected him; for God *sees* not as man sees, for man looks at the outward appearance, but the LORD looks at the heart'" (1 Sam. 16:7).

Jesse sent the next six sons in birth order before Samuel, and each time Samuel shook his head. "Is this all your sons?" Samuel asked in confusion. He was told the youngest was tending sheep and would be sent for immediately.

It's interesting that Jesse had not even thought to include his youngest in this great honor. He loved the boy but dismissed him as somewhat insignificant. Jesse probably didn't think of it as having favorites; it was just the way it was.

The teenage son David ran into the room, smelling of sheep and more than a few days without a bath, and the Lord said, "Arise, anoint him; for this is he" (1 Sam. 16:12).

We haven't changed much since that time, have we? Even now, parents, teachers, and coaches have favorites. Star athletes or musicians are still thought to be more significant than an "average" person. Money, age, gender, looks, brains, college degrees—they all determine a person's value in our society today, just as they always have.

You may feel like David, that you don't matter and are pushed into the background, familiar but not appreciated. There are moments when you feel greatness stir inside, but you shove it down before someone tells you you're a daydreamer. You look in the mirror and think, *It's not horrible, not supermodel material, but not scary either.*

Here's the truth. There is usually someone smarter, more talented, and better looking. The world runs to them. But God sees deeper. He is not opposed to a person having all those things. He's the One who gave them. But He never intended for those gifts to only be on the outside. The beauty of humility and honor were to glow from the heart out. The strength of mind and body were to reflect the spirit's power. It's what's inside that makes us great.

A man stutters, and God uses him to lead His people out of slavery. A woman is a beautiful ornament, and God uses her to save a nation. A teenager has an unskilled job, and God anoints him king.

Man looks at the outward appearance, but the Lord looks at the heart.

Bible Reading: 1 Sam. 16:1–13, Luke 9:48

Day 2

David had just been anointed king of Israel. What he did next showed why God chose him. He went back to his sheep. David completed his current job. His work was not finished, and he truly cared that it was done right. He trusted God to give him the throne in God's time.

We can picture the stunned silence in the room as Samuel poured oil over David's head and told him the purpose. This was completely against society's norm. Resentment or envy may have taken root in the eldest son's heart. The youngest was chosen. Yet David did not gloat. He did not command his other brothers to take over the sheep.

What God saw in David was a humble, modest heart. This shepherd had nothing to prove. God uses those who are accustomed to being in the background for the same reason He used David. Recognition and praise were not what motivated a behind-the-scenes worker. It's not about them; it's about the job, the results, the long-term goal. That kind of person doesn't quit when the going gets tough. They don't stop mid-job because they feel unappreciated. Their schedule is not focused on how it will affect their résumé.

Not only was David humble, but he was honorable. He had integrity. God says in 1 Kings 9:4, "As for you, if you will walk before Me as your father David walked, in integrity of heart and uprightness, doing according to all that I have commanded you *and* will keep My statutes and My ordinances. . . ." The word *integrity* in Hebrew means "to be complete, be finished, be upright ethically, innocent and simple."

A person with integrity isn't just a good first impression. They aren't a beautiful package with nothing inside. What you see is the genuine product, complete all the way through. There are no hidden agendas and double meanings; they are straightforward and innocent in all their words, actions, and intentions. That was David. He said what he meant and meant what he said. Whatever he did, he did it all to the best of his ability. There were no small tasks and nothing he would compromise on whether alone or in front of others.

God said, "I HAVE FOUND DAVID the son of Jesse, a MAN AFTER MY HEART, who will do all My will" (Acts 13:22). You see, God wanted a king who would promote God's Kingdom, not the king's own earthly kingdom. Also, the newly anointed king of Israel had a servant's heart, just like God's. Jesus said of Himself, "For even the Son of Man did not come to be served, but to serve, and to give His life a ransom for many" (Mark 10:45).

The greatest leaders are the greatest servants. They get in the trenches and work alongside their people. They never expect someone to do something they wouldn't do. In the end, they realize that the responsibility lies with them to get the job done. Dictators are insecure, petty bullies who force their will on others and fear discussion. Leaders are self-confident, big-hearted servants who people follow out of respect and admiration.

Humility, integrity, and a servant's heart do not happen overnight. "*Thy* kingdom come, *Thy* will be done" takes the training ground David had in his solitary work as a shepherd. Alone time is a hard thing to find and to endure, yet it is essential in order to make someone a person of character and strength. Take time to talk with God and listen to Him.

Enjoy solitude to see yourself as you really are. Welcome privacy to admit your sins and embrace your successes.

Bible Reading: Psalm 78:70–72, 1 Chronicles 28:9, Luke 22:41–42

Day 3

Saul, king of Israel, was extremely depressed and angry. He called for David to come and soothe him by playing his harp. David alternated from Saul to tending his flock at Bethlehem. Goliath, a Philistine giant, and his army came against Israel, and King Saul and his army went out to meet them. Jesse sent his son David to the battle with food for his three brothers who were in the army and to get information about the war.

When David heard Goliath mock God and saw Israel's army flee in fear, he asked, "For who is this uncircumcised Philistine, that he should taunt the armies of the living God?" (1 Sam. 17:26). To most of Israel, God was just a paper God, a national or family tradition, a God they trusted with the little things. But David showed us another reason God had chosen him as the next king. God was living and real and active to David. He not only wanted to defend God's honor, but he believed God had the power to defeat this enemy.

> Now Eliab his oldest brother heard when he spoke to the men; and Eliab's anger burned against David and he said, "Why have you come down? And with whom have you left those few sheep in the wilderness? I know your insolence and the wickedness of your heart; for you have come down in order to see the battle."
> —1 Sam. 17:28

Eliab was harboring resentment that God had chosen David instead of him. It wasn't David's fault, but he would have to endure the jealousy and mean-spirited treatment anyway. David handled it with dignity. He said, "'What have I done now? Was it not just a question?' Then he turned away from him to another and said the same thing; and the people answered the same thing as before" (1 Sam. 17:29–30).

When dealing with petty jealousy, it's best to step away. David let Eliab know his response was unreasonable by his respectful but brief questions, and then he turned away. Resentful, envious people cannot be reasoned with. They won't listen to anything that doesn't reinforce their mindset. David didn't defend his motives when he was attacked. He had more important things to do, so this man after God's own heart let the unjust snub go and moved on.

With five stones and a slingshot, David went out to war.

> *Then David said to the Philistine, "You come to me with a sword, a spear, and a javelin, but I come to you in the name of the Lord of hosts, the God of the armies of Israel, whom you have taunted. This day the Lord will deliver you up into my hands . . . that all this assembly may know that the Lord does not deliver by sword or by spear; for the battle is the Lord's and He will give you into our hands."*
>
> —1 Sam. 17:45–47

God would give the battle into "our" hands, not "my" hands, said David. He allowed the frightened army the dignity of sharing in God's victory—humble leadership.

Conventional wisdom said to armor up and strategize. David said, "God's God. I'll ask Him what to do and then do it." You see, the giant in David's life was God, not a 9'9" giant of a man. The biggest, most powerful thing in David's life was his God, not his enemy. The reason God chose David to be king was because David had already chosen God to be his King.

We have many giants in our lives—the courts, people, bad health, horrible memories—and they are huge, bigger than you or me. Step back, and get some perspective. God is bigger than any of it. It's His battle. It's His victory.

Bible Reading: 1 Samuel 17:1–11, 38–50

Day 4

David's defeat of Goliath ushered him into the hearts of his people. Saul took him back to his palace to marry his daughter, and Saul's son Jonathan became best friends with David. As David's popularity grew, so did Saul's jealousy and rage. David played his harp to soothe his king, and Saul tried to kill him twice. Through a series of events, Jonathan confirmed that his father, King Saul, did indeed intend to kill David, and David went on the run for his life.

Running to Gath, the home of Goliath, seemed like a good idea, but by the time David realized his mistake, he was standing in front of the Philistine king. David's world was crumbling before his eyes and about to get worse. He pretended to be insane, scratching on doors and drooling down his beard (1 Sam. 21:13).

With his self-respect shattered, David escaped to the cave of Adullam. When his brothers and his father's household heard about it, they went down to him.

> *Everyone who was in distress, and who was in debt, and everyone who was discontented gathered to him; and he became captain over them. Now there were about four hundred men with him. And David went from there to Mizpah of Moab; and he said to the king of Moab, "Please let my father and my mother come and stay with you until I know what God will do for me."*
>
> —1 Sam. 22:1–3

You're David. What are you thinking now? *This is it, God? You anointed me to be king, and this is Your plan? My palace is a cave, my people are losers and malcontents, my family is in danger, and I've lost my wife and best friend, not to mention my self-respect. Oh, and I need to be looking over my shoulder because the king of my country has a price on my head. He lied and ruined my reputation. I have nothing. There is no way I can recover from this.*

All of us will experience time in a cave. At some point we will have some of our crutches, or supports, knocked out from under us. David's experience was extreme. He lost everything that holds a person up, gives a person identity, supports a person's heart and mind, and makes a person feel whole, effective, and useful. Every reason to get up in the morning, everything that brings a smile or offers peace and gives strength—all of it was gone, stripped away. David had a faith crisis. *Was any of this ever real? Did I really ever hear Your voice? Do You exist—care—even know?*

> *I cry aloud with my voice to the LORD; I make supplication with my voice to the LORD. I pour out my complaint before Him; I declare my trouble before Him. When my spirit was overwhelmed within me, You knew my path. In the way where I walk they have hidden a trap for me. Look to the right and see; for there is no one who regards me; there is no escape for me; no one cares for my soul. I cried out to*

> *You, O LORD; I said, "You are my refuge, my portion in the land of the living. Give heed to my cry, for I am brought very low; deliver me from my persecutors, for they are too strong for me. Bring my soul out of prison, so that I may give thanks to Your name; the righteous will surround me, for You will deal bountifully with me."*
>
> —Ps. 142:1–7

The lonely desolation of David's cave drove him to his knees and then to his God. We can allow these times to be our boot camp for life, or we can let them crush us. We will sob and ache until we feel empty, and God will care. "You have taken account of my wanderings; put my tears in Your bottle. Are *they* not in Your book?" (Ps. 56:8). God allows the caves to prepare us for our calling. But He'll hold us through it all.

Bible Reading: 1 Sam. 19:1–2, 8–18

Day 5

The man who caused all David's problems was his king. Saul had been chosen by God and anointed by His prophet Samuel, and it was only after Saul rejected God that God rejected him as Israel's king.

> *Then Saul took three thousand chosen men from all Israel and went to seek David and his men in front of the Rocks of the Wild Goats. He came to the sheepfolds on the way, where there was a cave; and Saul went in to relieve himself. Now David and his men were sitting in the inner recesses of the cave. The men of David said to him, "Behold, this is the day of which the LORD said to you, 'Behold; I am about to give your enemy into your hand, and you shall do to him as it seems good to you.'" Then David arose and cut off the edge of Saul's robe secretly. It came about afterward that David's conscience bothered him because he had cut off the edge of Saul's robe. So he said to his men, "Far be it from me because of the LORD that I should do this thing to my lord, the LORD's anointed, to stretch out my hand against him, since he is the LORD's anointed."*
>
> —1 Sam. 24:2–6

Revenge is such a no-brainer. When we've been as wronged and hurt as David was, retaliation makes all the sense in the world. What's to think about? Why would we have to pray when the solution to our problem was right in front of us and vulnerable?

When we spend time in our cave praying and gaining God's view of our life, and when the Lord's eyes show us the big picture—that there are small details we've never considered and long-term consequences we'd like to ignore—when we learn to trust God because everything, absolutely everything, is beyond our control—when God's sandpaper of adversity refines us to the point where integrity matters more than a quick solution, then revenge is not appealing, and payback is not an option. We trust God to solve it His way in His time.

Then David went out of the cave, called out to King Saul, and showed him he had cut his robe. David asked Saul why he listened to lies about him, and in front of all of Saul's men—men who would one day serve under King David—he proved he was a man of integrity and honor. David said, "May the Lord judge between you and me, and may the Lord avenge me on you; but my hand shall not be against you" (1 Sam. 24:12).

Saul wept and said this to David:

> "You are more righteous than I; for you have dealt well with me, while I have dealt wickedly with you. Now, behold, I know that you will surely be king, and that the kingdom of Israel will be established in your hand. So now swear to me by the Lord that you will not cut off my descendants after me and that you will not destroy my name from my father's household." David swore to Saul. And Saul went to his home, but David and his men went up to the stronghold.
>
> —1 Sam. 24:17, 20–22

God had told David He would give his enemy into his hands for him to deal with as he wished. David could have killed King Saul if he had wanted to. Wisdom told him to hold off, to honor a king God had called. Some men were loyal to King Saul, and David would've always had to be alert for revenge if he assassinated the king. Showing honor may prolong his time in the cave, but it would also ensure that his time in the palace would be secure. If he wanted the Israelites to follow him with respect and loyalty, he needed to live that example in the hardest of circumstances. His time of bleakness and devastation had not been wasted. A man of deep strength and honor was formed, and a king was created.

***Bible Reading*: 1 Samuel 24**

Day 6

A week with David has exhausted me! Whoever says being a godly person is dull and boring has never read the Bible or tried it. Some of the things I love about David are that he was rugged and tough, a warrior. Yet he played the harp and other instruments beautifully and cared deeply for the people in his life. I think that is one of the reasons God said their hearts were alike. God is both extremes. He is our Banner and our Warrior in battle, and He is also the Lover of our soul who collects our tears. God loves music and is the artist who created today's sunrise.

To that point, let's remember what God told Samuel. "God *sees* not as man sees, for man looks at the outward appearance, but the Lord looks at the heart" (1 Sam. 16:7). This is so important for us to get. God looks all the way through us, all the way into us, to make His judgments of us. He said in Isaiah 29:13, "This people draw near me with their words and honor Me with their lip service, but they remove their hearts from Me." God doesn't want us to look good, say the right things, and just do good. He wants our hearts to be close to Him, love Him, and honor and obey Him. David proved that good actions and words flowed continually—no matter who saw or what the circumstance—from a godly heart.

Not only do we want our hearts to reflect God's, but we should be just as discerning as God called Samuel to be. Go deeper than the cute face, obvious talent, education, and money. We should watch people through the tough times and in the little things in order to know their heart.

A heart after God's own heart is humble, honorable, and ultimately a servant's heart. That's what we are looking for in ourselves and the people we befriend or follow. Is it all about us, or are we willing to give the glory to God and those around us? Integrity is bone-deep and straightforward, there for the public and there in the background. A servant's heart rolls up its sleeves and does what's required, working with others even if they are the king.

This is not the first time we've seen that others will hate us or misinterpret our intentions when we live a life of integrity. Even David's brothers were jealous of him. But a person with God's heart lets the petty things go and gets on with the big stuff—like proving the "giant" problems are dwarfed when put against our giant God. This heart of God has some steel in it.

With or without God, we'll all experience time in a cave with our support systems knocked out from under us. Making that time productive instead of destructive depends on who we turn to. David said, "Guard my soul and deliver me; do not let me be ashamed, for I take refuge in You. Let integrity and uprightness preserve me, for I wait for You" (Ps. 25:20–21). Let's allow our lonely, miserable times to shape us into leaders in God's service.

Integrity honed by adversity results in perspective. David had the chance for revenge and a quick end to his enemy, and he did not take it. He saw a bigger picture where showing respect was right, and he instilled respect for him in the hearts of the people who were watching. He realized it was worth a little more time in his cave to ensure that his time in the palace was safe, honorable, and pleasing to God.

We need to see God when nothing turns out like we expected. Our perspective must be that God is bigger than our enemies and the only foundation that will last. David showed us that having God's heart takes us from insignificant to influential.

Bible Reading: **1 Samuel 16:7, 11–23, 1 Samuel 17:31–58**

Week 9

JONATHAN

Day 1

Our first introduction to King Saul's son Jonathan was when he was a military leader. The life of this warrior prince was one of walking a tightrope between loyalty and honor.

King Saul was a religious man who talked a good talk about God, but his actions showed that his love of God stopped at his mouth. By the time Jonathan is mentioned, Saul has already sinned so often and so grievously that God said He would give the kingdom to someone else. During that time, the Philistines, as many as the sand, swarmed over Israel and would not allow any blacksmiths in all of Israel, so the Israelites weren't able to fashion weapons. As a result, no one in all of Israel but King Saul and Jonathan had a sword or spear.

Saul had started out with 2,000 men and Jonathan with 1,000, but by the time the Philistine garrison (a battlefield command center) camped nearby, they were down to 600 soldiers all together with most of Israel hiding in caves and crevasses in the hillside. "Now the day came that Jonathan, the son of Saul, said to the young man who was carrying his armor, 'Come and let us cross over to the Philistines' garrison that is on the other side.' But he did not tell his father" (1 Sam. 14:1).

On this one day that seemed like so many other days, Jonathan decided that enough was enough. Israel was in a conflict where defeat was inevitable. The odds were greatly stacked against them, and some of their men had gone over to the enemy. Jonathan was made of stronger stuff. *This is ridiculous. What do we have to lose? I can die like a coward or trust the God of our fathers and go for it.*

A couple of chapters before this account, Samuel had told Israel that God would not forsake them and would defeat their enemies to keep His promise to them. Jonathan took that to heart. It appeared that only Jonathan believed God could and would destroy the Philistines, and the weapons and sheer numbers were of no importance.

> *Then Jonathan said to the young man who was carrying his armor, "Come and let us cross over to the garrison of these uncircumcised; perhaps the LORD will work for us, for the LORD is not restrained to save by many or by few." Then Jonathan said, "Behold, we will cross over to the men and reveal ourselves to them. If they say to us, 'Wait until we come to you'; then we will stand in our place and not go up to them. But if they say, 'Come up to us,' then we will go up, for the LORD has given them into our hands; and this shall be the sign to us."*
>
> —1 Sam. 14:6, 8–10

Jonathan knew some things that caused him to step out so boldly. He knew there was a great need. Also, the past had taught Jonathan that God wanted to work with someone, and he was willing to be used of Him. He could have just prayed for God to miraculously zap the bad guys, but God loved working with the bold and fighting spirit of His people.[2]

Most of Israel believed in theory that nothing could stop God. Jonathan got it. That truth was deep inside of him, real and tried out.

Jonathan proves that being born into the right or the wrong family will not dictate how we turn out. Our parents' wrongs do not have to be our wrongs. Each of us chooses to live with integrity, trust in God, and courage—or not. Every day is a new chance to get it right.

Bible Reading: 1 Samuel 13:16–23, 14:6–23

Day 2

Jonathan and his armor bearer climbed up to the garrison and killed about 20 men, and God delivered the Philistines into the hands of Israel. The men of Israel were worn out that day because Saul had made them take an oath, saying, "Let a curse fall on anyone who eats before evening, before I have full revenge on my enemies." So no one ate a thing all day. But Jonathan had not heard his father's command, and he dipped a stick into a piece of honeycomb and ate the honey. After he had eaten it, he felt much better. But one of the men saw him and said, "Your father made the army take a strict oath that anyone who eats food today will be cursed. That is why everyone is weary and faint."

"My father has made trouble for us all!" Jonathan exclaimed. "A command like that only hurts us. See how much better I feel now that I have eaten this little bit of honey? If the men had been allowed to eat freely from the food they found among our enemies, think how many more we could have killed!" That day, after the Israelites had struck down the Philistines, they were exhausted (1 Sam. 14:24–31).

Back to today . . . one of our parents does something harmful to us and our family. What do we do? The boss tells us to change the numbers on a billing code in order to receive more money. We're told not to address an infidelity or misconduct so it doesn't ruin an athlete's, pastor's, or politician's career. We're asked to participate in fraud or abuse. How do we handle that? Where do our loyalties lie? In a split second, we must decide to speak the truth and go against authority or play it safe. In only a moment, we need to make a decision that could help many but get us into trouble.

Loyalty and honor collide. It's been suggested that Jonathan should not have said anything to his men and gone to speak to his father privately. That would be protocol, the correct code of etiquette. But this was war in the midst of survival, surrounded by danger.

Living in a family with a parent like King Saul causes us to have to make tough choices—choices that many people, including ourselves, will second-guess and criticize. Saul's authority pressured his soldiers into promising something they knew would hurt them. He put on his religious act and pushed them to fast for him, not for God. It was dangerous and foolish.

Jonathan, fresh out of his death-defying heroism, didn't blink. His men mattered. The war mattered. The women and children they were defending mattered. His father's pride and authority could be handled later. He told them to eat.

The Bible teaches us to respect all authority, and that all authority was given by God (Rom. 13:1–7). But Jesus did not tolerate abuse of power. In Matthew 23, Jesus raked the religious leaders over the coals in front of all the people. That would be like telling our parent or boss in front of others that they are wrong—like Jonathan changing his father's order.

We must be careful. Jesus stood against leaders who were putting heavy burdens on people (Luke 17:2). But He only opposed leaders to protect others and defend God's holy way. Never does Jesus condone rebellion, disrespect, or hatred. "Children, obey your parents in the Lord, for this is right" (Eph. 6:1). For the Lord's sake, respect all human authority (1 Pet. 2:13). Honor the Lord, but when someone needs protection, God calls His children to action.

Bible Reading: **Matthew 12:10–15 (one of Jesus's examples), Acts 5:27–29, Romans 13:1–7**

Day 3

Have you ever looked around and felt as if you were the only one who believed a certain thing—that you were alone in your willingness to stand up for something or fight for what was right? Imagine, then, that you discovered another person who demonstrates the same strength of spirit and courage to act as you have. It's a person who does not merely talk tough but lives tough. What would your reaction be?

The heart of the warrior who believed God could and would defeat an enemy who outarmed him. The mind of the soldier who was willing to risk everything to stand in that faith met another man with the same heart and mind. After David finished talking with Saul, he met Jonathan, the king's son. There was an immediate bond of love between them, and they became the best of friends (1 Sam. 18:1).

We were not meant to do life alone. God created us in His image, and God does not stand as a single, isolated individual. "Then God said, 'Let Us make man in Our image, according to Our likeness'" (Gen. 1:26). *Us* and *Our*—God the Father, God the Son, and God the Holy Spirit—worked, planned, and talked together as They created us. We were made to be like our God, working, planning, and talking to others who believe, think, and act like us.

If we come from a background where the closest people in our lives caused pain, it could make us want to keep a distance from others. Look closely at that attitude. It seems smart. But is it? Look at what Solomon says:

> *Two are better than one because they have a good return for their labor. For if either of them falls, the one will lift up his companion. But woe to the one who falls when there is not another to lift him up.*

Furthermore, if two lie down together they keep warm, but how can one be warm alone? And if one can overpower him who is alone, two can resist him. A cord of three strands is not quickly torn apart.
—Eccles. 4:9–12

I'm not like you. I don't need people in my life. I'm not a people person. People can't be trusted, so why try? Can you think of other defenses for keeping to yourself? It's understandable to be leery when you have been surrounded by people who betrayed your trust, were selfish, and totally disregarded what was best for others. Once again, we need to look at what is motivating our decisions. Boil the whole thing down. It starts with *I don't care . . . It's just smart to be cautious.* Keep going. Dare to be honest. *I'm afraid. I don't ever want to hurt this way again.* We should never—ever—let fear motivate any of our decisions. Over and over in the Bible we are told "do not fear them," "do not fear," "don't be afraid."

Is it scary to imagine our affection and trust being rejected? You bet. We can't let it stop us from searching for and accepting a good friend. Does the idea of being betrayed by a person we trusted make us nauseous? Of course. We must not let the people who have betrayed us control our life forever. We can take our life back and live the way we were meant to live. We can surround ourselves with a few good friends.

The key is to be discerning when choosing our friends. Remember what God told Samuel. Look at the heart of a person, not the package. Watch them day in and day out. Like Jonathan, observe a person in the most stressful of times, in the little details they think no one sees. Listen to their words, and watch how they treat the "smallest" people and the most important people. Be careful when choosing your friends, but do not be fearful.

Bible Reading: 1 Samuel 18:1–4, Proverbs 17:17, 18:24, 27:6, James 2:23

Day 4

Jonathan gave an example of how to honor a parent when they are publicly embarrassing and morally wrong. Throughout Jonathan's life, we see the grief of a child, no matter the age, when a mother or father is out of control and bent on destruction. His example of standing up to his father for rightness and quietly walking away from issues of lesser importance is impressive.

From the start, we saw Jonathan accepting the poor leadership of his father. He did not condemn or criticize his father and king for sitting under a tree while the country was in chaos and under siege. On his own, Jonathan quietly went up to the enemy's garrison and started the offensive that saved Israel. Jonathan was willing to accept the punishment for eating on that day, even though it was a foolish oath to have taken. His friendship with David, whom his father praised and then hated jealously, placed Jonathan in a volatile position.

"Now Saul told Jonathan his son and all his servants to put David to death. But Jonathan, Saul's son, greatly delighted in David. So Jonathan told David . . ." (1 Sam. 19:1–2). Saying no to murder, even if your dad or a government authority orders it, is right. The Bible does say for children to obey their parents, but "in the Lord" means just that. God plainly said don't murder. In the book of Acts, government officials told the disciples to stop talking about Jesus, and the disciples said, "We must obey God rather than men" (Acts 5:29).

You and I look at this and see in our own lives that God has protected us by His clear rules and guidelines. Sometimes the right and wrong are clear, and we don't have to guess at it. If any authority figure tells us to do something God has already said is wrong, we obey God and disobey them. No, we won't participate in sexual immorality. No, we won't steal or lie.

A person in Jonathan's situation will not avoid some lumps. If he pleased his father, he would be a murderer as well as lose his best friend and the respect of his nation, not to mention the damage it would cause to his conscience. If he did not obey his father, he faced his wrath. At one point, King Saul threw his spear at Jonathan because he was so angry. How humiliating to have your father publicly throw a temper tantrum.

Some may say it was good for Jonathan not to kill David, but he shouldn't have warned him. He should have stayed neutral. We've already discussed the importance of protecting the innocent, which alone vindicated Jonathan's decision to tell David. There comes a time, though, when we do need to draw a line and let the world know which side we stand on. Light and dark don't mix. Paul asked, "What partnership have righteousness and lawlessness?" (2 Cor. 6:14). At some point, we, like Jonathan, need to say, "This is what I stand for. This is how I will live." Sometimes it means we physically walk over and stand beside our friend instead of our parent.

No parent should put their child in that position. But they do. If you have wrestled with the guilt of not choosing well or going against your parent or spouse, know that you are not alone. Jonathan was a grown man, and this was incredibly hard for him. He didn't bad-mouth his dad or yell at him in disgust, but he did stand up to him. The price could be high, but here's a promise, "If God *is* for us, who *is* against us?" (Rom. 8:31). We can do this in His strength.

Bible Reading: 1 Samuel 20:18–42

Day 5

Besides Jesus, I think Jonathan is the best example of a friend in all the Bible.

First, Jonathan initiated the friendship. He had to because he was the crown prince, the next in line, while David was a shepherd and a war hero. Social position was not what Jonathan looked for in a friend, however. Integrity, courage, honor, bravery, quiet leadership, humbleness, respectfulness, faith, love of God—Jonathan had these qualities and recognized them in David. He was drawn to the good in David and sought him out to befriend him.

It's not clear if Jonathan knew David was the man God had chosen as the next king of Israel when they met, but he soon found out. Another quality of a good friend is a lack of jealousy. This situation could have been very awkward for both David and Jonathan. David was to take Jonathan's place because his father, King Saul, had failed so miserably. Jonathan respected God's decision and recognized that his friend was the perfect man for the job. He was happy for his friend's success and satisfied that his people would finally have a leader who would have their best interest at heart.

A friend defends our reputation. When Saul bad-mouthed David and lied about the fact that David wanted to kill him, Jonathan stood up for the truth.

> *Do not let the king sin against his servant David, since he has not sinned against you, and since his deeds* have been *very beneficial to you. For he took his life in his hand and struck the Philistine, and the* LORD *brought about a great deliverance for all Israel; you saw* it *and rejoiced. Why then will you sin against innocent blood by putting David to death without a cause?*
>
> —1 Sam. 19:4–5

Not only did Jonathan defend his friend, but he held his dad accountable for his intentions and words.

True friendship is willing to sacrifice. Jesus said in John 15:13, "Greater love has no one than this, that one lay down his life for his friends." Jonathan willingly risked his life to protect David. His father might have hated him, disowned him, or treated him terribly, but Jonathan did the right thing and developed a plan to help David run for his life. A true friend goes out of their way to encourage us.

> *And Jonathan, Saul's son, arose and went to David at Horesh, and encouraged him in God. Thus he said to him, "Do not be afraid, because the hand of Saul my father will not find you, and you will be king over Israel and I will be next to you; and Saul my father knows that also." So the two of them made a covenant before the* LORD*; and David stayed at Horesh while Jonathan went to his house.*
>
> —1 Sam. 23:16–18

These two friends hadn't seen each other in a while, but Jonathan knew David was probably feeling discouraged and depressed. Friends seek each other out, take time to connect, and encourage each other. When things are the darkest and you feel swallowed up by your enormous problem, a good friend will not tire of your tears. They will listen to you and pray with you. And if needed, they will push you into the truth.

Jonathan also reassured David that things were good between them. He held no resentment because David would be the next king. "You will be king, and I will be second to you." A true friend has your back, and you can count on them. They want what's best for you.

What a friend Jonathan was! The greatest friend you could ever know is Jesus. Like Jonathan, Jesus has initiated the friendship. Take Him up on it.

Bible Reading: 1 Samuel 23:10–18, John 15:9–17

Day 6

What a friend we've made in Jonathan! One of the most exciting things for me as a mother is for my two sons to be rugged and manly, and yet sensitive with a great capacity to love at the same time.

JONATHAN

As a woman and mother of a daughter, I am thrilled to know there are men like Jonathan and David—men of integrity and courage who are protectors, not predators. I love the fact that music and military strategy flowed together in the minds of Jonathan and David. Friendship and family—relationships—were important to these men, and they weren't afraid to show it. Mostly, my heart swells with emotion to see that these strong, good-looking men loved God. They believed in His power and sovereignty and love for them.

We are starting to see that God works through us in different ways. Moses and Esther had time to pray, fast, and think before speaking and acting. David and Jonathan were in the middle of a battle and had to go into instant action with a quick prayer darted up to God.

Jonathan knew God. He knew how God had fought in his nation's history. God was real to him, and his faith was deep and strong. Unlike his father, Jonathan listened to the prophet Samuel and drank in the wisdom and promises of God. He spent time with the Lord.

That is how we can survive and win in our life's battles. We need to be prayed up. We need to spend time alone with God, talking with Him and listening to Him. Reading our Bibles not only tells us God's methods and provisions for us, but it also gives us a history with Him. When a crisis slams us into a panic, we can have past experience to draw from—maybe not our personal experience but our God's personal experience. However and whenever we are ambushed by our enemies, we can be ready. Like Jonathan, we can say, "Let's go. If it's their many against my few, it doesn't matter to God. He can take them. He's done it before."

Our battles are not just about facing a huge enemy. Like Jonathan, we need to be ready to speak hard words to our parents, authority figures, or friends when they are endangering others. It's one of those circumstances when all we have time for is a quick "what do I say?" to God while the other person is talking.

Thank God for the training grounds of our lives. Would you or Jonathan have wished for better dads? Probably. But growing up with King Saul prepared Jonathan to be the soldier and man we met. As he grew up and when the going got tough, Jonathan ran to God. He paid attention to what worked and how God worked.

Jonathan died fighting alongside his father in defense of his country. That brings tears to my eyes. He was, indeed, an extraordinary man. His dad did nothing to deserve such loyalty. However, his position as father and king did merit honor. And we all know that no matter what our parents are like, some part of us loves them and needs to be loved and respected by them. Jonathan did the hard thing. He stood up to and against his dad when needed, and he loved his dad to the end, taking his orders in battle and dying beside him in a fight against their common enemy.

My prayer is that we will run to God and allow Him to transform our broken, angry hearts into warrior hearts full of honor and love. May Jonathan's life lead us to Jesus.

Bible Reading: **1 Samuel 31:1–7, 1 John 3:16–24**

Week 10

JOSEPH

Day 1

Joseph's story is fascinating and rich in meaning and application. We'll spend a week with him but will cover only a few points. Joseph was the second-youngest of Jacob's 12 sons. Jacob had two wives—Leah and Rachel—and Rachel was the one he loved most. The two youngest sons were born to Jacob and Rachel, and because of that, they were Jacob's favorites.

Jacob made a special coat of many colors for Joseph, which hurt and angered his other sons who not surprisingly took it out on Joseph. They hated Joseph and could not speak to him on friendly terms. At 17, Joseph was a good kid. He loved God and all his brothers and sisters; he sincerely wanted to do what was right. However, he often didn't think before he spoke. One day he was watching the flocks with his brothers and noticed they were doing things they shouldn't be doing. When he went home, he told his dad.

Adding to his marks against him, Joseph told his brothers two dreams he had in which objects that represented the brothers were bowing to an object that represented Joseph. Their hatred grew until they acted on it. They decided to kill Joseph, but one brother stopped them. So they tore off his coat and threw him into a well. A caravan came by, and the brothers sold Joseph into slavery. They took his coat and dipped it in goat's blood to show to their father, which led him to believe that a wild animal had killed Joseph.

Knowing when to speak and when to keep quiet is an important skill. At 17 or younger, we most likely will learn this by making some mistakes, just as Joseph did. The Bible spends a lot of time teaching us about the words we speak. Colossians 4:6 tells us, "Let your speech always be with grace, *as though* seasoned with salt, so that you will know how you should respond to each person." Titus 2 tells us to be sensible in speech. Proverbs 10 instructs us a couple times that a wise person listens and gains knowledge, but a person who talks a lot will be ruined.

Joseph's heart was good, but he needed to learn to keep his mouth closed. Just because we know something doesn't mean we have to tell everyone. It could be something good, even some amazing thing God has revealed to us. Maybe it's something exciting that will thrill others. Be wise. Don't ever let a thought go straight from popping up in our brain to shooting out of our mouth. We need to stop and pray over it. We need to spend time thinking about if it really needs to be said, who should hear it, and who shouldn't.

The book of James talks about our tongues being like the bits we put in a horse's mouth. We change the horse's direction by that little thing in its mouth. So also the tongue is a small thing, but what enormous damage it can do. A tiny spark can set a great forest on fire (James 3:5).

Truthfully, Joseph's problems were caused by more than his ill-considered words. However, he could have gone a long way toward making peace with his brothers if he had used a little wisdom when he talked to them and about them.

All of us have hurt someone with our words. We've all been cut or angered by other people's words. That's why it is so important to close our lips and ask God if and when we should say what we know, feel, or think. David wrote in Psalm 19:14, "Let the words of my mouth and the meditation of my heart be acceptable in Your sight, O Lord." Wise counsel.

Bible Reading: Genesis 37:1-4, 23-28

Day 2

Here are some ideas about parts of Joseph's life. From his dirt-walled captivity in the well, his thoughts would have raced. *The looks on my brothers' faces were terrifying. I know they were always angry with me, but, this?*

God, where are You? You know my heart. Okay, maybe I shouldn't have told them my dreams, but they were amazing. They were not really dreams; they were from You, weren't they? Even Dad got mad at me, so I guess I should have kept them to myself. Looking up at a noise, Joseph grabbed his brothers' arms, thinking they were going to rescue him. But all around were camels and dust and men, and behind them was a line of slaves. Joseph started breathing harder. His brothers were selling him. They were selling him like a common slave.

JOSEPH

Look at me, one of you—look at me! Don't do this. What will Dad do? This is wrong. Joseph turned to look back at his brothers as the caravan moved on, and one of the slave traders hit him in the head. Resolve hardened in his heart as he stumbled to stay upright. *God! God! Are You there? Do You see this? Help me. Please. I don't understand this.*

By the second day Joseph had learned how to keep his eyes ahead and his mouth shut. *God! You are my only hope. Save me. I don't see how those dreams can come true if I am a slave in some far-off place. This can't be what You want. I shouldn't have said so many things. I was so stupid! But it was punishable by this? They have done worse and gotten no punishment! Where is the justice there? How does this happen to a man who loves You?*

Finally, the caravan arrived in Egypt. Buckets of water were thrown on the slaves to clean them up so they would fetch a good price at the market. They were led to the auction block and bartered like goats. *I will not hang my head. I am Joseph, son of Abraham, Isaac, and Jacob.* He went stiff as someone poked at his stomach. *I did not know humiliation could feel this degrading, Lord.* Joseph squeezed his fists together and looked up. *You are my strength and my salvation. My life is in Your hands, Lord God.*

Potiphar, an Egyptian officer of Pharaoh, the captain of the bodyguard, bought Joseph. The Lord was with Joseph, so he became a successful man. And he was in the house of his master, the Egyptian (Gen. 39:1–2).

Is that a stretch for you? The Lord was with Joseph and yet terrible things happened to him. He became successful, yet it was as a slave. We are reminded again that God sees things differently than we do. Let's be very clear on the fact that God does not cause sin. Deuteronomy 32:4 says, "The Rock! His work is perfect, for all His ways are just; a God of faithfulness and without injustice, righteous and upright is He."

However, God allows us to choose how we will live, and if we choose sin, He allows its harm and destruction to touch us and the people around us. At the end of his life, Joseph said, "As for you, you meant evil against me, *but* God meant it for good in order to bring about this present result, to preserve many people alive" (Gen. 50:20).

God is good. He sees you in your pain and fear, living in the disaster of someone else's choices. Give Him your next step and then your next one . . . trust Him to work all things for good in your life. He has a plan for you, and as with Joseph, it will prosper you and others.

Bible Reading: Genesis 39:1–6, Romans 8:24–28

Day 3

Joseph was a 17-year-old spoiled boy when he was betrayed and sold into slavery. A situation that had the potential to destroy any person strengthened him. By the time he was brought to Egypt he was a determined, unshakable man of God.

God was with Joseph, and everything he did succeeded, so Potiphar put him in charge of all his possessions. When Potiphar's wife came on to Joseph, he said an insightful thing. "With me *here*, my master does not concern himself with anything in the house, and he has put all that he owns in my charge. There is no one greater in this house than I, and he has withheld nothing from me except you, because you are his wife. How then could I do this great evil and sin against God?" (Gen. 39:8–9).

Joseph realized that if he sinned, he would betray Potiphar. There is never a time that we can say, "This is my life. I can do what I want. It's nobody's business but mine." Sin has a ripple effect. We are touched, the people closest to us are affected, people further out and maybe even into the next generation experience the effect of our choice.

While the sin would hurt Potiphar, it would be against God. Joseph reminded himself and this woman that it was God and not his Egyptian master who was in control of his life. Ultimately, he would answer to God. Maybe the sin could stay hidden from the boss but not from God.

In retaliation, the woman accused Joseph of attacking her, and he was sent to prison, but the Lord was with Joseph there. Some of us probably smirked at that. Yes, God was kind to Joseph in prison, and Joseph prospered. He became in charge of the whole prison.

If we're getting the hang of how God works, we can see that He is getting Joseph ready for something—training him, refining him. And Joseph was doing great. No matter where he was, he worked hard and did his best. He treated others with respect. He thought and planned and made things better. Most importantly, he listened to God.

Soon two of Pharaoh's servants were imprisoned with Joseph, and they told him their dreams. Joseph asked God and interpreted their dreams. One servant was hanged, and one was sent back to serve the king, just as Joseph had said. The servant forgot all about Joseph until two years later when the king had a dream no one could understand. The king told Joseph his dream, and Joseph explained it to him. The king put Joseph second only to him in all of Egypt.

It took 13 years for God's plan to unfold in a way Joseph could plainly see. He went to bed that first night not only free from prison but second in command over all Egypt! How could he take it in? It was overwhelming. His mind wandered back to walking in the caravan with all the other slaves. Until then, he never knew how little a person could have and still survive. He'd never considered that a slave or prisoner had as much need for dignity as (he laughed) a second in command of a country. Those experiences were vital to being a good leader. The dreams of a teenage boy were starting to make more sense.

How desperately I want you to get this. Where you are may not be any place you would have wished for. No one dreams of having a broken family or being jobless or sick. Be a Joseph here. Right now, know God, do your best, and work carefully. People who go through stuff this hard are being readied for something great. Trust God. You are a leader in the making.

Bible Reading: **Genesis 39:20-23, Genesis 40:12-15, 23, Genesis 41:38-44**

Day 4

From Pharaoh's dreams, God revealed there would be seven years of abundance and then seven years of severe drought and famine. Joseph married and carried out his duties of storing up grain for the famine years. During the time of plenty, he had two sons. "Joseph named the firstborn Manasseh, 'For,' *he said*, 'God has made me forget all my trouble and all my father's household.' He named the second Ephraim, 'For,' *he said*, 'God has made me fruitful in the land of my affliction.'" (Gen. 41:51-52).

What's in a name? God's healing and Joseph's maturing were reflected in each of the names of his sons. Manasseh means "causing to forget" in Hebrew. Joseph had obviously not forgotten his family or the painful days in his past. He had chosen to not recall the feelings his family's behavior had stirred up in him. As Joseph gave God his life, he also gave Him the anger, hurt, bitterness, and unforgiveness in his heart toward his family.

We cannot be free to move forward when we are weighted down with the burden of those destructive feelings and thoughts. By their very nature, they overcome everything else in our minds until they are all we think and talk about. Revenge will boil up in our plans instead of the positive strategies that caused Joseph success in all he did. Added to that was God. He forgives and chooses to forget. Maturing and reflecting our Lord's nature produces forgiveness in us. God said in Isaiah 43:25, "I, even I, am the one who wipes out your transgressions for My own sake, and I will not remember your sins." It is not that God is incapable of remembering; it is that He chooses not to think of it and bring it up.

Ephraim's literal meaning is "double ash-heap: I shall be doubly fruitful." Joseph had found success and love in Egypt, but it was still the land of his suffering and difficulty. And in a nod to honesty, Joseph said Egypt had acted as a double ash-heap or compost heap for him. The pain and ugliness fertilized Joseph until he was "doubly fruitful."

It is all true. I've experienced it too. Times of fear and soul-deep pain fertilize us. Fertilizer acts as a stimulant and a nourishment to soil and plants—and to you and me. Our roots go deeper, our stems grow stronger, and our leaves and fruit show the rich color of healthy ripeness, or readiness. The good and easy times can fatten us up, but if our base is not sturdy and our roots are not deep, that added excess will break us or rot us.

These two things—forgetting past wrongs and growing because of them—take time. Years. And they both happen because we intentionally choose for them to happen. That is what we put our energy into. When the negative claws our memories, we tell God every dark, angry detail and ask Him to help us forget. On the days we can't move forward, let alone be productive, we tell God. "This is a bunch of poop!" I can almost laugh as I think of asking God to spread the manure of my hurts all over my life so, like Joseph, I could double my fruitfulness.

Famine did come for Joseph, and in time, he would be called to draw upon all God had grown in him. Seeing his family again would be a dream and the biggest challenge yet.

***Bible Reading*: Genesis 41:45–57, Philippians 3:12–14**

Day 5

Canaan was also experiencing the famine, and Jacob, Joseph's father, told his older sons to go to Egypt to buy grain. But he kept Benjamin, the youngest son, with him.

> *Now Joseph was the ruler over the land; he was the one who sold to all the people of the land. And Joseph's brothers came and bowed down to him with their faces to the ground. When Joseph*

saw his brothers he recognized them, but he disguised himself to them and spoke to them harshly. And he said to them, "Where have you come from?" And they said, "From the land of Canaan, to buy food." But Joseph had recognized his brothers, although they did not recognize him.
—Gen. 42:6–8

Joseph spoke harshly to his brothers, causing them to recall all they had done to him, although they thought he was dead. He heard them admitting their guilt and remorse, which moved him to tears. Joseph kept his identity hidden, and the next time his family needed food, Benjamin came too. Finally, Joseph revealed himself to his brothers in a deeply emotional scene. Great fear overcame the 10 older brothers, and Joseph said to them, "Now do not be grieved or angry with yourselves, because you sold me here, for God sent me before you to preserve life. Now, therefore, it was not you who sent me here, but God."
—Gen. 45:5, 8

How do we handle the people in our lives who have caused us great pain and treated us unjustly? Joseph is one of many examples in the Bible of someone who holds the person responsible for his harm accountable. "I am Joseph, the brother you sold into slavery," he said. Forgiving does not mean lying about the facts. It is not about pretending the person did not do something bad and wrong. In fact, forgiveness cannot take place until we are completely honest about what happened, how it happened, and why it happened.

David told Saul he had lied and listened to lies and that he was wrong to try to kill him. God told Israel they disobeyed and were hard-hearted. Esther clearly stated that Haman was evil for wanting to slaughter an entire race. Jonathan told his dad it was wrong to want to kill a man who was innocent.

Here's the thing. We are to speak the truth . . . in love. We can get so wrapped up in the "in love" thing that we forget the truth, yet each part of this is important. We're also afraid to come off as judging others. Let's figure out how to do this right. Accusing and condemning are not what God wants. Stating the facts without being hateful, without being abusive with our words, is what works. We and God have already dealt with our feelings, so when we face the one who hurt us, we state the facts and move forward in a positive and productive way. While we can offer forgiveness to someone for the hurt they've caused, we cannot offer forgiveness from God who they sinned against. That is up to them. They have to accept Jesus's payment for sins and His forgiveness, and honestly confess their sins.

Joseph had forgiven long ago, and then spoke the truth and moved on. He reflected God's mercy by protecting and providing for his family. Like Jesus, who was sent not to condemn the world but to save it (John 3:17), we should speak the truth and act in love.

Bible Reading: Genesis 45:1–11, Ephesians 4:14–32

Day 6

Joseph's father, Jacob, died.

> *When Joseph's brothers saw that their father was dead, they said, "What if Joseph bears a grudge against us and pays us back in full for all the wrong which we did to him!" So they sent a message to Joseph, saying, "Your father charged before he died, saying, 'Thus you shall say to Joseph, "Please forgive, I beg you, the transgression of your brothers and their sin, for they did you wrong."' And now, please forgive the transgression of the servants of the God of your father." And Joseph wept when they spoke to him. Then his brothers also came and fell down before him and said, "Behold, we are your servants." But Joseph said to them, "Do not be afraid, for am I in God's place? As for you, you meant evil against me, but God meant it for good in order to bring about this present result, to preserve many people alive. So therefore, do not be afraid; I will provide for you and your little ones." So he comforted them and spoke kindly to them.*
>
> —Gen. 50:15–21

Matthew Henry wrote, "A guilty conscience exposes men to continual frights, even where no fear is, and makes them suspicious of every body, as Cain . . . . Those that would be fearless must keep themselves guiltless. If our heart reproach [blames] us not, then have we confidence both towards God and man."[3]

These men could not believe that Joseph had forgiven them because they could not forgive themselves and found it hard to forgive others. It is a terrible way to live—always afraid, always manipulating to stop retaliation, never surrendering to God and accepting His forgiveness and restoration, and never forgiving when we've been hurt.

Forgiveness is a difficult thing to accept from anyone. Accepting it from God is especially hard at first for a couple of reasons. First, He is completely holy and pure and good, and we have made such a mess of our lives and hurt others. The gap between God and us is just so obvious, so huge.

Second, we want to do something to make up for it. We want to promise to be His servants, as Joseph's brothers did, to somehow earn the favor of God. Then we watch nervously, wondering if He'll decide to take His forgiveness away.

Romans 10:9 says, "If you confess with your mouth Jesus *as* Lord, and believe in your heart that God raised Him from the dead, you will be saved." It's all His work. Our forgiveness never goes away; we can't undo it. "For the death that He died, He died to sin *once for all*; but the life that He lives, He lives to God" (emphasis added) (Rom. 6:10). Galatians 2:16 tells us that a person is not justified (made right) by the works of the Law (doing good things) but through faith in Christ Jesus. We do not need to live in fear. Accept Jesus's death and resurrection as payment for your sins, a debt He finished paying once for all. Then believe Him, and live in confidence and peace.

***Bible Reading*: Genesis 50**

Week 11

JESUS'S ARREST

Day 1

Jesus began to be sorrowful and troubled. Then He said to His disciples:

"My soul is deeply grieved, to the point of death; remain here and keep watch with Me." And He went a little beyond them, and fell on His face and prayed, saying, "My Father, if it is possible, let this cup pass from Me; yet not as I will, but as You will." And He came to the disciples and found them sleeping, and said to Peter, "So, you men could not keep watch with Me for one hour? Keep watching and praying that you may not enter into temptation; the spirit is willing, but the flesh is weak." He went away again a second time and prayed, saying, "My Father, if this cannot pass away unless I drink it, Your will be done." Again He came and found them sleeping, for their eyes were heavy. And He left them again, and went away and prayed a third time, saying the same thing once more. Then He came to the disciples and said to them, "Are you still sleeping and resting? Behold, the hour is at hand and the Son of Man is being betrayed into the hands of sinners. Get up, let us be going; behold, the one who betrays Me is at hand!"

—Matt. 26:38–46

Jesus's Arrest

The purpose of Jesus's coming was to pay the penalty for our sins because it was a debt we were incapable of paying. He always knew He would die on the cross, but taking God's full wrath was agonizing to Him. The night before He was to die, He was so upset that He asked His three closest friends to pray with Him. And they fell asleep. The first time Jesus woke them up, He was very stern with them. "Couldn't you men keep watch with Me for one hour?"

Does that sound loving? When a nightmare is coming down on us hard, we need help. We need our friends. Jesus was desperate for their strength and prayers, and He let them know they had let Him down. They were physically and emotionally exhausted; He knew that. Sometimes life isn't about us. Sometimes another person has needs that outweigh our needs.

With an anguished heart, Jesus loved His friends enough to warn them, "Watch and pray so that you will not fall into temptation. The spirit is willing, but the body is weak." Is that amazing love? Really, put yourself in Jesus's place. You're grieved because one of your friends betrayed you. Dread and fear are pounding in your heart until you think it'll explode, and you feel as if you can't take a deep breath. You'd begged your best friends to stay with you and pray, and they fell asleep. Along with the fact that you're irritated and hurt, you look at them and think, *I have to protect them. They aren't ready for what's going to happen.*

Jesus told them in essence, "I believe in you. I know you want to do the right thing. You don't want to deny Me, and you want to be strong and have faith; but your nature, your humanness, is weak. You can't do it on your own. You need the help of God, so you need to be prayed up in order to hold up in what's coming."

The second time Jesus found them sleeping, He turned around and left them. They were in a dangerous way, and He'd already warned them. They would regret it. He'd tried to teach them. Sometimes God leaves us where we've chosen to be, even when it's harmful.

What kind of friendship do you have with Jesus? In the hardest of times, He proved that He loves us enough to push, He believes in us enough to trust, and He cares enough to be tough.

***Bible Reading*: Luke 22:39–47**

Day 2

"Then [Jesus] came to the disciples and said to them, 'Are you still sleeping and resting? Behold, the hour is at hand and the Son of Man is being betrayed into the hands of sinners. Get up, let us be going; behold, the one who betrays Me is at hand!'" (Matt. 26:45–46).

Would you have given up by now? *Forget them! I've got enough on my plate without worrying about a bunch of "friends" who apparently aren't that good of friends.* Jesus is tenacious. I love that in a friend. He is persistent and steadfast, loyal and consistent. Remember how I said that sometimes life isn't just about you? The same went for Jesus. The same goes for you and me when we are the ones in deep pain with problems. Sometimes life isn't all about us. Sometimes we need to look at our friends and see them with God's eyes. They're weak or scared, and they feel so inadequate. They need us.

Because Jesus was watching and alert to what was going on, He warned the disciples. Look, watch out, pay attention! Again, the temptation would be to let them get whopped upside the head with what was coming. It would serve them right.

Then Jesus told them to get up. Here's the thing. Whether we are prayed up and ready or not, life is going to hit us. Jesus said, "You need to get up and get going. You can't close your eyes again and pretend it isn't there. Get up because, ready or not, here comes trouble."

In what I think are the most beautiful words of friendship I have ever heard, Jesus said, "Let *us* go." Do you understand what He did? He knew he'd be beaten and whipped, and Jesus knew the night would be horrific before being crucified and facing the wrath of God. But He looked at His friends and saw that they were not ready to face that. They had not prayed and been filled with God's strength, insight, and peace—but He had. So He said, "I'll go with you. I'll help you in this fight. I'll hold your hand. I'll walk you through this. Let's do this together."

Then Jesus took the initiative. That was His choice. He went down and met Judas and the soldiers, and the next words Jesus spoke were again words of loving friendship. Judas approached Jesus to kiss Him, and Jesus said, "Friend, *do* what you have come for" (Matt. 26:50). That was it. Friend. He was reminding Judas one last time that he didn't have to do this. Jesus was willing to still be his friend. That one word said, "Remember all we've been through together? Remember how we laughed and cried, the amazing things we've seen and done? We were friends. We can still be friends."

Jesus's Arrest

Jesus says the same things to us. Get up. I'll go with you into this hard time. I'll help you. Friend, I'm going to allow you to do what you choose, but remember the time we've spent together. I am your friend. You don't have to follow through with a bad plan.

"You are My friends if you do what I command you. No longer do I call you slaves, for the slave does not know what his master is doing; but I have called you friends, for all things that I have heard from My Father I have made known to you" (John 15:14–15).

Bible Reading: John 10:17–18, 15:1–17

Day 3

So Jesus, knowing all the things that were coming upon Him, went forth and said to them, "Whom do you seek?" They answered Him, "Jesus the Nazarene." He said to them, "I am He." And Judas also, who was betraying Him, was standing with them. *So when He said to them, "I am He," they drew back and fell to the ground. Therefore He again asked them, "Whom do you seek?"* And they said, "Jesus the Nazarene." *Jesus answered, "I told you that I am He; so if you seek Me, let these go their way,"* to fulfill the word which He spoke, "Of those whom You have given Me I lost not one." Simon Peter then, having a sword, drew it and struck the high priest's slave, and cut off his right ear; and the slave's name was Malchus. So Jesus said to Peter, "Put the sword into the sheath; the cup which the Father has given Me, shall I not drink it?"

—John 18:4–11

Luke 22:51 gives us a little more detail on this scene. "But Jesus answered and said, 'Stop [Peter]! No more of this.' And He touched the servant's ear and healed him."

How did Jesus go from deep distress and grief to the point of sweating blood, to a man in control of this mob scene? What enables a person to see their friends' need and take care of it during a crisis? From where does the command presence to control a battalion of enemy soldiers and sword-wielding crowd come?

It comes from honest words with God. Jesus told His Father this plan was not one He wanted or looked forward to. We can say the same things to God. Jesus cried and begged and gave God all His emotions, fears, wishes, and thoughts about what was going on in His life. He was completely transparent, not trying to sound spiritual and wise and strong. *I hate this. I'm scared. Are You sure there isn't a better way? This hurts, and I don't think I can take it.*

Then there were the words that give resolve and determination. "Not my will but Yours, Lord God." In Jesus's humanness, it was easy for Him to get caught up in the moment and only see, feel, and think about what was right in front of Him. Remember Hebrews 4:15: "For we do not have a high priest [Jesus] who cannot sympathize with our weaknesses, but One who has been tempted in all things as *we are,* yet without sin." He was short-sighted for a time, but when He released Himself to His Father's will, His vision cleared. His mind remembered the power, purpose, wisdom, and ability of God. Jesus went from hunched over in pain and fear to walking confidently into the fight. God's strength in Him transformed Jesus from fear to confidence.

Perspective is as vital to us today as it was to Jesus that night. Focusing on the coming days or the past traps us in anxiety and dread. Our eyes see all we cannot control, the many people we cannot trust, and the hopelessness of broken systems, and the world shrinks to just that. When we pray for God to take those dilemmas away, to change our life, to protect us, we are on the right track. But if that is where we end, if we get up after telling God what we want but not listening to Him, we'll end up on our faces in short order.

Telling God "not my will but Yours" is the key to breaking us free. "I believe You are good, Lord. Your will is done in heaven, and that is . . . heavenly . . . amazing . . . wonderful. So now I want Your will done on earth, in me, with my life. Whatever it is, I trust You."

Bible Reading: Matthew 6:9–13, Mark 14:43–49

Day 4

Today we are going to focus mainly on Jesus—not how we can be like Him in similar situations but the wonder that is Christ Jesus. Did you know that from the beginning of time, since the plan for redemption was first made, Jesus chose to be the sacrifice (Heb. 4:3–4)?

Jesus's Arrest

Jesus was fully God and fully man, and that is not something we can understand totally. God the Son, Jesus, was in heaven surrounded by angels, seated near His Father, working with God the Spirit. He was in His heavenly body when the time came for their plan to begin. Jesus willingly gave up the comfort and splendor of heaven and agreed to be put in the form of a baby inside of Mary. The King of kings was born with the body and mind of a baby. He got diaper rashes and tummy aches. He fell as He learned to walk, went through potty training, lost His teeth, had His body change through His preteen years, got sick, and felt pain and hunger and embarrassment and fear—all because He chose to. He did it because He wanted us to know that He knew how we felt. He wanted us to believe that He intercedes for us and prays for us because He knows how hard it is to be a human (Rom. 8:27, 34, Heb. 7:25).

He could have used His power and knowledge as God, but for most of the 33 years of His life on earth, He chose not to. He lived as a man, and yet He did not sin. He was tempted, but because He really believed that life was eternal—not just here and now and that God wanted us to choose holiness and goodness and purity and gave us the ability to do so—Jesus did the right thing. He saw the big picture. He chose to obey God the Father because He loved Him and had a devoted relationship with His Father (John 14:31).

In the garden, Jesus said to His disciples:

> *"Put your sword back into its place; for all those who take up the sword shall perish by the sword. Or do you think that I cannot appeal to My Father, and He will at once put at My disposal more than twelve legions of angels? How then will the Scriptures be fulfilled,* which say *that it must happen this way?" At that time Jesus said to the crowds, "Have you come out with swords and clubs to arrest Me as* you would *against a robber? Every day I used to sit in the temple teaching and you did not seize Me. But all this has taken place to fulfill the Scriptures of the prophets." Then all the disciples left Him and fled.*
>
> —Matt. 26:52–56

Jesus Christ, our Friend, our Savior, the Son of God, did not have to let Judas betray Him. He did not have to let the battalion of soldiers, which was around 600 men, arrest Him. It was the right time. The plan to pay off our debt had come. Jesus assured His friends then and now that He is in control. Life looked crazy! Scary! The odds were against the good guys. There was so much evil and corruption and selfishness and greed that it was overwhelming. Jesus says to all of us, "Look at Me. Look at Me. Do you think that I can't ask My Father and He will at once send more than 12 legions of angels?" As our eyes dart back to the mob with weapons and anger and power, Jesus says again, "Don't look at them. Look at Me. It must happen this way to fulfill Scripture. This is just one part of a big and beautiful plan. I'm okay. This is what I have chosen—not My will but My Father's." God allowed a power of darkness to be at work for that time, but it was not in control.

***Bible Reading*: Matthew 26:36–56**

Day 5

Earlier, Jesus told His followers that they would all scatter when He was arrested, and Peter told Him he would never do that. Jesus told Peter before the cock crowed on the night of His arrest that he would deny knowing Him three times. The scene was set. Jesus's friends had fallen asleep repeatedly when Jesus had begged them to pray with Him. The angry mob had come, and all the disciples left Jesus and ran. Those who had seized Jesus led Him away. Then they spit in His face and beat Him with their fists; others slapped Him (Matt. 26).

> *But Peter was following at a distance. After they had kindled a fire in the middle of the courtyard and had sat down together, Peter was sitting among them. And a servant-girl, seeing him as he sat in the firelight and looking intently at him, said, "This man was with Him too." But he denied it, saying, "Woman, I do not know Him." A little later, another saw him and said, "You are one of them too!" But Peter said, "Man, I am not!" After about an hour had passed, another man began to insist, saying, "Certainly this man also was with Him, for he is a Galilean too." But Peter said, "Man, I do not know what you are talking about." Immediately, while he was still speaking, a rooster crowed. The Lord turned and looked at Peter. And Peter remembered the word of the Lord, how He had told him, "Before a rooster crows today, you will deny Me three times." And he went out and wept bitterly.*
>
> —Luke 22:54–62

Jesus's Arrest

Nothing about this night had been good. After failing to stay awake, Peter tried to make up for it by drawing a sword and fighting the crowd. It was now embarrassingly apparent to the world that he was a fisherman and not skilled with weapons. Yet he couldn't let Jesus go alone. Everyone else had fled, but not Peter. He followed at a distance. Jesus might need someone to stand up for Him, and Peter needed to know what was going on. The atmosphere was hostile. So he hung back, just watching and listening. But the servants couldn't keep quiet. Peter's mind was numb with fear and disbelief, and they kept yakking on about him.

Frightened and angry by the moment, Peter denied who he was and that he knew Jesus. Then everything happened at once. Soldiers led a beaten and bleeding Jesus out a door just as Peter denied Him a third time and a cock crowed. The world seemed to be still as Peter's head snapped up in the direction of Jesus. The Lord turned and looked at Peter.

Jesus knew. He knew that Peter had failed; He knew that Peter had denied Him. And by the look on Peter's face, Jesus knew that Peter was at the breaking point. It was a short look, a glance, yet it was full of compassion and forgiveness. It was a look that begged Peter to remember what He had said earlier. Jesus had warned him that Satan asked to sift him like wheat. But Jesus had said, "I have prayed for you, that your faith may not fail; and you, when once you have turned again, strengthen your brothers" (Luke 22:32).

Jesus knew Peter would fail, but His prayer was that Peter's failure would not cause his faith to break. The eyes of Jesus told Peter to remember that Jesus believed in him. Jesus knew Peter would turn back, and when he did, he would be able to strengthen his brothers. He would be needed and useful. Peter's Friend loved him through it all.

Bible Reading: Colossians 1:9–14

Day 6

What a friend we have in Jesus. We've met Him at the most traumatic time in His life, and He has proven worthy to be called our Lord. His life is one we should try to copy. In the hours before Jesus died, He gave his friends love and received it from them. Added to that was frustration, irritation, hurt, fear, disappointment, acceptance, courage, betrayal, power, purpose, sorrow, and pain. Did we miss anything? Jesus knows how you and I feel.

In His time here, Jesus formed deep and abiding friendships and showed us in His last day how necessary they were. There were times when Jesus wanted to be alone, but when life was at its hardest, He needed and wanted His friends.

Jesus was a tenacious friend, never giving up and always encouraging. He loved His friends enough to be honest and tell them when they had failed, and then He gave them another chance. He protected and helped them, regardless of how He was feeling. Jesus is the best friend any of us could have.

Our Savior didn't talk as much as He lived, and He lived out the truth that telling God "Your will be done" was empowering. At the moment Jesus most wanted to change, He could have pushed His feelings. But He didn't. Honest and transparent, Christ shared His fear and grief with His friends and His Father. Then He said, "Nevertheless, not My will but Yours be done." He told us to pray it, and He prayed it too. He told us to live it, and He lived it too.

Jesus was authentic and real. He said what He meant and lived what He said. When at last He completely released His fears and worries to God, He got up with steel in His spine, walked over to help His friends, and then faced His enemy.

We saw that as much as Jesus did not look forward to the cross, He still walked toward it with purpose. That was His plan—His choice. The bigger picture was clear. The shame, the pain, and the Father's wrath would be huge, but only for a time. "Let us run with endurance the race that is set before us, fixing our eyes on Jesus, the author and perfecter of faith, who for the joy set before Him endured the cross, despising the shame, and has sat down at the right hand of the throne of God" (Heb. 12:1–2).

Compassion and encouragement shined through the swollen eyes of Jesus as He looked at Peter when the cock crowed. His words to Peter earlier are echoed to you and me. "I have prayed for you, that your faith may not fail. And when you have turned back, strengthen your brothers." He says *when* you turn back because you and I will turn back after we've blown it. Jesus believed in His friend; He believes in all His friends. He lives to intercede for us, praying that our faith will not fail when we do and that we'll get back up, grab His hand, and turn and strengthen our brothers and sisters. That's what friends do.

Bible Reading: John 15:4–17

Week 12

THANKSGIVING

Day 1

I am so excited! Thanksgiving is my favorite holiday for many reasons, but the biggest reason is the food. Does that make me shallow? I love the smell and the look and the taste of all things Thanksgiving. Abraham Lincoln made this a legal holiday after decades of celebrating God's grace on the people of America. Our forefathers loved God and recognized that our mere survival was due to His blessings. With that in mind, I would like to share some old hymns and their history with you. Let's spend Thanksgiving week giving thanks and praise to our Lord God.

Saint Francis of Assisi was born to a rich merchant in Italy in 1182. In 1201, he joined the army and was taken captive as a prisoner of war for one year. It is thought that he came to know Christ as his Savior a few years after his return from the war and then chose to live a life of poverty serving the Lord. He loved nature and in 1225 wrote the words to "All Creatures of Our God and King."

> All creatures of our God and King, lift up your voice and with us sing, Alleluia! Alleluia! Thou burning sun with golden beam, thou silver moon with softer gleam! O praise Him! O praise Him! Alleluia! Alleluia! Alleluia!
>
> Thou rushing wind that art so strong, ye clouds that sail in Heaven along, O praise Him! Alleluia! Thou rising moon, in praise rejoice, Ye lights of evening, find a voice! O praise Him! O praise Him! Alleluia! Alleluia! Alleluia! . . .

Let all things their Creator bless, and worship Him in humbleness, O praise Him! Alleluia! Praise, praise the Father, praise the Son, and praise the Spirit, Three in One! O praise Him! O praise Him! Alleluia! Alleluia! Alleluia!

Praise, praise the Father, praise the Son, and praise the Spirit Three in One! O praise Him! O praise Him! Alleluia! Alleluia! Alleluia![4]

The week before Jesus was crucified, He entered Jerusalem on a donkey. The people laid their coats and palm branches on the road and praised Him loudly, shouting, "'BLESSED IS THE KING WHO COMES IN THE NAME OF THE LORD; Peace in heaven and glory in the highest!' Some of the Pharisees in the crowd said to Him, 'Teacher, rebuke Your disciples.' But Jesus answered, 'I tell you, if these become silent, the stones will cry out!'" (Luke 19:38–40). Romans 1:20 tells us that since the beginning of the world, God's invisible qualities, His eternal power, and His divine nature can be seen in His creation. Even if you and I don't praise Him, His creation does and will.

Bible Reading: Isaiah 51:3–4, Luke 19:28–40

Day 2

Horatio G. Spafford was a lawyer and real estate investor in Chicago in the late 1800s. In 1871 the great Chicago fire blazed throughout the city killing thousands and leaving hundreds of thousands homeless. Spafford lost a fortune but determined to help the people of Chicago rebuild. During this time, Horatio's young son died.

In November 1873, Horatio put his wife and four daughters on a luxury ship bound for Europe for an extended vacation. He planned to meet them when his work was finished. On November 22, the ship hit another vessel and sank. His wife, Anna, survived but their four daughters were lost. As Horatio was sailing across the Atlantic to meet his wife, he wrote the hymn "It Is Well with My Soul" as his ship passed the site of his daughters' resting place.

When peace, like a river, attendeth my way, when sorrows like sea billows roll; Whatever my lot, Thou has taught me to say, It is well, it is well, with my soul. It is well, with my soul, it is well, it is well with my soul.

Though Satan should buffet, though trials should come, Let this blest assurance control, that Christ has regarded my helpless estate, and hath shed His own blood for my soul. It is well, with my soul, it is well, it is well, with my soul.

My sin, oh, the bliss of this glorious thought! My sin, not in part but the whole, is nailed to the cross, and I bear it no more, praise the Lord, praise the Lord, O my soul! It is well, with my soul, it is well, it is well, with my soul. . . .

And Lord, haste the day when my faith shall be sight, the clouds be rolled back as a scroll; the trump shall resound, and the Lord shall descend, even so, it is well with my soul. It is well, with my soul, it is well, it is well, with my soul.[5]

God said in Isaiah 57:18-19, "'I have seen his ways, but I will heal him; I will lead him and restore comfort to him and to his mourners, creating the praise of the lips. Peace, peace to him who is far and to him who is near,' says the Lord, 'and I will heal him.'"

There are some pains that only dull, but they never completely go away. Horatio and Anna experienced such astounding loss and were never the same. It is a moment-by-moment thing to be able to say it is well with my soul after such loss. They staggered in their faith at times, but in the instances when their eyes fixed on God, it was well with their soul.

***Bible Reading*: 2 Corinthians 1:2–7**

Day 3

The day before his wedding, a 25-year-old man watched in horror as the body of his fiancée was pulled from a lake. The tragedy rocked him to his core, and he determined to leave his home of Dublin, Ireland, and move to America. Joseph Scriven sailed to Canada in 1845, leaving his family behind.

In 1855, Joseph's mother became very sick, and Joseph wrote her a poem, "What a Friend We Have in Jesus," to encourage her through the difficult time. His mother sent the poem to a friend who published it anonymously, and it quickly became a popular hymn. About 30 years later, Scriven was named as the author of these beautiful and true words.

> What a Friend we have in Jesus, all our sins and griefs to bear! What a privilege to carry everything to God in prayer! O what peace we often forfeit, O what needless pain we bear, all because we do not carry everything to God in prayer.
>
> Have we trials and temptations? Is there trouble anywhere? We should never be discouraged; take it to the Lord in prayer. Can we find a friend so faithful who will all our sorrows share? Jesus knows our every weakness; take it to the Lord in prayer.
>
> Are we weak and heavy laden, cumbered with a load of care? Precious Savior, still our refuge, take it to the Lord in prayer. Do your friends despise, forsake you? Take it to the Lord in prayer! In His arms He'll take and shield you; you will find a solace there.
>
> Blessed Savior, Thou hast promised Thou wilt all our burdens bear, may we ever, Lord, be bringing all to Thee in earnest prayer. Soon in glory bright unclouded there will be no need for prayer. Rapture, praise, and endless worship will be our sweet portion there.[6]

This week of Thanksgiving does not erase the hard times we have endured. The fact that we may not be spending this holiday with our family could cause pain and loneliness and anger. Joseph Scriven's experience taught him the truth about our Friend Jesus, a truth each of us can know too. First Peter 5:7 tells us to cast all our anxiety and cares on Him, because He cares for us.

"You are my friends," Jesus said, "if you do what I say." Jesus told us to trust in Him. Believe that He loves us. Know that He is the Son of God. Accept His gift of salvation, and be called a friend of God's.

Bible Reading: Matthew 11:28–30, Philippians 4:4–9

THANKSGIVING

Day 4

John Newton was born in England in 1725 to a mother who prayed for him and taught him God's Word. She died when John was seven, and he drifted in his faith. He joined the Royal Navy where he was flogged after deserting. His spirits were at an all-time low. Newton's life choices got worse as he began a career as a slave trader. One day a great storm arose on the sea, and many on board were swept away to their death. This prompted him to take stock of his life, and he started reading *The Imitation of Christ* by Thomas à Kempis. Newton soon asked Jesus into his heart and life.

John Newton eventually became a minister and outspoken opponent of the slave trade in England. In 1779, he completed the words to what became this famous song, "Amazing Grace."

> Amazing grace! How sweet the sound that saved a wretch like me! I once was lost, but now am found; was blind, but now I see.
>
> 'Twas grace that taught my heart to fear, and grace my fears relieved; how precious did that grace appear the hour I first believed!
>
> Through many dangers, toils and snares, I have already come; 'tis grace hath brought me safe thus far, and grace will lead me home....
>
> When we've been there ten thousand years, bright shining as the sun, we've no less days to sing God's praise than when we'd first begun.[7]

Romans 8:1–2 says, "Therefore there is now no condemnation for those who are in Christ Jesus. For the law of the Spirit of life in Christ Jesus has set you free from the law of sin and of death."

How much we have to be thankful for! God's amazing grace saved us from our sins, and He has kept us in His arms and provided us with food and shelter and love.

Bible Reading: Ephesians 1:1–8

Day 5

Life in gangs, drinking, and being on the streets was no different in the 1700s than it is today. Robert Robinson's father died when he was young. His mother could not control him, so she sent him to London to learn a trade. Instead, Robert joined the gangs that roamed the streets. When he was 17, he and his friends went to see a fortune teller, which left Robert feeling a little out of sorts. After drinking, he talked his gang into going to a local church to hear George Whitefield preach. The message sobered Robert, and three years later he gave his heart to Jesus.

In 1758, at age 23, Robert was a minister in Norfolk, England, when he wrote "Come, Thou Fount of Every Blessing" to accompany his sermon.

> Come, Thou Fount of every blessing, tune my heart to sing Thy grace; streams of mercy, never ceasing, call for songs of loudest praise. Teach me some melodious sonnet, sung by flaming tongues above. Praise the mount! I'm fixed upon it, mount of Thy redeeming love. . . .
>
> Jesus sought me when a stranger, wand'ring from the fold of God; He to rescue me from danger, interposed His precious blood; how His kindness yet pursues me mortal tongue can never tell, Clothed in flesh, till death shall loose me I cannot proclaim it well.
>
> O to grace how great a debtor daily I'm constrained to be! Let Thy goodness, like a fetter, bind my wand'ring heart to Thee. Prone to wander, Lord, I feel it, prone to leave the God I love; here's my heart, O take and seal it, seal it for Thy courts above.
>
> O that day when freed from sinning, I shall see Thy lovely face; clothèd then in blood washed linen how I'll sing Thy sovereign grace; come, my Lord, no longer tarry, take my ransomed soul away; Send Thine angels now to carry me to realms of endless day.[8]

Our testimonies, or life stories, are one of the most powerful ways to touch other people's lives. All of us have a story to tell. We have all been hurt by others or by circumstances in life, and we all have made choices for how we react to that. No matter what our age, we have the ability to blow it, and no matter how big or small the mess, we have a God who is waiting to bring us home to Him.

But you must not forget, dear friends, that a day is like a thousand years to the Lord, and a thousand years is like a day. The Lord isn't really being slow about His promise to return, as some people think. No, He is being patient for your sake. He does not want anyone to perish, so He is giving more time for everyone to repent (2 Pet. 3:8–9).

Bible Reading: 2 Peter 3:8–15

Day 6

The words to "Be Thou My Vision" are attributed to Dallán Forgaill in the eighth century. Christ was in his life because of the earlier evangelism of Ireland by St. Patrick, who was born in AD 373. As a young boy, Patrick was kidnapped from his home in modern-day Scotland and brought to Ireland as a slave. Patrick escaped and returned home. God spoke to him in a dream, and Patrick knew he was to go back to Ireland as a missionary.

The Druids, a superstitious religious group that had their hold on Ireland, fought him fiercely. Patrick planted around 200 churches as he spread the gospel of Christ Jesus to his former captors.

Many hymns were written because of his work, and in the eighth century, people began singing "Be Thou My Vision" throughout Ireland. In 1905, the words were set to the music of "Slane," a traditional Irish folk song.

> Be Thou my Vision, O Lord of my heart; naught be all else to me, save that Thou art. Thou my best thought, by day or by night, waking or sleeping, Thy presence my light.
>
> Be Thou my wisdom, and Thou my true word; I ever with Thee and Thou with me, Lord; Thou my great Father, and I Thy true son; Thou in me dwelling, and I with Thee one.
>
> Be Thou my battle shield, sword for the fight; be Thou my dignity, Thou my delight; Thou my soul's shelter, Thou my high tower: raise Thou me heav'nward, O Pow'r of my pow'r.

Riches I heed not, nor man's empty praise, Thou mine inheritance, now and always: Thou and Thou only, be first in my heart, high King of Heaven, my treasure Thou art.

High King of heaven, my victory won, May I reach heav'n's joys, O bright heav'n's sun! Heart of my own heart, whatever befall, still be my vision, O ruler of all.[9]

We need to have God's eyes, His vision of our life and circumstances. The way for us to be victorious is to see things the way God does. His perspective is the truth and our salvation.

Bible Reading: **Colossians 1:9–12**

Week 13

ISAIAH 40

Day 1

Isaiah was a prophet in the Old Testament who saw Israel through their godly kings, followed by a God-fearing people and wicked kings whose people were rebellious as well. He told of God's love, judgment, and salvation, his words turning our eyes to the sovereign God of the universe. Isaiah chapter 40 points out the smallness of people and the magnificence of God, which is our hope. Isaiah's passion was for us to gain God's perspective and realize that our problems—the powers of governments and people—are nothing compared to the powers of God.

> *"To whom then will you liken Me that I would be* his *equal?" says the Holy One. Lift up your eyes on high and see who has created these* stars, *the One who leads forth their host by number, He calls them all by name; because of the greatness of His might and the strength of* His *power, not one of them is missing.*

> *Why do you say, O Jacob, and assert, O Israel, "My way is hidden from the* Lord, *and the justice due me escapes the notice of my God"? Do you not know? Have you not heard? The Everlasting God, the* Lord, *the Creator of the ends of the earth does not become weary or tired. His understanding is*

> *inscrutable. He gives strength to the weary, and to* him *who lacks might He increases power. Though youths grow weary and tired, and vigorous young men stumble badly, yet those who wait for the* Lord *will gain new strength; they will mount up* with *wings like eagles, they will run and not get tired, they will walk and not become weary.*
>
> —Isa. 40:25–31

This fall we have learned through the lives of others to wait on the Lord, to look for Him in our circumstances, to expect to see God's plans unfold and His power come to our rescue to defeat our enemies. Another meaning of the word *wait* in the Hebrew is "to bind together." In the middle of our everyday life, whether in good and successful times or difficult and painful times, we need to be still. We need to stop and listen to God, pray to Him, and be bound together with Him. This time of waiting for the Lord ties us to His heart and mind. We become securely fastened to Him so His strength and wisdom will carry us through the rough waters of life.

When firefighters rescue people from high-rise buildings, rivers, or mountains, they sometimes tether themselves to the victim. The rescuer and the injured party are securely bound together with a harness and strong clasps. They become one with the strong, skilled firefighter in control of all movements and thoughts. If panic causes the victim to thrash around or fight the directions, the one in control calms them by telling them of his experience and familiarity with this rescue mission. He's done this before; he's practiced and studied, and he knows what will happen next. "So trust me," he says. "Relax, and let me do the work."

In the same way, those who wait on the Lord will gain new strength— His strength. Being tied securely to the Lord will make us firm. Fear and fatigue melt us into weakness after a time if we are on our own, but those who wait on the Lord will be firm, solid, and strong. Zechariah 4:6 says, "This is the word of the Lord to Zerubbabel saying, 'Not by might nor by power, but by My Spirit,' says the Lord of hosts." It is by God, in God, and through God that we will be strong throughout the whole of our life. Wait with God, and gain His strength.

Bible Reading: Isaiah 40:1–20

ISAIAH 40

Day 2

Those who wait on the Lord will mount up with wings like eagles. Isaiah was talking to Israel who was once again surrounded by military enemies, and he writes to you and me today as we find ourselves in various levels of distress. Wait on the Lord. Stop thrashing about, and quiet down; tie yourselves to God, and mount up with wings like eagles. Get a bird's-eye view of your life.

Can you picture this with me? God is our eagle, and we are securely strapped on His back as He takes off to give us a better perspective. From ground level, it's ugly and scary. Destruction and blood are all around. Dark shadows cast creepy images through the forest, and we can't see if there is danger lurking or if it's our imagination. The eagle starts its ascent, and we see things we hadn't noticed before. There's a clearing on the other side of the deep forest that is sunlit, warm, and safe. As we go a little higher, we see there were people living pretty close to us, and we had thought we were so alone. Finally, the eagle reaches its flying altitude of 10,000 feet, and we gasp. The forest seems so small from this vantage point, not all-consuming as we had thought. There were rugged mountains that had come before it, as well as lush valleys. Streams run out of the mountain through the forest and into the meadow, full of fish and life-giving water. From on high, we can see nests in the trees and deer running into the forest for shelter. The place we had thought of as fearfully dark and dank, a place where our dreams of safety and peace would die, appears so different from the eagle's vantage point.

Not only that, but it is just one part of a much bigger picture. The world and sky stretch on forever, and we are only one small piece of it—a rich and vibrant part. The forest we live in is made up of beautifully intense features in this painting of God's. But there are bright, sunny yellows and splashes of vivid colors too. What we see is full—full of life and death and light and darkness.

The eagle tells us to put on its goggles, and we will be able to see through its eyes. Eagles have two centers of focus in each eye, which allow them to see both forward and to the side at the same time. Finally, we are able to view the scene of our life in its fullness, from all directions. It's amazing! What had seemed like chaos and madness looks good from up here. The complete picture is right; it's balanced with color, light, drama, and humor. What we had thought was too much gloomy darkness stands out from 10,000 feet as a focal point. That is what is at the center of this entire view.

Slowly the eagle starts its decent back to the forest floor. We hold on tightly, not wanting this time to end but knowing it must. We're rested now, which is good because we know God wants us to run and not get tired, and walk but not become weary. And we can do that. Our eyes have cleared, and we know we will not be in this hard place forever. There's something else we know. This bad, painful, and dark time has some life in it. Some good and beautiful things are being born in this place.

Bible Reading: **Isaiah 40:21–31**

Day 3

Those who wait for the Lord will run and not get tired; they will walk and not become weary. Running and walking are metaphors or descriptive images the Bible uses for different things in our life. Our walk is how we live every step of every day. It's basic life—the motives, ideas, actions, and feelings of a normal day. The day in, day out routine of walking through life can become tiresome and wear us down, and we can become weary.

Running is a specific workout we do in order to reach a certain goal. It's getting it on for a cause, being challenged by the wrongs in our life or tested by the hardships. So we take the challenge and run. We plan and train for it, and we have a goal and objective. There are different types of running that call for certain degrees of endurance and conditioning. A marathon is long-distance and takes stamina. The sprinter needs a sudden and extreme burst of speed for a short time. In a football game, the runners need to be able to plant their feet and cut and then, when rushed by the opponent, juke to stay on their feet, hopefully all with great speed and agility. In the midst of the running, exhaustion sets in. Our lungs and muscles burn, our hearts pump hard, and we are physically spent.

Hebrews 12:1–2 says to "lay aside every encumbrance and the sin which so easily entangles us, and let us run with endurance the race that is set before us, fixing our eyes on Jesus, the author and perfecter of faith, who for the joy set before Him endured the cross, despising the shame, and has sat down at the right hand of the throne of God."

Jesus Christ—that's our goal, our reason for training, working out, and running. Our eyes are on Him. We are spending all our strength performing in a way that will show Jesus to others as Lord and Savior. When life throws us a curveball of pain or someone's hatefulness, we cut to the side and keep on toward our goal. If our trial is a marathon, we dig deep for God's strength, keep on, and endure. We don't give up, and we never quit. Throwing aside anything that slows us down—unforgiveness, fear, resentment—we fix our eyes on Jesus.

Vigorous young men may stumble, and the strongest of those who follow God may mess up and fall down, but those who wait for the Lord will gain new strength. We attach ourselves to God and soak up His power and energy. Then we get back up, bruised and maybe a little embarrassed, and get back in the race—because it's still on. It's not time to walk on the road of everyday life. We are in a battle for justice, a race for our families' safety. The match is about righteousness and goodness beating evil.

And at the end we are invigorated. Our muscles burn, and our bodies are soaked with sweat, but our hearts and minds are refreshed and ready to go again. The run feels great. But it's the prize that makes it worth it—the joy set before us—knowing inside that we did it, we did our best, we got back up, and we did it all with God's strength in us. We experienced Christ.

The joy set before us—it's not only about the here and now. There is a bigger picture, God looking at you and me saying, "Well done, My good and faithful servant." What joy!

Bible Reading: 1 Corinthians 9:23–27, Isaiah 40:29–31

Day 4

Walk with me through some weeks of everyday life, the life where nothing out of the ordinary happens. We wake up near our family and friends all the time, every morning. Some eat breakfast, and some don't. We rush to school or work—or both. It's the same as always—same teachers, same coworkers, same people, same routine, same timetable, same issues.

The surroundings may be constant, but God presses us to walk outside the lines of normal—outside the same as everyone else who is living. In Ephesians 4:1–3, Paul says, "Therefore I, the prisoner of the Lord, implore you to walk in a manner worthy of the calling with which you have been called, with all humility and gentleness, with patience, showing tolerance for one another in love, being diligent to preserve the unity of the Spirit in the bond of peace."

All of a sudden, our same ordinary day gets a little challenging, doesn't it? We have to help with breakfast and get off to work and school in a way worthy of the calling of Jesus. Day after day, we need to respond to our family and friends in a way God would find admirable. With God in our lives, we are to look different from the people who don't know Him.

The steps we take today ought to reveal our humbleness. We are unpretentious. Knowing God loves us fills us with such confidence that we don't need to put others down or act big-headed and stuck-up. It becomes easy to be pleased when others succeed. The things that used to threaten us and make us feel as if we were losing ground as an important person become clear to us when we have God's eyes. Being humble means we let our actions speak louder than our words.

A gentle person is kind and tenderhearted. Not everyone is made that way, but God enables us to live and feel exactly how He wants us to. Proverbs 15:1 says, "A gentle answer turns away wrath, but a harsh word stirs up anger." Apply that to the same people in your same, everyday routine. The reason we can speak gently with our families is because we are patient with them. They keep making the same mistakes, and we take a deep breath, forgive, and answer gently. Our teacher was completely unfair, and without complaining, we calmly and respectfully ask for clarification of the situation. We wait, we're understanding, we're kind—bearing with others in love. We put up with their little quirks, their sloppy rooms, their whiney voices—with love and gentleness and patience.

A person who walks with God guards the unity of the people in their life. A discussion on how, why, or when things are done is great, but in the end, we should agree to be at peace with each other, even if we have to agree to disagree. There is to be a bond of peace, tranquility, and safety. The steps of our days should be wrapped up in the security of God's humble, gentle, patient, long-suffering love that unifies us in peace.

Living this way day in and day out in our own strength is wearisome and ultimately impossible. Yet those who wait for the Lord will gain new strength; they will mount up with wings like eagles, they will run and not get tired, they will walk and not become weary.

Bible Reading: Colossians 1:9–12

Day 5

Throughout the Bible, we are told to remember—remember what you were, remember that God took you out of Egypt, remember how He defeated Pharaoh. Do not fear this new enemy; remember what the Lord your God did to Pharaoh and to all Egypt. Remember that Jesus fed thousands with five loaves of bread. Remember.

Isaiah says this:

> *Do you not know? Have you not heard? Has it not been declared to you from the beginning? Have you not understood from the foundations of the earth? It is He who sits above the circle of the earth, and its inhabitants are like grasshoppers, who stretches out the heavens like a curtain and spreads them out like a tent to dwell in. He it is who reduces rulers to nothing, who makes the judges of the earth meaningless. Do you not know? Have you not heard? The Everlasting God, the* Lord, *the Creator of the ends of the earth does not become weary or tired. His understanding is inscrutable.*
> —Isa. 40:21–23, 28

I'm talking to myself as well. Stop running scared. Quit whining and complaining and wringing your hands. Take stalk of your life right now, and then remember who God is. Remember what He has done in your past and in the lives of others. Do you not know that if God can create your body with all the big and little systems and chemicals and thoughts and feelings that work together perfectly, He can also heal it?

Have you not heard how God directed the stone from David's slingshot to the one place on Goliath that wasn't covered and would be fatal? Do you remember reading about Esther and Elijah and Jesus? Have you not heard the stories from the Revolutionary War when God moved in so many ways in order for General George Washington to defeat the much greater British army? Pay attention. Focus on the right thing, not your problems.

Have you not understood that from the foundations of the earth, the One who could make all there is, is beyond understanding? Scientist have only scratched the surface of everything from the farthest known galaxy to the most minute microscopic organism. And they are all woven together, independent of each other yet part of a huge system that connects. The Creator of the universe does not grow tired. He reduces the most powerful men and nations to meaningless grasses. He is the One in control. He has fought for justice and righteousness and peace. He is the One who is fighting for you now and in the future.

Do you not know? Have you not heard? The Everlasting God, the Lord, the Creator of the ends of the earth loves you. He wants to take you up with wings like eagles so you can have His view of all this. He wants to be bound to you in a close and loving relationship.

Life in poverty, the foster system, or depression hurts, and it is scary and hard. Being a parent, student, man, or woman hurts, and it is scary and hard. God wants us to remember that He is "able to do far more abundantly beyond all that we ask or think, according to the power that works within us, to Him *be* the glory in the church and in Christ Jesus to all generations forever and ever" (Eph. 3:20–21).

***Bible Reading*: Hebrews 11**

Day 6

Isaiah 40 starts out with God saying, "Comfort, O comfort My people." That was the goal of every day this week, to ease our heavy hearts and soothe our burned-out spirits. Our Lord desperately wants to reassure and encourage us in this life we live.

Wait on the Lord. Look at God, and securely strap into the harness He offers us. Our hearts start beating as one, and His soft words calm us as His plan starts to unfold. It's His strength that propels us off the cliff and over the dangerous waters. What a comfort to know that the One we are bound to has done this before and is strong enough to do it again.

Our perspective changed completely as we soared with wings like eagles. Every elevation gave us a different view of the dark places in our lives. The higher we got, the more clearly we saw that there was so much more than our story going on. But together it all made such a beautiful and rich picture. Descending back to the ground, we were comforted to know that we would only be in this place a little while. Good times and bad times—and just small ones at that—are only for a season. The view from the eagle went on to eternity.

We've always known we would be running in the race of our lives at some point, so learning how to focus on our goal and knowing what that goal is has strengthened our resolve. There were times we thought we just needed a shot of energy for a sprint, yet here we are two years into the nightmare of our life. We're a marathon runner now, and God has given us endurance. The comfort we have knowing Jesus fixed His eyes on the joy set before Him in order to get through the cross is immense. We're just like

Isaiah 40

Him. We need a goal, an ending to look forward to. We run this race to win and for an eternal, imperishable prize.

Sometimes the monotony of our everyday life can be as hard to endure as the running. Walking God's way kicks up the intensity a little, but still, day in and day out gets long. We get tired, bored, and sloppy. Thank goodness for God's perspective. From His view, we see that the boring little details matter. They're carrying us toward that prize just as surely as the race is. Living our life in a worthy way is a daunting task, but oh the comfort to know that God said He would renew our strength and sharpen our focus so we can see this through to the end.

We can do this—the surviving, the waiting, the running, the walking, the winning—if we remember. See God's fingerprints on the stunning successes and horrifying tragedies in our past and in other people's lives. Every time we read *have you not heard* or *do you not know*, we will sit a little straighter. Yes, we have heard. The God of the universe is all-powerful. We know that God performed miracles in the past and is doing it today. He is the giant in our lives. And what a comfort and relief to know that God, the Everlasting God, loves us.

He gives strength to the weary, and to him who lacks might, He increases their power. Though youths grow weary and tired and vigorous young men stumble badly, those who wait for the Lord will gain new strength; they will mount up with wings like eagles, they will run and not get tired, and they will walk and not become weary.

***Bible Reading*: Isaiah 40:28–31**

WINTER

INTRODUCTION

Winter—what autumn was slowly changing, winter kills off with one frigid breath. The season that hosts Christmas and Valentine's Day has the ability to immobilize our hearts with soul-deep sadness and hopelessness.

Alcohol and drugs may dull the sting for those who feel like losers because their families don't match the commercials about warm dinners and festive packages under a beautiful tree. The love in Christmas and Valentine's Day is sorely missing in many lives, so these holidays can cause despair and depression. More suicide attempts happen during these months than any other time in the year.

There is some beauty in winter, though. Nothing compares to seeing soft and silent white snow falling from the sky and drifting around trees and homes. Very slowly, all that was dead becomes blanketed with sparkling, frosty snow.

God looked through the windows of each of our homes and saw that some of us had nothing—no trees, no presents, no love. He saw into the packages in other homes and knew how empty those boxes really were. And He knew our hearts would break. So the Trinity—God the Father, God the Son, and God the Holy Spirit—agreed and came up with the perfect gift for you and for me, and for each person everywhere. Like the blanketing snow, His gift promises to cover our dying souls with the Son's light, beauty, and life.

Curl up with me next to the fire, and let's allow our heavenly Father to slowly open His gift to us. Don't rush this. We are going to want to take in every little thing our gift has to offer and all the love our Father has poured out to us in the giving.

Week 1

DAVID THE SHEPHERD

Day 1

King David, a shepherd himself, wrote Psalm 23 about the Lord as our Shepherd. He wrote it from the sheep's perspective. In the first verses, David wrote to the "sheep" of the world, the sheep that had a different shepherd than he had. His goal was to entice the world's sheep over to the Shepherd who loved and cared for His flock.

The second section of Psalm 23 is the sheep talking directly to the Shepherd. Summer is a time when the hardworking, careful shepherds drove their sheep to the high country in the mountains. It was a long, lonely, and difficult task but one that allowed the pastures close to home a rest from winter grazing. The trip was fraught with dangerous paths next to cliffs, as well as predators such as bears and mountain lions. Yet David praised his Shepherd personally for His care and protection throughout this time.

> *The Lord is my shepherd, I shall not want. He makes me lie down in green pastures; He leads me beside quiet waters. He restores my soul; He guides me in the paths of righteousness for His name's sake. Even though I walk through the valley of the shadow of death, I fear no evil, for You are with me; Your rod and Your staff, they comfort me. You prepare a table before me in the presence of my enemies; You have anointed my head with oil; my cup overflows. Surely goodness and lovingkindness will follow me all the days of my life, And I will dwell in the house of the Lord forever.*
>
> —Ps. 23:1–6

The Lord is our Shepherd, and we are His sheep (Ps. 100:3). God is our Father, and we are His children (2 Cor. 6:18). God's perfect plan for fathers and mothers, for parents, are for them to be like Him. He lives out Fatherhood and fleshes out His mother's heart perfectly in our lives now, just as He did throughout the entire Bible.

This is a Father we want to get to know. He is our Abba, our Daddy, our Papa. He loves us and takes care of all our needs. Our Father shepherds us, leads us to safe places, and gives us rest. When we're scared, our Daddy holds us in His arms, and suddenly, we aren't afraid anymore, no matter who's around. He is never the cause of our fear; our Abba protects us and gives us so much love that our cup runs over. We will be His children, and He will be our Father.

What a foreign concept this kind of father is to many people. The foster system is in place because mothers and fathers are not like the heavenly Father. But let's not reject God because of our bad experience. We as children are not always like God's Son either. None of us gets it right all the time. In this case, God the Father and God the Son are our models, and God the Holy Spirit is the enabling force we need to live like them.

We cannot change the parents we have, but we can allow the love and guidance of our heavenly Father to have a place in our lives. Here's a fact: most of you will become moms and dads someday. Don't take this time getting to know your Father only for the here and now; learn to be a parent like Him. Let Him help you be more loving and careful than what you faced in your family. Copy how God disciplines, forgives, teaches, protects, and provides for His kids. Learn to be a shepherd kind of parent by giving our Shepherd and Father a place in your life.

Bible Reading: **John 10:1–17, Galatians 4:4–7**

Day 2

David said, "The LORD is my shepherd; I shall not want" (Ps. 23:1). What does that mean? Well, if the Lord is our shepherd, He's our parent, our caregiver, the one we trust. We don't like to use that word nowadays, but whoever is calling the shots is the master.

Think carefully on this. Whatever or whoever we love "owns us" to some extent. We look to them whenever we have a need or want. It is that thing or person that is in our thoughts all the time. We'd be willing to forfeit things in order to get more of who or what we love.

Jesus said, "No one can serve two masters; for either he will hate the one and love the other, or he will be devoted to one and despise the other. You cannot serve God and wealth" (Matt. 6:24). Only one thing can be number one in our lives.

David was a good shepherd, so he recognized the Lord as one too. There is a lot of work and sacrifice that goes into taking care of another person or animals. If they're sick, they are the master's priority. The shepherd is alert to any dangers that could be lurking around his sheep. He wants them to eat healthy food and stay within safe boundaries. Spending time with them gives the sheep a feeling of security, and they can rest easily. That time maintains a relationship so that when there is danger and the shepherd urges them to come, they obey without argument.

Let's step away from the pasture for a moment. Our moms and dads may not be the picture of David and the Lord, and that is undeniably painful. But this goes deeper than the obvious. It's bigger than the physical. The "world system" is run by Satan (Luke 4:6). We really have the choice of only two masters—God or Satan. We follow, do things for, are motivated by, and are provided for by the Good Shepherd—God—or the bad shepherd—Satan. If we think we are the masters of our lives, not God or anyone else, then we are following Satan's teachings.

Author Phillip Keller said, "I have known some of the wealthiest men on this continent . . . and some of the leading scientists. . . . Despite their dazzling outward show of success, affluence and prestige, they remained poor in spirit, shriveled in soul, and unhappy in life. They were joyless people held in the iron grip and heartless ownership of the wrong master."[10]

Everything the world tells us will bring success, happiness, and peace is temporary. It may start out strong and good, but it's all fleeting. When anxiety creeps into the place of peace, we find out that the system we had counted on doesn't care. Look at Hollywood to verify this. Satan doesn't want you or me; he just doesn't want us to be with God.

The Good Shepherd, however, does want us. Jesus said if one of His sheep gets lost, He leaves the others in a safe place and goes looking for that one lost sheep. And all of heaven rejoices when He finds that sheep. With our Good Shepherd, we do not want—for anything.

Bible Reading: Luke 15:4–10, 2 Thessalonians 2:16–17

Day 3

Whoa! This is perfect . . . everything I've ever dreamed of right here in front of me. If I get that family and that house, I would be so happy. That person, they've got it all—looks, smarts, and always up for a good time. When we're together, I feel loved and special; they fill me up. I'm going to Hollywood or to play ball 'cause it's the money and fame that counts in this world. With that in my pocket, I'll be loved and secure forever.

Have you ever had any of those daydreams—closing your eyes and imagining your perfect world? I have. What's silly is that I would see someone in a magazine or on TV who had what I wanted and later read that they were reeling from a broken relationship and moving on to the next one, and the next one. They did something crazy and embarrassing while partying and seemed to need a lot of shopping, boozing, and constant attention. It wasn't the happiness or peace I was looking for, but it'd probably be different with me. I would stop when I got just enough so I wouldn't get into their problems, right?

Our Father lets us rest in green meadows; He leads us beside peaceful streams. Sheep find it impossible to lie down when things around them aren't right. They need to be free from all fear and conflict with the other sheep in the herd. Flies, bugs, and outside troubles drive them to distraction, and rest becomes impossible. They also need to be released from the worry of hunger and thirst. When all those needs are met, they can lie down and rest.

Green pastures take time and work, and the shepherd is the one who puts in the effort. He pulls weeds that look good to the sheep but will end up bloating them or even killing them. The shepherd plants the right mix of grasses while clearing out rocks and making the terrain even for safe walking. Animals smell water and run to it whether it is churning with mud, stagnant with algae, or fresh and clear. A good shepherd leads them past the bad and on to clear waters.

The love and care of our Shepherd combined with His perspective are ultimately what will fulfill our dreams. We think excitement and living on the edge makes us feel alive because—why? Relationships give us security and fulfillment—why? Money, things, and attention give us confidence and pleasure because—why? What is it we are looking for?

All of us were created in God's image. All of us have a God-shaped hole in us that makes us crave being filled up with lasting goodness, love, purpose, and peace. On our own, we grab whatever looks good and is convenient. We're like sheep, so we follow the crowd and try what they're doing to fill that void. We're starving and thirsty, but nothing satisfies for long. Throughout history, people's insatiable thirst for God has led them to a variety of religions, philosophies, and rituals. We'll try anything to take away the gnawing hunger within us.

Jesus said, "I am the bread of life; he who comes to Me will not hunger, and he who believes in Me will never thirst" (John 6:35). "I am the door; if anyone enters through Me, he will be saved, and will go in and out and find pasture.... I came that they may have life, and have *it* abundantly" (John 10:9–10).

***Bible Reading*: Jeremiah 15:16, John 4:9–34**

Day 4

In this Christmas season, we have talked of how depressed some people become. Never have the warm Christmas movies been a reflection of their lives. It is a time of spending money they don't have and trying desperately to fit in. The smells and sounds trigger nausea, headaches, and a sickened heart instead of joy and anticipation. Then we have to move into the new year, hoping above all hope that it is a happy one, a better one than the others before it. We scarcely have time to take a deep breath before Valentine's Day shows up. *Please don't let the schools have those stupid Sadie Hawkins dances. I won't be asked ... and if I ask, I won't be accepted.*

Winter isn't only a season; it is a place some people live in year-round. Life is difficult. Rejection and failure kick harder than a mule. Some of the problems in our families started before our birth and may never end, and they're devastating. Divorce, betrayal, bitterness, hatred, abuse, feeling unappreciated and unloved—we are cast down in our despairs and fears.

A "cast" sheep is an old English term for a sheep that has turned over on its back and can't get up on its own. Picture this. Their legs frantically flay back and forth, but they bleat only once in a while to call for help. Cast sheep can become distressed and die within a short period of time if they are not rolled back into a normal position. When back on their feet, they may need support for a few minutes to ensure they are steady.

Does that sound familiar? Life knocks us down, and we thrash around wildly trying to get back up. We call out to God for help every so often, but for the most part, we just fight and work to fix ourselves on our own. Finally, the Lord gently puts us on our feet, and we find ourselves wobbly and unsteady. We need something to hold on to.

The shepherd is not the only one who keeps an eye out for cast sheep; so do predators. In the animal world, buzzards, cougars, and coyotes are looking for the weak and vulnerable. First Peter 5:8 says, "Your adversary, the devil, prowls around like a roaring lion, seeking someone to devour." His weapons of choice—substance abuse, rebelliousness, and more—vary for people. "This knowledge that any "cast" sheep is helpless, close to death and vulnerable to attack, makes the whole problem of cast sheep serious for the manager."[11]

Our Father restores our soul. He brings us back, sometimes repeatedly. As a parent, I can tell you this is a very intimate thing. When my little ones fell, I'd bend over and gently pick them up. Sometimes they got tangled up in a place they shouldn't have been, so the whole time I calmed them with my soft voice, I also instructed them, *Mama said not to go over here. This can hurt you, and you need to be a good listener. You're okay; hold my hand, and we'll get you out of this.* Our Good Shepherd restores our soul and returns us to safety and dignity.

Bible Reading: Psalm 23, 1 Peter 5:6–11

Day 5

Tell me this . . . why do we imitate behavior we hate? The person in our life who has hurt us most is self-centered, foul-mouthed, and mean. If someone crosses us, we respond in a mean-spirited, foul-mouthed, selfish way. It looked so bad on that other person, but when we do it—hey, the person deserved it. Someone in our lives judges harshly everything we say or do, condemns us, and accuses us. It makes us so angry. Yet others in our lives can see the same characteristics in us. We stay with familiar people and places, and copy them, like it or not.

It's really no wonder the Bible compares us to sheep and not some other animal. Sheep live the same way. Wherever they are they want to stay, and they'd eat from the same contaminated place their adversaries eat from. Morning, noon, and night they take the same path to the same place, and the whole flock follows whoever gets going first. Without careful shepherding, the land can become barren with deep ruts from frequent walks and predators who know the sheep's routine. There will be another way to go and another place to eat, but sheep are creatures of habit. They may be miserable where they are, but they are also comfortable with it.

We hate change. A good shepherd keeps his flock moving so the land or his sheep are not destroyed. He guides them along new paths to good food and clear water. Some of the footing is scary and new to the sheep, but the shepherd has already gone over it. He knows his flock can make it, and the end result will be worth the effort.

God is moving us out just as He moved Israel out of slavery in Egypt. And listen to this: the Good Shepherd moves us before the pasture gets bad. To us, things are still okay. We're comfortable, and the people around us aren't unpleasant; the school and friends are good. We don't want to go. Besides, He isn't telling us where we're going; we're just supposed to follow. We need to remember that He has a better view than we do. He can see the ruts we're in, the muddied water, and exactly how sparse our food is. He knows a better place, a place where we'll grow and exercise and find out new things about ourselves and our God.

There's something else to consider. God wants to move us for our own good but also for His name's sake. He has a reputation to uphold. He wants other sheep to look at the good shape we're in and want to follow Him too. The Shepherd wants us to value our relationship with Him, and He wants the world to know that He does His job well. He wants the predators to know not to mess with His sheep because His sheep hear His voice and follow Him so they don't stand a chance.

"There is a way *which seems* right to a man, but its end is the way of death" (Prov. 14:12). Jesus said, "I am the way, and the truth, and the life; no one comes to the Father but through Me" (John 14:6).

Let's do it. Let's follow our Shepherd wherever He leads, even when it seems all right where we are. He's guiding us in the paths of righteousness for His name's sake.

Bible Reading: John 14:1-7, 2 Thessalonians 3:3, 5

Day 6

The 23rd Psalm was written from the sheep's point of view. David said, "The LORD is my shepherd" (Ps. 23:1). That's remarkable because what we've read so far in David's life has not been all green pastures and cool waters. Yet still he said, "I don't want for anything." As a shepherd himself, he understood that his Good Shepherd had a perspective the sheep did not have. So David didn't sweat the stuff he didn't know. He didn't want for more security or information, food, or rest. What he had for that day was sufficient. What he needed for tomorrow his Shepherd would supply.

David shared how easy it was to lie down in green pastures because he felt secure. Our Father, our Shepherd, spends a lot of time with us, walking with us through our life so we feel secure and safe. This sense of well-being not only allows us to lie down, but it is what gets us up to follow our Shepherd out of those same fields when, from our view, there is no reason to leave.

Taking the Shepherd's route to tranquil water may mean that we walk past watering holes that look good to us and offer relief from our immediate thirst. The relationship between the sheep and the Shepherd shows its importance once again. We may never know why our Father tells us not to take in the water, the short-term refreshment, from a specific place, but we should know that He is trustworthy and His perspective is faultless. If He prods us past a relationship or activity, it is guaranteed to be in our best interest.

When we fall, and we will, our Good Shepherd sets us back on our feet. And if we've wandered to a remote place in His field and then been cast down, He notices that we are gone and looks until He finds us. By that time, we will need more than just the help to stand up; our Father will gladly steady us until we are able to walk again on our own.

Restoring our soul is so much more than setting us on our feet again. It's not that God just brings us back to what we used to be or where we used to live. When you and I land flat on our back in a mess or in abject despair, our Father picks us up and teaches us. His goal is to prevent this from happening again, so as He calms our fears and soothes our embarrassment, He reprimands us for not following His directions. Sometimes discipline could be part of our restoration. It lovingly teaches but never crushes us.

All our Father, our Shepherd, does is to protect us from every harm and predator and provide us with health, peace, and dignity. He guides us in the paths of righteousness for His name's sake. It is for His glory that you and I are content, full, and rested. Our good fortune speaks well of Him as our Father. When people who don't know Him notice the difference between them and those in His care, they'll want to be part of His flock. God's name being glorified draws the hurting and hungry into His safe and loving arms.

Jesus said, "I am the good shepherd, and I know My own and My own know Me" (John 10:14). God is our Father, our Shepherd, and we are loved by Him. To be His sheep is as easy as telling Him you want to be.

Bible Reading: John 10:1–17

Week 2

DAVID THE SHEPHERD

Day 1

David then looked up at his Shepherd and said, "Even though I walk through the valley of the shadow of death, I fear no evil, for You are with me" (Ps. 23:4).

The valley of the shadow of death—that place where our greatest fears are lurking, where our enemies are hiding, where our imaginations run wild with memories. This valley harbors our greatest pain and may even be a raging anger over events and people in our lives. Temptations lie in wait for us, ready to entice us to go back to our old ways, to believe there is no hope, to do things our way. A loss of our faith, dreams, and peace darken our paths.

Most fearful of all is death—real death, our bodies dying, whether in a peaceful way or by violence—terrifies a lot of people. What happens then? Is that it? Is it over and we're gone, and none of our life really mattered?

A person who has not asked Jesus into their life is like a sheep from another pasture. They have a different shepherd, so the valley is in complete darkness. There is not the "shadow of death"; there is only death. When the Bible talks of death, it means the separation of our bodies from our spirits. It's as if we are walking and take our coat (our bodies) off, and what was inside the coat keeps on walking—into judgment and hell (Luke 12:5, 2 Pet. 2:4) if we have rejected Jesus or into heaven and eternal life (Matt 25:46, John 3:16) if we have accepted Jesus as the Son of God and our Savior.

The reason David did not fear is because God was with Him. Think about this. There cannot be a shadow unless there is light. God is light (John 1:4). So when we walk with Jesus through the scariest, darkest times in our lives, His light hits the evil, death, and pain like the sun hits a rock or tree, and we stand in the shadow of it. The bad stuff is still there with the power to hurt, but its power has been diluted, or weakened, by the light and power of our Shepherd and Lord. Its effect is temporary instead of permanent.

Because God's children are human beings made of flesh and blood, Jesus also became flesh and blood by being born in human form. For only as a human being could He die, and only by dying could He break the power of the devil who had the power of death. Only in this way could He deliver those who have lived all their lives as slaves to the fear of dying (Heb. 2:14–15).

There are bodies in the heavens, and there are bodies on earth. The glory of the heavenly bodies is different from the beauty of the earthly bodies. It is the same way for the resurrection of the dead. Our earthly bodies, which die and decay, will be different when they are resurrected, for they will never die. When this happens—when our perishable, earthly bodies have been transformed into heavenly bodies that will never die—then at last the Scriptures will come true: "DEATH IS SWALLOWED UP in victory. O DEATH, WHERE IS YOUR VICTORY? O DEATH, WHERE IS YOUR STING?" How we thank God who gives us victory over sin and death through Jesus Christ our Lord! (1 Cor. 15:40, 42, 54-55, 57).

Bible Reading: John 10:22–30, John 11:21–26, Revelation 1:17–18

Day 2

"Even though I walk through the valley of the shadow of death, I fear no evil, for You are with me; Your rod and Your staff, they comfort me" (Ps. 23:4). We are not only free from fear because our Father, our Shepherd, is with us but because of the equipment He has at His disposal. A shepherd's rod was a long club that was used to chase off predators as well as discipline sheep who wandered away or got themselves into dangerous situations. His staff was a cane-like pole with a hook on the top that was usually the same height or a little taller than the shepherd.

Let's take the rod first. It's a scary thought to those who've been beaten and abused in the name of discipline. So again, I will tell you this truth: abusive, mean, selfish parents are *not* following God's instructions and do *not* in any way look or act like our heavenly Father.

A shepherd carried a literal rod with him, but it is most often used in the figurative sense in the Bible as the Word of God. "He is *on* the path of life who heeds instruction [God's Word], but he who ignores reproof goes astray" (Prov. 10:17). Second Timothy 3:16 says, "All Scripture is inspired by God and profitable for teaching, for reproof, for correction, for training in righteousness." We talked yesterday about how fear, grief, rage, sorrow, our enemies, memories, imaginations, and temptations grab us in the valley. So . . . pay attention to God's rod.

> *Only be strong and very courageous; be careful to do according to all the law which Moses My servant commanded you; do not turn from it to the right or to the left, so that you may have success wherever you go. This book of the law shall not depart from your mouth, but you shall meditate on it day and night, so that you may be careful to do according to all that is written in it; for then you will make your way prosperous, and then you will have success. Have I not commanded you? Be strong and courageous! Do not tremble or be dismayed, for the LORD your God is with you wherever you go.*
>
> —Josh. 1:7–9

Jesus used Scripture as His weapon of choice to combat Satan when he tempted Jesus at the beginning of His ministry. Every time Satan presented an attractive alternative to Jesus to turn away from His purpose of dying on the cross, Jesus said, "It is written . . ." and quoted the Bible. Jesus used the most powerful tool at His disposal—the God-inspired, Holy Spirit–breathed words of Scripture. Our Shepherd wields His rod for our protection and correction, and to combat lies and temptations for us. His example teaches us how to use our "rod" effectively.

The staff symbolizes concern and compassion. A shepherd uses the crook of his staff to gently pick up a sheep and bring it to him for inspection or to unite a lamb with its mother. The Holy Spirit draws us toward God. He draws all His children together for intimate fellowship and care. A long staff guides us in our walk. When we do go on our own and land in a tangle of thorns, our Shepherd uses the crook of His staff to lift us out and put us back on our feet, scratched up and bleeding but safe again.

How desperately we need our Father's presence, His rod and staff in this valley of the shadow of death. Have you asked Him to be your Shepherd? Do you trust Him in your pain?

***Bible Reading*: Proverbs 3:11–17, Isaiah 11:2–4, Matthew 4:1–11**

Day 3

I feel as if we need to spend one more day in this valley of the shadow of death because I struggled with the fact that this could sound so trite. On this flat piece of paper, words can tell you your physical abuse or hunger and fear are a shadow of death—not the real thing and not as bad as it seems. When someone tries to comfort a person by saying things like "God is in control" or "this is just a shadow of a problem," quite honestly you may want to punch them. I don't want you to feel as if the terror of your life is being glossed over by me or by the Bible.

Do you remember back to Elijah? In his fear, exhaustion, grief, and pain he wanted to die. The intensity of his pain did not lessen because he knew God. Though the pain is severe for everyone, the god of this world does not offer rest, food, and water. The God of Elijah did. He stood in the gap for Elijah who could not even stand at all, and He stood between Elijah and the enemy. It was God's shadow that hid Elijah against the prying eyes of the darkness of death, grief, and fear. The psalms repeatedly ask to be hidden in the shadow of God's wings.

I'm not sure at what point in his life David wrote Psalm 23, but we've seen that his early life was filled with jealous lies, betrayals, murder attempts, fear, depression, loneliness, hunger, humiliation, fatigue, and more. David knew what it was like to be in the valley of the shadow of death. He was a man who was talking from experience, and he said that even though he walked through the valley of the shadow of death, he feared no evil, for God was with him; His rod and staff comforted him.

It's interesting that David said he didn't fear evil, not that he didn't fear death. In the Hebrew, *evil* means "cruel, vicious in disposition, hurtful, to break or shatter." Death only came about because of sin, which was defeated by Jesus's death and resurrection. But still, it ends the only thing we can see and touch. It's scary to think about it for ourselves, and it hurts desperately when a person we love dies. But with our Good Shepherd standing between us and death, we don't fear being shattered by it. The vicious pain will not destroy us by breaking us in pieces.

When we live through the darkness of abuse and neglect, the intent of Satan and the people hurting us is cruel and vicious. They want to break us into a million hurt and useless pieces. That is why it is so important to accept Jesus's offer to be our Shepherd. He will stand between our enemies and us with His rod and His staff. We may get beat up in the valley of the shadow of death, but we will not be destroyed. Our enemies will have no victory over us, and in the end, we will move on to the table our Lord has prepared for us.

We do not need to fear evil in the darkest places in our lives. Our giant of a God and Father is casting the shadow of His rod over our enemy. He will keep us moving through this valley and into a place overflowing with whatever is true and honorable, whatever is right and pure, whatever is lovely and of good reputation, whatever is excellent (Phil. 4:8).

Only God can be our Father of Lights while at the same time dwarfing evil in the shadow of His presence. Hold on tightly to Him. He will not let you break in your pain.

Bible Reading: **Psalm 68:4–6, Psalm 91:1–7, Romans 16:20**

Day 4

Still looking into the eyes of his Shepherd, David says, "You prepare a table before me in the presence of my enemies; You have anointed my head with oil; My cup overflows" (Ps. 23:5). The Bible teaches that this world is under Satan's control right now. Ephesians 2:1-2 tells Christ-followers that they were dead in their sins in which they formerly walked according to the course of this world, according to the prince of the power of the air, of the spirit that is now working in the sons of disobedience. Second Corinthians 4:4 says that "the god of this world has blinded the minds of the unbelieving so that they might not see the light of the gospel of the glory of Christ, who is the image of God."

Whether we have asked Jesus into our lives or not, Satan is our enemy. He hates us all, and his goal is evil—to destroy us and keep us from God and in darkness, guilt, and fear. The world eats at a table in the presence of their enemy all the time, but with no protection.

Those of us with God as our Father and Shepherd still live in this world. We are surrounded by the forces of evil. Yet our God prepared a table for us in the presence of our enemy. He wants good things for us here on earth and protects us while we are here.

If you don't have much experience fixing dinner for guests, I'd like to invite you into my kitchen as I prepare a meal for you. Days or weeks in advance I thought of the foods you would enjoy most. I found recipes, shopped for the food, and began the preparations. The day of our dinner, I cleaned my house and set my dining room table. As I cooked, I was thrilled to see there was so much food, and we would be able to have seconds and even leftovers.

Our Father puts even more thought and effort into preparing and providing for all things essential for our body and soul for now and eternity. Right here in the presence of our enemy, in the middle of our broken homes and hearts, God has prepared an overflowing abundance of goodness, sweetness, and healthy experiences for us.

In David's day, a host would honor his guests by applying oil to their heads to cool them from their travels and rid them of the dust of the road. A shepherd poured oil on his sheep's head to keep insects away. David was thanking his Shepherd for keeping all bothersome worries and discomforts from him so he could eat at the table prepared for him.

Paul told us in the New Testament, "The Lord is near. Be anxious for nothing, but in everything by prayer and asking with thanksgiving let your requests be made known to God. And the peace of God, which goes beyond all understanding, will guard your hearts and your minds in Christ Jesus" (my paraphrase of Phil. 4:5–7). We can sit at the table prepared for us in the presence of our enemies in peace and comfort. Life all around is loud and angry, uncertain and scary, but our Lord is near, and He has prepared an overflowing abundance of life and goodness for us.

Bible Reading: Hosea 14, Philippians 4:12–13, 18–19

Day 5

With great confidence, David proclaims, "Surely goodness and loving-kindness will follow me all the days of my life, and I will dwell in the house of the LORD forever" (Ps. 23:6). David's strength and hope had risen because of his daily walk with his Shepherd and because of the intense exercise of getting through the valley of the shadow of death.

With God as our owner and Shepherd, goodness will follow us wherever we go all the days of our lives. Goodness is everything that brings benefit to us spiritually, intellectually, and physically. It is a sure thing that a bounty of valuable, excellent things and experiences will follow us as we follow our Shepherd. By now we know that in God's estimation, painful and uncertain times can be good, so we do not assume we are being promised all feather beds and flowers. We are being promised that the hard times and the evil intentions of others will work out for our good and the good of others when we are God's children. That is what Paul meant when he said, "We know that God causes all things to work together for good to those who love God, to those who are called according to *His* purpose" (Rom. 8:28). That doesn't mean that all things are good, but that all things—terrible, sinful, wonderful—work together for good for God's children.

Mercy or lovingkindness will follow us all our lives when we follow our Good Shepherd. That means compassion, kindness, and forgiveness will follow us. God will lovingly wait for us to grasp that He is enough for us. He will tenderly lift us up when we cave in to our fears and with great kindness will hold our hands as we stumble through some of our life.

Goodness and lovingkindness all flow from the heart of our Father and Shepherd. He is the source of our hope and our strength. God is the guide, the shield, and the support for our journey through life—all of our life until the very end. God told us in Hebrews 13:5 that He will never leave us; never will He abandon or forsake us. He is with us for the long haul, no matter what.

Because of all this, David looked at his Shepherd and promised his loyalty. I will dwell in the house of the Lord forever. I will remain in Your sheepfold all the days of my life. I choose to live with You and for You forever because life with You, God, is one of security and goodness.

David chose to live under God's management and direction whether he was in green pastures with cool, clear water or in the valley of the shadow of death. He chose loyalty to his Shepherd whether he was being disciplined or pushed in a direction he didn't feel like going or lying down to rest in a cool place. No matter what, through it all, David recognized that life with his Good Shepherd was so much better than life with the world's ruler.

At the end of Moses's life, he said to Israel that today "I have set before you life and death, the blessing and the curse. So choose life in order that you may live, you and your descendants, by loving the Lord your God, by obeying His voice, and by holding fast to Him; for this is your life and the length of your days" (Deut. 30:19–20).

***Bible Reading*: Psalm 118:1–9, Revelation 3:20–21**

Day 6

The L<small>ORD</small> is my shepherd, I shall not want. He makes me lie down in green pastures; He leads me beside quiet waters. He restores my soul; He guides me in the paths of righteousness For His name's sake. Even though I walk through the valley of the shadow of death, I fear no evil, for You are with me; Your rod and Your staff, they comfort me. You prepare a table before me in the presence of my enemies; You have anointed my head with oil; My cup overflows. Surely goodness and lovingkindness will follow me all the days of my life, And I will dwell in the house of the L<small>ORD</small> forever.

—Ps. 23:1–6

These are the words of a sheep about his Shepherd and to his Shepherd. These are the words of a child about his Father and to his Father. None of these words or truths can be said of the world's leader. So to that point I want to ask you to consider who your leader is. Who do you run to, trust in, and listen to? Remember that there are only two choices—God or Satan. We may think being in control of our own lives is a third option, but that is Satan's lie. The devil's goal is for us to serve him, but if we won't do that, he at least wants us to serve and follow anyone or anything but God. Jesus said we cannot serve two masters (Matt. 6:24, Luke 16:13). The line has been drawn in the sand. We must choose.

Romans 6:23 says that the wages of sin is death, but the free gift of God is eternal life in Christ Jesus our Lord. In Romans 3:10 we're told that no one is spotless and clean, not one single person, and verse 23 says all have sinned and fall short of the glory of God.

"But God demonstrates His own love toward us, in that while we were yet sinners, Christ died for us" (Rom. 5:8). John 3:16 tells us that because God so loved us all, He gave His only Son, Jesus, that whoever believes in Him will not die but have eternal life.

Do you know how much Jesus loves us? Isaiah 53:5 says He was pierced with nails and a spear for our rebellion, and He was crushed for our immorality; the punishment that brought us peace was upon Him, and by His wounds we were healed. See how very much our heavenly Father loves us, for He allows us to be called His children, and we really are! (1 John 3:1).

You can say with David that the Lord is my Shepherd. As Romans 10:9-10 says, all you need to do is confess with your mouth that Jesus is Lord and believe in your heart that God raised Him from the dead, and you will be saved. For it is by believing in your heart that you are made right with God, and it is by confessing with your mouth that you are saved.

How could we not want a Shepherd who has conquered our most feared thing—death? God raised Jesus from the dead, freeing Him from the agony of death because it was impossible for death to keep its hold on Him (Acts 2:24). Death has no sting. We can be faced with it or with incredible physical and emotional pain, anger, or harm, but we will not be broken. Jesus Christ has conquered it all, and when He is our Lord and Shepherd, we are seated with Him in victory at the right hand of God (Col. 3:1). Think carefully, and choose your Abba Father and Shepherd today.

***Bible Reading*: Romans 10:8-13**

Week 3

ADAM AND EVE

Day 1

This week we will look at how God parents in everyday life as well as when discipline and punishment are required. Let's meet in the Garden of Eden and watch the heavenly Father interact with Adam and Eve. The first thing we see is that God created men and women in His image. No other animal, plant, or thing was created in His image or is a reflection of God.

God gave Adam a purpose by assigning jobs for him. "Then the LORD God took the man and put him into the garden of Eden to cultivate it and keep it" (Gen. 2:15). "Out of the ground the LORD God formed every beast of the field and every bird of the sky, and brought *them* to the man to see what he would call them; and whatever the man called a living creature, that was its name" (Gen. 2:19). Before sin, there was work. Are you surprised?

Having jobs and responsibilities gives us value and meaning. We sometimes wonder why we are even here. Is it just to be miserable and take up space? In God's plan, there is always work to be done, and though He doesn't need us, He wants us to be part of the process. To that purpose, our heavenly Father has gifted us in different ways.

Exodus 23–39 reveals the gifting of artistic, building, sewing, and craftsman skills. First Corinthians 12–14 shows gifts God has given us such as healing, teaching, hospitality, and more that should be used in the church and world today. Work is good and was given to us as a gift of love and trust. God believes we can accomplish much and proves it by placing us in situations where we must perform. Our Abba, Daddy, gives us the freedom to accomplish our tasks in our own creative ways, just like Adam named all the animals. What fun we can have!

Adam and Eve

Genesis 3:8 says, "They heard the sound of the LORD God walking in the garden in the cool of the day." The Father spent time with Adam and Eve, walking and talking with them. They had a relationship of joy, friendship, and time, and the Lord came to them. Throughout the Bible we have seen God search out His children. Moses, Samuel, David, Isaiah, the disciples, and Jesus are wonderful examples of God's love of us and desire for a relationship.

Today, right now, God the Father wants you and me. He yearns for us to spend time with Him and share our thoughts with Him. Revelation 5:8 tells us that in heaven there are golden bowls full of incense, which are the prayers of the saints. (Remember, saints are all who believe in Jesus as Lord and Savior) (Rom. 1:7, 1 Cor. 1:2). Can you imagine that—having your words, thoughts, and your conversations so valued that they are kept in a golden bowl?

This Parent doesn't tell us to be quiet, and He doesn't ignore us. He listens and then saves our words in golden bowls. He loved us before we loved Him (1 John 4:19). We know His love by this, that He laid down His life for us (1 John 3:16). Ephesians 1:4 says that long ago, even before God made the world, He loved us and chose us in Christ to be holy and without fault in His eyes.

Our heavenly Father created us on purpose. He values our input and efforts, and looks for us to spend time with Him. There will never be another Daddy like Him. Soak in His love.

Bible Reading: Genesis 2:8–25, Ephesians 1:1–8

Day 2

Out of the ground the LORD God caused to grow every tree that is pleasing to the sight and good for food; the tree of life also in the midst of the garden, and the tree of the knowledge of good and evil. Then the LORD God took the man and put him into the garden of Eden to cultivate it and keep it. The LORD God commanded the man, saying, "From any tree of the garden you may eat freely; but from the tree of the knowledge of good and evil you shall not eat, for in the day that you eat from it you will surely die."

—Gen. 2:9, 15–17

What a good and perfect parent God is. He gave instructions and responsibilities to His children. He gave great freedom and opportunities but also limits and restrictions. There were a lot of yeses. Yes, eat from dozens of trees. Yes, name and play with the animals. Yes, cultivate and be creative with the garden. But there was one no. No, you may not eat from the tree of the knowledge of good and evil. God didn't owe Adam an explanation, but He gave him a partial one anyway, that when he ate from that tree he would surely die. There would be a consequence. That wasn't a threat; it was a warning, a caution to be careful when making choices.

As a parent, I find it interesting that God didn't hide the tree that had the potential for bad and harmful consequences. It was sort of like hiding the chocolate so the kids won't get a stomachache, or forbidding all TV so they won't see the immorality and violence.

In essence, our Father said, "This is the world. Everything that is real and exists is here. I made you because I wanted to. I love you and want you to love Me." Sweeping His arms wide, He went on. "Look at it all—it's full and beautiful and good. You can choose any of the good things I have made for you. But there is one good thing I want you to not choose. Don't eat from that center tree." It wasn't because the tree was bad but because choosing self-control and obedience was better—the best thing God could give us.

God wants to be loved the same way we are loved. Remember, He chose us and loved us. He wants us to choose Him and love Him too. So He put a "no" in front of us, not to set us up to fail but to give us a choice. Our Father wants us to choose to love Him and follow Him.

After Adam and Eve ate from the forbidden tree, God came to them as He usually did in the evening. They were hiding because they felt guilty and realized they were naked. God knew they had disobeyed and, in effect, rejected Him, yet He didn't come yelling and accusing. He asked where they were. Adam answered, "I heard the sound of You in the garden, and I was afraid because I was naked; so I hid myself." And God said, "Who told you that you were naked? Have you eaten from the tree that I commanded you not to eat?" (Gen. 3:7–11).

Our Father had every right to be furious. Yet He came in love and gentleness and asked questions instead of condemning and accusing. He allowed Adam and Eve to tell their side of the story before He acted. Even after their disobedience, God wanted them to know they and their words had value. Their Father loved them. The consequences would come for a time, but His plan to provide payment for the penalty and restore their relationship was in motion.

***Bible Reading*:** Genesis 3:7–11, Deuteronomy 30:19–20, Acts 13:38–39

Day 3

After God asked if Adam and Eve had eaten from the forbidden tree, Adam replied, "'The woman whom You gave *to be* with me, she gave me from the tree, and I ate.' Then the Lord God said to the woman, 'What is this you have done?' And the woman said, 'The serpent deceived me, and I ate'" (Gen. 3:12–13). Neither person took responsibility for their actions. Adam even had the nerve to blame God for giving him the woman.

The heavenly Father didn't waste His time responding to their self-serving, blame-throwing comments. He held the three parties involved responsible for what they had done.

God told the serpent he would be cursed and people would hate snakes forever. One of the beautiful creatures God created and Adam named was now a slithering, hissing, dust-eating, vile animal. The next part of this punishment went to Satan himself who had taken on the image of a serpent. God placed a natural animosity between Satan and mankind. Satan had always hated God's creation, but now people would have antagonism toward Satan. In a foretelling of Jesus's death and resurrection, God told Satan that one of Eve's offspring (Jesus) would bruise him on the head, and Satan would bruise Him on the heel.

> *To the woman He said, "I will greatly multiply your pain in childbirth, in pain you will bring forth children; yet your desire will be for your husband, and he will rule over you." Then to Adam He said, "Because you have listened to the voice of your wife, and have eaten from the tree about which I commanded you, saying, 'You shall not eat from it'; cursed is the ground because of you; in toil you will eat of it all the days of your life. Both thorns and thistles it shall grow for you; and you will eat the plants of the field; by the sweat of your face you will eat bread, till you return to the ground, because from it you were taken; for you are dust, and to dust you shall return.'"*
>
> —Gen. 3:16–19

The enjoyable experiences of childbirth and tending the garden, of producing life, were now turned into painful, labor-intensive tasks. The ground itself was cursed so it would naturally yield weeds instead of life-giving food.

In rejecting God, mankind rejected His gifts and life, and in punishment, God made the joy and reward of them a difficult thing to attain.

God's love was still so great that His desire was to protect His children. Adam and Eve had tried to cover their nakedness and shame with fig leaves, which were inadequate, so the Lord made clothing for them from animal skins. First Corinthians 13 is called the love chapter, and verse seven says that love always protects. The Greek word *protect* means "hide or conceal, covering to keep off something that threatens." God covered their shame to protect them from the elements of creation that had now turned hostile, from Satan's assaults, and from ridicule and attack from other people. Pointing to Jesus, God shed the innocent blood of an animal in order to cover Adam and Eve. His love wiped out our sins on the cross with His Son Jesus's blood, and He covers us today to protect our dignity, hearts, and minds. Our Father hides us in the shadow of His wings from the threat of all evil and helps us bear the burden of this hostile world. Again, I say, see how great a love our Father has for us!

Bible Reading: **Genesis 3, 1 Peter 1:18–25**

Day 4

Cain and Abel were two of Adam and Eve's children, and their story is familiar to most of us. At harvest time, Cain brought to the Lord a gift of his farm produce, while Abel brought several choice lambs from the best of his flock. The Lord accepted Abel and his offering, but He did not accept Cain and his offering. This made Cain very angry and dejected. "Why are you so angry?" the Lord asked him. "Why do you look so dejected? If you do what is right, will you not be accepted? But if you do not do what is right, sin is crouching at your door; it desires to have you, but you must master it" (Gen. 4:1–7).

Hebrews 11:4 gives us a little more insight into why God accepted Abel and his gift and not Cain and his. "By faith Abel offered to God a better sacrifice than Cain, through which he obtained the testimony that he was righteous, God testifying about his gifts, and through faith, though he is dead, he still speaks." It was about the sacrifice. It's always about the quality of the sacrifice for our sins. What we offer in our own power and ideas (like Adam and Eve's fig leaves) is not acceptable to God. Only blood can wipe out and cleanse us from sin. So God, pointing toward the cross, was the first to shed blood to reconcile the sinner. Abel offered the blood of choice and innocent lambs, following God's example. Cain wanted to come to God on his own terms, so he offered something God had cursed: the fruit of the ground.

Both Cain and Abel had sin in their lives. Like today, God accepts us based on the sacrifice, not our gift or behavior. He wants us to trust in His plan and follow His lead. Our faith in His sacrifice, Jesus's death and resurrection, is the only thing that is pleasing to God.

How did the Father respond? He showed approval and pleasure to Abel for doing the right thing. That's what a good parent does. They don't just shrug and say that was what was expected of their child; they recognize and appreciate a job well done.

Then, good parent that He is, God talked with Cain. "Why are you so angry? Why do you look so dejected? If you do what is right, will you not be accepted? But if you do not do what is right, sin is crouching at your door; it desires to have you, but you must master it." Did you notice that just as He did with Adam and Eve, God asked Cain questions instead of yelling and condemning? He used every opportunity to teach and cause His kids to think. He was also direct with His words. "Why are you angry and depressed? Have you considered the fact that it's because you haven't made good choices? Would you feel this way if you did the right thing?"

A warning came next. Be careful; you're walking on dangerous ground. Sin is crouching at your door. The word *sin* here means "condition of sin or sin offering." In this context, God told Cain that his wanting to come to God in his own efforts, Cain's desire to be in control, was crouching at his door; it desired to have him. Haven't we all experienced this? Haven't we wanted God to accept us based on our behavior and reject others for the same reason? Our Father said we must master that. Take that thought captive. Believe what God says is the only way to the Father. Have faith in Jesus, not ourselves. God's love has always pointed to the one thing that will save us—the blood of the Lamb.

Bible Reading: Hebrews 9:11–28

Day 5

Cain said to his brother, Abel, "Let's go out to the field." While they were in the field, Cain attacked his brother and killed him.

> *Then the LORD said to Cain, "Where is Abel your brother?" And he said, "I do not know. Am I my brother's keeper?" He said, "What have you done? The voice of your brother's blood is crying to Me from the ground. Now you are cursed from the ground, which has opened its mouth to receive your brother's blood from your hand. When you cultivate the ground, it will no longer yield its strength to you; you will be a vagrant and a wanderer on the earth."*
>
> —Gen. 4:8–12

Our loving Father gave Cain the chance to confess his sins by asking where Abel was, but when Cain lied and got defensive, God did not even blink. So Cain couldn't hedge further, God said, "What have *you* done?" There would be no blaming anyone else.

I love that God cared about the victim and made sure his name and murder were not glossed over. Abel's blood cried to God from the ground. That is true today. Your blood, scars, and pain cry out to God for justice. Psalm 89:14 says, "Righteousness and justice are the foundation of Your throne." God sees, cares, and is actively working out justice for each of us.

Notice that God took away Cain's ability to grow crops, which Cain had chosen to give as a sin offering. God's punishment could have been a blessing to Cain. But Cain still wanted to be in charge, so he said, "My punishment is too great to bear! Behold, You have driven me this day from the face of the ground; and from Your face I will be hidden, and I will be a vagrant and a wanderer on the earth, and whoever finds me will kill me" (Gen. 4:13–14). Instead of appreciating that God had not sentenced him to death, instead of being sorry for killing his brother, Cain continued to show his rebellious heart and made himself out as the victim. He wanted God to do things his way.

The Father showed His love again, not by taking away Cain's punishment but by protecting him in the midst of it. "Whoever kills Cain, vengeance will be taken on him sevenfold" (Gen. 4:15). Then the Lord put a mark on Cain to warn anyone who might try to kill him.

Our first reaction may be to think how unfair it was that God protected Cain when he had committed murder. Romans 3:23 says we all have sinned and fall short of the glory of God. Yes, we all want justice when we've been hurt. And yes, we want mercy when we're the ones who've sinned. Our

Father gives us both. His desire is for us to be reunited with Him in a loving relationship. Colossians 1:20 says the Father reconciled us with Himself by Jesus's blood.

Cain had the same opportunity that you and I have—to choose to turn around from our self-centered way of living and have a relationship with our Father. That is God's longing. God's heart is also for the victims. He is greatly angered by injustice and cares for those hurt by it (Deut. 10:18, Rom. 12:19). We will be disciplined, but His hope is that correction will draw us back to Him.

Bible Reading: Genesis 4:1–15, Romans 12:19, Colossians 1:19–23

Day 6

What a special love the Father has for us—creating us in His image, meeting with, talking, and listening to us. The Father has given us gifts and abilities, and He values our efforts and input.

Listen to some of the names God is called that give us a picture of who He is. He is the Lord God, God Most High, the Everlasting God, Almighty, the I Am, Eternal God, the Living God, God of Hosts, the Holy One of Israel, Mighty God, Lord God of Heaven, King Eternal, Sovereign, and the heavenly Father. God is Creator, Defender, Shepherd, Ancient of Days, Incomparable, Invisible, Unchangeable, Unequaled, Unsearchable, All-Powerful, All-Knowing, Ever-Present, Abba, and Father of Lights. And this magnificent God chooses to love you and me.

We've learned that whoever the Lord loves, He chastens. Discipline means to instruct, correct, and teach. Punishment means to discipline, penalize, and chew out. The heavenly Father has shown us through His dealings with Adam, Eve, and Cain how a loving parent accomplishes these things. Without backing down from the harsh price their actions demanded, the Father covered them with His love and protection. His goal is to teach us what is right and restore us to the good relationship He planned for us from the beginning.

There is no abuse or degrading in God's discipline and punishment. Like Adam, Eve, and Cain, our pitiful attempts to cover our failures are flimsy. We think that education, money, toughness, or fame will make us look acceptable and people won't see the mess we are. When we are God's children, He gently replaces our inadequate "fig leaves" with the lasting cover of His Son's cleansing blood, with His everlasting love and forgiveness. The results of our choices may last our lifetime or even into generations after us, but God's love and forgiveness last throughout eternity.

Adam and Eve experienced God's unconditional love. By accepting Satan's explanation of the forbidden tree, they had rejected God's. After God had given them all His creation, they rejected His love and provision in order to do things their way. You and I know how bad rejection feels and how much it hurts. Yet God's love didn't stop. It was not based on whether or not people loved Him. God's love was based on who He is. The Father chose to love us from the beginning because He is love—not that God feels love but that He is love (1 John 4:8, 16).

Before sin, people never feared anything, but God's punishment was also His protection. We learned that Satan had always hated God and His creation, but one of his punishments was that God put a natural hostility in our hearts toward Satan. That distrustful ill feeling is designed to keep us from being easily led into Satan's traps. That fear protects us.

God told Satan that one of Eve's offspring (Jesus) would bruise him on the head, and Satan would bruise Him on the heel. In the Father's greatest act of love, He sent His perfect Son, Jesus, to die on the cross for our sins. Satan bruised Jesus's heal for that short time, but the victorious Lord Jesus crushed Satan's head when He rose from the grave and now lives forever in heaven (1 John 3:8). Our Father God has protected and provided for our every need because He is love.

Bible Reading: I John 3:1–12

Week 4
CHRISTMAS

Day 1

Christmas week has finally arrived! The wrapping has been torn off our gift, and we gasp at what is revealed. It looks like a baby, but something leaps in our heart as we stare at Him. He is more than just another little boy. "His name is Immanuel," someone whispers, "God with us."

The 400 years between the Old Testament of the Bible and Jesus's birth at the beginning of the New Testament make this name a tender gift from God. He had ceased talking through prophets. Like today, His children had only His written words, and there was little recorded history of Israel. Because of this, these years are sometimes referred to as "the Silent Years."

One harsh regime after another took over the land. Israel had been occupied or taken away and treated cruelly. God allowed this because the people had rejected Him and completely disobeyed His teachings, yet when things got bad enough, the people had a history of calling out to Him for help. God worked for 400 years, but it was silent and without the close relationship He had enjoyed before with His children.

Do you know how that feels to believe you're unheard in the midst of an angry world, to cry out to God and feel as if your words bounced off the ceiling and echoed back to you? You may have been taken from your home because of your rebellion or for your protection, and you may have gone through heartaches and troubles where fear, despair, and rage warred within you.

We've read about some of the times when God moved slowly to show His plan and His love, but 400 years? In your case, you may be thinking, "My whole lifetime?" Is God gone? Did He just walk away and dust His hands to be rid of us?

This winter of frozen hearts and spiritual death lasted for a long time. It was into this season—into your time of winter—that God gave us our first Christmas. Joseph, God's chosen stepfather for His Son, was assured that God's silence had finally ended.

> *An angel of the Lord appeared to him in a dream, saying, "Joseph, son of David, do not be afraid to take Mary as your wife; for the Child who has been conceived in her is of the Holy Spirit. She will bear a Son; and you shall call His name Jesus, for He will save His people from their sins." Now all this took place to fulfill what was spoken by the Lord through the prophet: "BEHOLD, THE VIRGIN SHALL BE WITH CHILD AND SHALL BEAR A SON, AND THEY SHALL CALL HIS NAME IMMANUEL," which translated means, "GOD WITH US."*
>
> —Matt. 1:20–23

Jesus is our gift. Jesus—Jehovah—is salvation. He is the existing One, the I Am, our rescuer, our freedom, our salvation. Immanuel is our present—God with us, next to us, living with us; God experiencing our emotions and limitations and life. No longer would God be up there in beautiful, safe heaven working from a distance. He would crawl with us and walk with us. Jesus would eat with us and go hungry like us. Our gift would feel love and joy and laughter. And He would feel betrayal and sadness and fear. His very presence said, "I love you," louder than any spoken words in the past. Our Christmas present is Immanuel—God with us.

Bible Reading: Matthew 1:18–25

Day 2

Why is Jesus such an amazing gift? What makes His willingness to be born as a person and live among us so extraordinary? Let's take a peek into heaven to gain a better understanding of our first and best Christmas present.

> *I [John] was in the Spirit on the Lord's day, and I heard behind me a loud voice like the sound of a trumpet, Then I turned to see the voice that was speaking with me. And having turned I saw seven golden lampstands; and in the middle of the lampstands I*

> *saw one like a son of man, clothed in a robe reaching to the feet, and girded across His chest with a golden sash. His head and His hair were white like white wool, like snow; and His eyes were like a flame of fire. His feet were like burnished bronze, when it has been made to glow in a furnace, and His voice was like the sound of many waters. In His right hand He held seven stars, and out of His mouth came a sharp two-edged sword; and His face was like the sun shining in its strength.*
>
> —Rev. 1:10, 12–16

This was Jesus as God—fully glorified, looking as He does in heaven. John said he fell at His feet as a dead man. We cannot even fathom the splendor, wonder, and magnificence of God. Did you know that in heaven there is no sun or moon because the brilliance of the Lord shines and lights up everything? (Rev. 21:23, 22:5). Close your eyes, and try to picture Jesus, not as a baby, Mary's son, or a man leading the disciples and talking with people. Don't picture Him as the beaten man hanging on the cross. Picture Jesus Christ as God the Son in all His glory.

Now let's try to grasp the power and purpose of God the Son. Jesus said, "Do not be afraid. I am the first and the last, and the living One; and I was dead, and behold, I am alive forevermore, and I have the keys of death and of Hades" (Rev. 1:17–18).

Baby Jesus—helpless, dependent, newborn Jesus—is the first and the last. He is eternal. For people, the life process and the death process start at the same time, at the moment of conception. Jesus Christ was born to die, yet only in Him was death finally conquered (1 Cor. 15:54–57). He came that we may have life and have it abundantly (John 10:10). Our Christmas present did not begin 2,000 years ago. In Revelation 1:8, Jesus said, "I am the Alpha and the Omega . . . who is and who was and who is to come, the Almighty." Alpha—the beginning; Omega—the ending. A–Z, eternal, always, and forever. He is our all in all!

As we start to understand Jesus as God, we must consider one more thing. In order for His gift to be, Jesus died to self. Think about that for a moment. Dying to self means saying no to all our own desires, comforts, privileges, and protections. Jesus willingly gave up His glory, power, prestige, honor, and rights in order to be a baby who needed diapers and mushy food. He said yes to skinned knees, a pimply face, family, love, rejection, serving, and pain because He looked at you and me and burst with love for us.

The glory of the magnificent Lord was wrapped snugly in strips of cloth and laid in a manger because there was no room for them in the inn (Luke 2:10). Unwrap this Gift with care. Hold Him up to the light, and see the brilliance of love and grace. This is a priceless Gift that lasts forever. This gift is God's Son.

Bible Reading: Luke 2:1–20

Day 3

Who would be the first to hear your announcement if you were in charge of proclaiming the birth of the King of kings? The heavenly Father heralded this birth in a grand way to a surprising group of people.

> *In the same region [as Bethlehem] there were some shepherds staying out in the fields and keeping watch over their flock by night. And an angel of the Lord suddenly stood before them, and the glory of the Lord shone around them; and they were terribly frightened. But the angel said to them, "Do not be afraid; for behold, I bring you good news of great joy which will be for all the people; for today in the city of David there has been born for you a Savior, who is Christ the Lord. This will be a sign for you: you will find a baby wrapped in cloths and lying in a manger." And suddenly there appeared with the angel a multitude of the heavenly host praising God.*
> —Luke 2:8–13

Micah, an Old Testament prophet, said hundreds of years before the first Christmas that out of Bethlehem a ruler would come who would shepherd His people, Israel. Jesus Christ was born in the city of David, the first shepherd king. So, it is no surprise that birth announcements were sent to the people who would most appreciate and understand the Gift God had just given.

Shepherds—they stay out in the fields keeping watch over their flock at night. A shepherd goes to where his sheep live. He would be more comfortable in his own home, but his sheep cannot function there, so he goes to them. Christ Jesus did the same thing for us. Taking it one step further, He came as one of us. His goal was to guide and watch over us, but it was also to let us know He understood how hard it was to be a person. Hebrews 2:17 tells us that Jesus had to be made like His brothers and sisters in all things so He could reconcile us to God. That's hard to understand, so let's think about it.

Jesus became a person so He would experience life as we live it. He was tempted to fight with His siblings, argue with His parents, and say He knew it all. Anger, fear, desires, and resentment knocked on the door of His mind and heart. Yet He never let those temptations take over and control Him. He never sinned. However, the experience of being human gave Him such a heart for us that now He stands by the Father to reconcile or patch up our relationship when we are being accused. When we blow it, Jesus says to the Father, "It's hard for them. But they are in Me, and I am in them. Justice has been satisfied. My blood covers all of them, Father. They are forgiven." His goal is to keep us and guide us into right living.

Our Christmas present is the Shepherd King. He came to stay with us in our homes and live our lives. Jesus was born to watch over us in the darkest night and walk with us through our days. He was not a king who lived in a palace of wealth and privilege, unaware of the poverty and injustice in his kingdom. He was a Shepherd living among His sheep day and night, seeing the dangers and hardships that His flock lived in. He was providing for our needs while protecting us from all harm and judgment. This is our good news of great joy, the greatest Gift ever given.

Bible Reading: **Isaiah 40:11, Micah 5:1-4, Hebrews 2:17-18, 4:15-16**

Day 4

Merry Christmas! We can say that. We can feel that down to our toes because the angels brought good news of great joy to all people—the news that Christ Jesus was born. Our Christmas present is joy.

What is joy? The simple definition is "gladness and great delight." But according to the Bible, joy is not just an emotion we feel on occasion. When a person asks Jesus into their lives, the Holy Spirit gives them fruits, or results, that come from Him living and working in them. One of the results of the Holy Spirit being in our lives is joy (Gal. 5:22).

Joy is not based on what is going on in our lives. It is based on what Jesus did for us. He loved us, came to us, lived, died, and conquered death for us. With Jesus in our lives, our joy is always with us. However, joy will not always bubble up within us as a feeling.

Jesus dreaded going to the cross because great physical pain was involved in it. Emotionally, He would have to endure betrayal, humiliation, and abandonment. Spiritually, He would have to carry every disgusting, horrible sin any person would ever commit. So Hebrews 12:2 says we must fix our eyes on Jesus, "the author and perfecter of faith, who for the *joy set before Him* endured the cross, despising the shame, and has sat down at the right hand of the throne of God" (emphasis added).

Christ Jesus did not feel great delight in the pain and shame; He endured it. Jesus knew His joy was at the end of the trial. It was at the finish line, and it was a prize worth fighting for. And because Jesus endured to the end, He secured joy for each of us too.

James tells us to "consider it all joy . . . when you encounter various trials, knowing that the testing of your faith produces endurance. And let endurance have *its* perfect result, so that you may be perfect and complete, lacking in nothing" (James 1:2–4).

That tells us that recognizing our joy is a choice. We are to count all our problems as joy. It is our choice how we consider the hurts and injustices we live through. If we believe God is good and in control—which He is—we will be able to say in the midst of our tears or battles that we claim the joy of the Lord (Mark 10:18, 1 Tim. 6:15). Pushing on, never giving up, persevering in devastating emotions and physical hardships, we can choose to chalk up the trials as joy because we are getting lasting and valuable life skills that we keep for eternity.

Joy—it is not shallow or empty, not just a giggle or a short thrill, but a deep and abiding gladness that the God of the universe loves us enough to grow us and strengthen us and carry us when needed. We rejoice that God in us turns our trials from destruction to glory.

Do not be afraid; for behold, I bring you good news of great joy which will be for all the people; for today in the city of David there has been born for you a Savior who is Christ the Lord.

Bible Reading: Romans 15:13, 1 John 1:1–5

Day 5

No matter what part of the world a person lives in, whether south of the equator where it is summer during the Christmas season or in the Northern Hemisphere where it is winter, some things are the same. We are people of churning emotions, worries, fears, and discontent. People who don't know Jesus or don't know Him well are apprehensive about where they stand with God after death. Does one "good" deed erase one "bad" deed? Who gets to choose the definition of "good" and "bad"? If we die in the midst of a bad time, what then?

Have you finished unwrapping your Gift yet? Did you see the part where the angels said, "Glory to God in the highest, and on earth peace among men with whom He is pleased"? What a beautiful part of our Gift. Peace. Tranquility, harmony, serenity, and calm restfulness.

For the Christian, or follower of Christ (the only ones with whom He is pleased) (Hosea 6:6, Micah 6:6, Col. 1:10), that means the tranquil state of a soul guaranteed their salvation through Christ and so fearing nothing from God and content with its earthly life, no matter what that is. We who have asked Jesus into our hearts are at peace with God. There is no fear of His judgment. Romans 8:1–2 assures us that "there is now no condemnation for those who are in Christ Jesus. For the law of the Spirit of life in Christ Jesus has set you free from the law of sin and death."

That answers so many questions. It is the work of Jesus—not our "good" works—that allows us to stand calmly and right before God. Nothing we do can erase our sin, and nothing we do can erase the salvation we have through Christ. We are told it is by grace we are saved through faith and not anything of ourselves. It is the gift of God. Salvation is not a reward for the good things we have done, so none of us can boast about it (Eph. 2:8–9).

Many verses assure us that we or Satan cannot undo what Jesus did on the cross. First Peter 3:18 confirms, "For Christ also died for sins once for all, *the* just for *the* unjust, so that He might bring us to God, having been put to death in the flesh, but made alive in the spirit." Other references are Romans 6:10, Hebrews 9:12, 10:10, and Jude 1:3. Our gift of peace is that we do not fear anything from God after we accept His gift of Jesus Christ. Once and for all His death and resurrection paid our debt and cleansed us of all our bad doings and thinking.

This peace is reason enough to rejoice, but God offers us more. Peace with individuals, security, safety, and prosperity are ours in Christ. We may experience this in the physical sense, but that is not necessarily guaranteed. The promise is that we will have this peace and completely know it as we go through the ups and downs of life. When faced with the person who abused you, as far as you're concerned, the hatred and war is over. Inside, no bitterness, malice, and unforgiveness rage. You don't respond to the people or situations the way you did before Christ's peace lived in you. Your heart and mind are safe; you prosper and grow rich in knowledge, skill, strength, and love. "The peace of God, which surpasses all comprehension, will guard your hearts and your minds in Christ Jesus" (Phil. 4:7). We can't do that on our own. Stand firm in God's strength, power, and love. Our Gift is peace.

Bible Reading: John 14:27, John 16:33

Day 6

One of the things I love about God is that He keeps His word. When the Lord promises something, it will happen without fail, every time, exactly how He said.

Like little children, we think every promise should happen when we want it to—quickly while we're thinking about it. And like an adult who can see a bigger picture, God waits until just the right time to carry out His word.

The Old Testament points to the promise of a Savior, our Redeemer, a Shepherd King, the Son of Man, the Son of God. Historical documentation proves the book of Isaiah was written around 701 BC. Isaiah wrote in chapter 7 verse 14, "Therefore the Lord Himself will give you a sign: Behold, a virgin will be with child and bear a son, and she will call His name Immanuel."

> *For a child will be born to us, a son will be given to us; and the government will rest on His shoulders; and His name will be called Wonderful Counselor, Mighty God, Eternal Father, Prince of Peace. There will be no end to the increase of* His *government or of peace, on the throne of David and over His kingdom, to establish it and to uphold it with justice and righteousness from then on and forevermore. The zeal of the* Lord *of hosts will accomplish this.*
>
> Isa. 9:6–7

Hundreds of years passed. Life was good and a celebration. Life was grueling and a bitter hardship. Would you believe God was trustworthy? In the middle of your life right now, in a place of unresolved problems, pain, and rejection, can you believe that God keeps His promises?

The Gift we are now holding, our Christmas present, is the proof we need to get through the long wait we sometimes face. Galatians 4:4–5 says, "But when the fullness of the time came, God sent forth His Son, born of a woman, born under the Law, so that He might redeem those who were under the Law, that we might receive the adoption as sons." Remember perspective, to get the eagle's eye view. God sees the biggest picture possible and knows when the right time is. He will fulfill all His promises to us. He will. But it will be when the right time fully comes, and that may not be when we want it.

We could fill ourselves up with what we think will give us joy and peace and make us good because we grew tired of waiting on God to come through. Our efforts last a short time and require constant feeding and work. The danger with that, with our impatience and distrusting hearts, is that when the right time finally comes, our hands will be full of our own stuff, and we won't be able to grab hold of God's gift. Or we will be so busy trying to fulfill God's "obligation" to us that we will totally miss the Promise being born.

The angel told Mary that the right time had finally come, and she would give birth to the Son of God. She asked how that could be, and the angel answered, "For nothing will be impossible with God" (Luke 1:37). Our gift is the fulfilled promise of God.

Bible Reading: Luke 1:26–38; 2:1–20

Week 5

MICAH

Day 1

The prophet Micah wrote one of the Old Testament books at a time when the rich, the religious, the politically powerful, and the civic leaders were greedy, full of bribe-taking corruption and wickedness. Foreign armies raided the poor, small villages with no help arriving from the fortified cities. God called Micah to speak hard truth as well as encouragement to people who had heard of Him but didn't all have a relationship with Him.

Many of us are afraid to say or believe that a loving God rebukes and disciplines us, yet God tells us repeatedly throughout the Bible that He does. He does not abuse; however, the results of sin definitely have a sting. This is a reminder for us to make wise decisions. His patience is long. Those of us who've been hurt by someone may not like that He doesn't strike them immediately. The Bible reminds us that God sees all of us, and we have all done wrong and hurtful things (Rom. 3:23). Each of us benefits from His patience.

His warnings are like a slap on the wrist, a time-out, or a privilege taken away. When our choices hurt others, are unjust, or lead someone off the right track, God's discipline will be strong.

Yet this punishment is loving. Recall with me the definition of sin. It's missing the mark or disagreeing with God's thinking, feeling, or ways of doing something. The results of sin are a separation between us and God (Isa. 59:2), death, shame, guilt, sorrow, destruction, pain, fear, and more. Sin stains us. God loves us. So He reprimands us to cause us to recognize what we have done. Those of us who are covered by Jesus's grace from the cross still fight a spiritual battle. While there is no formula to follow, the components of recognizing our sin, repenting, confessing to God, rejecting the sin and its place in our life, and removing it are an active part of our choice to walk with Jesus. Our Father's love saves us from many natural consequences now and has taken away the penalty of His wrath and eternal separation from Him.

God is also just. Psalm 89:14 says, "Righteousness and justice are the foundation of Your throne; lovingkindness and truth go before You." Sin deserves the penalty of eternal death—hell. God's love aches at the thought of us having to go to hell, yet His justice and righteousness demand that the penalty for the wrongdoing be paid. So Jesus covered our sin and released us from the results once and for all. Any reproof God gives the unbelieving world now is small compared to the penalty of eternal separation from Him in hell. Micah's warnings were strong. God had had enough and was about to severely punish His chosen people in various ways. His goal was to bring the lost to salvation in Him and His children back into the close relationship a Father and child should have.

> *Who is a God like You, who pardons iniquity and passes over the rebellious act of the remnant of His possession? He does not retain His anger forever because He delights in unchanging love. He will again have compassion on us; He will tread our iniquities under foot. Yes, You will cast all their sins into the depths of the sea. You will give truth to Jacob* and *unchanging love to Abraham, which You swore to our forefathers from the days of old.*
> —Mic. 7:18–20

***Bible Reading*: Micah 7:18–20, Hebrews 7:25–27**

Day 2

In Micah 1:2, the whole earth is told to hear God's judgments. Micah 3:1 and 9 tell the rulers of God's people to hear God's words. Micah 6:1 is addressed to God's people and says, "Hear now what the Lord is saying."

I want to stress again that God is not an abusive parent who jumps out from behind a door to ambush us in order to accuse and punish us. He repeatedly talks to us and tells us His will for us and what He sees us doing right and wrong. When our Father's discipline comes, we will know every reason why if we have listened to Him.

The word *hear* is *shama* in the Hebrew language and means "to listen to with interest, to agree and obey." God wants us to stop what we're doing and give Him our complete attention. We should hear every word He speaks and be interested in the meaning and intent of God's heart. When we listen that way, we will understand that God's desire is to protect us from the ravages of sin and from punishment. He wants to provide a strong foundation for us so we'll be able to choose the correct lifestyle, as well as live in peace, joy, and confidence.

As God moves past discipline and into punishment, He tells us to hear why He is stepping up the seriousness of His response. Again, the heavenly Father does not punish us to destroy and humiliate us. Hebrews 12:10–11 says, "For they [our earthly fathers] disciplined us for a short time as seemed best to them, but He *disciplines us* for *our* good, so that we may share His holiness. All discipline for the moment seems not to be joyful, but sorrowful; yet to those who have been trained by it, afterwards it yields the peaceful fruit of righteousness." The Father disciplines and punishes out of love and with love in order to help us improve and grow in goodness, justice, peace, and honesty.

That shows a relationship between God and the people with whom He is talking. Don't you love that? The Creator of the universe looks at you, pays attention to your feelings, thoughts, and actions, and then talks to you. He wants you to do the same with Him. God longs for us to look at Him; pay attention to His feelings, thoughts, and actions; and talk to Him. When Daniel prayed (Dan. 9:17), he said, "Listen (*shama*) to my prayer, God." Isn't that amazing? That's a relationship. We listen with great attention and agree with God, and He listens with great attention to us. When our lives harmonize with God's, He is able to agree with us because our thoughts and motives will be right with Him. From this intimate and open relationship, our Father comes to us as in Micah and lets us know when we've stopped listening to Him and how that's caused us to go off in the wrong direction.

Just as in Micah 6, the Lord reminds us of all He has done for us and asks us why we have left Him. My people . . . listen. My people . . . remember in order that you might know the righteous acts of the Lord. "Truly, truly, I say to you, he who hears My word, and believes Him who sent Me, has eternal life, and does not come into judgment, but has passed out of death into life" (John 5:24). God gives us the chance to listen and avoid punishment. That is love.

Bible Reading: Micah 3:1–4, 9, Micah 6:1–2, John 12:46–50

Day 3

Micah foretells, or prophesies, Jesus Christ's birth, life, and liberation of His people.

> "Now muster yourselves in troops, daughter of troops; they have laid siege against us; with a rod they will smite the judge of Israel on the cheek. But as for you, Bethlehem Ephrathah, too little to be among the clans of Judah, from you One will go forth for Me to be ruler in Israel. His goings forth are from long ago, from the days of eternity." Therefore He will give them up until the time when she who is in labor has borne a child. Then the remainder of His brethren will return to the sons of Israel. And He will arise and shepherd His flock in the strength of the LORD, in the majesty of the name of the LORD His God. And they will remain, because at that time He will be great to the ends of the earth. This One will be our peace.
>
> —Mic. 5:1–5

Like all the prophets, Micah blended near and distant ages in his prophecy. Some of these things happened during Micah's lifetime when Assyria took over Israel. Some happened hundreds of years later when Jesus was born and then went to trial before the cross. Some will happen in the end times that are yet to come. It's like pulling a telescope open while looking through it.

What does this have to do with us today? Did you see the life choices being made in Micah's time? They practiced lies, rebellion, deception, scheming, evil, thievery, idolatry, sexual immorality, greed, injustice, robbery, arrogance, cheating, bribes, violence, strife, false religion, and more. God listed all the things He had against His people and reminded them of His previous warnings and care for them. The heavenly Father told the people they would be punished because of the way they chose to live. But in an act of irresistible love and compassion, He told them how He planned to rescue and free them.

This rescue mission was not only for the people of that time but for any of us who would accept it. God's Messiah was promised to this group of people who didn't really care and wanted to live life their own way. *Messiah* means "anointed one," the king of Israel, the high priest of Israel. *Messiah* in Greek is "Christ." Jesus Christ is more than a name. Every part of His birth, life, and death fulfilled prophecy from hundreds of years before. Matthew 1 and 2 tell us that all the events of Jesus's birth fulfilled what the prophets had said. The death and resurrection of Jesus fulfilled prophecy in Matthew 26 and 27. Hebrews 3 tells us that Jesus is our High Priest. Romans 11:25–27 says, "A partial hardening has come upon Israel, until the fullness of the Gentiles has come in. And in this way all Israel will be saved, as it is written, 'The Deliverer will come from Zion, he will banish ungodliness from Jacob'; and this will be my covenant with them when I take away their sins."

Even when God was rightly angry with His people, had run out of patience, and was about to punish them, He wanted to give them hope. "I will deliver you from your punishment." That is not just hell, which would be enough; the Father wants to free us from the devastation sin has on our lives today. Through Christ Jesus, the chains of addiction, bitterness, fear, and rage are broken. Feelings of insecurity, being unlovable, and rejection are exposed as lies when we stand in the light of Christ's love. Because "greater love has no one than this, that someone lay down his life for his friends" (John 15:13). Who is a God like this who calls us friends and forgives us?

Bible Reading: John 3:16–21, John 15:9–15

Day 4

Imagine you are in a courtroom on the witness stand, and you are the one on trial. The judge is God, and He has heard the list of all the crimes you have committed. In your heart you know it is all true, yet you are angry. "What do you have to say for yourself?" asks the Judge, and you scream your answer. "What do You want from me? You're impossible to please!" Sarcastically you exaggerate the amount of payment and sacrifice you think will make God happy.

That's exactly what Israel did in Micah 6:6–7: "With what shall I come to the Lord *and* bow myself before the God on high? Shall I come to Him with burnt offerings, with yearling calves? Does the Lord take delight in thousands of rams, in ten thousand rivers of oil? Shall I present my firstborn *for* my rebellious acts, the fruit of my body for the sin of my soul?" Would that make Him glad?

"Blinded to God's goodness and character, he [the guilty] reasons within his own depraved frame of reference. He need not change; God must change . . . His willingness to raise the price does not reflect his generosity but veils a complaint that God demands too much."[12]

Micah 6:8 answers back, "He has told you, O man, what is good; and what does the LORD require of you but to do justice, to love kindness, and to walk humbly with your God?" The Lord patiently stops our shouting by calmly reminding us that He has shown us before what He wants. Be just—treat others the way you want to be treated. Love mercy—don't just show mercy; love to show it. Give the same amount of mercy you want to receive from God. Walk humbly—remember who you are and who God is. This is a heart issue. True humility is thinking rightly, not meanly, about yourself. When you see yourself honestly, you will be humble. Walking humbly is not acting humbly; it is living "God first, others next, me last" all the time.

The prosecution rests. Israel, you, and I are troubled. But it is not because of the indifference or neglect of God. Our own sin brought our problems on us. What God required of us was not mysterious; we simply did not do it. We cannot do it without Him.

> *Therefore if you have been raised up with Christ, keep seeking the things above, where Christ is, seated at the right hand of God. For you have died and your life is hidden with Christ in God. And have put on the new self who is being renewed to a true knowledge according to the image of the One who created him. So, as those who have been chosen of God, holy and beloved, put on a heart of compassion, kindness, humility, gentleness and patience; bearing with one another, and forgiving each other, whoever has a complaint against anyone; just as the Lord forgave you, so also should you. Beyond all these things* put on *love, which is the perfect bond of unity.*
>
> —Col. 3:1, 3, 10, 12–14

With this the Judge's gavel strikes as He pronounces us "not guilty by reason of His Son's cleansing blood!"

Bible Reading: Psalm 51

Day 5

Micah ends his book by manning up to his sin and the sin of all Israel. Forgiveness comes today by believing in Jesus. When we sin, our everlasting but interrupted relationship with God is restored when we confess our sins and repent. Micah 7:1–4 tells us that sin leaves us impoverished, empty, and craving good. There seems to be no price for sin when we're in the middle of it, but our judgment day is coming swiftly.

Micah 7:5–6 points out one of the penalties of living in sinfulness is that we cannot trust friends and family members. Betrayal, deceit, and disrespect weave themselves into our closest relationships. While this is wrong and bad, good can come out of it as we discover that God is really the only One we can always trust and count on.

Taking responsibility for his actions and choices, Micah says, "I will bear the indignation of the LORD because I have sinned against Him, until He pleads my case and executes justice for me" (Mic. 7:9). Jesus executed justice on the cross and pleads our case now to the Father. Owning up to our wrong choices isn't what gives us salvation. But to get out of the pit of darkness and shame we are in when we sin, God wants our active honesty. "If we say that we have no sin, we are deceiving ourselves and the truth is not in us. If we confess our sins, He is faithful and righteous to forgive us our sins and to cleanse us from all unrighteousness" (1 John 1:8–9).

God promises to protect, comfort, pardon, and shepherd His people when they do this. He promises us a close relationship with Himself. This book in which God our Father, Protector, Judge, and Rebuilder is proclaimed ends in a beautiful praise and promise. Micah, whose name means "who is like God?" writes these words:

> *Who is a God like You, who pardons iniquity [evil, sin] and passes over the rebellious act of the remnant of His possession? He does not retain His anger forever; because He delights in unchanging love. He will again have compassion on us; He will tread our iniquities under foot. Yes, You will cast all their sins into the depths of the sea. You will give truth to Jacob and unchanging love to Abraham, which You swore to our forefathers from the days of old.*
>
> —Mic. 7:18–20

For a holy, righteous God to pardon our guilt is a love we cannot understand. He lifts the burden and carries the weight of our sin for us. God does away with our rebellion and chooses not to stay angry with us forever. The Lord delights in unchanging love. Nothing you or I do will change the love our Father has for us. It's more than a feeling; it is how He chooses to think about us. And He is not sighing deeply because He is at the end of His rope. He delights in loving us—all the time, no matter how we succeed, no matter how we blow it.

God will discipline us for a short time, but His compassion (mercy and love) will flow over us again. Our Defender will subdue and bring our guilt and sins under His foot. The Father will throw our sins into the depths of the sea, and as someone said, He will post a "no fishing" sign there. He will not bring our sins up again; He will not allow others to bring them up, and He doesn't want us to bring them up after He has thrown them out. Micah says that God will give truth—firmness, reliability, and faithfulness—to us, fulfilling all His promises. Who is a God like that?

Bible Reading: 1 John 1

Day 6

What have we learned this week about God? How has His love and justice been shown to us through His dealings with His rebellious children? Who is a God like Him? From any religion you've ever heard of, what "god" matches the one true God of the Bible?

It is as if Micah lived today. We are the same people who lived in Israel and Judah thousands of years ago. Our families are fractured and unsafe because of the blatant and defiant sins of our lives. Justice is polluted in our homes, schools, courts, jobs, and governments because of greed and selfish ambition. The weak are trampled or ignored by the strong and powerful. A person's value is determined by their physical appearance, bank account, and brains instead of the fact that they are a person created in God's image. Integrity, purity, kindness, strength of one's convictions, and truthfulness are talked about but not really admired or sought after. God has spoken to us through His prophet Micah. Have we heard?

One of the keys God has given us is to listen to Him. In order to unlock the doors of our prison cells and unchain our hearts and minds from sin's consequences, listen to Him. Hear His words; pay close attention to why He is saying things. Understand His heart so we can agree with our Lord's plans, even when they are bigger than anything we can think or imagine.

Amazingly we've seen that God listens to us in the same way He wishes to be listened to. Let's clear up the concept of Him agreeing with us. Ephesians 4:13–14 says we should listen to Him "until we all attain to the unity of the faith, and of the knowledge of the Son of God, to a mature man, to the measure of the stature which belongs to the fullness of Christ. As a result, we are no longer to be children, tossed here and there by waves and carried about by every wind of doctrine, by the trickery of men, by craftiness in deceitful scheming." Unity means become one, that our minds will become one with God's when we listen to the truth. He agrees with the truth.

Bankers are taught to recognize counterfeit dollars by only handling real money. They become so familiar with the feel, texture, color, design, and smell of real currency that they instantly recognize a fake bill. That is how we are to be with God. We listen to His truth and handle it all the time so we know when a lie is presented to us. When we talk to God and He listens to us, He agrees with us because the two of us are speaking truth to each other. For example, we no longer pray to be rich to solve all our problems because we know that isn't a true solution and that God will not usually agree with that. We ask God to help us be content and live within our income, and He agrees with us. He may give us riches, but that is a blessing and not a solution to a difficulty.

God is looking for honest hearts when we've done wrong. He doesn't require money or physical sacrifices to pay for our sins. "He has told you, O man, what is good; and what does the LORD require of you but to do justice, to love kindness, and to walk humbly with your God" (Mic. 6:8)?

Bible Reading: Psalm 130

Week 6

PAUL

Day 1

The Apostle Paul was a man of great passion for the gospel, or good news, of Christ Jesus. He was one of the earliest missionaries and started churches wherever he traveled. Paul wrote letters, or epistles, to the churches he "fathered" and treated the new believers as his children in faith. He wrote to encourage, teach, reprove, and train his spiritual sons and daughters. Let's open the letters and see what we can learn.

First Corinthians 4:14–21 says:

> *I do not write these things to shame you, but to admonish you as my beloved children. For if you were to have countless tutors in Christ, yet you would not have many fathers, for in Christ Jesus I became your father through the gospel. Therefore I exhort you, be imitators of me. For this reason I have sent to you Timothy, who is my beloved and faithful child in the Lord, and he will remind you of my ways which are in Christ, just as I teach everywhere in every church. Now some have become arrogant, as though I were not coming to you. But I will come to you soon, if the Lord wills, and I shall find out, not the words of those who are arrogant but their power. For the kingdom of God does not consist in words but in power. What do you desire? Shall I come to you with a rod, or with love and a spirit of gentleness?*

A father's or a mother's heart should be as Paul's—willing to warn their kids when their actions are headed for trouble but not willing to shame them. Moreover, Paul recognized it was his responsibility more than anyone's because he was their spiritual father. Taking his responsibility to an even higher level, Paul told his "kids" to follow his example of how to live for Christ. At first that may seem egotistical. "I'm so good you need to copy everything I do." Yet whether we know it or not, we do mimic our parents—the good and the bad.

When our parents got angry, did they yell, walk away, hit . . . ? Did our parents react to stress by listing ways to handle the situation, praying, drinking, leaving for good? The classroom of everyday living teaches children more than any book. Paul was right to recognize that his actions spoke louder than his words. He lived knowing people were watching, and he represented Christ Jesus, so he said what we all should be able to say, "Follow my example."

The Corinthians thought talking, dressing fashionably, and saying spiritual things made them important and better than others, even Paul. Some said Paul was unimportant and totally not cool. Paul addressed that head on and challenged the big talkers to see if their words carried the power of God or just sounded good. He said they were like a pretty bag of hot air saying arrogant words that meant nothing and held no power. God's kingdom was not about politically correct, empty words but rather about His life-giving power. The rule and authority of God are proven by our living like Christ, not speaking religion.

Finally, Paul said, "The ball's in your court. Start thinking and praying and doing right. It's up to you if I come with punishment and scolding or with quiet love and gentleness." God says the same to you and me today. Consequences and rewards are attached to our life choices.

Bible Reading: **1 Corinthians 2:1–5, James 1:21–27**

Day 2

In chapter 3 of Paul's second recorded letter to the Corinthians, he tells them there are a lot of false teachers using fake letters of recommendation from him so people will give them money and listen to them.

> *Are we beginning to commend ourselves again? Or do we need, as some, letters of commendation to you or from you? You are our letter, written in our hearts, known and read by all men; being manifested that you are a letter of Christ, cared for by us,*

> *written not with ink but with the Spirit of the living God, not on tablets of stone but on tablets of human hearts.*
>
> —2 Cor. 3:1–3

Again, Paul is teaching that the kingdom of God is not about fancy words or knowing the right people but about powerfully affected and changed lives. My mom led me to know Jesus as my Savior. I could write her a letter to show others so they would listen to her, but it would be more beneficial if others could look at how I live my life every day in every way. They would see that Jesus Christ has changed me from a shy, scared girl into a woman of confidence, willing to speak and teach God's truth. Which one is a more effective letter of reference?

It is said that the only Bible some people will ever read is us. That is what Paul was getting at. You (believers in Christ) are letters that recommend Christian living, written on the hearts of your spiritual parents as well as yourself, known and read by everyone. Actions speak louder than words. Our lives vouch for Christ Jesus as well as other believers and the church.

Paul's letter of recommendation—the believers in Corinth—was written by Christ Jesus, not Paul, who does not take credit for the changed hearts but gives it to Jesus. However, he was the tool or pen God used to write the letter. God doesn't need us, but out of love He values us and uses us to bring others to Him. The ink in Paul's pen was the Holy Spirit, and the paper he wrote on were the hearts of each person. All of this was very personal.

In verses 4–6, Paul went on to say, "Such confidence we have through Christ toward God. Not that we are adequate in ourselves to consider anything as *coming* from ourselves, but our adequacy is from God, who also made us adequate *as* servants of a new covenant, not of the letter but of the Spirit; for the letter kills, but the Spirit gives life."

Paul admitted he was not good enough by himself to lead all those people to Christ. He also recognized that we may never feel ready or that we know enough to share our faith with someone. It's not about our adequacy; it's about God. Go out and live Christ. Others will ask how we can have peace in the middle of our hardships; how we can forgive the person who hurt us; how we have joy even through our tears. We can trust God to empower us and the Holy Spirit to give us the words we need. He will use our lives, the letters written on our hearts, to change other people. We are a valuable tool to God.

***Bible Reading*: Jeremiah 31:31–34, Ezekiel 11:19–20, Ezekiel 36:25–28**

Day 3

Scrolling down farther in this letter, we see that Paul wrote this:

> *Now in a like exchange—I speak as to children—open wide to us also. Do not be bound together with unbelievers; for what partnership have righteousness and lawlessness, or what fellowship has light with darkness? Or what harmony has Christ with Belial, or what has a believer in common with an unbeliever? Or what agreement has the temple of God with idols? For we are the temple of the living God; just as God said,*
>
> "I WILL DWELL IN THEM AND WALK AMONG THEM; AND I WILL BE THEIR GOD, AND THEY SHALL BE MY PEOPLE. *Therefore,* COME OUT FROM THEIR MIDST AND BE SEPARATE," *says the Lord.* "AND DO NOT TOUCH WHAT IS UNCLEAN; *and I will welcome you. And I will be a father to you, and you shall be sons and daughters to Me," says the Lord Almighty.*
> —2 Cor. 6:13–18

Paul keeps hammering the fact that having Christ in our lives is more about our changed hearts than religious words and spiritual ideas. Our old selves—the ways we thought, reacted, and lived—are gone, and in all ways we are made new in Christ Jesus (2 Cor. 5:17).

From those five verses we see that our old selves were unbelievers, wicked, dark, of Satan, worshipers of images and false gods, dead, and filthy. By contrast, Christ-followers are good, light, believers, God's temple, belonging to the living God, and clean. Those two lists do not live together in harmony or agreement. They do not coexist. They're complete opposites.

Let's make this simple. How can a follower of Christ be amused by sexually immoral or violent books, songs, or movies? One is pure and clean; one is dirty. Is it possible to spend most of our time with people who use drugs or steal and remain free of those activities? Would the people living that way want the new us hanging out with them?

If we walk out of our house clean, in pure white clothing, and then walk in mud, the mud will show. We can't pretend it isn't there because the contrast is so stark. Just touching the world's smut gets some pollution and contamination on us. There is just no way to stay clean while mixing it up with things that are dirty.

So what is Paul telling us? Are we supposed to be rude and ignore our old friends and family? I don't believe so. He's saying our hearts are not the same as each other anymore. The most important part of a believer is not in agreement with the most important part of a nonbeliever. We can still care for unbelievers, but we cannot be tied to them as a best friend, intimate companion, blood brother, or partner in any way. We have no right to condemn or judge them, but out of love for God, we must be sure we separate our hearts from their hearts. God in us will not coexist with the darkness of the world in them.

> *This is the judgment, that the Light has come into the world, and men loved the darkness rather than the Light, for their deeds were evil. For everyone who does evil hates the Light, and does not come to the Light for fear that his deeds will be exposed. But he who practices the truth comes to the Light, so that his deeds may be manifested as having been wrought in God.*
> —John 3:19–21

Bible Reading: 2 Corinthians 5:14–21

Day 4

One of the most important and loving things a parent can do for their children is pray for them. It is an expression of selfless love as they go to God, not for their own needs but for someone else's. Paul did this for his "children" in faith who lived in Ephesus.

> *For this reason I bow my knees before the Father, from whom every family in heaven and on earth derives its name, that He would grant you, according to the riches of His glory, to be strengthened with power through His Spirit in the inner man, so that Christ may dwell in your hearts through faith; and that you, being rooted and grounded in love, may be able to comprehend with all the saints what is the breadth and length and height and depth, and to know the love of Christ which surpasses knowledge, that you may be filled up to all the fullness of God. Now to Him*

> *who is able to do far more abundantly beyond all that we ask or think, according to the power that works within us, to Him be the glory in the church and in Christ Jesus to all generations forever and ever. Amen.*
> —Eph. 3:14–21

Background is key here. Paul was in prison when he wrote this letter because he had stuck up for the Gentile believers, saying they were as much a part of God's family as the Jews were. The church in Ephesus was mostly made up of non-Jews, or Gentiles. At the persuasion of the angry Jewish religious leaders, Paul was arrested by the Romans and thrown into prison.

Guilt can cause discouragement to sink us into despair faster than almost anything else. You can imagine how terrible the believers in Ephesus felt thinking they were the cause of Paul's imprisonment and harsh treatment. Paul told them not to be discouraged and then addressed the four areas discouragement hits in the order they usually fall. In Chuck Swindoll's radio message on this, he said (I'm paraphrasing), "Physically we lose energy when discouraged. We just don't have what it takes to keep going. Emotionally we lose touch with reality, thinking no one cares about us and that things are so bad we will never survive. Mentally we lose our memory, forgetting truths we know from God's Word and past experience, not able to remember the steps toward the solution. Spiritually, discouragement takes away our intimacy with God. It acts as a wall between us, and we feel so alone and unheard."

Paul's prayer covered each of these areas of discouragement. He prayed that God would grant them according to the riches of *His* glory to be strengthened with power through *His Spirit* in the inner man. The power of the Holy Spirit is the Greek word *dynamis* from which we get our word *dynamite*.

When we're feeling as if we can't get up much less go on, when we don't have the energy to eat let alone problem solve, it is time to pray for the Holy Spirit to strengthen and empower us. The power of the Holy Spirit in us gives us the ability to physically do something, enables us to see God, and then centers our feelings and minds on the Lord. Paul didn't pray for a shot of caffeine-induced energy that would last a few hours. He prayed that according to the riches of God's glory, God would energize us with the Holy Spirit's dynamic power.

Bible Reading: Acts 1:8, Colossians 1:9–14

Day 5

Paul's prayer asked God to supply all the needs his children had because of their discouragement. He prayed for them to be strengthened with the dynamic power of the Holy Spirit in their inner being. Moving from their physical needs, Paul asked God to fill them emotionally. They needed the Holy Spirit's power so Christ would dwell in their hearts through faith and they'd be rooted and grounded in love.

Rooted is the picture of a tree with thick, strong roots flowing deep into the ground that keep the tree firmly planted even in the midst of severe storms. *Grounded* is an architectural term that means "to lay a foundation." Again, we see the image of a building able to withstand earthquakes, floods, and other disasters because it has a firm and solid foundation. And what made the roots and foundation strong? Love. God's love.

Only the person who is rooted and grounded in love and tested by the storms of life can understand what are the breadth and length and height and depth of God's love. Ephesians 3:17–19 says "that you, being rooted and grounded in love, may be able to comprehend with all the saints what is the breadth and length and height and depth, and to know the love of Christ which surpasses knowledge, that you may be filled up to all the fullness of God." We can hear these words and believe they are true. But until we experience them in the flow of our lives, we will not get how widely forgiving, wide-ranging, and large His love is; how very long-suffering and long-lasting His love is; how much higher than our imaginations His love is; and how deeply intimate, personal, and private His love is.

After experiencing the love of Christ, although it is so great we will never fully understand it, we will be filled with the fullness of life, love, and power that comes from God. That is when God addresses our mental weariness. Now to Him who is able to do far more abundantly beyond all that we ask or think, according to the power that works within us—this is God doing God-sized things, more than we ask for, more than we even think could be done. Far more. God is able to do far more abundantly—richly, lavishly, largely, bountifully—than we would ask or think; far more abundantly beyond—ahead of, outside our imaginations, further than—*all* we will ever ask or think. Don't ever forget, no matter how tired and discouraged you are, that God is an amazing, awesome, powerful God.

All of this—God filling us with His Holy Spirit's dynamic power, grounding us on the solid foundation of His enormous surrounding love, doing so much abundantly more than we could ever ask or think—brings us back into spiritual intimacy with our heavenly Father. The walls of despair crumble as we start to understand just how magnificent God is and how much He loves us. He is our Father—from whom every family in heaven and on earth derives its name. Jews and Gentiles, men and women, rich and poor, any color, any language—every person who has ever believed in God and His Son, Jesus, carries God the Father's name. None of us are illegitimate. We belong in God's family, and we belong to the Father who gave us His name.

With Paul we can all say, "To Him *be* the glory in the church and in Christ Jesus to all generations forever and ever. Amen" (Eph. 3:21). The power, love, and knowledge of God go into infinity, past the next generation and the next, forever and ever. What a glorious God we have!

Bible Reading: Ephesians 1:13–23

Day 6

We've just taken a peek into a few of Paul's letters to his "kids" and seen that a father's heart is full of love, accountability, instruction, sacrifice, prayer, and—did we mention—love?

Paul has taught us this week that the proof of our believing in Jesus Christ is in our changed lives. The sacrifice of Jesus and the power of the Holy Spirit combine to turn our broken hearts into whole hearts filled with the Father's love. Through His love, power, and knowledge, our discouragements, bitterness, fears, and insecurities are healed. Our changed lives are God's love letters to the world.

All of this points to a loving and forgiving Father and a loving and victorious Jesus Christ. The main thing in all of Paul's writings is this: Jesus is our Savior, and God is our loving Father.

May grace and peace be yours, sent to you from God our Father and Jesus Christ our Lord. How we praise God, the Father of our Lord Jesus Christ who has blessed us with every spiritual blessing in the heavenly realms because we belong to Christ (Eph. 1:2–3).

Do you believe this? Think of how often we joke that if a food is good for us, it's going to taste bad, or if something feels good, it's probably wrong. Paul is telling us that is not how God the Father operates. "Every good thing given and every perfect gift is from above, coming down from the Father of lights" (James 1:17). He pours blessings on us from heaven. How I want this to go from our head knowledge to our hearts, that we know and understand and get that our Father is good and tastes good and feels good and smells good. Everything He wants for us, allows to happen to us, and provides for us is sweet and for our good. When we mess up the plan with rebellion, He still stands there waiting for us to repent and then turns our ashes into beauty (Isa. 61:3). Know this. Believe it, and let it free you from your broken heart and feelings of being uncared for and unloved.

I'm trying to picture all your faces and hearts as I pray Paul's words for you personally. "I have never stopped thanking God for you. I pray for you constantly, asking God, the glorious Father of our Lord Jesus Christ, to give you spiritual wisdom and understanding, so you might grow in your knowledge of God. I pray that your hearts will be flooded with light so you can understand the wonderful future He has promised to those He called. I want you to realize what a rich and glorious inheritance He has given to His people. I pray that you will begin to understand the incredible greatness of His power for us who believe Him. This is the same mighty power that raised Christ from the dead and seated Him in the place of honor at God's right hand in the heavenly realms" (Eph. 1:16–20).

God offers all of this to His children. Being His child starts with believing Jesus is God's Son who died on the cross for your sins and rose from the dead to live forever. By that faith, you are His child. Then you admit to God you have made a lot of wrong choices (sinned), accept His forgiveness in Jesus's name, and tell Him you want to repent (turn yourself around) and go in God's direction. Be ready . . . He will pour His good blessings out until you overflow!

Bible Reading: **1 Corinthians 1:1–9, Galatians 1:1–5**

Week 7

PAUL

Day 1

During one of the times Paul was in prison for preaching about Jesus, he wrote a letter to the church in Philippi. A new theme—joy—emerged in this writing. Approximately 16 times Paul used some form of that word as he pressed the point that a life with Christ Jesus is a life in which we can rejoice, no matter the circumstances.

> *In this way stand firm in the Lord, my beloved. Rejoice in the Lord always; again I will say, rejoice! Let your gentle spirit be known to all men. The Lord is near. Be anxious for nothing, but in everything by prayer and supplication with thanksgiving let your requests be made known to God. And the peace of God, which surpasses all comprehension, will guard your hearts and your minds in Christ Jesus.*
>
> —Phil. 4:1, 4–7

    Paul had been under house arrest and had been thrown into dungeons and prison cells. Each of those situations was included in the "always." Your situation, mine, your family's . . . if we are in the Lord, we have reason to rejoice.

    What Paul is saying is not for the physical part of us as much as the spiritual. His joy, and ours, was based on the peace of God—not peace in God or peace with God but the peace *of* God. It's supernatural, spiritual, and not a human peace, which is why it is beyond understanding.

    If we are being physically hurt in any form, we are not being told we should praise God for it. Jesus certainly didn't do that during His court hearing, beatings, and crucifixion (Heb. 12:2). Our emotions, thoughts, and body will respond to being harmed instantly and in the days and even years to follow, but with God as our center, we have His peace inside of us. This battle is spiritual, not physical. And our weapons are joy in the Lord, prayer, and the peace of God.

> *For though we walk in the flesh, we do not war according to the flesh, for the weapons of our warfare are not of the flesh, but divinely powerful for the destruction of fortresses. We are destroying speculations and every lofty thing raised up against the knowledge of God, and we are taking every thought captive to the obedience of Christ.*
> —2 Cor. 10:3–5

The verses in Philippians 4 are about taking our thoughts captive. We won't let our mind race with bitterness, anxiety, or hatred. We'll turn our eyes from our wounded selves, tear them off our enemy, and look full on at God. A stronghold is any excuse or reason we rely on to reinforce our opinion or way of living. God and our parent didn't protect us *from* pain, so we start to believe we are unlovable, not worth protecting, and that no one can be trusted.

Stop! In everything, by prayer and asking, with thanksgiving, present your requests to God. And the peace of God, which surpasses all comprehension, will guard your hearts and your minds in Christ Jesus. His peace, not a bumper sticker's peace, will guard our hearts and minds. We are not equipped to destroy the lies and fiery arrows of Satan. God is. Ask Him. Give your thoughts and emotions to Him, and I promise that you will experience the peace of God in the middle of your worst nightmare. And then you will rejoice—in Him.

Bible Reading: John 14:26–27, Philippians 4

Day 2

There is still more to gain from Paul's message in Philippians 4.

> *In this way stand firm in the Lord, my beloved. Rejoice in the Lord always; again I will say, rejoice! Let your gentle* spirit *be known to all men. The Lord is near. Be anxious for nothing, but*

> *in everything by prayer and supplication with thanksgiving let your requests be made known to God. And the peace of God, which surpasses all comprehension, will guard your hearts and your minds in Christ Jesus.*
> —Phil. 4:1, 4–7

Why is "let your gentle spirit be evident to all men, the Lord is near" stuck in the middle of this section? At first glance, it doesn't fit. *Gentle spirit* has a different twist to it than our English words. Those two words describe the heart of a person who will let the Lord fight their battles. They know that "vengeance is Mine, says the Lord" (Rom. 12:19). It describes a person who is really free to let go of their anxieties and all the things that cause them stress because they know the Lord will take up their cause.[13]

Believing the truth that the time is near ("the Lord is near") for Jesus to come back makes it easier for us to show our gentle hearts to everyone. We know that Jesus will settle the score at His return, and we can trust Him to make things right in our falling-apart world.

Ask God to fight the battles we are in—the battles against evil; against faulty beliefs that we are worthless, alone, and forgotten; the war against fear, bitterness, hatred, vengeance, envy, self-destruction, and depression. Thank the Father that He is able to defeat our enemy who is so much stronger than we are. Thank Him that 1 John 4:4 is true. "You are from God, little children, and have overcome them; because greater is He who is in you than he who is in the world."

Paul's heart was for his children and for us to stand firm in the midst of life's victories and storms. His instructions were simple. We stand firm by focusing on the Lord. Rejoice in Him, not our success because He gave it to us. Rejoice in God, not our failure because He will grow us through it and bring about a lasting victory because of it. Rejoice in the Lord during pain, tears, and injustice because God is in control. After God defeated the Egyptians at the Red Sea, Moses declared, "The LORD is a warrior; The LORD is His name" (Exod. 15:3). Rejoice in your warrior Lord and Savior.

Don't be anxious, worried, or frightened about anything. That means don't live in anxiety. Here is an oversimplified example: seeing a car speeding straight at you would cause a natural and good fear. Always being afraid and worried when you see a car after that is wrong. Take that anxiety captive, give it to God, and ask Him to free you from not trusting Him to care for you and from living in fear instead of in victory in Christ.

Doing that enables us to have the peace of God as the guard of our hearts and minds. Guard is a military term. God in His full armor will stand guard, protecting our hearts and minds. Everything has to go through Him and His peace in order to get to our feelings and thoughts.

Bible Reading: **Ephesians 6:10–18**

Day 3

Paul's first letter to the Thessalonians was basically to praise and encourage the young believers of that city. He revealed his heart, which was a reflection of God's heart, as tender like a new mother's and lovingly firm like a father's.

> *But we proved to be gentle among you, as a nursing mother tenderly cares for her own children. Having so fond an affection for you, we were well-pleased to impart to you not only the gospel of God but also our own lives, because you had become very dear to us. For you recall, brethren, our labor and hardship, how working night and day so as not to be a burden to any of you, we proclaimed to you the gospel of God. You are witnesses, and so is God, how devoutly and uprightly and blamelessly we behaved toward you believers; just as you know how we were exhorting and encouraging and imploring each one of you as a father would his own children, so that you would walk in a manner worthy of the God who calls you into His own kingdom and glory. For this reason we also constantly thank God that when you received the word of God which you heard from us, you accepted it not as the word of men, but for what it really is, the word of God, which also performs its work in you who believe.*
>
> —1 Thess. 2:7-13

One of the most loving statements I've ever heard is Paul saying they gave not only the gospel, which is a huge gift of love, but also their own lives. There have been times when believers have gone out shouting God's Word while ignoring the people. These teachers in the Bible worked various jobs to support themselves so they wouldn't be a financial burden. Pastors and missionaries should be paid by the church (1 Cor. 9:14). Paul gave up that right and gave even more of himself in order to live Christ to these new believers.

Giving of himself in a personal and sacrificial way gave Paul the right to push and encourage his children to live in a way that was worthy of God. It has been said that people don't care how much you know until they know how much you care. Paul gave both his care and his knowledge to the Thessalonians, and in response they believed his message was from God and not just made up by men. Living the way Christ Jesus did accomplishes a lot. Others will have a close-up example to follow—like a father-son relationship—and people will believe in the power of God to change lives. It is not within our nature to be completely selfless and giving; therefore, it must be Christ in Paul (or you or me) that produces that lifestyle.

Like a good parent, Paul praised his kids for doing the right thing with the gift he had given them. What an important example! We are so quick to criticize but so stingy with our praise. When our mom makes dinner, we think, "Well that's her job." When a doctor listens to us and makes us feel better, we think, "For the money I'm paying, he'd better." Paul said, "I recognize you could have chosen a couple different ways to handle the words I gave you. I thank God you chose right, believed it was from Him, and took it to heart." Finally, Paul assured his new children in faith that the Word of God was effectively at work in those who believed. "I can see God in you. If I needed an example to follow, it would be you." What a shot of encouragement!

Bible Reading: 1 Thessalonians 2

Day 4

Paul called Timothy "my true child in the faith." Their love and respect for each other was sincere and deep. In his second letter to Timothy, Paul was alone in a dungeon as a prisoner of Nero, one of the most bloodthirsty, deranged, and vicious leaders of all time. Paul knew that his life was about to end, and he wanted desperately to see and encourage Timothy one last time. The theme of 2 Timothy is being a good soldier of Christ. We are not called to be a terrorist or to kill; we are called to live and spread God's love and truth, and stand up to Satan's lies and destruction. Paul reminded Timothy of a soldier's call to courage and faithfulness and of the character

God requires in His soldiers. He cautioned about some of the dangers and gave Timothy the orders of a soldier of Christ.

Paul told Timothy, "I solemnly charge *you* in the presence of God and of Christ Jesus, who is to judge the living and the dead, and by His appearing and His kingdom: preach the word; be ready in season *and* out of season; reprove, rebuke, exhort, with great patience and instruction" (2 Tim. 4:1-2).

A soldier's life is hard. Fighting for anything, including God's truth, takes its toll. Yet there are comforts to being a good soldier that one cannot buy, including the soul-deep knowledge that you made a difference and were strong and tenacious. Paul told Timothy, "For I am already being poured out as a drink offering, and the time of my departure has come. I have fought the good fight, I have finished the course, I have kept the faith" (2 Tim. 4:6-7).

While this is somber, it is also incredibly beautiful. Poured out has the idea of a complete giving, with no reservation. The liquid is entirely emptied from the cup. Paul's love for Christ caused him to willingly give his life to live for Him and to die for Him.

Oh, the peace we have when we have a clear conscience, when we can say, "I did my best, I fought the good fight, I can hold my head up." Paul had completed his service, gone through the difficulties of his warfare, and been instrumental in the victories of Christ Jesus over the powers of darkness. He knew he fought for a good cause and that victory was sure.

Paul finished the course. He did just as commanded over the long haul, passed all the tests, and closed the books on his finished work. Knowing he was going to die, Paul had no regrets, no worries of being embarrassed at the life he had lived.

May we all be able to say we have kept the faith; we have guarded the grace, mercy, and love of Jesus Christ and His death and resurrection. Paul said he had taken great care of the faith, protecting it from being twisted and dirtied up; he had fought to protect its reputation.

One of the comforts of being a good soldier is the guarantee of a good finish to life. This is a sweet and precious gift from God, to know we are going to die and be able to smile in peace at the picture of our life. You can know that right now, no matter what your age. Trust in Jesus, and live for Him.

***Bible Reading*: Romans 8:35-39, 2 Timothy 4:1-18**

Day 5

We will all look at ourselves honestly at the end of our life, whether we admit it to others or not. Death has a way of stripping away the pretense, denials, and excuses, leaving the stark truth of who we were. Paul was there in his second letter to Timothy, and he shared that being right with God gives us tremendous comfort. Yesterday we saw the comfort of a good finish to life. Today we will look at two other reassurances Christ offers.

At the end of our life, we have a future. "In the future there is laid up for me the crown of righteousness, which the Lord, the righteous Judge, will award to me on that day; and not only to me, but also to all who have loved His appearing" (2 Tim. 4:8). Heaven and hell are real and forever. Every person who has accepted Jesus as their Savior will go to heaven. The good choices we've made will be evaluated by God, and we will be publicly rewarded. The unrecognized good we did will be noticed in heaven (Heb. 6:10).

Not one friend came to Paul's defense when he was arrested the last time. He stood alone. "But the Lord stood with me and strengthened me, so that through me the proclamation might be fully accomplished, and that all the Gentiles might hear; and I was rescued out of the lion's mouth. The Lord will rescue me from every evil deed, and will bring me safely to His heavenly kingdom; to Him *be* the glory forever and ever. Amen" (2 Tim. 4:16–18).

Beth Moore's study on the book of Daniel opened my eyes to an amazing truth about God's deliverance. There are three scenarios when people of God face a fiery trial. We can be delivered *from* the fire—our faith is built on this. We can be delivered *through* the fire—our faith is refined as the fake and useless parts of us are burned away. We can be delivered *by* the fire into God's arms—our faith is perfected because we are in heaven at last.[14]

All of us, like Paul, will experience freedom from and through some fires in our lives. Paul knew God was about to deliver him into glory in heaven *by* using the evil intents of others.

How many times have we questioned how a good God can let bad things happen? It doesn't seem fair that Christians are hurt and killed for their faith. Paul faced his certain death with peace, confidence, and the joy of the Lord, along with his pain, loneliness, and exhaustion, because he understood these truths of how God worked.

For a follower of Christ, death is the ultimate healing. The end of our earthly body rescues us from all danger, pain, and hardship. We should be able to say with Paul, "For to me, to live is Christ and to die is gain" (Phil. 1:21).

The comforts offered good soldiers of Christ at the end of our lives are confidence in a good finish to life, a good future after life, and knowing our good Friend is faithful in life and in death. God wraps us in His peace that passes understanding every step of our life and death.

Bible Reading: **2 Timothy 2:1–19**

Day 6

Let's go to the movies, to an action thriller. Deep within enemy territory, a town is recovering from the recent attacks of the enemy's army. People are on cots bleeding and dying, and a group is burying the dead. Some are finding weapons and preparing for future battles, some are gathering supplies to help the wounded, and a few are yelling for the fighting to stop. There are several people preparing dinner for themselves and pretending nothing is wrong, and there is a group of enemy sympathizers who secretly want them to succeed in order to prove there is more than one right way to govern.

This picture of a physical war zone reflects the very real spiritual war zone of our world. Christians are not the only ones living here and experiencing the results of the war. Everyone gets deeply wounded by the enemy, and some die at his hands. There are people, even in the church, who pretend there is no war. They say, *Jesus took care of me at the cross, and nothing else is real. I don't need to fight.* Yet that is not Paul's experience or teaching. Ephesians 6:10–12 tells us in the present tense to continually be strong in the Lord and put on the full armor of God. Our fight is present tense continually, not against flesh and blood but against the rulers, against the powers, against the world forces of this darkness, and against the spiritual forces of wickedness in the heavenly places.

There are those who reject the Bible and Jesus as trivial or wrong and many who fight against our rights and freedoms. Some believers caution us not to get "too religious" and want us to compromise in order to get along. Paul's letters to his spiritual children cautioned them against such talk. "For the time will come when they will not endure sound doctrine; but *wanting* to have their ears tickled, they will accumulate for themselves teachers in accordance to their own desires" (2 Tim. 4:3).

God had allowed Paul to live in great comfort, success, and acceptance and be beaten, falsely accused, imprisoned, and hated. We talked about the strongholds, or faulty thinking, we build in our lives when bad things happen. We may believe that because God and our parent didn't protect us from abuse or neglect they are bad, absent, or uncaring. At the end of Paul's life, he shared God's faithful truth. People will let us down, but the Lord stands with us and strengthens us. The Lord will rescue us from every evil deed and bring us safely to His heavenly kingdom (2 Tim. 4:16–18).

Fiery trials are guaranteed. So is God's deliverance. We will be delivered *from* the fire, *through* the fire, or *by* the fire—each one carrying a benefit. God's goal is to build our faith, refine us, and finally perfect us when we reach heaven.

How will our part finish in this movie? Paul told his children they had done well. Their lives showed the power and work of Christ Jesus, and they were good soldiers. They would be able to say at the end of their lives, "I have fought the good fight, I have finished the course, I have kept the faith; in the future there is laid up for me the crown of righteousness, which the Lord, the righteous Judge, will award to me on that day" (2 Tim. 4:7–8).

***Bible Reading*: Philippians 1:3–11**

Week 8

LUKE 15

Day 1

Jesus often taught with parables, or earthly stories with heavenly meanings. Luke 15 is one parable with three scenarios in it, picturing people from God's house who were lost in some way. Jesus was eating with people who lived in sin (possibly Gentiles) and with tax collectors, hated Jews who worked for the Roman government. His disciples and the Scribes and Pharisees (religious leaders) were also present. The religious leaders grumbled and criticized that Jesus said He was good and righteous but ate with the tax collectors and sinners.

> So He [Jesus] told them this parable, saying, "What man among you, if he has a hundred sheep and has lost one of them, does not leave the ninety-nine in the open pasture and go after the one which is lost until he finds it? When he has found it, he lays it on his shoulders, rejoicing. And when he comes home, he calls together his friends and his neighbors, saying to them, 'Rejoice with me, for I have found my sheep which was lost!' I tell you that in the same way, there will be more joy in heaven over one sinner who repents than over ninety-nine righteous persons who need no repentance."
>
> —Luke 15:3–7

The religious leaders were so serious about not associating with the ungodly that they would not even teach them the Word of God. Through this story, Jesus pointed out that the Good Shepherd leaves the good sheep in His safe pasture and goes after the lost sheep. The leaders said God would only receive a sinner who came to Him in the right way, yet in the parable Jesus taught that God actively seeks out the lost while they are lost and in the wrong place. Romans 5:6 says, "For while we were still helpless, at the right time Christ died for the ungodly."

Jesus told this group who believed they were righteous because they followed rules that there was more joy in heaven over one sinner who repents than 99 good sheep. He taught that God's heart was not thrilled by people obeying man-made or God-made rules, looking good and sounding respectable. God looks at our heart. Heaven rejoiced when a sinner repented. The truth was that the 99 sheep had been lost at one time. Paul said in Romans 3:23, "For all have sinned and fall short of the glory of God."

Those men knew the words of Isaiah well. "All of us like sheep have gone astray, each of us has turned to his own way; but the LORD has caused the iniquity of us all to fall on Him" (Isa. 53:6). Jesus's parable highlighted this truth. He carried the burden of every person's sin.

Note the attitude of our Good Shepherd. On His shoulders He laid the lost sheep that had caused the Shepherd a good deal of trouble and grief and rejoiced. The Shepherd was not fed up, angry, or stressed out. The lost sheep was not treated roughly, dragged through the mud, or publicly humiliated. Lifting His treasured, soiled sheep onto His shoulders, the Shepherd carried it home with exceedingly great joy. And He celebrated this recovery with others.

Whatever dirty place you've gotten into while lost, know that God is looking for you, even there. The mess He finds you in will not define you. The fact that Jesus found you, that you allow Jesus to carry you, will. That is repentance, and all of heaven will rejoice because of it.

Bible Reading: Luke 15

Day 2

There are three pictures of the lost shown in the Luke 15 parable. *Lost* in the Greek means "to destroy, kill, ruin; to separate." The lost sheep shows a sheep of God's flock who sinned and, in its foolishness, wanders away into dangerous territory without being aware of doing so. God says in Hosea 4:6, "My people are destroyed for lack of knowledge. Because you have rejected knowledge." The sheep lived close to the Shepherd and had seen His provisions and protections, yet it had still wandered away aimlessly, looking for what was right in front of it.

Jesus went on to the second scenario in His parable.

> *Or what woman, if she has ten silver coins and loses one coin, does not light a lamp and sweep the house and search carefully until she finds it? When she has found it, she calls together her friends and neighbors, saying, "Rejoice with me, for I have found the coin which I had lost!" In the same way, I tell you, there is joy in the presence of the angels of God over one sinner who repents.*
>
> —Luke 15:8–10

This coin was lost in the house. Jesus was pointing to all the precious souls who had been lost in the Scribes' and Pharisees' house of God, buried under the Law and rules. The religious leaders didn't like Jesus offering grace to those they considered dirty. They wanted Him to "throw the book" (the Law) at them and condemn them. "There is now no condemnation for those who are in Christ Jesus. For the law of the Spirit of life in Christ Jesus has set you free from the law of sin and of death. For what the Law could not do, weak as it was through the flesh, God *did:* sending His own Son in the likeness of sinful flesh and *as an offering* for sin, He condemned sin in the flesh" (Rom. 8:1–3).

The lost coin was buried by all the regulations of the law. Jesus told a people of the law that God was bringing in His grace to sweep the dirt from the grave that held condemnation and death and to offer salvation and life through faith in God's Son. The law only reveals our sin and need for God's grace. His grace empowers sinners to repent or turn from sin to Him.

> *When you were dead in your transgressions and the uncircumcision of your flesh, He made you alive together with Him, having forgiven us all our transgressions, having canceled out the certificate of debt consisting of decrees against us, which was hostile to us; and He has taken it out of the way, having nailed it to the cross. When He had disarmed the rulers and authorities, He made a public display of them, having triumphed over them through Him.*
>
> —Col. 2:13–15

God nailed the law to the cross. By canceling the list of requirements against us, Jesus took the weapons out of Satan's hands. The devil beats us with condemnation, with our failures, with accusations and criticisms. But the grace and mercy of Jesus take those weapons away.

The woman reveals how God seeks for us until He finds us. Romans 2:4 says, "Or do you think lightly of the riches of His kindness and tolerance and patience, not knowing that the kindness of God leads you to repentance?" Knowing that God loves us, searches for us, and sent Jesus to die for us when we were a mess leads us to change our life. The law shows a holy way to live and condemns us when we fail. But the kindness of God empowers us to live right.

Bible Reading: **2 Corinthians 3:5–18**

Day 3

The story of the prodigal son is well-known. Jesus showed us someone who knowingly and willingly estranged himself from God. That person lived with his father and yet looked him in the eyes and rejected him personally while still wanting some of the stuff he possessed. The child's rebellious heart saw the good things of God as chains that limited his fun and freedom.

Quite honestly, the younger son's sin was the basis of all our sins—we want to be in control of our life and be the god of our life. That's what Satan tempted Eve with in the garden. Every time you and I consciously want what God has but reject a relationship with Him, our hearts are rebellious like this son's. *I deserve a break, but they don't. Just don't tell me to forgive—that person was horrible, and You should support my getting even. I am taking my brains and my talents and will become successful by whatever means necessary. Don't tie me down to all Your restrictions. You say I can only have peace or happiness doing things Your way, but I see a lot of fame, fortune, and excitement out there that looks better than anything You have to offer.*

Our heavenly Father is just like the father in this story. When He sees that His input, provision, and protection are no longer wanted, He will let us go. He will let us, through trial and error, find out what He knew all along—that to depart from Him is not to throw off the yoke but to exchange a light yoke for a heavy one and one gracious Master for a thousand imperious tyrants and lords.[15]

The prodigal son found after a time how very harsh the world is as a master. It demands that you give all you have, and when you're running low, it pushes harder. We feel as if everyone loves us when we're on top, but hitting the bottom shows us that they only loved what we could do for them. They don't care who gives it to them; they only care that they get what they want.

A prodigal's heart is a heart that is distant from God. This young man didn't suddenly become so rebellious that he wanted to leave; his heart and mind had been separating from his father for a long time. The walk to a far-off place takes time. Another mark of rebellion was his wasteful heart. He wanted the money and things he felt his father owed him, but he did not value them. All his resources were wasted on parties, buying friends, and living large. He was in a state of continuous dissatisfaction. No fun, no piece of clothing, no food, no party, no drug, no person satisfied him. He needed to do it again, over and over, bigger and more.

Yet when he reached rock bottom, he finally saw his father and his father's house for what they really were—full of goodness and caring, clean, and honest. His father had gentle expectations of him and gave more than he took. The son wanted to go home. And this is when he found a father with a receiving love, a father who ran out to meet him; hugged his filthy, stinking shoulders; and kissed his cheek. He found a father who called out to all his house to rejoice with him. His son who was lost was home.

Bible Reading: **Proverbs 14:12–16**

Day 4

Jesus was mainly talking to the religious leaders who were grumbling about Him eating with sinners. His three-part parable was insightful to all three groups listening, but the main thrust of the message was to the 99 sheep, the nine coins not lost, and the older brother. Jesus said in essence, "Take this personally" when He said, "What man among you" (Luke 15:4). That is His call to you and me—take this personally. Who are you in this story? How do you feel about people who live in open sin, people who've betrayed you and your beliefs? What is your view of how God responds to the rebellious believer, the outright sinful, and the religious?

The religious leaders identified with the older brother in the story of the prodigal son. When he came in from working in the fields and heard about the party, he was angry and resentful and refused to celebrate with his father. Just as the shepherd went out to look for the lost sheep, just as the woman carefully looked for her lost coin, and just as the father went out to meet his wayward youngest son, the father also went out to meet his oldest son. Sin separated them all.

> *His father came out and began pleading with him. But he answered and said to his father, "Look! For so many years I have been serving you and I have never neglected a command of yours; and yet you have never given me a young goat, so that I might celebrate with my friends; but when this son of yours came, who has devoured your wealth with prostitutes, you killed the fattened calf for him." And he said to him, "Son, you have always been with me, and all that is mine is yours. But we had to celebrate and rejoice, for this brother of yours was dead and* has begun *to live, and* was *lost and has been found."*
> —Luke 15:28–32

The older brother distanced himself from his younger brother by calling him "this son of yours." It's so much easier for us to resent, hate, and condemn others if we don't look at them personally. Rejecting people is easy when all we see is their sin. Jesus said *this brother of yours*. He's looking you and me in the eye and telling us to take this personally, realize He created that other person just as He created you and me. Those are flesh and blood people, and the Father sees them as our brothers and sisters. We are not more valuable or better than they are.

Being a Scribe or Pharisee was hard work. So many people today slave just as hard to follow rules, say the right words, go to church, do good deeds, work... work... work to please God and earn their way to heaven. And just like this older brother, there is no joy in the service. Working to earn what God has freely given is as heavy a yoke as the world's demands. Both put us in slavery; both leave us empty. There was little difference in the two sons' hearts. They saw the father's house as repressive and took the food, shelter, clothing, and safety, as well as the father's love, for granted, resenting him for any love or mercy he showed to others.

Jesus's heart was to assure us that God's joy in a reconciled relationship didn't lessen His joy in His righteous child. When we have chosen to live faithfully with God, we have a daily relationship with the King of kings.

All He has is at our disposal. Our wealth in Christ grows as we mature with Him until it far exceeds anything our rebellious brother took when he left. Every day with our Father is a celebration free of guilt, shame, and regrets.

Bible Reading: Ephesians 2:8–9, 1 John 4:7–21

Day 5

Luke 15 gives us a beautiful picture of God's love for us, His seeking love, His saving love, and His receiving love. Receiving love means God runs to meet us and receive us when we come to Him in repentance. All of heaven has great joy in our reconciliation.

We've talked of repentance before, and it's an important concept for us to understand. Jesus Christ did all the work for us when He died on the cross to pay for our sins and rose from the dead three days later, conquering death—the penalty of all sin—forever. There is absolutely no work or thing we can ever do to earn our freedom from the penalty of our sins. It is a bigger debt than any person is capable of paying. All we have to do is believe that Jesus completed that for us (Acts 16:31, Rom. 10:9). That faith in His love will cause us to want to repent.

There are a couple of definitions from the Old and New Testaments for the word *repent*. It means "to be sorry and regret, to turn back or return, to change one's mind and turn from sin to God." The younger son in the story of the prodigal son gives us a step-by-step picture of repentance. First, he came to his senses; he compared his father and his father's house to the ruler of the world and the world itself, and he finally recognized how good it was with his father (Luke 15:17). He regretted ever leaving home.

The second step in repentance is found in Luke 15:18: "I will get up and go to my father, and will say to him, 'Father, I have sinned against heaven, and in your sight.'" We need to understand that everything we do or think that is wrong is a sin against God. Also, we must acknowledge that other people have been hurt by our sins. Verse 19 completes this honest look at ourselves: "I am no longer worthy to be called your son; make me as one of your hired men." When we truly repent of our sins, we see ourselves and God clearly. God doesn't owe us a good life, comfort, or a get-out-of-jail-free card. He is completely holy and good, and we're not worthy to be His children. Our relationship is dependent on His love, mercy, and grace.

Repentance takes action. The son got up and went back to his father. We can imagine the feelings of fear, guilt, and regret that assaulted him each step of his way home. Yet before he got to the front door, his father ran out to meet him, hugging and kissing him and rejoicing in the fact that the son had chosen to come home. A repentant heart is filled with immense gratefulness and awe that the Father would receive us back in such a way.

This three-part parable shows that Jesus is our focus and the reason we repent. The lost lamb repented by willfully staying on the shepherd's shoulders and going back home with him. The woman lived repentance by cleaning up her act and looking for the coin her actions lost. The coin was passive and uninvolved but still benefited from the woman's repentance, and, in fact, she repented like the lamb, remaining and living in the light and truth of the clean house. And the younger son remembered who his father was and chose to leave the sin and go home.

The choice of repentance brings great joy in heaven, to God, and in our lives. Repentance starts in our hearts, moves to our minds, and shows in our actions.

Bible Reading: Ezekiel 18:27–32, Acts 3:17–19

Day 6

Suppose on your 18th birthday your grandparents gave you $10 million. For the rest of your life, you would be financially secure. You would always have plenty to eat, beautiful clothes, a large home, and reliable cars. Additionally, you'd be able to help other people with your money, which would bring you deep satisfaction. You and your grandparents would have a close relationship, and they would guide you and watch you prosper.

One of your cousins, however, was rebellious, in and out of trouble his whole life. When he turned 40 years old, he finally straightened up his life, and your grandparents gifted him with $10 million as well and spent time with him reestablishing a relationship.

Later on, you learned that your aunt, who had treated your grandparents cruelly and lived a selfish and wasteful life, had reconciled with your grandparents. She was 70 years old and dying, yet your grandparents still decided to give her $10 million.

What response would you have in each of these situations? Many times, like the religious leaders, we resent the fact that a vile criminal can be forgiven and saved just before they die. Christians may think it unfair that a person who lived a partying, self-centered life can be saved and get the same rewards we have. After all, we never got to have fun.

Yet through the years, our gift from our grandparents would have grown substantially. Looking back, we see that our life has changed countless people for the better, and we can look at pictures and remember sweet moments spent with our grandparents.

Jesus told us through this parable that when we choose to stay home with the Father, we have chosen the better thing. Every day we have the ability to live in the rich rewards of being in His presence. The God who is able to do far more abundantly beyond all that we ask or think is close enough to talk with anytime we want. We are free to throw a party for our friends, free to open the pantry or refrigerator anytime—because God's home is our home. God's blessings and provisions are always there for our use and enjoyment. And when our heart is breaking with sorrow or fear, He's right there to hold us and strengthen us with His power.

Three groups of people listened to Jesus's story. The lost heard that God is looking for them and that He, along with all the angels in heaven, rejoices when they repent. The disciples who were following Jesus with loving hearts heard that their goal should be finding the lost and bringing them to God. They should join with God, rejoicing when each and every person is reconciled to Him. Pharisees and Scribes, religious workers, heard that God wants us to see each other personally, not look down on or judge each other but look at each other as brothers and sisters. They learned that God's rejoicing over a sinner who comes home takes nothing away from His child who was always faithful. And they saw that a heart can be far from the Father, even when the body stayed home and worked for Him. All heard that grace, not rules, restores the lost. No matter how far a person had wandered, heaven rejoiced when they repented.

***Bible Reading*: Ephesians 3:14–21**

Week 9

ISAIAH 43

Day 1

Isaiah wrote to warn Israel of God's punishment for the way they had repeatedly sinned. They had walked away from God and worshiped false, make-believe gods, lived immoral lifestyles, and forgotten all that the one true God had done for them in the past. They would be punished, and it would be harsh, being taken from the land God had promised them and made slaves of the Babylonians. Yet in Isaiah 43, God shows His remarkable love for His children by promising to be with them through their punishment. He assures them that He will not allow the harshness of their much-deserved discipline to overcome and completely destroy them. And God tells His people that He will lift them up and forgive them. All of this was said before His children were sorry for their behavior or repented. Isaiah tells us who our God and Father is and how strong our Father's love is for us.

> *But now, thus says the* Lord, *your Creator, O Jacob, and He who formed you, O Israel,* "Do not fear, for I have redeemed you; I have called you by name; you are Mine! When you pass through the waters, I will be with you; and through the rivers, they will not overflow you. When you walk through the fire, you will not be scorched, nor will the flame burn you. For I am the* Lord *your God, the Holy One of Israel, your Savior; I have given Egypt as your ransom,* Cush and Seba in your place. Since you are precious in My sight, *since you are honored and I love you, I will give* other *men in your place and* other *peoples in exchange for your life. Do not fear, for I am with you; I will bring your offspring from*

the east, and gather you from the west. I will say to the north, 'Give them up!' And to the south, 'Do not hold them back.' Bring My sons from afar and My daughters from the ends of the earth, everyone who is called by My name, and whom I have created for My glory, Whom I have formed, even whom I have made."

—Isa. 43:1–7

In this passage God gave us a sense of dignity, purpose, worth, and distinction. When a person believes in evolution or the Big Bang or any other "chaos-producing order" theory of our existence, a person's worth is greatly diminished. They are an "accident" of some force out there, not planned, having no purpose, just another life form that popped up unexpectedly for an undetermined amount of time.

God says, "I have created you; I have ransomed you. I have called you by name; you are Mine. You are precious to Me, you are honored, and I love you. All who claim Me as their God will come, for I have made them for My glory. It was I who created them." In 1 Peter 2:9, all believers in Christ are told, "But you are A CHOSEN RACE, a royal PRIESTHOOD, A HOLY NATION, A PEOPLE FOR *God's* own possession, so that you may proclaim the excellencies of Him who has called you out of darkness into His marvelous light."

Our Father made us very specifically and purposefully to fulfill a valuable objective. For as long as a person has breath, they have a purpose and are worth a great deal to God. If our bodies are beautiful, sick, or deformed, if our minds are feeble or wise, young or old, even in a comatose state, God calls us by name, interacts with us on a spiritual and physical level, and has a reason for us to be alive. God made us for His glory. We're designed and meant to possess and display God's glory to showcase and benefit from being made in His image.

Bible Reading: Isaiah 43

Day 2

The Lord guaranteed that we would go through hard times in our life. He said, "When you pass through the waters, I will be with you; and through the rivers, they will not overflow you. When you walk through the fire, you will not be scorched, nor will the flame burn you" (Isa. 43:2). When—not if, but when—it will happen. Whether it is because we are being punished as in Isaiah; because Satan is evil and attacks us for living a godly life as in the case of Jesus and Paul; to fulfill God's plan in our life and His world; or as unbelievers living in this world where Satan works and hurts—we will go through tough times. Expect it.

By now we know that being in floodwaters or walking through fire is not always literal, although sometimes it could be. God is reminding the Israelites how their forefathers walked through the Red Sea safely and how their enemy, Egypt, was destroyed by those very waters. He foretold how three Israelite men, Shadrach, Meshach, and Abednego, would be thrown into a burning furnace because they would not bow to a false god, and the fire would not burn them (Dan. 3:20–30).

We need to understand this in order to remain strong when terrible things smash into our lives. God is aware of it. He is still in control. We may only see the waves crashing overhead or the flames leaping into the air, destroying everything in their path. God sees all of that and us too. He tells us not to be afraid. Trust Him. Know that He has proven Himself as our Savior in the past, and He will rescue us now and in the future.

If we stare at God and not our huge troubles, the waves will be cleansing waters that wash away sins and wrong beliefs we stubbornly cling to. The fires will be refining fires, burning away the impurities and false securities that pollute our lives.

David said in Psalm 138:7–8, "Though I walk in the midst of trouble, You will revive me; You will stretch forth Your hand against the wrath of my enemies, and Your right hand will save me. The LORD will accomplish what concerns me; Your lovingkindness, O LORD, is everlasting; do not forsake the works of Your hands." David was a man who had learned to keep his eyes on his God. He realized he had never been promised a life of ease, wealth, and comfort. He and we have been promised a life with God conquering our fears and enemies, making us strong in His might and fulfilling His purpose through us. The Lord will not desert or abandon us. We are the works of His hands, His creation. Do you believe that?

Once again, Isaiah 43 tells us that God will deliver us. He will deliver us *from* the raging waters and burning fires, *through* them, or *by* the terrible trials we will endure and into His arms in heaven. *Everyone* who is called by God's name will be rescued and set free.

Today, wherever you are and in whatever circumstance you are living, God loves you. He says to you, "Do not fear, I am with you." Our Father spent time forming you and creating you, and He knows your name. You belong to Him as a precious daughter or son. In your hard times, He will not abandon you. He guarantees He will rescue you—because He loves you.

Bible Reading: Isaiah 43:11–13, John 10:27–30, Philippians 1:6

Day 3

God reminds us in Isaiah 43 who He is and how powerless false gods are. Paul told us this in 1 Corinthians 8:4–6:

> *Therefore concerning the eating of things sacrificed to idols, we know that there is no such thing as an idol in the world, and that there is no God but one. For even if there are so-called gods whether in heaven or on earth, as indeed there are many gods and many lords, yet for us there is* but *one God, the Father, from whom are all things and we exist for Him; and one Lord, Jesus Christ, by whom are all things, and we* exist through Him.

Simply, every so-called god that is not the real God is make-believe. People make up in their imaginations the god of the air, fire, gold, whatever, and assign the powers they think should go to these deities. There are religions today that say Jesus was good and powerful and a prophet, but not God. Jesus said He is God (John 10:30), so either He is God or He is lying and bad. The option of Jesus just being a good man is not possible. That is a false religion.

The names God and Jesus Christ are pronounced differently in every language; however, His person, character, powers, will, and love are always the same. The Bible is the one authentic Word of the living and true God. No matter what language is being spoken, truth is always true, and whatever is not true is always false. Truth does not change with the times. An inch is always an inch, a kilometer is always a kilometer, good is always good. Jesus said, "I am the way, and the truth, and the life; no one comes to the Father but through Me" (John 14:6). Always.

If we need proof of the Bible's authenticity, there are many books on apologetics that take historical documentation and scientific and archaeological facts found in secular writings and discoveries and give irrefutable proof that the Bible is true. I encourage you to read *Don't Check Your Brains at the Door* by Josh McDowell and Bob Hostetler, *The Case for Christ* by Lee Strobel, *The New Evidence that Demands a Verdict* by Josh McDowell, and *Defending Your Faith: An Introduction to Apologetics* by R. C. Sproul, to name a few.

Isaiah 43 says the world has blind eyes so they don't see the truth of God and deaf ears so they don't hear His truth. Yet we take the testimony of these people when they tell us something about God. That's like going to court and asking a blind person to tell what they saw and a deaf person to tell what they heard. God tells us to quit relying on the world to tell us the truth about Him. Second Corinthians 4:3–4 says, "And even if our gospel is veiled, it is veiled to those who are perishing, in whose case the god of this world has blinded the minds of the unbelieving so that they might not see the light of the gospel of the glory of Christ, who is the image of God."

"'You are My witnesses,' declares the LORD" (Isa. 43:10). Believers who have experienced God's peace in the midst of great turmoil, wisdom when there seemed to be no clear answer, strength to move on when physically and emotionally exhausted—you are the ones who know in the depths of your souls that God is real. It is you who have been freed of fear or bitterness or addiction. You can testify for God because He's taken your guilt and shame away. All who have seen God work in their lives and heard His comfort, direction, and truth—you are witnesses to who the one true God is.

Bible Reading: Isaiah 32:1–8, 43:8–13

Day 4

Who is God? Let's listen to His own words.

> *"Since you are precious in My sight,* since *you are honored and I love you, I will give* other *men in your place and* other *peoples in exchange for your life. Do not fear, for I am with you; I will bring your offspring from the east, and gather you from the west. I will say to the north, 'Give* them *up!' and to the south, 'Do not hold* them *back.' Bring My sons from afar and My daughters from the ends of the earth, Everyone who is called by My name, and whom I have created for My glory, whom I have formed, even*

whom I have made. Bring out the people who are blind, even though they have eyes, and the deaf, even though they have ears. All the nations have gathered together so that the peoples may be assembled. Who among them can declare this and proclaim to us the former things? Let them present their witnesses that they may be justified, or let them hear and say, 'It is true.' You are My witnesses," declares the Lord, *"and My servant whom I have chosen, so that you may know and believe Me and understand that I am He. Before Me there was no God formed, and there will be none after Me. I, even I, am the* Lord, *and there is no savior besides Me. It is I who have declared and saved and proclaimed, and there was no strange god among you; so you are My witnesses," declares the* Lord, *"And I am God. Even from eternity I am He, and there is none who can deliver out of My hand; I act and who can reverse it?" Thus says the* Lord *your Redeemer, the Holy One of Israel, "For your sake I have sent to Babylon, and will bring them all down as fugitives, even the Chaldeans, into the ships in which they rejoice. I am the* Lord, *your Holy One, the Creator of Israel, your King."*

—Isa. 43:4–15

God said, "What false god or powerful person can say they brought Israel's forefathers out of Egypt and performed the miracle of parting the Red Sea? Who but Me can tell you what will happen in the future and then it happens?" That's what the Lord was doing—reminding them He had foretold the famine and Joseph's reign in Egypt, Israel's slavery in Egypt, and God's rescue through Moses. Isaiah also told rebellious Israel they would be captured by Babylon but eventually brought back to their Promised Land years before it happened. Many people can make vague predictions, but only the true God always knows exactly what, when, and how the future will unfold. He is proven by getting it 100 percent right every time.

Our one true God has always been, from eternity to eternity. No one—not Satan, a powerful government leader, the courts, a man, or a woman—no one can take something out of God's hands. No one can reverse something God has acted on. He is omnipotent—all-powerful. God is omniscient—all-knowing. The Lord is holy—set apart as all good and completely pure.

Why do you and I need to know these things about God? First, we need to know them because they are true. Additionally, God's absolute authority, power, knowledge, love, holiness, and justice center us as we live. If you or I are rebellious like Israel, the reminder of who God is will hopefully snap us out of our self-indulgent defiance before our consequences become too great. When trials hit us, knowing the attributes of God will anchor us to His solid foundation and hold us steady through the storms. And when we succeed with fame and fortune, we will know our power and importance do not match God's. There will be no place for arrogance in a person who sees God for who He is. The Lord's character, knowledge, and power warn us, secure us, encourage us, and center us. He alone is God. He alone is worthy of worship and praise.

Bible Reading: John 17:1–17

Day 5

Isaiah repeatedly said to remember the work of God in the past, so Isaiah 43:18–19 may seem odd at first glance. It says, "Do not call to mind the former things, or ponder things of the past. Behold I will do something new."

People's tendency would be to think that if God rescued Israel by sending a man (Moses) and parting the Red Sea, that is how God will always work. We might resist being freed or rescued because we believe God only works the way He did the last time. You and I feel comfortable putting God into a box that fits our imagination. Isaiah 55:8 reminds us, "'For My thoughts are not your thoughts, nor are your ways My ways,' declares the LORD." God wants to do a new thing with us and show us details about Him we've never seen before. God told Israel to remember Egypt and Moses so they would remember that He was capable of miraculous rescues but not to limit Him to what they knew from the past.

New and remarkable workings awaited Israel, and they await you and me today. We need to be open to God being God. Your solution may not look like your friend's. Micah said, "But as for me, I will watch expectantly for the LORD; I will wait for the God of my salvation. My God will hear me" (Mic. 7:7). God's new things keep us on our toes.

So why don't we cry out to God if we know about His past rescues? Are we like Israel who became weary of God, tired of feeling as if we're supposed to do it the hard way—God's way? God pointed out that though they (and we) know what to do, we don't do it. "You have not brought to Me the sheep of your burnt offerings, nor have you honored Me with your sacrifices. I have not burdened you with offerings, nor wearied you with incense. You have bought Me not sweet cane with money, nor have you filled Me with the fat of your sacrifices; rather you have burdened Me with your sins, you have wearied Me with your iniquities" (Isa. 43:23–24).

Our perfect Father honestly pointed out all the reasons His children were going to be punished. We can't say *What? What did I do?* and put on an innocent act. God doesn't ambush us with His discipline. In detail He reminds us of our actions and then reminds us what a loving and merciful Father He is. "I, even I, am the one who wipes out your transgressions for My own sake, and I will not remember your sins" (Isa. 43:25). Like the father of the prodigal son, our Father loves us unconditionally. For the sake of His love, He wipes our sins out until we are clean. Our Father chooses to not remember what we've done wrong. He will put away the list of why we were being punished, never to be brought out again. By the blood of Jesus Christ on the cross, our debt has been paid in full. God chooses not to remember what you and I did to nail His Son to that cross—because He loves us.

For the sake of God's love, He disciplines us wisely. For the sake of His reputation, He forgives us for everything. For the sake of His glory, He makes us new. For the sake of His promises, He restores us to a close relationship with Him. For the sake of His kind mercy and grace, the heavenly Father washes us clean. For the sake of His Son's sacrifice, God chooses not to remember what made us so filthy dirty. This is a Father's perfect love. He offers it to you.

Bible Reading: Acts 10:34–43, 1 Corinthians 13:4–8

Day 6

But now, thus says the LORD, *your Creator, O Jacob, and He who formed you, O Israel, "Do not fear, for I have redeemed you; I have called you by name; you are Mine! When you pass through the waters, I will be with you; and through the rivers, they will not overflow you. When you walk through the fire, you will not be scorched, nor will the flame burn you. For I am the* LORD *your God, the Holy One of Israel, your Savior; I have given Egypt as your ransom, Cush and Seba in your place. Since you are precious in My sight,* since *you are honored and I love you, I will give other men in your place and other peoples in exchange for your* life. *Do not fear, for I am with you; I will bring your offspring from the east, and gather you from the west. I will say to the north, 'Give them up!' and to the south, 'Do not hold them back.' Bring My sons from afar and My daughters from the ends of the earth, Everyone who is called by My name, and whom I have created for My glory, whom I have formed, even whom I have made.*

"Bring out the people who are blind, even though they have eyes, and the deaf, even though they have ears. All the nations have gathered together so that the peoples may be assembled. Who among them can declare this and proclaim to us the former things? Let them present their witnesses that they may be justified, or let them hear and say, 'It is true.' 'You are My witnesses,' declares the Lord, *and My servant whom I have chosen, so that you may know and believe Me and understand that I am He. Before Me there was no God formed, and there will be none after Me. I, even I, am the* Lord, *and there is no savior besides Me. It is I who have declared and saved and proclaimed, and there was no strange god among you; so you are My witnesses," declares the* Lord, *"And I am God. Even from eternity I am He, and there is none who can deliver out of My hand; I act and who can reverse it?"*

Thus says the Lord *your Redeemer, the Holy One of Israel, "For your sake I have sent to Babylon, and will bring them all down as fugitives, even the Chaldeans, into the ships in which they rejoice. I am the* Lord, *your Holy One, the Creator of Israel, your King." Thus says the* Lord, *who makes a way through the sea and a path through the mighty waters, who brings forth the chariot and the horse, the army and the mighty man (they will lie down together and not rise again; they have been quenched and extinguished like a wick): "Do not call to mind the former things, or ponder things of the past. Behold, I will do something new, now it will spring forth; will you not be aware of it? I will even make a roadway in the wilderness, rivers in the desert. The beasts of the field will glorify Me, the jackals and the ostriches, because I have given waters in the wilderness and rivers in the desert, to give drink to My chosen people. The people whom I formed for Myself will declare My praise.*

ISAIAH 43

Yet you have not called on Me, O Jacob; but you have become weary of Me, O Israel. You have not brought to Me the sheep of your burnt offerings, nor have you honored Me with your sacrifices. I have not burdened you with offerings, nor wearied you with incense. You have bought Me not sweet cane with money, nor have you filled Me with the fat of your sacrifices; rather you have burdened Me with your sins, you have wearied Me with your iniquities. I, even I, am the one who wipes out your transgressions for My own sake, and I will not remember your sins."

—Isa. 43:1–25

Bible Reading: Ephesians 2:1–10

Week 10

1 JOHN

Day 1

Ninety years after Jesus was here, people who believed in Him, or professed to, started to take in false teachings of the world, and the Apostle John was intense in his response. Walking away from the truth breaks, or interrupts, our fellowship with God. It could indicate that we never truly believed Jesus is the Son of God since that belief always leads to truthful action. The book of 1 John was written to believers to combat the false Gnostic teachings that there was no one God or creator, God never became man, and no one can resurrect from the dead. Because they believed only a spirit could be good, Gnostics acted immorally. Their spiritual arrogance resulted in a lack of brotherly love, and believers in Christ were following in their footsteps.

Doubt and confusion developed among believers. How do we know what is true and if we really are children of God? John provided his "children" with tests or criteria by which they can evaluate the claims of others and strengthen believers in the assurance of their salvation.

This was obvious spiritual warfare, and John fought back with the simple and straightforward sword of truth. His letter is filled with contrasts of light and darkness, love of God and love of the world, children of God and children of the devil, the Spirit of God and the spirit of antichrist, love and hate. There were no hazy areas in which to stand. With John in the crowd, Jesus had taught that we cannot serve two masters, that we will either hate the one and love the other or be devoted to one and despise the other. We can't serve God and wealth (Matt. 6:24). Life is extreme contrasts: right or wrong. When we choose anything to serve, believe, love, and follow besides God, we are rejecting all of God. We can't love God and love money. It isn't possible to believe that Jesus *and* other religious ideas and prophets lead to heaven. Jesus said, "I am the way, and the truth, and the life; no one comes to the Father but through Me" (John 14:6). Clearly, Jesus left no room for other gods or religions. Knowing who Jesus is roots us in solid ground.

> *What was from the beginning, what we have heard, what we have seen with our eyes, what we have looked at and touched with our hands, concerning the Word of Life—and the life was manifested, and we have seen and testify and proclaim to you the eternal life, which was with the Father and was manifested to us—what we have seen and heard we proclaim to you also, so that you too may have fellowship with us; and indeed our fellowship is with the Father, and with His Son Jesus Christ. These things we write, so that our joy may be made complete.*
>
> —1 John 1:1-4

As an eyewitness to the life and ministry of Jesus, John was stating the case that Jesus is fully God who became fully man. John and many others saw Jesus, heard Him, touched Him, and were present at His crucifixion. Then they saw, heard, and touched Jesus after He resurrected from the dead. John assures us that Jesus is indeed one part of the Trinity and was present at creation; He is eternal. Jesus conquered death when He rose from the dead after His crucifixion; He is eternal life. The words Jesus said spoke creation into existence. His teachings give us light and a path to follow that lead us to salvation and fellowship with God the Father; He is the Word of Life. We can know this for a certainty. Jesus is our solid foundation of truth and life.

Bible Reading: 1 John 1, Genesis 1:1-3, 26-27, John 1:1-4

Day 2

The Bible is God's Word, His most prominent way of talking to us. John is the writer of this letter, but he is passing on God's message to us. First John 1:5 states, "This is the message we have heard from Him and announce to you, that God is Light, and in Him there is no darkness at all." Light defines God's character. God is all pure—no impurities darken or shadow His light. He is all good, and no badness dims His shining light. The Lord is clean with no dirtiness to hide His light. God is right and righteous—nothing wrong or evil defiles or taints His brilliant light.

John is very simple and straightforward about how this part of God's character applies to our lives. "If we say that we have fellowship with Him and *yet* walk in the darkness, we lie and do not practice the truth; but if we walk in the Light as He Himself is in the Light, we have fellowship with one another, and the blood of Jesus His Son cleanses us from all sin" (1 John 1:6–7). If we believe creation and evolution mix to give us the truth about how we all began, we have combined the darkness of Satan's lies with the pureness of God's truth and are not walking in God's light. His light has *no* darkness. If we live our lives continually being bitter about a person's mistreatment of us, unwilling to forgive them, we are not living in God's light. Living in addiction, fear, lying, stealing, rejecting responsibility for ourselves, and hatred defiles and stains us and is dark. God's light may be in us (if we believe Jesus is God and our Savior), but we've covered it and blocked it out. We are not practicing truth or living in close friendship with God.

Kindness and gentleness are sometimes best achieved by sharp, quick action. When we have cancer, we want the surgeon to make careful, precise incisions in us and aggressively take out all the dangerous impurities in our bodies. Our souls have much more eternal importance than our bodies. So John tells us that if we say we have fellowship with God and yet walk in the darkness, we lie and do not practice the truth. Ouch! That is sharp but easy to understand. We can easily put our ideas, excuses, lifestyle choices, thoughts, and feelings to the test. What does God's Word say about it? If we are different from what God says, we are wrong. Let's not lie to ourselves and others and say we are close to God in this.

But if we walk in the Light as He Himself is in the Light, we have fellowship with one another, and the blood of Jesus His Son cleanses us from all sin. Living each step of our days in God's light gives us fellowship, which is close friendship, partnership, and sharing with other believers in Christ. We won't be alone. God provides a tangible lifeline, a sturdy foundation, a loving safety net for us by giving us our church family. He designed this family to work correctly by all of us walking in His light.

Another benefit of walking in God's light is that as it shines in our lives, we can see the areas that are shadowed with sin. We're promised that if we walk in close intimate partnership with God's light, the blood of Jesus cleanses us from all sin. As soon as the dark smudge of sin is evident to us, we turn to God, admit our wrongdoing, and accept Jesus's continual cleansing in our lives. So we must stop rationalizing our sin. Let's not call it a disorder or disease. We are not sin's victims; we are responsible for the sin in our lives. That is freeing because we then have the ability to repent (turn), confess, be washed clean, and walk in light.

Bible Reading: **Proverbs 4, 1 John 1:5–10, 2:1–6**

Day 3

Have you ever wondered, "How do I know for sure if I'm saved?" Here's a test—1 John 1:6–10. Verse 9 reassures us of the truth. If you confess your sins, God is faithful to forgive. So be confident; you are forgiven. When God promises, He delivers. Always. The word *if* in these verses lets us know we have choices to make about how we think and live, and those choices reflect the truth of our relationship with God. *If* we say that we have no sin, we are deceiving ourselves, and the truth is not in us. *If* we confess our sins, He is faithful and righteous to forgive us our sins and to cleanse us from all unrighteousness. *If* we say that we have not sinned, we make Him a liar, and His word is not in us.

The Greek word for *confess* means "to say the same thing as or to agree with." We need to say the same thing about our sins as God says—agree with Him. Living immorally because "everybody's doing it" is choosing darkness and impurity over God's light and holiness. Condemning others shows arrogance and hatred, not virtue and wisdom. Saying sin is not really sin is a lie, not tolerance. But when we confess our sins, He forgives us and cleanses us.

Deceiving ourselves is a dangerous game. John loved his spiritual children enough to not let them get by with it. We're only fooling ourselves if we say we don't have any sin in our lives. In reality we're calling God a liar. And if we call God a liar by our lifestyle choices, feelings, and conversations, His truth and word are not in us. These words are sharp and loving at the same time. We don't have to stay in our miserable, dangerous place of self-deception. Stop believing all our bad decisions are the result of bad parenting, pain from our past, or injustice. Take one thing at a time. Be honest with yourself, and then agree with God's view of that part of your life.

John wants us to realize that we can be close to God. It is possible for us to have the same fellowship—intimate friendship—with Jesus that John had. Confession is key to this promise because intimacy is rooted in honesty. Think about that.

If you told your best friend the deepest parts of you and were honest and open with her, just as she was with you, and you found out she had lied to you about her life, what would that do to your relationship? There would be no possibility to carry on in a close, intimate friendship, would there?

It would be difficult, but with God's help it would be possible for you and me to forgive our friend if they confessed their lies, repented (changed), and apologized. But could we have a close, intimate, trusting, friend relationship with them again? Here's the amazing thing. God willingly risks His heart being hurt again by saying yes to that. If you and I confess our sins, God will forgive us and clean us. He wipes the stains from our confessed sins off us so we can stand without embarrassment next to Him and pick up our personal, in-depth, warm, close, and loving fellowship with Him. God restores our intimate relationship with Him through our honesty.

The choice is yours. If you want to be close to God, be honest with yourself and Him.

Bible Reading: Psalm 38:18–22

Day 4

Remember that John was writing to people who went to church and said they had accepted Jesus as their Savior yet had allowed beliefs from the world to become part of their lives. Because the Gnostics made up their own beliefs about God, they also made up their rules of life as they went. Their ethical standards were low, and the Christians were starting to follow that lifestyle. That means they believed there was no definite right and wrong. Stealing, cheating, lying, sex outside of marriage, revenge, bad language, overt sensuality, and disrespect for authority are just some of the ways people show unethical behavior. And there is always a good reason for it. *It's only a little white lie. We didn't steal; we just took that to feed our family. Sex outside of marriage is okay if we love the person.* On and on we try to justify ourselves.

John pulled no punches in letting us know that God is not buying our excuses for sin. He said in 1 John 2:3–6:

> *By this we know that we have come to know Him, if we keep His commandments. The one who says, "I have come to know Him," and does not keep His commandments, is a liar, and the truth is*

> *not in him; but whoever keeps His word, in him the love of God has truly been perfected. By this we know that we are in Him: the one who says he abides in Him ought himself to walk in the same manner as He walked.*

This is so simple. Our lives prove if we know God personally or if we are lying when we say we do. Now let's be clear on what this doesn't mean. It does not mean that a believer in Jesus never sins and that if they do sin, they lose their salvation. Verse 5 in the New International Version says "if anyone obeys his word," but the New American Standard Bible gives a closer translation and says, "whoever keeps His word." That means to continually guard, to preserve, to take care of. The person who continually lives the way God tells them to in His Word, the Bible—anyone whose ongoing way of thinking, talking, living, and feeling is how Jesus lived—who guards God's truth and doesn't fall for ideas that are different from God's, is the one who has God's love in them.

Every person who believes in Jesus as their Savior will sin. But the sin won't be how they continually live. There is no given time span in the Bible for this. Some God-followers lived in sin for years, months, or just days. God is the only One who knows our hearts. But true children of God are miserable living far from Him. Their conscience bothers them and draws them back. Ultimately, they won't keep and guard the lie that it's okay to live in that sin but will go back to the truths from God's Word. So if anyone obeys God's Word, His love is truly made complete, carried through to the finish, accomplished in them. That is how we know we are in God.

We're not on our own in this. Jesus lived as a man and faced all our temptations and hardships. First, Jesus knew God's Word. He read and studied God's personal letters of love and instruction. Jesus was prayed up. He continually talked to His Father, and He purposefully went away by Himself to talk with God. Doing this gave Jesus His Father's eyes—the ability to see the big picture, to understand that doing the right thing now when it was hard and scary or dangerous and painful would result in the least painful, most successful ending. Knowing God's Word and being close to Him through prayer enabled Jesus to experience love and friendship, hatred and betrayal, power and popularity, vulnerability and rejection, security and confidence, fear and dread—and never sin. He showed us how to live for God day in and day out.

***Bible Reading*: Ephesians 4:17–32, 5:1–10**

Day 5

Every level of believer in Jesus is being instructed by John's words. Little children in Christ are people of any age who have recently confessed Jesus to be Lord of their lives. Young men are those who have known Jesus for a while and have been praying and studying His Word and practicing God's truth in their everyday lives. Fathers are very mature believers who have taught and encouraged others and have an ongoing, intimate relationship with God.

John wants us to remember what we know. Remember that God is. He exists and has existed forever. Remember that your sins are forgiven because of Jesus's death on the cross and His resurrection. Remember the power you have through Jesus to overcome the evil one, to stand strong and fight the lies and attacks of the world.

Little children, young men and women, fathers and mothers, when you remember the truths of God, you will be able to break free from the world system because in some ways it is very appealing. "Do not love the world nor the things in the world. If anyone loves the world, the love of the Father is not in him. For all that is in the world, the lust of the flesh and the lust of the eyes and the boastful pride of life, is not from the Father, but is from the world. The world is passing away, and *also* its lusts; but the one who does the will of God lives forever" (1 John 2:15–17).

We are to love and care for the people of the world and the earth, but we are not to love the world system or its way of doing things. The world system, which is run by Satan, wants us to give it our time, attention, and money—our devotion and love. Think about all the commercials and billboards we see. They tell us that in order to be cool, accepted, valuable, and happy, we must spend time, money, and attention on clothes, makeup, alcohol, cars, gadgets—things. Athletes, movie stars, politicians, wealthy people—they're the ones we want to be like, look like, and sound like. When we get caught up in this, our focus shifts. We go to college to gain respect and get a good-paying job so we can live in a nice house, have cool cars and great clothes, throw amazing parties, and go on fun vacations. The lust of the flesh—we want to feel it all, taste it all, experience all the world offers. The lust of the eyes—we want what that person has, the "good life," all that money can buy. The boastful pride of life—we want others to know how smart we are, the title of our job, how we've volunteered and accomplished great things. These are *not* from the Father. They are from the world, and the world is passing away.

When we define ourselves by what we have, what degree we got from school, our job, talent, and looks, we are on dangerous ground. All of that is passing away. Almost no one remembers who the MVP of the 1959 World Series or Super Bowl X was. Do you care which banker, doctor, or businessperson got their degree from Harvard in 1940, 1980, or 2000? Which 90-year-old model or movie star looks as beautiful as they did when they were 20? Have you ever heard of a multimillionaire taking their money with them when they died? Everything the world system says matters, slips away. But the person who does the will of God lives forever, and their work done in God's will continues on and lasts for all eternity. Love what matters and lasts. Choose to live for God, in this world but not controlled by it. Live in God's love. Live for Him.

Bible Reading: 1 John 2, John 6:40

Day 6

What a hard-hitting week. The plain talk of 1 John is exactly what we need to combat the subtle enticements and deceptions of the world. We are worn down by the constant pressure to believe and act in a way the world thinks is right and to be tolerant of sin.

God gave us an easy checklist. If we say one thing and live another, we are double-minded or hypocrites. If we don't think there is any sin in us, we are self-deceived. If we buy the idea that everyone is good, that we have never sinned, we're calling God a liar. If we say we know God but don't obey Him, we're lying. If we say we're in the light but hate someone, we're really living in darkness. If we love the world's way of living and thinking, then we don't love God. If we live for the world, it will all fade away and count for nothing.

But . . . there's hope! "But if we walk in the Light as He Himself is in the Light, we have fellowship with one another, and the blood of Jesus His Son cleanses us from all sin" (1 John 1:7). "If we confess our sins, He is faithful and righteous to forgive us our sins and to cleanse us from all unrighteousness" (1 John 1:9). "But the one who does the will of God lives forever" (1 John 2:17).

This week has taught us to look carefully at ourselves. Our flesh pulls us toward sin, and we can at any point choose light or darkness. Being honest with ourselves is the first step to being clean, reflecting God's light, and living in fellowship with other believers and Christ Jesus. Our life proves where our heart is. God is interested in our motives. Taking care of our environment is right, but worshiping the creation instead of the Creator is wrong. Dressing attractively, making healthy choices in exercise and diet, going to school, and taking care of the money and things God gives us is responsible and wise. Letting any of those things control us, loving them, or making them the most important things in our lives is wrong.

There are so many distractions, so many lies coming at us. Some of them sound religious and loving and good. We have the ability to test all philosophies through the Bible. Any teachings that reject Jesus as God's Son are lies (1 John 2:18). "Who is the liar but the one who denies that Jesus is the Christ? This is the antichrist, the one who denies the Father and the Son. Whoever denies the Son does not have the Father; the one who confesses the Son has the Father also" (1 John 2:22–23).

Again, how does this work out in our lives? Basically, remember what you know to be true and have learned from God's Word. Jesus is God's Son, eternal, and the Creator of the universe. Jesus came to live here for a time, died to pay for our sins, and rose from the dead three days later. After conquering death, Jesus Christ now lives in heaven with the Father and intercedes, or appeals, to the Father on our behalf when we confess our sins. God is life and light, righteous and true. By walking in God's grace and power, we can live in a way that shows we love Him. Believing in Jesus gives us eternal life, and living for Christ has eternal rewards. Knowing this, living this, keeps us close to God, free of guilt and shame, clean and confident.

Bible Reading: 1 John 1, 2

Week 11

1 JOHN

Day 1

We're told that everyone who remains in and practices sin for a period of time is not of God. First John 3:6–10 reads:

> *No one who abides in Him sins; no one who sins has seen Him or knows Him. Little children, make sure no one deceives you; the one who practices righteousness is righteous, just as He is righteous; the one who practices sin is of the devil; for the devil has sinned from the beginning. The Son of God appeared for this purpose, to destroy the works of the devil. No one who is born of God practices sin, because His seed abides in him; and he cannot sin, because he is born of God. By this the children of God and the children of the devil are obvious: anyone who does not practice righteousness is not of God, nor the one who does not love his brother.*

It's possible to say we're a Christian without truly believing Jesus is God's Son. Believing there is a God doesn't mean we've given God control of our lives. People who tell us false things about God and continually live against God's words may have never been saved. We can't lose our salvation, but we need to know there is only one way to be saved—and saved people show Jesus in their lives.

Paul helps us understand this. Believers in Christ have our old selves, sometimes referred to as the flesh or our sinful nature, and we have our new selves created in God's likeness—righteous, holy, and true (Eph. 4:24). We are to consider the sinful parts of our old self as dead. Our sinful thoughts, feelings, words, and actions were crucified on the cross with Jesus, and we need to leave them there. Colossians 3:9–10 says to not lie to one another since you laid aside the old self with its evil practices and have put on the new self who is being renewed to a true knowledge according to the image of the One who created him.

Nonbelievers have only one nature: the sin, devil-controlled nature. People who are not Christ-followers can do "good" things, but we've already learned that we can never do enough good to erase the debt we owe God for not being perfect. Once a person accepts Jesus's payment for their sin and believes He is the Son of God, they have a new "God nature," born from the perfect, sinless seed of God the Father. When Christ-followers die and go to heaven, they will be perfected. They will then have only one nature—the new and completely sinless God nature. They will not be gods, but they will be like God—sinless and pure, working and glorifying the Lord. However, while believers are still in this world, they have two parts to them: their old, sinful selves and their new, sinless God nature. Our job is to turn away from our old, sinful ways and choose to grow and live our new nature in Christ.

As Christians, we can actively seek to have "God in us" be the biggest part of us and have our natural, old way of thinking, feeling, talking, and acting become the smallest part of us. We'll still sin, but the goal is to recognize the sin immediately, confess it to God, and stop doing that sin. Sometimes believers start living in a sin, practicing it and allowing it to stay in their lives. Slowly we allow our old natures to become the biggest part of us and squeeze our new, sinless God nature into a tiny corner of our lives. We have been sealed by the Holy Spirit with the promise that we will always be God's children (Eph. 1:4), but it is our choice if we allow God or a sin to be the biggest part of our lives. Let's choose to look and live like our Father.

Bible Reading: 1 John 3:1–10, Galatians 5:13–25

Day 2

Solomon said in Ecclesiastes 1:9 that there is nothing new under the sun. This proves to be true in 1 John, doesn't it? All the false teachings that were seeping into the churches in AD 90 are being taught to us today. Families were broken, the weak were stomped upon, and justice and integrity were words to be loftily spoken and then traded in back rooms for money or power. That was yesterday's news and today's reality, and it will be the same tomorrow.

There's only one way to live in victory and be more than survivors today. Jesus asked His disciples, "'Who do the people say that I am?' They answered and said, 'John the Baptist, and others *say* Elijah; but others, that one of the prophets of old has risen again.' And He said to them, 'But who do you say that I am?'" (Luke 9:18–20).

That is the question. Who do you say Jesus is? Do you want to know how to go through the foster system and the challenges of this world and come out strong and healthy in every way? Are you trying to figure out how to rise above instead of be a victim to family problems, addictions, hatred, bitterness, and fear? Answer Jesus's question: "Who do you say that I am?"

The people said Jesus was a good teacher and a miracle worker but not the "main event." The prophets were like the opening act at a concert—good but not the best, not who we're waiting for. Peter answered Jesus, "You are the Christ of God." Jesus is it—the Son of God, the Christ, the Promised One. Christ Jesus is our Savior for today and into eternity.

John tells us, "This is His commandment; that we believe in the name of His Son Jesus Christ, and love one another, just as He commanded us" (1 John 3:23). "Whoever confesses that Jesus is the Son of God, God abides in him, and he in God" (1 John 4:15). "Whoever believes that Jesus is the Christ is born of God. Who is the one who overcomes the world, but he who believes that Jesus is the Son of God?" (1 John 5:1, 5).

Jesus told His disciples that they would run to their homes and leave Him alone after He was arrested. He kept telling them life would hurt and be hard. They would be betrayed, mocked, physically hurt, and treated unjustly. But He would endure those things too. And even though all His friends and family would abandon Him, Jesus said, "And *yet* I am not alone, because the Father is with Me. These things I have spoken to you, so that in Me you may have peace. In the world you have tribulation, but take courage; I have overcome the world" (John 16:32–33).

This world offers temporary happiness and peace, all based on what is going on around us. But Jesus offers eternal security. His peace and joy, His rest and protection, His wisdom and strength last through all life's circumstances. Jesus went through being degraded verbally, emotionally, and physically during His trial. He experienced the world's "justice" and abuse of power. Betrayal and aloneness were stark realities to Him. None of the laughter and good times He'd had before was enough to get Him through the tribulations. Only His relationship with His heavenly Father gave Him courage. Jesus Christ overcame this world. In Him we have the same victory. Victory comes down to the answer to this: "Who do you say Jesus is?"

Bible Reading: 1 John 4

Day 3

> *Whoever believes that Jesus is the Christ [Messiah] is born of God, and whoever loves the Father loves the* child *born of Him. By this we know that we love the children of God, when we love God and observe His commandments. For this is the love of God, that we keep His commandments; and His commandments are not burdensome. For whatever is born of God overcomes the world; and this is the victory that has overcome the world—our faith. Who is the one who overcomes the world, but he who believes that Jesus is the Son of God?*
>
> —1 John 5:1–4

John shows an urgent need for us to get the point that Jesus is the Promised One, the Son of God, the Christ. He stresses that we should take it a step further and *believe* that Jesus is the Son of God. *Believe* is an action word. We don't merely think Jesus is God; it's more than being pretty sure that Jesus is the Son of God. John tells us to be certain, to know beyond a doubt that Jesus is the Son of God. *And* that belief will cause us to act.

When you sit down on a chair, you sit there because you believe the chair will hold you. You are certain that the chair will be a safe place for you to sit, so you put your belief into action and sit. When we believe Jesus is who He says He is—the Son of God, the promised Messiah—we can safely rest on that belief. We put our belief into practice and do the things God has told us to do; namely, to love Him and love His other children.

This is incredible. Doing good things, treating others the right way, standing strong when life crumbles around us, fighting for justice and goodness when we feel like giving up, discerning truth from all the lies we hear—all that eventually wears us down. The world overcomes us with its pressures and ugliness. But! When we believe that Jesus is the Christ, He fills us with His Spirit. Believing in Jesus enables us to live God's way, to feel, think, and speak His way. Living according to God's commands does not burden us because Christ in us empowers us. Since Jesus overcame (triumphed over, conquered) the world, our faith in Jesus enables us to overcome the world too.

Jesus Christ is the Son of God who became a person so He could live for us and then die to pay the penalty for our sins. He rose from the dead three days later, conquering Satan and death. Do you believe this is true? You can put your faith in these facts and stand securely on the foundation of Jesus. You can sit down and rest on the "chair" of Christ Jesus that is strong and true. He will hold your weight. If you are tired of fighting to stay emotionally whole and safe, stop. Believe in Jesus, and let Him who has overcome the world fight for you. John said this:

> *These things I have written to you who believe in the name of the Son of God, so that you may know that you have eternal life. We know that we are of God, and that the whole world lies in the power of the evil one. And we know that the Son of God has come, and has given us understanding so that we may know Him who is true; and we are in Him who is true, in His Son Jesus Christ. This is the true God and eternal life.*
> —1 John 5:13, 19–20

Bible Reading: 1 John 5

Day 4

There are a couple major points that stand out in the first letter of John. Jesus is God who became man. He overcame the world, and we can, too, through Him. Believing in Jesus gives us eternal life and victorious life, and our belief in Him will be evident in how we live every day. John takes these facts and gives us a reason for them. God loves us. That's why He sent His Son to us. That's why He empowers us to overcome this difficult and evil world. God loves us. "See how great a love the Father has bestowed on us, that we would be called children of God; and *such* we are. For this reason the world does not know us, because it did not know Him. Beloved, now we are children of God" (1 John 3:1–2).

Beloved, let us love one another, for love is from God; and everyone who loves is born of God and knows God. The one who does not love does not know God, for God is love. By this the love of God was manifested in us, that God has sent His only begotten Son into the world so that we might live through Him. In this is love, not that we loved God, but that He loved us and sent His Son to be the propitiation for our sins. We have come to know and have believed the love which God has for us. God is love, and the one who abides in love abides in God, and God abides in him. By this, love is perfected with us, so that we may have confidence in the day of judgment; because as He is, so also are we in this world. There is no fear in love; but perfect love casts out fear, because fear involves punishment, and the one who fears is not perfected in love. We love, because He first loved us.

—1 John 4:7–10, 16–19

God—the Creator of the universe, the completely pure and holy God, the most powerful and always victorious God, the absolutely just and righteous God—is love. It's not merely that God loves you and me; God *is* love. The dictionary defines *love* as "feeling tender affection for someone or something, a passionate or romantic feeling, intense compassion and affection, having a deep interest in something or someone." The Bible describes God as perfect love.

God, our Father, pours His love all over us. He fills us with it. Our Lord's love moved Him to action. Because God is just, or completely honorable and fair, as well as love, He had to come up with a plan that would satisfy both of those parts of Him. From the beginning of time, our affections have been divided. A lot of people say they love God but also love themselves and want to put "me" first in many ways. We don't have perfect, complete love for God on our own. No matter how ugly our motives and lives look, God still loves us—not our sin, but us. So our God—the Trinity (the Father, Son, and Holy Spirit)—sent the Son into this world to live among us as one of us. Then the Son of God, Jesus Christ, died on the cross as the acceptable sacrifice that paid the price for each and every person's sins. That was where God's justness and love converged. When you and I acknowledge and believe in Jesus and His payment for our sins, we live surrounded by, soaked in, and completely covered by God's love. We have no fear of His judgment. With confidence in His love and Jesus's sacrifice, we can face God as His forgiven child. And then, because He first loved us, we are finally able to love Him.

You and I don't deserve God's love, but He still wants us to receive it. He knows you, yet He still loves you. He wants you. All you have to do is believe in His love and His love gift, Jesus. The Father wants you to be His child, called by His name, loved unconditionally forever.

Bible Reading: John 3:16–18, Romans 8:31–39

Day 5

Sir Isaac Newton's third law of physics states that for every action there is an equal and opposite reaction. That principle works with the book of 1 John. Because God first loved us, we have the ability to love Him and other people. Jesus was once questioned by a group of religious leaders.

> *One of them, a lawyer, asked Him* a question, *testing Him, "Teacher, which is the great commandment in the Law?" And He said to him, "'You shall love the Lord your God with all your heart, and with all your soul, and with all your mind.' This is the great and foremost commandment. The second is like it, 'You shall love your neighbor as yourself.' On these two commandments depend the whole Law and the Prophets."*
>
> —Matt. 22:35–40

Let's be honest with ourselves. There are times when we are not lovable. Sometimes we go out of our way to be obnoxious and rude, and sometimes we have no idea why we keep screwing up. Regardless of our behavior, God loves us. And He takes His love to an extreme. The entire love story of Jesus's sacrifice for us is so hard to believe because that kind of love is just astounding. Even now with more than 50 years of being God's child, I cannot completely grasp His love for me. However, when you and I tell God we believe in His Son and want Him in our lives, God's love floods our love-starved hearts and minds. Being loved like that is irresistible.

Discovering that our Father created each of us in detail for a purpose fills us with value. Knowing that God wants us to talk to Him and He listens to us makes us feel like we matter. His strength when we are weak, His courage when we're afraid . . . His love for us makes us fall in love with Him. That causes a reaction: we want to do the things that will let God know we love Him too. Love is the reason we willingly follow His instructions and stay within His boundaries. Jesus knew that if we loved God with all our heart, all our soul, and all our mind, we would obey Him. It's just natural to want to please the one we love.

The second commandment is as logical as the first. We would never murder a person's reputation with gossip if we loved them. Love would have us speaking kindly to others, treating them with respect, caring for the other person's needs above our own. If we truly love others like we love ourselves, we will not steal from them, kill them, or lie about them.

Love is not just a feeling, is it? Love is an action word. God's love for us propelled Him to save us from judgment and eternal separation from Him. That action fills us with His love, which causes us to love Him in return. Our love for God initiates our obedience and our love for other people. This isn't complicated . . . it's a natural law of physics. Accept God's love, and the rest will happen automatically. Our job is to keep our eyes on the Father, our hearts open to His guidance and love, and our minds constantly aware of the ways God wants us to show our love. Keep God first in our hearts, and let His love do the work. We love because God first loved us.

Jesus said, "A new commandment I give to you, that you love one another, even as I have loved you, that you also love one another. By this all men will know that you are My disciples, if you have love for one another" (John 13:34–35). Taking in God's love results in pouring out His love to others.

Bible Reading: 1 John 4

Day 6

Let's review who and what God is. Do you remember? It's the three "L's": God is LIFE, God is LIGHT, God is LOVE. Jesus spoke the universe into existence, gave us eternal *life* by His death and resurrection, and His words lead us to a full *life* on earth now and for eternity in heaven. Christ Jesus is the *light* of the world, and in Him there is no darkness. His *light* shows us the way to live and keeps us safe and free from fear. It is pure and clean and completely true. Our Savior's *love* is sacrificial, unselfish, freeing, and unconditional. God's *love* is so great that it overflows in us and causes us to think, feel, and act in a new way. His *love* causes us to love. Our love for God and other people shows the unbelieving world God's *Life*, *Light*, and *Love*.

John wrote his letter to people in the church who claimed to have accepted and believed in Jesus Christ as their Lord and Savior. The reason he wrote was because those believers had allowed some of the worldly philosophies about God to come in and pollute their beliefs. He was almost childlike in his "day and night" statements. When we become God's children, we will change how we live. We either live in light or in darkness (1 John 1:1-4, 2:8-11). Our hearts either love the world or love God (1 John 2:15-17). We're children of God or children of the devil (1 John 3:4-10). You and I are listening to and following the spirit of the antichrist or the Spirit of God (1 John 4:1-3). Our hearts, minds, and actions are the result of that and show love or hate (1 John 4:7-12, 16-21).

First, we are to put our own selves under this microscope of truth to see where we stand. Second Corinthians 13:5 says, "Test yourselves *to see* if you are in the faith; examine yourselves! Or do you not recognize this about yourselves, that Jesus Christ is in you—unless indeed you fail the test?" Next, we are to put the people in our lives and their beliefs under this same microscope.

In Matthew 7, Jesus clearly told us not to judge others so we won't be judged. That can seem like a contradiction. Let's clear up our responsibilities. We are not to judge and condemn other people according to our own standards. We are, however, to take God's standards and determine if a person is living and speaking in line with God's truth. That's making a judgment. God wants us to come to wise and discerning conclusions about the people we choose to have close in our lives and the people we choose to believe and follow. When we see that the person is not living according to God's ways, we must use Christ's *life*, *light*, and *love* to guide us. Use prayer and His Word (the Bible) to know how to handle our relationship.

Since light and darkness cannot be intertwined, we will not be able to have a close, intimate relationship with a person who is living outside of God's will. But we'll be able to treat them with respect and love while we clearly live according to God's standards. Any teaching and belief that is not in line with God's truth are from the spirit of the antichrist and evil (1

John 4:1). We are to reject false ideas and not allow a false teacher to teach us or be in our churches. Our loyalty is always to God, not a person. Never mistake being nice for being loving. Love demands honesty, and the truth is that God is love, God is light, and in Him there is no darkness. Jesus is the only way, the truth, and the life, and no one comes to the Father but through Him (John 14:6). Walk in truth and in faith.

Bible Reading: **John 14**

Week 12

LOVE

Day 1

With Valentine's Day being celebrated sometime soon, I want us to learn about real love. There are many kinds of love. Friendly love, or fondness, comes from the Greek word *phileo*, which is where we get Philadelphia, the City of Brotherly Love. *Éros* isn't in the Bible but is Greek for romantic love with strong emotions and physical feelings. Then there is the word *agape*, which is the way God loves us and the way He wants us to love Him and others.

Paul wrote of love to the church in Corinth because that city was controlled by two things: open sexuality and a reverence for philosophy. Like today, their view of love was formed by sensuality and intellectualism. The warped ideas that love meant tolerating sinfulness or was shown sexually without restraint seeped from society into the church and were about to be corrected. However, Paul opens our eyes to *agape* love.

> *If I speak with the tongues of men and of angels, but do not have love, I have become a noisy gong or a clanging cymbal. If I have the gift of prophecy, and know all mysteries and all knowledge; and if I have all faith, so as to remove mountains, but do not have love, I am nothing. And if I give all my possessions to feed the poor, and if I surrender my body to be burned, but do not have love, it profits me nothing. Love is patient, love is kind and is not jealous; love does not brag and is not arrogant, does not act unbecomingly; it does not seek its own, is not provoked, does not take into account a wrong suffered, does not rejoice*

in unrighteousness, but rejoices with the truth; bears all things, believes all things, hopes all things, endures all things. Love never fails.

—1 Cor. 13:1–8

What do you think? It struck me that although I say I love some people, according to God's definition, I don't. How wonderful that we studied 1 John last week and learned that we don't need to be overwhelmed by the task of loving people. We won't be able to do this on our own. Left to our old natural instincts, our love would be based on our own needs; it would be selfish at the core. But all that changes when we accept God's *agape* love for us. We *agape* because He first loved us. We can do a lot of things that look loving and look like God without our motive being love. We find out quickly if our motives are loving or selfish when people don't respond to us the way we want.

The reason Jesus's life makes such an impact is because His motive for living here in this world was love. No other person in history has made the lasting impression Jesus makes. No other person's sacrifice but Jesus Christ's shakes people to the core, causes such strong positive and negative emotions, and endures throughout thousands of years—for the simple reason that Christ did what He did because He loves His Father, and He loves each of us.

You and I have received a beautiful Valentine. We're part of an incredible love story. Jesus Christ loves you; Jesus Christ loves me. His love is patient and kind; it is not jealous or boastful or proud or rude. Christ's love for us does not demand its own way nor is it irritable, and it keeps no record of when it has been wronged. It is never glad about injustice but rejoices whenever the truth wins out. His love never gives up, never loses faith, is always hopeful, and endures through every circumstance. Jesus's love for you and for me will last forever without fail.

Bible Reading: 1 Corinthians 13

Day 2

Let's take these verses apart to learn how we are loved and how to love. Love is patient. *Patient* in the Greek means "doesn't lose heart or become discouraged." It sticks with the loved one tolerantly and bravely while enduring misfortunes and troubles. Love is uncomplaining in bearing the offenses and injuries of others. *Patience* means "slow to anger and slow to punish, mild." Wow! Already this is a challenge. Do you love your parents and family, friends and coworkers? Do you love the people who've let you down and hurt you?

We could put ourselves in danger if we aren't wise in applying this in our lives. If the person we love is abusive or neglectful in any way, God does not mean we should tolerate and bravely endure the abuse. Paul said to the believers at Corinth, "Do you not know that you are a temple of God and *that* the Spirit of God dwells in you? If any man destroys the temple of God, God will destroy him, for the temple of God is holy, and that is what you are" (1 Cor. 3:16–17). Clearly, we have a responsibility to keep our bodies, hearts, and minds safe.

It may be that we need to separate ourselves from a person if they are dangerous and harmful to us, but our attitude toward them—even when they are not with us—can be one of love. We are not told to love the abuse or trouble, or to patiently sit there while they injure us. Love can happen from a distance. That aspect of love takes God's perspective. We need to see the person with our Father's eyes—eyes that separate the sin from the sinner. Without becoming discouraged or angered with the loved one who is hurting us, we can commit to pray for them as God prompts us. With love it will be possible to let go of bitterness and vengeance and release the person and situation completely into God's just and loving control.

You see, this love is not dependent on another person's behavior. It is about you and me being right with God. It is about His love, which is patient with us, filling us, and then we love Him in response. Our love for God will enable us to obey Him, and He wants us to love the people He's allowed into our lives. Even if the wisest choice we can make is never seeing a person again, we can love them with an *agape* kind of love.

Jesus gave us an example of this patient love in Matthew 26:50. Judas came with soldiers in order to betray Jesus for money. Jesus said, "Friend, *do* what you have come for." Then they came and laid hands on Jesus and seized Him. Jesus called Judas a friend even though He knew Judas intended to hurt Him because Jesus's love was not based on Judas. He called Judas "friend" to let him know that was how He still felt about him. Jesus wanted Judas to remember the relationship they once shared, and He gave him another chance to do the right thing. His love was patient with Judas. His response was mild. Because Jesus loved Judas, He was willing to put His heart at risk in order to give Judas the chance to get it right. Jesus had spent many hours praying to His Father and studying Scripture, which enabled Him to make this decision at the right time. Wisdom comes from prayer, God's Word, and the counsel of godly people. There are many people we can love patiently without any danger to ourselves. But if the person does pose a threat, use wisdom in how you go about loving them.

Bible Reading: 1 Thessalonians 5:11–15, 1 John 4:7–12

Day 3

Love is kind. Going again to the original language of the New Testament, we see that the word *kind* means "mild, fit for use; the opposite of harsh, sharp, and bitter." So our love gives us the ability to use kind, mild words and actions. When things are going well, this isn't a problem. But there are times when we snap sharply at someone who has irritated or hurt us. Sometimes other things in life are the triggers, but our loved one is the person to lay into.

We all have people in our lives who have hurt us. Whether we see them again or not, we should show kindness to them in how we speak and feel about them. In order for us to be able to live out that love, we will have to open up to the Father.

Unforgiveness, bitterness, condemnation, fear, and clinging to victimization and rage enslave us to events and people who hurt us. Those emotions bind us to the very ones who have caused us pain and treated us unjustly. However, Jesus came to set us free. When we recognize that we are living with those harmful feelings, we need to tell God, remember His forgiveness for us, forgive who we need to forgive, and ask our Father to free us from the power of that sin in our lives.

Second Corinthians 10:3–7 tells us this is a spiritual battle, and we are to destroy and take these thoughts, imaginings, and feelings captive. So do it. Tell the sin of bitterness to leave and not return, in Jesus's name. Use Scripture. Say, "Greater is He who is in me than he who is in the world." Or use another verse that applies. In the name of Jesus, you've pulled that weed of sin out of your life. Now fill that hole with something of God. Thank God for His freeing work in your life, and ask Him to fill you with His love, truth, and kindness. You are now fit for use, able to function effectively as a child of God, loved by Him, and loving kindly, like Him.

Love is not jealous. Another translation says it does not envy. Interesting. Love does not manipulate or use control. It does not boil with envy, hatred, and anger. Fear and selfishness jump out as two main reasons for these feelings. So does a lack of trust in God. We grab control when we don't think He'll get it right or will allow us to be hurt. No one likes to be rejected or abandoned. But we cannot control others. No matter how much we try to manipulate people and situations, in the end we can't make things turn out the way we want. Doing all that focuses on ourselves; it's self-centered. In reality, the person we love is us, not the one we're trying to control and feeling envious and angry toward.

God loves you and me, but He doesn't manipulate us. He sent Jesus as a love gift, and He passionately wants us to accept His gift and love Him back. But He doesn't force us. His love is pure. It is patient, kind, and not envious. If it takes us five years, 30 years, or 90 years to respond to Him, God is patient and kind. He loves us with *agape* love.

The question is this: have we accepted His love? If we have, do we *agape* God and the people He's allowed in our life? We can because the love of God has been poured out within our hearts through the Holy Spirit who was given to us (Rom. 5:5).

Bible Reading: John 15:8–14, 2 Corinthians 10:3–7

Day 4

Love does not brag and is not arrogant. These two things have "self" at the center. Boasting or bragging means a self-display, making up extra embellishments or frills in praising oneself excessively. If I loved you, I would not feel the need to "one-up" you. I would be thrilled with your success, not threatened by it. So when you made the sports team or got a musical or academic award, I did not brag about the awards I had received. There would be no desire to top what you did. My love for you would be all about you; it would delight in your achievements.

Agape does not allow me to brag about my strengths compared to another person's weaknesses or how I was right and they were wrong. With God's eyes, we can see that while a person struggles in one area, they are strong in another. That truth fits us as well. Love enables us to celebrate each other's strengths and be kind and patient in our weaknesses.

Arrogant means puffed up, conceited, big-headed, superior, and proud. Love is not arrogant. Opposite of arrogant is humble. Our best example of humble love is Christ Jesus. He is better than us, He's the Creator of the universe, the King of kings, and yet He agreed to live as one of us. In His time on earth, Jesus served the people He loved. Humble love also makes us willing to forgive instead of feeling superior to someone who blew it. It allows us to appreciate people with diverse points of view and feelings as we realize God made us all differently.

What enabled Jesus to not have arrogance toward us? I think it was because He was secure in who He was. That is the key to being able to humble ourselves and truly love other people. Jesus knew He was the Son of God and was sure of His purpose. He was confident because His motives were to honor His Father and obey His Word. So Jesus had nothing to prove to Himself or to others. He believed God's view of Him, not the world's.

If we are going to be able to love, we must first be secure in the Father's love. We need to believe the fact that we are fearfully and wonderfully made, skillfully woven together in the depths of the womb (Ps. 139:14–15). We are God's masterpiece, created in Christ Jesus to do good works, which God prepared in advance for us to do (Eph. 2:10). Believe it or not, knowing our worth and value to God does not make us arrogant; it is humbling. His loving regard and respect for us makes us secure and confident. We have nothing to prove to ourselves or anyone else when we believe what God has said about us.

Being filled with the fullness of God enables us to love without bragging or arrogance. We will be able to value a person's differences instead of belittle them, and, in fact, we will be thrilled to see the world through their eyes. God created us all distinctively. Together we make the whole body of Christ. Living securely in who we are in Christ is the only way to love as He loves us, to celebrate others' success instead of feeling threatened by them, to forgive weaknesses and failures, to encourage strengths and accomplishments. God's love in us flows out so we can serve, help, and care for people who don't appreciate our work or who seem to always make mistakes. *Agape* is centered on God and others but benefits us as well.

Bible Reading: Ephesians 3:14–21, Philippians 2:5–11

Day 5

Love is patient; love is kind and is not jealous; love does not brag and is not arrogant; love does not act unbecomingly (is not rude). The Greek for *rude* means "indecent, acting or behaving unbecomingly, preparing disgrace for a person." At first glance, rudeness is easy to grasp. It's disrespect, mockery, sneering at someone. Maybe it's even letting a door shut in a person's face instead of holding it for them or not stepping aside so there is room for them to pass without bumping into us. Those things seem spontaneous to me, based on selfishness and even mean-spiritedness but without a lot of prior planning.

Preparing to disgrace a person goes a little deeper. It takes premeditation. Deep-rooted sin is involved in order for a person to plan to embarrass someone or publicly snub them. Resentment, unforgiveness, and bitterness are just a few of the reasons for this behavior. If the other person has hurt us, those feelings are natural. But God does not give us a free pass on sin because of other people's actions. Their sin does not excuse our sin. If you or I start imagining ways we could show a person up or let them know how it feels to be treated the way they treated us, we are falling short of God's standard. We're sinning.

Peter tells us to honor all people. Love your Christian brothers and sisters. Fear God. Show respect for the king. "For what credit is there if, when you sin and are harshly treated, you endure it with patience? But if when you do what is right and suffer *for it* you patiently endure it, this *finds* favor with God" (1 Pet. 2:20). Peter then reminds us that Christ suffered and did not sin. When they hurled their insults at Him, He did not retaliate; when He suffered, He made no threats. Instead, He entrusted Himself to Him who judges justly.

Don't ever think Jesus was a wimp. I dare you to try this the next time someone smaller or less influential than you gets in your face. It takes a lot of strength to hold back. Jesus is God. He could have called 12 legions of angels to protect Him from being taken by the Romans and crucified (Matt. 26:53–54). He didn't hurl insults back or retaliate because He was strong, not because He was weak. Christ in us gives us that same strength. The love of Jesus Christ caused Him to speak the truth and act on the truth. After studying 1 John, we know the truth is not wishy-washy and sweet all the time. But Jesus and His followers were never rude with the truth. They never set people up to make them look bad or stupid. They spoke the truth in love (Eph. 4:15).

Love doesn't behave rudely, but it also doesn't think rudely. We may never act out what we feel, but God looks at our hearts too. Every part of us is involved in love.

Love doesn't seek its own way; it isn't self-centered. We're seeing that, aren't we? Real love is focused on the one we love, not on our needs, feelings, and desires. Real love is as pure as the God who gives it to us. It says, "I'll forgive." Love patiently and kindly waits for others to get it right, is thrilled with their success, and is humble enough to serve. Love is not rude. Love is not selfish. All that builds up, all that nurtures, all that is good and true, honorable and right, all that is pure, lovely, excellent, and worthy of praise is love. Love is amazing—and it is yours.

Bible Reading: 1 Peter 2:9–25

Day 6

"But now faith, hope, love, abide these three; but the greatest of these is love" (1 Cor. 13:13). The Message version of the Bible tells us to love extravagantly because the greatest of the three—faith, hope, and love—is love. What a wonderful picture these words give us. We are to love extravagantly, and *agape* is an extravagant, generous, outrageous love. If we truly love like God loves us, there is no other description than that.

Read 1 Corinthians 13 in The Message (below), and take in the fact that you have a Father who loves you like this. Ask Him to enable you to love others in the same way.

> *If I speak with human eloquence and angelic ecstasy but don't love, I'm nothing but the creaking of a rusty gate. If I speak God's Word with power, revealing all His mysteries and making everything plain as day, and if I have faith that says to a mountain, "Jump," and it jumps, but I don't love, I'm nothing. If I give everything I own to the poor and even go to the stake to be burned as a martyr, but I don't love, I've gotten nowhere. So, no matter what I say, what I believe, and what I do, I'm bankrupt without love.*

Love never gives up. Love cares more for others than for self. Love doesn't want what it doesn't have. Love doesn't strut, doesn't have a swelled head, doesn't force itself on others, isn't always "me first", doesn't fly off the handle, doesn't keep score of the sins of others, doesn't revel when others grovel, takes pleasure in the flowering of truth, puts up with anything, trusts God always, always looks for the best, never looks back, but keeps going to the end.

Love never dies. Inspired speech will be over some day; praying in tongues will end; understanding will reach its limit. We know only a portion of the truth, and what we say about God is always incomplete. But when the Complete arrives, our incompletes will be canceled.

When I was an infant at my mother's breast, I gurgled and cooed like any infant. When I grew up, I left those infant ways for good.

We don't yet see things clearly. We're squinting in a fog, peering through a mist. But it won't be long before the weather clears and the sun shines bright! We'll see it all then, see it all as clearly as God sees us, knowing Him directly just as He knows us!

But for right now, until that completeness, we have three things to do to lead us toward that consummation: Trust steadily in God, hope unswervingly, love extravagantly. And the best of the three is love.

Wow! *Agape* is not the love of romantic novels, Hollywood shows, or tabloid magazines. *Agape* is love we can count on. God is *agape*, and you are the one He loves. Instead of learning how to love, let's learn how much God loves us. His *agape* will flow out of us as we learn to accept and live as His beloved children.

Bible Reading: John 15:9–17

Week 13

LOVE

Day 1

There's still more to learn about love. Let's jump back in. Love is not provoked. That means love is not easily made angry or exasperated; it isn't sharp. For some reason, we tend to be irritated by our loved ones much easier than our casual friends. They know how to push our buttons, or maybe we let them get to us too easily. We should not let familiarity breed contempt. God planned it so that the longer we live together, the longer our fuses become. Yet life seems to work the opposite way. It's difficult to have more love and patience the longer we live with someone. That kind of love comes only from God.

Stretching our limits a little, let's think about how we treat waitresses and store clerks, anyone we come in contact with. Are we easily provoked? Do we roll our eyes when they inconvenience us or make a mistake? Remember, Peter told us to honor all people, not just fellow believers in Christ or loved ones. Love for God demands respect and a mild response for others, along with patience and kindness.

Next is possibly the most challenging aspect of love. It keeps no record of wrongs. That's hard. We can forgive, but forget? And how do we keep the lesson we learned if we forget how it was taught? God says in Jeremiah 31:34, "For I will forgive their iniquity, and their sin I will remember no more." The word *remember* in Hebrew means "recall, call to mind." God's choice for how He will treat our rebellious, selfish behavior is to not call it to mind. He decides not to recall our bad choices. Our Father makes a conscious decision not to dredge up our past sins. We may not be able to forget all the painful things that happen to us, but through prayer we can give them to God and be freed from their control. Like the Father, we should not throw past mistakes in people's faces whenever we are angry or want our own way. Issues do need to be discussed and resolved, but then they are over. The account is balanced. Nothing is owed.

The reason for this is simple. That's the way God loves us.

> *The* LORD *is compassionate and gracious, slow to anger and abounding in lovingkindness. He will not always strive with us, nor will He keep His anger forever. He has not dealt with us according to our sins, nor rewarded us according to our iniquities. For as high as the heavens are above the earth, so great is His lovingkindness toward those who fear Him. As far as the east is from the west, so far has He removed our transgressions from us. Just as a father has compassion on his children, so the* LORD *has compassion on those who fear Him. For He Himself knows our frame; He is mindful that we are but* dust.
> —Ps. 103:8–14

That last sentence is crucial. God understands how weak we are, that we're only human. He doesn't expect us to get it right all the time because He knows us. If a perfect God has such gentle expectations of us, why can't we have gentle expectations of other people? The Bible's not saying our weaknesses are an excuse to be hurtful and wrong. Read those words again. It says God is slow to anger, not that He never gets angry. He will not always reprimand, but He will when necessary. When our Father does get angry, He won't carry that anger forever, but He will get angry. We can get angry, too, but remember to let people be human, make mistakes, and struggle. Love tells us to choose to not recall all the past problems while at the same time we remember the lessons learned through the pain. This love takes God's heart beating in us.

Bible Reading: Ephesians 3:14–21, Colossians 1:9–12

Day 2

Continuing our in-depth look at love, we see it does not rejoice in unrighteousness. Have you ever known someone who jumps on every mistake you make and tries to make a huge issue of it? Have you ever secretly, or even openly, rejoiced when they blew it, wanting to prove to them they were human too? Sometimes we want a person to do a bad thing in order to prove we were right or so we can be freed from a relationship with them.

The damage of this mindset is far-reaching. Unrighteousness always hurts God. Jesus died for it. God is separated from His loved ones because of it. That is not cause for rejoicing. The person who sins is hurt by it. You know very well how awful it feels to do the wrong thing. There are times when the shame and guilt from sin could cause a person to lose all hope and feel as if God could never forgive them. That is utterly sad and tragic. When a person is unrighteous, many outside people are hurt as a result. People's lives can be damaged in various ways by another person's sin, and the harm can last for generations.

Perfect love does not rejoice in unrighteousness but does rejoice with the truth. When we see a person or situation through God's eyes, we see the truth. We are able to see their strengths and weaknesses honestly. Our hearts, minds, and eyes will not be clouded with emotional issues, prejudices, past hurts, or traditions. Truth means we see objectively, and we see what is true in any matter under consideration—the reality and the facts.

The Greek for *rejoice* is fascinating. Rejoice is used twice in 1 Corinthians 13:6, but it is two different words. Love does not rejoice is *chairo*, which means "to be glad, to be well, and to thrive." Love does rejoice is *sugchairo*, which means "to rejoice with or together, to take part in another's joy." When we rejoice over someone's failing, we are doing it all alone. We may thrive on their mistakes, but they do not, and neither does anyone else. This is an act of selfishness, which is why it is not love. On the other hand, when we rejoice in the truth, we are not alone. Together, as one, we all rejoice in the truth. We bask in each other's accomplishments. Love allows us to revel in other people's victories over obstacles and be glad that God honestly sees them and works in them.

Another truth that should cause us great joy is the fact that God loves us. God loves you; He loves each person in your life, and He loves me. The Father's love is not based on who is in a better place, who is living right, or who is blowing it. He loves us because He is love.

God has shown us a different way of being right in His sight—not by obeying the law but by the way promised in the Scripture long ago. We are made right in God's sight when we trust in Jesus Christ to take away our sins. And we all can be saved in this same way, no matter who we are or what we have done. We all have sinned and fall short of the glory of God, but God in His gracious kindness declares us not guilty. He does this through Christ Jesus who has freed us by taking away our sins. Can we boast, then, that we have done anything to be accepted by God? No, because our acquittal is not based on our good deeds. It is based on our faith (Rom. 3:21–24, 27).

Bible Reading: 1 Peter 1:17–25

Day 3

"[Love] bears all things, believes all things, hopes all things, endures all things" (1 Cor. 13:7). The Greek word for *bears* means "to cover or protect, to preserve; to hide or conceal the errors and faults of others by covering to keep off something which threatens."

The application of this in our lives is big. Having a counselor, whether professional or a wise and godly friend, is important and good. Being honest with them and ourselves about what someone did to us or said to us is vital and wise. However, our time with them should not be blaming and shaming the one who hurt us. Speak the truth in that safe and private place, and reveal it all, but not for the sake of gossip or revenge. It should not be to shred the other person's reputation. The reason to tell our story is to help ourselves see the truth; figure out how to handle the damage, lies, and people in our life; and live victoriously where we are.

When telling our story to inspire others, we must be careful to leave out names and give the account without becoming distasteful or coarse with our details. Not everyone can relate to each detail of our life, but they can connect with the insecurities, rejections, and fears. What is important is that we were chained to certain lies and sins, and God freed and healed us. It is quite possible to help others with our story and bear or cover the people in our lives. We don't lie about what they did, but we are wise and discreet in the telling. Saying they did the best they could is untrue when, in fact, addiction, neglect, betrayal, and abuse are not the best anyone can do. Calling them names or trying to embarrass and discredit them is also unproductive and displeasing to our Lord. Speak the truth in love. Tell your story truthfully and tastefully. Love God first and others next. We are not the focus.

"Love believes all things" means we have confidence in the person we love to eventually get it right. We give them credit when they do and trust them when they say they want to do what is good and right. Most importantly, we believe God is powerful enough to change them. Does this sound a little naive to you? Usually an addicted person wants to live healthy when they're sober, but they seem to always let us down and fall back to their addiction. Maybe the person honestly doesn't care at all to change. So what does that mean for us?

In Matthew 19, Jesus told the disciples that following the Law would not save anyone and that wealthy people would find it hard to get to heaven because they love and trust their money. Someone asked Him, "Then who can be saved?" Jesus said, "Humanly speaking, it is impossible. But with God, everything is possible."

That is our confidence. Our first, one true love is Jesus, and we believe all things about Him. We believe He loves us. We believe He loves each person in our lives. We believe He is good all the time; He is all-knowing and all-powerful. Our faith is in the fact that God doesn't want anyone to die but wants everyone to repent (1 Pet. 3:9). It isn't humanly possible for people to break all their destructive life patterns, but with God, all things are possible. When we love someone, we commit them to our Father. We pray for them, believing He is faithful. Our love for God and for them causes us to believe all things as we patiently wait for God's good will.

Bible Reading: Ephesians 4:17–32

Day 4

When Paul tells us that love hopes or believes all things, he is saying we should have an expectation of good for those we love. First, let's look at the people in our lives who are positive and safe. Have you ever anticipated the worst from them? Do you expect a person to be slow getting a project done and say as much to them and others? Love demands that we eagerly anticipate that a person will do well or do something for a good reason. That is part of believing in them. Our personal and in-depth knowledge of them is what allows us to hope. When we do not understand or even like what they are saying or doing, we can still expect it to be for good. And when they are on a roll of making poor decisions, we hope all things. We expect them to figure out what's wrong and make appropriate changes.

Our hope in unsafe and negative people is a little different. They may never have given us a reason to believe they will do the right thing, but we do still have reason to hope. Our ultimate hope is that God has the ability and desire to clean up their painful and messy lives now and give them eternal life in heaven. Paul told us this:

> Remember *that you were at that time separate from Christ, excluded from the commonwealth of Israel, and strangers to the covenants of promise, having no hope and without God in the world. But now in Christ Jesus you who formerly were far off have been brought near by the blood of Christ.* AND HE CAME AND PREACHED PEACE TO YOU WHO WERE FAR AWAY, AND PEACE TO THOSE WHO WERE NEAR; *for through Him we both have our access in one Spirit to the Father.*
> —Eph. 2:12–13, 17–18

Our hope is in God and His power to reach into people's hearts, to change them just as He has changed and healed us.

Love endures all things. *Endures* means "to remain, to bear bravely and calmly ill treatments, not recede or flee." It also means not to become another or different; to maintain unbroken fellowship. Fleeing or receding emotionally is easy to do. When a person hurts or angers us, we step back, and when we don't talk about it, the situation grows increasingly worse. The walls start to go up, and we take our feelings and go to an easier or safer place. Enduring doesn't just mean we stick it out in the ugly parts of a relationship; it means we don't become a different person. We've all imagined showing someone how awful their actions and words are by doing the same thing to them. That is willingly allowing someone who's hurt us to change us, imitating behavior we don't respect or like. How does that make sense? God wants to protect us from becoming bitter, angry people who react to others instead of living in control of our own behavior. So He has told us and enabled us to endure when life gets tough.

After Jesus rose from the grave, He showed what enduring love was all about. His disciples had run away and left Him during His trial and crucifixion. Peter had denied knowing Him three times. Yet Jesus rose from the grave and sought them out to encourage and love them. Their fellowship had been interrupted, but Jesus modeled *agape* love.

Love is patient, love is kind, love is not jealous; love does not brag and is not arrogant; it does not act unbecomingly; it does not seek its own, is not provoked, does not take into account a wrong suffered, does not rejoice in unrighteousness, but rejoices with the truth; it bears all things, believes all things, hopes all things, endures all things. Love never fails.

Bible Reading: Ephesians 2:12–18

Day 5

The love we have just discovered never fails. Ever! The Greek is again very descriptive for the word *fails*. It means "love never falls out of, one cannot lose it." *Agape* never falls from an upright to a prostrate position; it never decays and never loses its power.

Seriously, this is not the stuff of movies and magazines. Unfortunately, this kind of love is becoming hard to find. Be very assured, *agape* love exists. It is real, and we can experience it and give it.

We have learned that love is a conscious choice. It is not a flighty, breathless, fickle emotion that sweeps us off our feet in a whirlwind. True love is strong and purposeful and requires thoughtful effort to maintain. Because of that, we cannot fall out of love with our spouses, children, siblings, fellow believers, or God. And they cannot fall out of love with us. We can choose to selfishly disobey God and not cultivate our relationship with each other, but that is not love failing. That is you and I failing. If we loved as 1 Corinthians 13 tells us to, our relationships would survive anything.

Living in a family ripped apart by divorce, experiencing abandonment or rejection, or being hurt by betrayal can knock our feet right out from under us. The blow of having someone yank their love from us takes our breath away as we fight to get through each day. When I read that *fail* means "to descend from an upright to a prostrate position," I was amazed. Losing love brought people to their knees 2,000 years ago, just as it does today. Love is real, and having someone choose to turn away from it is devastating.

At first glance, *agape* love may not seem exciting or passionate. It's just a list of does and does not. But I would disagree. There is something very exciting about being loved so completely and unselfishly. And the challenge to love with *agape* is never dull. God's love for us never waivers and is always as it should be. When we blow it, when we lose our patience or speak unkindly, we can get a do-over. What love requires is open and honest communication.

God says this in 2 Chronicles 7:14-15: "[If] My people who are called by My name humble themselves and pray and seek My face and turn from their wicked ways, then I will hear from heaven, will forgive their sin and will heal their land. Now My eyes will be open and My ears attentive to the prayer *offered* in this place." When we mess up and stop living as if God loves us, when we don't love God with all our heart, soul, mind, and strength, we can have a do-over. It takes being humble enough to say, "I was wrong and I'm sorry." It means we change and start living and loving the way He does. When we talk honestly and openly with our Father, He promises that He will listen and forgive us. God says He will also open His eyes and pay attention to us; He will see, hear, and understand us. Besides forgiving us, our Lord will heal us. Do you know why? Because He loves us with *agape* love.

Bible Reading: 1 Corinthians 13

Day 6

It's important to understand that most of the Bible is written to God's children—people who put their faith in Him—to teach, reprove, train, and equip them (2 Tim. 3:16-17). The first four books of the New Testament, the Gospels, are for unbelievers so they may believe that Jesus is the Christ, the Son of God, and with believing may have life in His name (John 20:31).

Look at 1 Corinthians vertically first—from God in heaven to you and me. *Agape* love is given by God to His children. Everyone in the world is loved by God; however, we must meet His requirement before He gives the gift of a relationship with Him. The only way to live in the Father's love is to become His adopted child. In the Gospel of John, it says, "There was the true Light [Jesus] which, coming into the world, enlightens every man. He was in the world, and the world was made through Him, and the world did not know Him. He came to His own, and those who were His own did not receive Him. But as many as received Him, to them He gave the right to become children of God" (John 1:9-12).

That makes sense. We may invite acquaintances into our homes, but it would be foolish of them to expect to have their pictures hanging on our walls or to be in our will. If they became part of our family by marriage or adoption, then we would put their pictures in our homes and include them in our inheritance. Becoming part of God's family opens the door of His love for us and gives us the ability to understand *agape* and give it to others.

Now that we've taken care of the vertical—believing in Jesus as God and being filled with His Spirit and love—we can move on to the horizontal; that is, you and me loving those around us. Remember, 1 Corinthians 13 was written to believers in the church about loving other believers. We know from the context of the whole Bible that we are to respect and show honor to all people, and the truth is that most of us have nonbelievers in our families and lives.

The principles of *agape* for followers of Christ can be difficult because we are all human. All of us make selfish decisions that hurt others, and we are hurt by others too. For those of us who are new to our faith in Christ and have people in our lives who don't know Jesus, another layer of difficulty is added to living out *agape* love. God gives us His wisdom when we ask for it, and that will be a vital part of loving the unsafe people in our lives. Following Jesus's examples will also guide us as we realize that love does not require us to stay close to people who have no intention of loving God or us. We can show love from a distance. Jesus loved His family and the town where He grew up; however, His purpose was to follow His Father's plan for Him. So when Jesus went home during His ministry and was rejected, He left without doing much healing or teaching (Mark 6:1-6).

Love that never fails is strong and purposeful. *Agape* is how we treat others, talk about them, and feel toward them. God in us enables us to love on the hard and ugly days when the pain is fresh and the anger is simmering. That is why this was written to children of God. We are the only ones who have the Father's love flowing through our veins. We are the only people capable of *agape*. God's love is so appealing and captivating, and seeing it is an open invitation.

***Bible Reading*: Romans 5:1-6, Romans 8:35-39**

SPRING

INTRODUCTION

The air is still a bit frosty, and snow is sure to come for at least one more visit, but little sprigs of green assure us that change is around the corner. It's spring! It's the season of new life and fresh beauty.

Winter seemed to have killed and buried all that was comfortable and promising. Bleakness and harsh reality blanketed the world and individual lives for what seemed like forever. Yet eventually, through the frozen hearts and hardened exteriors, we glimpse a fresh hint of life. It had been germinating unseen, deep beneath the surface, growing new and strong.

Recovering from the consequences of our past mistakes takes us through a valley so low and so cold that we may feel as if giving up is our only option. Being caught in the whirlwind of another person's sins and failings is painful in its injustice and has the potential to harden our hearts and freeze our souls.

Yet the promise of springtime is always within our grasp. Just as our Creator permits His world to change and die in order to bring new life, He allows His children to do the same. All along, the Father, Son, and Holy Spirit's plan was for the Son to live out the ultimate display of springtime renewal and beauty.

Find your umbrellas, and join me as we expectantly wait for the bare trees to bud with new life. Even though some rain may fall, let's rejoice in the warm feeling of the sun on our faces and the soft breeze of change whispering through our hair. All was not lost to the freezing destruction of winter. Life will always rise up victoriously. Because of the promise of spring, we can shout with Paul, "O DEATH, WHERE IS YOUR VICTORY? O DEATH, WHERE IS YOUR STING?" (1 Cor. 15:55).

Look for a special Mother's Day and Father's Day reading at the end of spring.

Week 1

DAVID AND BATHSHEBA

Day 1

David is the only person in the Bible to be called a man after God's heart. Hundreds of years after David reigned as King of Israel, Luke wrote of David's loving and obedient heart for the Lord in Acts when the New Testament church was beginning. I want to establish this fact in our minds before we look at the darkest time in David's life. He had suffered hardship at the hands of King Saul, but this time in David's life was more devastating because it was caused by his own sin.

That is what sin does. It destroys the person who engages in it by instantly submerging them into darkness with a tunnel vision of only what is in the moment. Then slowly the results of sin eat away at us with shame and guilt. Those mindsets cause us to feel isolated and alone, and our world caves in until our only reality is our tormented conscience and fear of judgment.

David dragged some victims with him into this dark place. David took Bathsheba, the wife of one of his most loyal soldiers, without any concern of the consequences for her. Uriah, Bathsheba's husband, was betrayed and murdered. Servants and soldiers who knew the truth about David's actions were put in a difficult position of loyalty to a man who had behaved horribly. Family members heard the whispers and saw the results of David's sin, and the entire nation weakened as their leader sank into the depths of the consequences of poor choices.

The account of this time is devastating. We see very clearly that no one is immune to the lure of sin. And we also see that God will not ignore our sin, no matter who we are. It doesn't end there, however, because the

God of justice is also the God of mercy and grace. We will see in both David's and Bathsheba's lives that life can come from death, and beauty can rise from the ashes. Our heavenly Father usually does not take the natural consequences of our choices away, but He will give us the strength to endure them. He will discipline His children because He loves us, but He will also restore us to a close relationship with Him. In addition to all that, God offers us a chance to be productive and valuable again, even after we have rebelled and sinned in a grievous way or been the victim of another's sin.

As we read of this time in King David's and Bathsheba's lives, put yourself in their place. It would be so easy to be angry at the injustice or to be judgmental of all the weaknesses on display. These people were real people, just like you and me. We face the same choices they faced. Each moment of every day we must choose to live with integrity or to follow the pull of our selfish desires. Getting it right today does not ensure we'll choose right tomorrow. If you are living in the aftermath of someone else's or your own sinful choices, look to this story for the hope it offers. God is a forgiving and loving Father. He will restore you to Him and fill your life with joy and purpose once again. Through repentance and a willingness to forgive, each of us can be freed of the power of sin in our lives to live in victory and light.

Finally, I want us to read the words directly from the Bible as they were written. This story has been told many times without a thorough look at the Word of God. Let us humbly put our own ideas down and ask God to show us His truth. May the Holy Spirit guide us in our reading of God's Word.

Bible Reading: **2 Samuel 11, 2 Samuel 12:1-15**

Day 2

Looking back, we see that David had led many successful military campaigns. As a king, David was expanding his country's borders, adding land and wealth to his nation under God's leadership. The story picks up in 2 Samuel 11 the following spring when kings usually went back out to battle. But we see an aimless and restless leader who wasn't leading.

There are few things as difficult to handle as success. The challenge of overcoming the next obstacle has been conquered; people admire and glorify our every move. We start to believe everyone's praise while pride and arrogance creep slowly into our hearts. That plays out with athletes and celebrities today. Everyone is watching them, yet they feel as if their sins are invisible. Pride makes a person feel invincible and unaccountable. Arrogance demands they be noticed and that their bad choices be ignored.

When we allow arrogance and pride to settle in our minds, we push God out of our hearts. The victories were our victories, and the success was because of our abilities. We have all the answers and believe we are self-made. Combine this attitude with a lack of purpose and direction, and disaster will always follow.

> *Then it happened in the spring, at the time when kings go out to* battle, *that David sent Joab and his servants with him and all Israel, and they destroyed the sons of Ammon and besieged Rabbah. But David stayed at Jerusalem. Now when evening came David arose from his bed and walked around on the roof of the king's house, and from the roof he saw a woman bathing; and the woman was very beautiful in appearance.*
> —2 Sam. 11:1-2

David got up in the evening. When most people were going to bed David was getting up. He had been lying around during the day when he should have been working or governing, and he got up at night. He went out onto the flat roof of his palace, which was higher than all the other buildings in the city, and walked around. He looked into one of his neighbors' houses and saw a woman taking a bath. Though he should have turned away, he didn't and fed his senses with self-indulgence.

So many red flags are waving from these first two verses. We would be wise to heed their warnings. In Genesis 4:7, God told Cain, "If you do well, will not *your countenance* be lifted up? And if you do not do well, sin is crouching at the door; and its desire is for you, but you must master it." Peter gave us similar council. "Be of sober *spirit*, be on the alert. Your adversary, the devil, prowls around like a roaring lion, seeking someone to devour" (1 Pet. 5:8).

Let's wake up if we've become complacent and smug. All of us, like David, have had some incredibly hard times in our past. When life becomes easier and the stresses start to ease, it is still important to keep our eyes open to the dangers in our world. Satan is prowling around seeking someone to devour. But we are from God and have overcome because greater is He who is in us than he who is in the world. Turn your eyes back to Jesus; humbly ask for His wisdom, guidance, and protection. We don't have to fall. We can overcome temptation.

Bible Reading: 2 Corinthians 10:3-7, 1 Peter 5:6-11, 1 John 4:4

Day 3

David did not merely glance at the woman taking her bath; he looked at, observed, and considered her. He did not run from temptation; he moved closer to it and drank in the images as his imagination took over. So David sent someone to find out about her. The man said, "Is this not Bathsheba, the daughter of Eliam, the wife of Uriah the Hittite?" (2 Sam. 11:3).

Consider all the subtle ways God uses information and people to show us the truth and warn us that we are in a danger zone. David was informed that he desired a woman who was married, the wife and daughter of loyal men in his kingdom. Only the closest advisors had the right to tell the king what to do or not to do. However, the information supplied by this servant warned David clearly. But when we push our conscience down in order to focus on our physical wants and cravings, we don't hear or see anything that keeps us from our desires.

Ignoring the warning, David sent messengers and took her (2 Sam. 11:4). David was the king, and he sent more than one messenger to Bathsheba's house at a time when her husband, her protector, was gone, and they took her to him. That was abuse of power. Women did not have a voice at that time; they were considered assets and property of their fathers or husbands. Even more, it was the king who had sent for her. David thought he had kept all of this a secret (2 Samuel 12:12), but it stands to reason that he did not tell his messengers to tell her why she was being summoned. We have no way of knowing what the men sent to take Bathsheba told her, but we do know that refusing to go when the king sent for her was not an option.

Abuse of power is not limited to kings and subjects. Today, authority figures still abuse their power and position for their own gratification and profit. Parents, teachers, politicians, clergy, law enforcement, judges, bosses, and doctors have all made the news with disturbing tales of using their positions to pressure, intimidate, and persuade the people under their care.

Both men and women are in positions of power today, and we have seen that gender is not the cause of this offense.

Every part of life takes careful consideration and a daily commitment to integrity. Jesus lived a perfect example of leadership—sacrificial, loving, willing servant, just, and honest. He also gave us guidelines. In Exodus 18:21, Moses was told what to look for in a leader. Select capable men from all the people, men who fear God, trustworthy men who hate dishonest gain. First Peter 5:2–3 instructs the leaders in the church. Be shepherds of God's flock that is under your care, not serving as overseers because you must, but because you are willing, as God wants you to be; not greedy for money but eager to serve; not lording it over those entrusted to you but being examples to the flock.

Leaders from the home to the throne stand before God. Write His requirements for your position down, and check yourself every day. Abuse of power undermines the leader's authority and weakens the fabric of the entire community. And the person who is the direct victim will bear the scars for the rest of their lives. The more power a person gets, the more time they need to spend on their knees seeking God's integrity, humbleness, and wisdom.

Bible Reading: **Joshua 1:1–9, 2 Samuel 5:2, 2 Samuel 7:8**

Day 4

Bathsheba later found out she was pregnant and sent the message to King David. In an effort to cover up his sin, David sent a message to the battlefield to bring Uriah, Bathsheba's husband, home. I think we've all been there to some degree, faced with the ugly and scary results of our wrong choices and desperate to hide them from ourselves and others. When we've been immersed in self-indulgence, we even believe we can hide things from God.

Because David found it difficult to resist satisfying his sexual urges, he most likely assumed Uriah would too. David's plan was to have Uriah sleep with his wife so the world would think the baby was Uriah's. Again, we see a common misconception of a self-indulged, arrogant person. They think everyone feels and acts like they do. That's why they think it isn't wrong. They don't believe they are weak or sinful; they say they're just human.

When we turn our eyes from the light of God and walk into the darkness of sin, it is hard to see the people who are still walking in God's light.

Uriah, however, proved to be a man of integrity with deep personal convictions and self-discipline. Even after David got him drunk, he would not spend the night in his home with his wife while his fellow soldiers were sleeping outside on the battlefield. Finally, David sent Uriah back to war with a sealed message for the commander. The King of Israel had one of his loyal soldiers carry the orders. It was a death sentence for the man who would carry out the plan. Commander Joab had to employ unwise military strategy to ensure David's plan, that Uriah would be killed in battle. Other Israeli warriors were also killed in this setup. David's list of victims kept growing. The position he had placed his military commander in was inexcusable. It caused him to be complicit (a responsible participator) in the murder of many good soldiers. Joab's unsound military decision could have weakened his credibility with his men.

David's goal was to make his own life as enjoyable and pleasurable as possible. A few short hours of selfish indulgence unraveled the entire fabric of his life. The choices he made in his personal life affected him spiritually and professionally. David wrote a psalm to express the effects of his sin.

> *Your arrows have sunk deep into me, and Your hand has pressed down on me. There is no soundness in my flesh because of Your indignation; there is no health in my bones because of my sin. For my iniquities are gone over my head; as a heavy burden they weigh too much for me. My wounds grow foul* and *fester because of my folly. I am bent over and greatly bowed down; I go mourning all day long. For my loins are filled with burning, and there is no soundness in my flesh. I am benumbed and badly crushed; I groan because of the agitation of my heart.*
>
> —Ps. 38:2–8

Satan is a liar and deceives the whole world (Rev. 12:9). He tells us if it feels good, it must be right. He says follow your heart, and don't be judgmental—tolerate sin. Times are different now, he claims, and it's no one's business what you do with your life. You have to grab what you want with both hands.

At creation God saw that all He had made was very good, yet He tells us not to make gaining all the things of the world our goal. "But seek first His kingdom and His righteousness, and all these things will be added to you" (Matt. 6:33). Living God's way is lavishly good and satisfying. He wants us to experience all His blessings without any of sin's consequences.

Bible Reading: Psalm 38

Day 5

> *Then Joab sent and reported to David all the events of the war. He charged the messenger, saying, "When you have finished telling all the events of the war to the king, and if it happens that the king's wrath rises and he says to you, 'Why did you go so near to the city to fight? Did you not know that they would shoot from the wall? Who struck down Abimelech the son of Jerubbesheth? Did not a woman throw an upper millstone on him from the wall so that he died at Thebez? Why did you go so near the wall?'—then you shall say, 'Your servant Uriah the Hittite is dead also.'" So the messenger departed and came and reported to David all that Joab had sent him to tell. The messenger said to David, "The men prevailed against us and came out against us in the field, but we pressed them as far as the entrance of the gate. Moreover, the archers shot at your servants from the wall; so some of the king's servants are dead, and your servant Uriah the Hittite is also dead." Then David said to the messenger, "Thus you shall say to Joab, 'Do not let this thing displease you, for the sword devours one as well as another; make your battle against the city stronger and overthrow it'; and so encourage him."*
>
> —2 Sam. 11:18–25

That is a hard heart. David was a seasoned warrior who had always taken the loss of his men personally. Yet now that his only goal was to save his hide, he shrugged and nonchalantly said, "War's tough. No telling who'll get killed. Don't let it bother you."

Look at your heart. Have you ever lied, stolen something, or cheated in school? While we have probably not resorted to murder as a cover-up, our hearts have been just as cold and calculating as David's. We don't care who is hurt or what kind of misfortune has to occur to save us from ruin. We just want to get out of our predicament without any trouble.

God passed His judgment on the arrogant Babylonians in Isaiah 47:7–9:

> *Yet you said, "I will be a queen forever." These things you did not consider nor remember the outcome of them. Now, then, hear this, you sensual one, who dwells securely, who says in your heart, "I am, and there is no one besides me. I will not sit as a widow, nor know loss of children." But these two things will come on you suddenly in one day: loss of children and widowhood. They will come on you in full measure in spite of your many sorceries, in spite of the great power of your spells.*

It is not just the powerful who believe they can cover up and get away with their bad choices. You and I do the same things. We shrug and think it was just a little thing we did—a white lie, looking at a magazine where adults displayed their bodies, copying homework just once. Those "little sins" work to callous our hearts and sealed the death sentence of our Lord Jesus Christ. Pay attention to the Bible's warnings. "Do not be deceived, God is not mocked; for whatever a man sows, this he will also reap. For the one who sows to his own flesh will from the flesh reap corruption, but the one who sows to the Spirit will from the Spirit reap eternal life" (Gal. 6:7–8).

We are told that the wages of sin are death, and they are—eternal death and hell for those who don't accept Christ's gift of salvation. Sin also brings the death of our reputation, our peace of mind, our joy, and our relationships. But the free gift of God is eternal life in Christ Jesus our Lord (Rom. 6:23). We do not have to stay in our place of self-deceiving sin. Our heavenly Father loves us and has provided a way out for us. Remember, the only person we are fooling is ourselves. Other people see the truth about us, and God cannot be fooled, so let's stop trying to save face and confess our sins. God has promised that He will forgive us.

***Bible Reading*: Romans 6:8–13, 1 John 1:6–10**

Day 6

We may think David's fall into sin began that spring when he stopped leading and became aimless and lazy. Perhaps it began that spring evening when he stared at the woman taking her bath. Nathan got to the root of the problem when he asked David, "Why have you despised the word of the LORD by doing evil in His sight?" (2 Sam. 12:9).

In God's opinion, King David despised His Word. David held the Lord's commands in contempt, which he showed by the way he lived. Deuteronomy 17:14–20 explains God's clear instructions for Israel's kings.

> *When you enter the land which the LORD your God gives you, and you possess it and live in it, and you say, "I will set a king over me like all the nations who are around me,"* you shall surely set a king over you whom the LORD your God chooses, one *from among your countrymen you shall set as king over yourselves; you may not put a foreigner over yourselves who is not your countryman. Moreover, he shall not multiply horses for himself, nor shall he cause the people to return to Egypt to multiply horses, since the LORD has said to you, "You shall never again return that way." He shall not multiply wives for himself, or else his heart will turn away; nor shall he greatly increase silver and gold for himself. Now it shall come about when he sits on the throne of his kingdom, he shall write for himself a copy of this law on a scroll in the presence of the Levitical priests. It shall be with him and he shall read it all the days of his life, that he may learn to fear the LORD his God, by* carefully observing all the words of this law and these statutes, *that his heart may not be lifted up above his countrymen and that he may not turn aside from the commandment, to the right or the left, so that he and his sons may continue long in his kingdom in the midst of Israel.*

All kings had scribes, secretaries, who wrote for them. Yet God told the king to write for himself a copy of the law and to do it in front of the priests. That accomplished a couple of things. Writing out the laws would help cement them in the writer's head. It would also give the king ownership of the laws. They would be in his handwriting, something he knew, participated in, and agreed to. Having the priests there gave the king accountability. He was not alone in his leadership but had godly men watching over him and watching out for him.

After personally handwriting God's laws, the king was to read them every day of his life. Leadership is not a haphazard activity. For the

David and Bathsheba

protection of the people and the king, God laid out precise instructions. Write the law, and then read it every day. Why? So the king's heart may not be lifted up above his countrymen and that he may not turn aside from the commandment.

When David saw a woman and took her, his heart was lifted above his countrymen. As king, he thought he could take whatever he wanted. He believed he was more important than other people, that his desires mattered more than their rights or needs.

We face the same sense of entitlement. With total disregard for others, we try to fulfill our desires for popularity, power, physical pleasure, and money. But we don't have to stay there. We can write out God's grace and instructions and read them every day. Our pastor, mentor, and friends can keep us accountable. It's our choice to either despise God's Word or live it.

***Bible Reading*: Psalm 119:1–19**

Week 2

DAVID AND BATHSHEBA

Day 1

Now when the wife of Uriah heard that Uriah, her husband, was dead, she mourned for her husband. When the *time* of mourning was over, David sent and brought her to his house and she became his wife; then she bore him a son. But the thing that David had done was evil in the sight of the Lord (2 Sam. 11:26–27). What exact "thing" of David's was evil in God's sight? Nathan tells David and us in 2 Samuel 12:1–9.

> *Then the* Lord *sent Nathan to David. And he came to him and said, "There were two men in one city, the one rich and the other poor. The rich man had a great many flocks and herds. But the poor man had nothing except one little ewe lamb which he bought and nourished; and it grew up together with him and his children. It would eat of his bread and drink of his cup and lie in his bosom, and was like a daughter to him. Now a traveler came to the rich man, and he was unwilling to take from his own flock or his own herd, to prepare for the wayfarer who had come to him; rather he took the poor man's ewe lamb and prepared it for the man who had come to him." Then David's anger burned greatly against the man, and he said to Nathan, "As the Lord lives, surely the man who has done this deserves to die. He must make restitution for the lamb fourfold, because he did this thing and had no compassion." Nathan*

David and Bathsheba

> then said to David, "You are the man! Thus says the Lord God of Israel, 'It is I who anointed you king over Israel and it is I who delivered you from the hand of Saul. I also gave you your master's house and your master's wives into your care, and I gave you the house of Israel and Judah; and if that had been too little, I would have added to you many more things like these! Why have you despised the word of the Lord by doing evil in His sight? You have struck down Uriah the Hittite with the sword, have taken his wife to be your wife, and have killed him with the sword of the sons of Ammon.'"

The entire incident of David with Bathsheba was evil in God's sight. From the words of Nathan, God says it was David who was wrong and guilty. Bathsheba is never condemned by God throughout the entire Bible. God has never spared the reputation of a person when they have sinned, whether they were the main focus of the story or a support player. Look at Lot's wife in Genesis 19, Potiphar's immoral wife in Genesis 39, the women in Samson's life in Judges, Queen Jezebel in 1 Kings, and Sapphira in the book of Acts.

In contrast, Bathsheba was portrayed as a little ewe lamb. Throughout the Bible, lambs are the picture of innocence. Nathan's God-given allegory said the rich man, who represented David, took the little lamb and used it for his own benefit. It's interesting that the story doesn't say the rich man killed the owner of the lamb, only that he killed the lamb. When a person is taken against their will sexually, a piece of who they are is destroyed. Paul tells us in 1 Corinthians 6:18 to flee immorality because every other sin that a man commits is outside the body, but the immoral man sins against his own body. While the victim of a sexual assault is not immoral and hasn't sinned, the principle that their body inside and out is broken remains true. No matter how poor a person is or how little power they have in their world, they own who they are. When someone by physical force or by abuse of power steals that, great damage is done. Bathsheba is a wonderful model of how to live with purpose and dignity after such degradation.

Bible Reading: **Isaiah 61, 2 Corinthians 1:2–4**

Day 2

From my studies at a young age until now, I have heard that Bathsheba took her bath on the roof and enticed David, that she should have said no and that she was a scheming woman after the throne. I heard that she pushed her son to be king and more. Yet reading the Word of God does not support any of that. In fact, we don't know what conversation took place between King David and Bathsheba, but we do know that God never condemned her for not thwarting the king's summons or sexual advances. Nor did God accuse Bathsheba of sensual misconduct and enticement. We read that David, not Bathsheba, was on the roof. And it was God's choice for Solomon, Bathsheba and David's son, to be the next king of Israel (1 Chron. 28:5, 29:1). When another son was going to usurp the throne, Nathan went to Bathsheba so they could remind David of his promise to make Solomon king. Again, Nathan, God's righteous prophet, supported this as God's will, and David said the Lord alone told him Solomon would be king.

The question is this: Why do people feel the need to blame the victim along with the person who committed the offence? One of the reasons is that we don't like to take responsibility for our sins. And if we feel there is any kind of similarity between us and the offender, it becomes natural for us to place some of the blame on the victim. We are uncomfortable with the idea that a person is completely responsible for controlling their behavior because that would make us responsible for the same.

This started at the first sin. After Adam and Eve ate the forbidden fruit, the blame game began. When God asked Adam if he'd eaten the fruit, Adam answered, "The woman whom You gave *to be* with me, she gave me from the tree, and I ate" (Gen. 3:12). He blamed God for giving him the woman and Eve for giving him the fruit. Adam said it was not his fault, that he was not responsible for his actions or lack of actions. God then asked Eve what she'd done, and she said, "The serpent deceived me, and I ate" (Gen. 3:13). Again, she said it was not her fault, that she was not entirely responsible. The serpent was.

In the Old Testament, God said this:

> *"The person who sins will die. The son will not bear the punishment for the father's iniquity, nor will the father bear the punishment for the son's iniquity; the righteousness of the righteous will be upon himself, and the wickedness of the*

wicked will be upon himself. But if the wicked man turns from all his sins which he has committed and observes all My statutes and practices justice and righteousness, he shall surely live; he shall not die. Therefore I will judge you, O house of Israel, each according to his conduct," declares the Lord God. "Repent and turn away from all your transgressions, so that iniquity may not become a stumbling block to you. Cast away from you all your transgressions which you have committed and make yourselves a new heart and a new spirit! For why will you die, O house of Israel? For I have no pleasure in the death of anyone who dies," declares the Lord God. "Therefore, repent and live."

—Ezek. 18:20–21, 30–32

No one should be blamed for another person's wrong choice. That is not justice, and it is not God's way. Nathan held David responsible for his choices and never condemned Bathsheba.

Bible Reading: 1 John 1:5–10

Day 3

Today we are going to look at Bathsheba's amazing life story. She was taken by her king in what was an abuse of power while her husband was away at war, and she became pregnant. In my estimation, it would have been a frightening thing and would have taken great courage for Bathsheba to inform the king of her pregnancy. Added to that, she could have been put to death if people believed she'd committed adultery. Next, Bathsheba's husband was killed in battle. The emotions swirling through her—fear, shame, grief, dirtiness, guilt, uncertainty, and anger—must have been tumultuous. After the allotted time of mourning, King David took her to be his wife, and if human nature was what it is today, the whispers and critical looks followed her throughout the palace.

The baby boy who was born to David and Bathsheba died while an infant. David went to Bathsheba, and they conceived another son, Solomon. The godly prophet Nathan trusted Bathsheba and found her to be a reliable and effective ally. He went to her first to ensure that Solomon was crowned the next king of Israel (1 Kings 1, 2). Solomon proved to be a man of great honor and wisdom who had a close relationship with his mother and with God. Many of David's other children were rebellious and disloyal, leading us to believe that Bathsheba was a mother who took her job seriously. Some of King David's wives had been mocking and contemptuous of him, yet at the end of his life, Bathsheba was treating him with genuine respect and loyalty.

Bathsheba doesn't show us how to be a good victim. She shows us how to be strong, dignified, honorable, forgiving, and productive, despite being a victim. Her life proves that being victimized does not have to make us victims. We have the power to shed that mindset and live victoriously. Physical and sexual abuse cracks something deep within our hearts and has the potential to kill our sense of worth and self-esteem. Know that this is one thing you have power over. No one can take what God made you to be. You are created in His image with a purpose for living that nothing can destroy. This healing is not easy or fast, but it is completely possible.

Jesus also showed us how to live through and handle victimization. I would add that He faced and still faces the same criticism most victims face. Why didn't He do something to stop it? Or maybe if He had done some things differently, none of this would have happened. When they hurled their insults at Christ Jesus, He did not retaliate. When He suffered, He made no threats. Instead, He entrusted Himself to God who judges justly . . . by His wounds you have been healed (1 Pet. 2:23–24). Jesus handled Himself with dignity when His clothes were stripped off and when He was beaten and mocked. People have the power to hurt our bodies and damage our emotions, but they don't have the power to touch our souls. Our dignity comes from who we are in God. We are created in God's image, and we are His masterpiece. Others may criticize and blame us as victims, but Romans 8:31, 33, and 37 say, "What then shall we say to these things? If God *is* for us, who *is* against us? Who will bring a charge against God's elect? God is the one who justifies. But in all these things we overwhelmingly conquer through Him who loved us."

We will never be the same after being victimized, but we can still be strong and graceful, valuable and useful, whole and healthy.

Bible Reading: Romans 8:26–39, 1 Peter 2:12–24

Day 4

Let's spend another day analyzing how Bathsheba was able to accept David as a constant in her life and live productively and fully after the blows she took. One of the greatest tools to facilitate freedom is forgiveness. Conversely, nothing imprisons and enslaves us more effectively than hatred and unforgiveness.

Corrie ten Boom, a Dutch woman who lived during World War II, hid Jews from the Nazis. Her family was arrested, and some were sent to concentration camps where her father and sister died. After the war, Corrie traveled throughout the world telling of God's work in her life and how He alone can heal and free the victims of hate, abuse, murder, and injustice. The Lord revealed to her the power of forgiveness. She has said that forgiveness is an act of the will, and the will can function regardless of the temperature of the heart. Usually, our minds will heal before our emotions. It will take our hearts time to soften from the fear and pain of victimization, but we can choose to let go of the consuming hatred and bitterness that follow such treatment.

Forgiveness is not releasing a person from their responsibility and accountability. It is letting go of their debt. We send the person's bill to God and let Him collect the debt, but we are free from the presence and reminders of that debt in our life. That is how Jesus was able to take the abuse of His trial and crucifixion. In 1 Peter 2, we see that Jesus *kept entrusting Himself to God who judges righteously.* The size of the debt and the power of the offenders were too big for Him to handle. So Jesus continually let go of their debt of guilt, abuse, and injustice and gave it to His Father in heaven.

Jesus taught us to pray in what we now call the Lord's Prayer. Part of it says, "And forgive us our debts, as we also have forgiven our debtors. For if you forgive others for their transgressions, your heavenly Father will also forgive you. But if you do not forgive others, then your Father will not forgive your transgressions" (Matt. 6:9, 14–15). Jesus says in Mark 11:25, "Whenever you stand praying, forgive, if you have anything against anyone, so that your Father who is in heaven will also forgive you your transgressions." Clearly, there is a part of forgiveness that has nothing to do with the other person. In these Scriptures, the offender is not required to repent or apologize. We are required to let go of our feelings about them and release their debt into God's hands. That is completely between God and us, to make our hearts right with our Father. We obey willingly and forgive like this to show that we recognize our debt that Jesus paid. Forgiveness means we must let go of all the notes of debt we hold on others. This forgiveness frees us, not our offender.

Repentance plays a role in the relationship we have with a person. Repenting means changing our mind and actions. This is not a quick "sorry." When we repent to God and ask for His forgiveness, it is life-changing. We turn from the darkness of sin and move into a restored relationship with God in His light. If an offender comes to us and truly repents and asks for forgiveness, we should forgive them as we are forgiven. Prayerfully we can then decide how to move into a new relationship with that person, as Bathsheba did with David.

The way to put our victimization behind us is to let it go into God's hands. We don't have to be defined as victims. We can live in such a way that people will see the strength and dignity of God in us instead of the damage of an evil person. You have the power to choose.

Bible Reading: Ezekiel 18:30–32, Matthew 6:9–15

Day 5

Turning our attention back to David, we see why God considered him a man after His own heart. Nathan told David the story of the little lamb and stated that David was the guilty man. Then David said to Nathan, "I have sinned against the LORD" (2 Sam. 12:13). That is truly amazing. He immediately took responsibility for his behavior. David could have killed the messenger, denied everything, or made excuses, but this man of God was miserable because of his sin. The mighty king humbled his heart before his Lord and repented of all his sins. He listened to what his punishment would be without asking for leniency and accepted God's judgments as just and reasonable. When God told David the baby would die, David humbly prayed and wept for his son to live (2 Sam. 12).

Let's pause here to understand that God was not cruel to the innocent baby. In no way was this baby guilty because of the circumstances of his conception. When he died, the baby went to be with the Lord, and David said, "While the child was *still* alive, I fasted and wept; for I said, 'Who knows, the LORD may be gracious to me, that the child may live.' But now he has died; why should I fast? Can I bring him back again? I will go to him, but he will not return to me" (2 Sam. 12:22-23). David knew that because of his faith he would go to be with the Lord when he died and see his baby there, but the baby would not be brought back to life here on earth.

David went on to lead his nation through peace and wartime according to God's will. There were occasions when he still sinned, but his daily desire was to live for the Lord. We read in 1 Chronicles 29:28, "Then he [David] died in a ripe old age, full of days, riches and honor; and his son Solomon reigned in his place."

Sin is destructive. Prolonged and progressively more heinous sins show hearts that are very dark and far from God. David's life has shown us that many people are hurt in the aftermath of such a storm of sinfulness. But his life also portrays a man who was willing to humble himself and repent. We have seen his brokenness turn to wholeness and his inadequacy change to effectiveness. God is willing to restore any heart that is repentant.

> *How blessed is he whose transgression is forgiven, whose sin is covered! How blessed is the man to whom the* Lord *does not impute iniquity, and in whose spirit there is no deceit! When I kept silent about my sin, my body wasted away through my groaning all day long. For day and night Your hand was heavy upon me; my vitality was drained away as with the fever heat of summer. Selah. I acknowledged my sin to You, and my iniquity I did not hide; I said, "I will confess my transgressions to the* Lord*"; and You forgave the guilt of my sin.*
> —Ps. 32:1-5

David spoke of his personal experience with sin and forgiveness at the beginning of Psalm 32. Then in the rest of the psalm, he put his life experience to good use by teaching others from his mistakes.

When you and I fall and choose to live in a wrong way, we, too, can experience God's cleansing forgiveness. We already know that if we confess our sins, "He is faithful and righteous to forgive us our sins and to cleanse us from all unrighteousness" (1 John 1:9). David proves to us that we can also be powerfully useful when we are humble enough to tell our story honestly for the glory of God and the benefit of others. Our Father blesses us even more by making us secure in relationships our sin damaged. He encourages us to stand with our heads up when others bring up our past but forgiven sins. "If anyone is in Christ, *he is* a new creature; the old things passed away; behold, new things have come" (2 Cor. 5:17).

Bible Reading: **Psalm 32, 2 Corinthians 5:14–21**

Day 6

David and Bathsheba have given us a look into two real people's lives. We've witnessed the fall of a great man and his ill treatment of many people in his kingdom. Bathsheba has shown us how to be dignified as she overcame the stigma of her victimization and her feelings for the man who took everything from her. Uriah lived and died with integrity. Even Nathan the prophet showed great courage as he boldly spoke the truth to the king.

I would submit to you that both David and Bathsheba are overcomers. Both their lives were open books to the kingdom where they lived and to us today. We all know it is incredibly hard to stand before people who know how badly we have behaved. David's sins left him vulnerable to others' attacks, yet he humbly admitted his actions and sought to teach others from his mistakes. Bathsheba lived as the mother of one of David's children, teaching the future king about God, loyalty, and life. She probably always faced whispered gossip about her character, as she indeed still does today. Yet through her pain, many can be healed.

We learn something about our God through their lives as well. Our Father is a God of second and third and sometimes 100 chances. He is a God who knows how frail we are and how hard it is to get life right. His desire is not to zap us when we get it wrong but for us to repent and choose life. God is a Father who will outline His discipline and tell us that He still loves us. Never whitewashing our sins, our Father is just and strong in His discipline. Yet He cleanses us and makes us pure again, as well as useful and prosperous. Our Father loves us through it all.

If we've been the victim of another's sin, God loves us and values us. He gives us the strength to move through the pain and anger to be whole again. Jesus said in Matthew 10:28–31, "Do not fear those who kill the body but are unable to kill the soul; but rather fear Him who is able to destroy both soul and body in hell. Are not two sparrows sold for a cent? And *yet* not one of them will fall to the ground apart from your Father. But the very hairs of your head are all numbered. So do not fear; you are more valuable than many sparrows."

Don't let being hurt by others be an excuse to sin. Refuse to stay a victim living in fear, anger, and bitterness, never leaving the control of the one who hurt you. Jesus told us not to fear a person who can only kill our body. Fear offending God instead since He has the power over our souls and bodies. Jesus means that instead of living focused on the bullies in life, focus on God and living in a way that pleases Him. He loves each of us so much that He knows how many hairs we have on our heads. Our Father has told us how to live a life of freedom and victory. Believe in Jesus, confess our sins, forgive others, be anxious for nothing, walk in the light of purity and honor. Remember, you can do all things through Him who strengthens you (Phil. 4:6–13).

Jesus told us, "The thief comes only to steal and kill and destroy; I came that they may have life, and have it abundantly" (John 10:10). Satan is the thief, and he tries to steal our identity and security when we've been the victim of abuse. His goal is to destroy our purpose in life by telling us we are too sinful or too broken to be useful. But the good news lived out in the lives of David and Bathsheba is that God is greater than Satan. And God's Son, Jesus, came so each of us could have abundant life—an abundantly rich, full, and prosperous life. Make no mistake—sin brings death to the sinner and the victims, but there is life after death in Christ Jesus . . . abundant life.

Bible Reading: **Psalm 51, Ephesians 3:13–21**

Week 3

JOB

Day 1

The book of Job, pronounced *Jōb*, is the Old Testament story of a non-Jewish man who was blameless and upright, fearing God and turning away from evil. What a gift God has given us, showing even in the Old Testament that although Israel was His chosen people, a person from any nationality could believe in God and please Him with their lives.

Job's story is a difficult one to embrace because he was a man of integrity and influence, yet God allowed Satan to afflict him and his family. The thought that our loving and good God allows disaster to strike His children when they are doing everything right is tough. In our minds, that's not fair. It is definitely not good. We support the idea of punishing bad behavior and rewarding good. God does do that. But let's remember that He is God—we're not. For us to expect the almighty God to only respond to our actions and motives would be putting us in control. Our behavior would dictate God's behavior.

God is the One who is God, the One in control. One truth we will learn through Job's life is that we should respond to God, not only to His blessings but also to what we know to be true about Him in any circumstance. When God blesses us and gives us love, security, and wealth, He shows His goodness and unearned favor to us. When God allows pain and injustice in our lives, He also shows His goodness and undeserved favor to us. You see, there are things going on behind the scenes that we don't know about. When we are God's children, we are under His protection, and He puts restrictions on the harm Satan can do to us.

The depths of Satan's wickedness and disgusting evil are beyond our imaginations. But our Father will not allow the devil to unleash all the powers of hell on us. So while the attacks we go through can be horrendous and make us wish we were dead, make no mistake, things could be worse. It is because of God's goodness and love that He does not leave us unprotected.

Many things are revealed in Job's life story. We will learn much about ourselves, and we will learn many things about God. As we've talked about before, God cares about our physical well-being, but to our Father, the most important part of us is our soul. James 1:2-3 tells us, "Consider it all joy, my brethren, when you encounter various trials, knowing that the testing of your faith produces endurance." Paul said, "But we also exult in our tribulations, knowing that tribulation brings about perseverance; and perseverance, proven character, and proven character, hope; and hope does not disappoint, because the love of God has been poured out within our hearts through the Holy Spirit who was given to us" (Rom. 5:3-5).

Every person—believers and nonbelievers—will go through trials and hardships to various degrees in life. Satan is evil and mean and wants to destroy us all. The difference for the child of God is that the garbage and misery Satan throws at us is used by God to strengthen us and refine us. "*We are* afflicted in every way, but not crushed; perplexed, but not despairing; persecuted, but not forsaken; struck down, but not destroyed. Therefore, we do not lose heart, but though our outer man is decaying, yet our inner man is being renewed day by day. For momentary, light affliction is producing for us an eternal weight of glory far beyond all comparison, while we look not at the things which are seen, but at the things which are not seen; for the things which are seen are temporal, but the things which are not seen are eternal" (2 Cor. 4:8-9, 16-18).

Bible Reading: Job 1

Day 2

God has given us a divinely inspired look into some of the activities in the spiritual world. "Now there was a day when the sons of God [angels] came to present themselves before the Lord, and Satan also came among them. The Lord said to Satan, 'From where do you come?'" Then Satan answered the Lord and said, "'From roaming about on the earth and walking around on it'" (Job 1:6-7).

Angels are accountable to God; they don't merely float on clouds playing harps. They have specific missions. Satan is a fallen angel. He is very powerful, but we see that even he is under God. When God asks the devil a question, the devil answers. When God puts restrictions on Satan's activities, he has to obey. Because Satan can't compete with God power-against-power, he is bent on obstructing God's relationship with humans. Using temptation, he tries to alienate people from God. With accusations, Satan attempts to alienate God from people.

Satan's accusation against Job was that his righteousness was self-serving because it paid for him to be good. Look at all God had given him. Job was good because God bribed him, Satan claimed. This tactic of calling good evil is still used today. The words and actions of Christ-followers are twisted, and our godliness is called wicked. It is Satan's classic challenge to God. If he can show that the godliness of righteous people is terrible sin, then there is a canyon of separation between God and man that should never be bridged. Satan is trying to say that even when we get it right, we get it wrong. He tells us there is nothing about us that is worth saving—that we're lost causes.

Since the accusation was spoken and wouldn't disappear, God determined to set the record straight and allowed Satan to take away what God had given Job—within certain boundaries. In one day, Job lost all his possessions, his livelihood, his children, and his grandchildren. Put yourself in Job's and his wife's place. To lose our business would be distressing; to lose everything we owned would be shocking; to know our employees had been killed on duty would be appalling; but to find out all our children and grandchildren had died would be devastating. Put all those events together in one day, and the trauma is unspeakable. In anguish, Job tore his robe, shaved his head, fell to the ground, and . . . worshiped? How could he do that?

Job had a mature perspective and saw God and himself honestly. He said, "Naked I came from my mother's womb, and naked I shall return there. The LORD gave and the LORD has taken away. Blessed be the name of the LORD" (Job 1:21). Job did not have a feeling of entitlement; God did not owe him a certain level of comfort or success. Job realized he had been born helpless and with nothing and that God had given him all he had. It is true that Job worked hard and was wise with his business, but he understood that he was not a self-made man. The Lord gave him his success and family, and the sovereign Lord had the right to take them away. Through all this, Job did not sin or blame God (Job 1:22).

Here is the truth. Our contentment and security cannot be in the people we have in our lives or the things we own. All that is temporary. God's love, security, and peace withstand the fires of pain and trouble, and they last forever. When we have our minds and hearts grounded in God, we can make it through great success and immense hardships.

Bible Reading: **Philippians 4:11–13, 1 Timothy 6:6–19**

Day 3

Consider the effect of these tragedies on Job's wife. This was a woman who had lost everything just as her husband had. She was barely hanging on to her composure, and then her husband broke out in boils. Satan's next attack was to cause boils to cover Job's body, and the pain was beyond words. Job would have looked horrible, and watching the strong man she loved groan and writhe in pain caused her to snap. I would caution us not to judge her too harshly for her words until we've spent a day in her shoes.

Then his wife said to Job, "Do you still hold fast your integrity? Curse God and die!" (Job 2:9). Those are the words of a woman who felt she had reached the end of the pain she could withstand. Not understanding why everything was happening, she just wanted it to end. So in desperation she told Job to give up, cry "uncle," tap out . . . surely they had reached the end and couldn't take anymore. She just wanted it all to go away.

Job's response is breathtaking. Picture him as he speaks. His head is shaved, and his clothes are torn from ripping them in grief. The pain of the boils covering his body is burning and fierce, yet it doesn't compare to the pain in his heart as he envisions his children's and grandchildren's deaths and the utter destruction of his servants and belongings. When Job looks at his wife, the woman he is supposed to protect and provide for, the anguish and sorrow on her face stabs his heart. Through that haze of grief and pain, Job says, "'You speak as one of the foolish women speaks. Shall we indeed accept good from God and not accept adversity?' In all this Job did not sin with his lips" (Job 2:10).

This is a question each of us will have to answer at some point in our lives. Is God really the Supreme Being in our life . . . or are we? Do we believe God is doing good work when He gives us our own way and we're comfortable? When the bad times come—family rejection, death, injustices, loss of a job, divorce, car accident, disease—is God still doing a good job? Thinking about this could be life-changing. If we believe God's responsibility is to answer yes to all our requests, we've reduced Him to a genie in a bottle fulfilling our wishes and then disappearing until we call on Him again. We've made ourselves god and God our servant.

Job saw God as sovereign, superior in every way. This man understood that God knew things he didn't know, saw into the future, and viewed the whole big picture of Job's life and everyone else's. Job had trusted the Lord when life was wonderful, and he chose to trust Him when it was terrible. Did he like what was happening in his life? Not at all. Did he understand what was happening and why? No. But Job did understand that God had a right to act like God. God had given Job more blessings than he ever thought possible, and God had the right to give him hardship. In Job's life, God was on the throne. Through peace or suffering, God reigned supreme.

> *Do you not know? Have you not heard? The Everlasting God, the* LORD, *the Creator of the ends of the earth does not become weary or tired. His understanding is inscrutable. He gives strength to the weary, and to* him *who lacks might He increases power. Though youths grow weary and tired, and vigorous young men stumble badly, yet those who wait for the* LORD *will gain new strength; they will mount up* with *wings like eagles, they will run and not get tired, they will walk and not become weary.*
>
> —Isa. 40:28–31

Give God your pain. Trust His leading.

Bible Reading: Job 2, Isaiah 40:18–31

Day 4

Job's grief eventually drove him into the pit of despair.

> *Let the day perish on which I was to be born, and the night which said, "A boy is conceived." May that day be darkness; let not God above care for it, nor light shine on it. As for that*

> *night, let darkness seize it; let it not rejoice among the days of the year; let it not come into the number of the months. Why did I not die at birth, come forth from the womb and expire? Why is light given to him who suffers, and life to the bitter of soul, who long for death, but there is none, and dig for it more than for hidden treasures, who rejoice greatly, and exult when they find the grave? For my groaning comes at the sight of my food, and my cries pour out like water. For what I fear comes upon me, and what I dread befalls me. I am not at ease, nor am I quiet, and I am not at rest, but turmoil comes.*
> —Job 3: 3–4, 6, 11, 20–22, 24–26

There are times of such desperation and deep sorrow in life that a person sinks into depression. They, like Job, wish they had never been born. We've all had days and even months when life sucked the joy and energy from us, when smiling took more effort than it was worth. Job reached an even deeper level of depression. None of the good years meant anything to him; their memory did not take away the grief he was experiencing. Job did not curse God; he only wanted to not be—to never have been born. At that point in his life, the pain far outweighed the joy, and every fear had become a reality.

These are the words of a desperate, suffering man. Any person going through divorce, the foster system, war, or a long-term disease knows some of that desperation. Great personal loss, injustice, or rejection propels us into hopelessness, and the downward, out-of-control spiral of fear and depression can sweep us off our feet.

One of the lessons of Job is this: when things go from bad to worse, the only thing that gives us a solid foundation on which to fall is knowing who and what God is. Life will kick our feet out from under us. Without God as the foundational rock, people are plunged into a bottomless pit that may swallow them whole. But sound knowledge of God and His Word saves us. When we fall in utter despair, we will hit the solid support of His truth and ride out the storm of life in safety. Jesus told a story to illustrate this point.

> *Therefore everyone who hears these words of Mine and acts on them, may be compared to a wise man who built his house on the rock. And the rain fell, and the floods came, and the winds blew and slammed against that house; and yet it did not fall, for*

it had been founded on the rock. Everyone who hears these words of Mine and does not act on them, will be like a foolish man who built his house on the sand. The rain fell, and the floods came, and the winds blew and slammed against that house; and it fell—and great was its fall.

—Matt. 7:24–27

Life may emotionally wipe us out. We may physically never be the same after tragedies we face. But we, like Job, can sink to our knees on the solid foundation of God's sovereign power. We can know that Jesus Christ has experienced what we are going through and that He talks to the Father on our behalf and tells His Holy Spirit to fill us with His strength and endurance. While wishing we were never born yet knowing we are in God's hands, we can pour out our pain to our Father. "Therefore, let us draw near with confidence to the throne of grace, so that we may receive mercy and find grace to help in time of need" (Heb. 4:16).

Bible Reading: Psalm 18:1–6, 28–36, Hebrews 4:15–16

Day 5

Friends came to visit Job when they heard of his troubles. One of the most necessary and special gifts God has given us is friendship. When it's done right, friendship can be the source of great encouragement, quiet rest, accountability, and shared tears and laughter. Job's three friends started well as they wept and grieved quietly with him, but soon their presence turned into his final trial. The haunting question of why God allows "senseless" tragedies to happen to people pushed these men to find an answer with which they could feel safe.

In Job 4–37, his friends took turns giving a total of nine arguments for why Job was suffering. The bottom line they offered to their friend was that he had sinned. First, they were sarcastic and a bit mocking, and then they begged Job to be honest and come clean. Even though these men had never known Job to be anything but upstanding and just, they accused him of specific wrongs. Finally, they acted miffed and sulked, saying Job should stop insulting them by refusing to confess what he'd done to deserve his punishment. Their argument, that God is just and therefore always blesses the righteous and causes the wicked to suffer, was to make them feel safe from enduring Job's hardships. They attacked his integrity and walked away feeling secure in their limited belief of how God operated. Like many of us, when we don't understand God, we put Him into a box we can understand and make the explanation simple—a matter of cause and effect. God always responds to our behavior—punishment or blessings. It couldn't possibly be that He was working out a greater purpose for now and eternity because that would be too hard to grasp. That would push us to admit God was bigger than we are and beyond our comprehension. So Job's friends comforted themselves instead of their friend.

Let's come away from this with a desire to be good friends, caring friends who are sensitive and know when to stay quiet and when and what to speak. Our goal should be to comfort a friend who is going through hardships and depression. David had two wonderful friends in his life—Jonathan and Nathan. Jonathan defended David's reputation when Jonathan's father tried to destroy it. He believed the best of his friend and protected him at risk to himself. Nathan was a friend who encouraged and guided David and, when necessary, truthfully kept him accountable for his life choices—good and bad. It's easy to second-guess and critique other people's performances after the fact when we have never experienced what they're going through. That is not the kind of friends we want, and that is not the kind of friends we should be.

Next, let's come away with the knowledge that God is beyond our understanding. Having all the answers is not possible and is not the key to our survival. Knowing that God is more knowledgeable and powerful than we are is where our security rests.

> *Then the* LORD *answered Job out of the whirlwind and said, "Who is this that darkens counsel by words without knowledge? Now gird up your loins like a man, and I will ask you, and you instruct Me! Where were you when I laid the foundation of the earth? Tell Me, if you have understanding, who set its measurements? Since you know. Or who stretched the line on it? On what were its bases sunk? Or who laid its cornerstone, Where is the way to the dwelling of light? And darkness, where is its place, that you may take it to its territory and that you may discern the paths to its home? You know, for you were born then, and the number of your days is great!"*
>
> —Job 38:1–6, 19–21

The Lord God is the One who created and upholds the universe. We can rest on the solid foundation that God is good and just, all-powerful and all-knowing. Wait for His plan to finish. Trust Him.

Bible Reading: Job 38

Day 6

Our first week in Job has taught us that while we don't know God's plans for us ahead of time, He does. We need to have a firm grasp of God's Word and know beyond a shadow of a doubt who God is. That foundation is what will help us stand strong. It will hold us when we fall into the pit of despair and depression after a prolonged period of pain and trouble. Being that grounded in the Lord also enables us to be people of integrity during life's trials.

> *"For I know the plans that I have for you," declares the* Lord, *"plans for welfare and not for calamity to give you a future and a hope. Then you will call upon Me and come and pray to Me, and I will listen to you. You will seek Me and find Me when you search for Me with all your heart. I will be found by you," declares the* Lord, *"and I will restore your fortunes and will gather you from all the nations and from all the places where I have driven you," declares the* Lord, *"and I will bring you back to the place from where I sent you into exile."*
>
> —Jer. 29:11–14

We may feel as if we've reached a dead end, that our life is ending in a horribly painful time, but God's plans will work out for our well-being. We most definitely have a future and a hope. God has promised, and He is faithful. We must remember our lesson learned in autumn. At times God delivers us *from* the fire, God sometimes delivers us *through* the fire, and there are times when God delivers us *by* the fire into His arms in heaven. We don't know how He is going to save us while we're living our difficult life, but we do know He will save us.

God has shown us that we should rejoice in our sufferings because we know that suffering produces "perseverance; and perseverance, proven character; and proven character, hope; and hope does not disappoint, because the love of God has been poured out within our hearts through the Holy Spirit who was given to us" (Rom. 5:3–5). Rejoice when we have Job-like lives because we are mature enough to know that God's up to something. He's working out His perfect plan in us. With joy through our tears we persevere. We keep going with integrity and strength, and that establishes strong character in us, which gives us hope. That expectation of God's good plan does not disappoint us because the lavishly, abundantly, poured-out love of God overflows our hearts through the Holy Spirit who is in us.

The lesson in friendship for Job was painful to watch. Caring and sensitive friends are a treasure. They know how to stay quiet and when to speak. Friends believe the best in us and comfort us, and when needed, they keep us accountable. We have seen how important it is to know God's Word so we can discern if we're receiving good or faulty advice. Job's friends showed us that well-meaning people don't always have the Lord's perspective. Speaking many truthful words about God, their knowledge was incomplete. Remember, His ways are unfathomable.

A thread woven throughout Job's story is that God is supreme and sovereign. Every knee will bow to Him in heaven and on earth. Satan answers to God and can only function within God's boundaries. God created the universe, the laws of science, and the math that keep the seas in their borders, the sunrise and sunset according to schedule, and the hawks flying. None of us can understand God's mind or grasp His plans—and all of that is reassuring. He is more than capable of taking us through life's hardships. God is in control and trustworthy.

Bible Reading: **Job 4:1–7, 6:24–30, 32:1–5, Isaiah 45:21–25**

Week 4

JOB

Day 1

There are times in our lives when we cannot hear God or see Him. We may read our Bibles, but nothing touches us or makes sense to us. When we pray, it feels as if our words bounce off the ceiling. Job experienced this. His suffering was so intense that he desperately cried out to God—and God was silent.

> *Oh that I knew where I might find Him, that I might come to His seat! I would present my case before Him and fill my mouth with arguments. I would learn the words which He would answer, and perceive what He would say to me. Behold, I go forward but He is not there, and backward, but I cannot perceive Him; when He acts on the left, I cannot behold Him; He turns on the right, I cannot see Him.*
>
> —Job 23:3–5, 8–9

With desperation Job searched for any sign of God, and all he got was silence. What should his response have been? How do we handle this?

Job remembered. He remembered that God is always with us, and He does see us. With certainty, Job said, "But He knows the way I take; *when* He has tried me, I shall come forth as gold" (Job 23:10).

Our challenge is this: when life is devastating, when God is silent, when we feel alone, we must choose to live for God. We must choose integrity because no matter what we feel and think we know, God is with us and watching over us. When at last we finally feel and hear and see God, we want to be able to say with Job, "You tested me, Father, and I came out like pure gold."

When we are confused and hurt and so very tired, that is the time to do the things we know to do. Put one foot in front of the other, and make sure our attitudes, words, and actions stay in tune with what's right—no bitterness, no cursing God, no retaliation, no sustained temper tantrums. There are days when the basics are our goal. Remember to eat and clean up; remember to talk to God, to trust Him for the next thing; remember that the people around us are hurting too; remember to count to 10 before we respond to them; remember that God looks at our heart and that He understands how difficult life is; remember that God loves us and is right next to us, protecting and guiding us. Remember that God loved you enough to send His Son, Jesus, to die for your sins. Remember that this pain will eventually end, and we will live with God in heaven forever.

You and I want to be able to say with confidence, "My foot has held fast to His path; I have kept His way and not turned aside. I have not departed from the command of His lips; I have treasured the words of His mouth more than my necessary food" (Job 23:11–12).

We've discovered that sometimes people around us may accuse us wrongly; they may not recognize that we are doing it right. But when we look at our thoughts, motives, and actions and know they line up with God's Word, then like Job we can be certain our walk is pure gold. Part of the growing-up process is being secure in what we know is true, even when those around us don't recognize it. Job didn't need his friend's stamp of approval. It would have been nice, but when he didn't get it, he didn't crumble. We can't control other people; we can't control much of our circumstances. We can control how we live and think and sometimes how we feel. We can choose to live for God in the good times and in the bad times, when we feel His presence and when we feel empty and alone. We can remember what we know to be true about God.

Bible Reading: Job 23, Psalm 66:8–15

Day 2

Let's recall what Job had been through.

> *Now on the day when his sons and his daughters were eating and drinking wine in their oldest brother's house, a messenger came to Job and said, "The oxen were plowing and the donkeys feeding*

> *beside them, and the Sabeans attacked and took them. They also slew the servants with the edge of the sword, and I alone have escaped to tell you." While he was still speaking, another also came and said, "The fire of God fell from heaven and burned up the sheep and the servants and consumed them, and I alone have escaped to tell you." While he was still speaking, another also came and said, "The Chaldeans formed three bands and made a raid on the camels and took them and slew the servants with the edge of the sword, and I alone have escaped to tell you." While he was still speaking, another also came and said, "Your sons and your daughters were eating and drinking wine in their oldest brother's house, and behold, a great wind came from across the wilderness and struck the four corners of the house, and it fell on the young people and they died, and I alone have escaped to tell you." Then Satan went out from the presence of the Lord and smote Job with sore boils from the sole of his foot to the crown of his head.*
>
> —Job 1:13–19, 2:7

Add to this Job's friends who accused and blamed him for the disaster that was now his life. Now sit for a moment in Job's boil-covered, heartbroken place.

What kind of pain are you sitting in right now . . . from your family situation, physical pain, injustices, unfair condemnation and blame, or betrayal? Job's friends assumed they knew the heart and mind of God and that God would not let terrible things happen to a "good" person, so Job started to question God. Running to God and telling Him we don't understand what's going on, crying out to our Father in our pain and anger and sorrow is what a Daddy is for. But if we cross the line and accuse God of not being fair, if we question His motives and demand that He explain Himself to us so we can determine if we agree with what He's done and why, our Father becomes angry. The reason for this anger is simple. We are turning the tables on God by making ourselves the most powerful and knowledgeable one, telling God He must answer to us. So God, the Creator of the universe, asked Job (and you and me), "Have you ever given orders to the morning or shown the dawn its place that it might take the earth by the edges and shake the wicked out of it? Have you journeyed to the springs of the sea or walked in the recesses of the deep? Have the gates of death been shown to you? Have you seen the gates of the shadow of death? Have you comprehended the vast expanses of the earth? Tell me, if you know all this. What is the way to the abode of light? And where does darkness reside?" (see Job 38).

Job's answer began the healing of his heart and life. "I know that You can do all things, and that no purpose of Yours can be thwarted" (Job 42:2). We can shake our heads to clear our thoughts and know the same thing there is *nothing—no thing—*that God cannot do. Jesus said in Luke 18:27, "The things that are impossible with people are possible with God." Elizabeth told Mary, Jesus's mother, in Luke 1:37, "For nothing will be impossible with God."

The way to survive your nightmare, the long month-after-month, sometimes year-after-year, heartbreak of injustice and pain is to recognize that God is omnipotent. He is all-powerful. Nothing is too hard for Him. Satan may have his way for a time, but God is still on the throne. He sees you and has a plan for you and the world around you for now into eternity. We must not allow ourselves or our enemies to take God's place in our lives. Know that God can do all things and that no plan of His can be thwarted. We're safe in the hands of the most powerful Lord God.

Bible Reading: Job 42:1–6, Jeremiah 32:17–27

Day 3

The first point Job said he knew about God was that God could do all things. In the same breath, Job also realized that no plan of God's could be thwarted. You and I need to get that. The devil does not have the power to cut off God's plans. There is no government, no situation, no person who is capable of fencing in or stopping God's plans.

Standing in your shoes right now may look as if God has disappeared, as if your world is full of chaos and God's plan has been thrown out the door. Pause, and ask God to give you His perspective. We are in the middle of a big picture being painted. Nothing makes sense, some things are incomplete, it's ugly, and the colors seem all wrong. Ask the Father to help you remember that His plan is good and perfect and working out in this very moment. Know that God can do all things and that no plan of His can be thwarted.

God had asked Job, "Who is this that hides counsel without knowledge?" Job answered, "Therefore I have declared that which I did not understand, things too wonderful for me, which I did not know" (Job 42:3). This is one of the core messages of the book of Job. God's plans, God's thoughts, God's feelings, and God's actions are beyond our understanding.

David said, "How great are Your works, O Lord! Your thoughts are very deep" (Ps. 92:5). Isaiah 55:8–9 confirms that: "'For My thoughts are not your thoughts, nor are your ways My ways,' declares the Lord. 'For *as* the heavens are higher than the earth, so are My ways higher than your ways and My thoughts than your thoughts.'"

God did not reveal His plan or the reason the plan was working out the way it was. In the middle of Job's loss and heartache, loneliness and anger, pain and suffering, God revealed Himself. Listen to that again. God doesn't always reveal His plan behind our pain, but He reveals Himself. Job did not see all the answers, but Job did see God.

So Job told God, "I have heard of You by the hearing of the ear; but now my eye sees You" (Job 42:5). We can know things intellectually. Our minds can receive the knowledge that God is all-powerful, and we can agree with that. But until we have experienced God's power holding us up in the middle of a raging storm, we have not seen His power personally. You and I can look at the world around us and think it's amazing how it all works, but that thought process will not keep us from sinking into depression or falling into sin when life gets rough. The only thing that keeps our hearts and minds sane and functioning when the bottom drops out of our world is experiencing God personally.

That's the reason we have the gift of Job's life story. God wants us to know that even if He told us all that was going on, we wouldn't be able to get it. Our Father wants us to realize that He doesn't have to explain Himself to us because He's God; He knows more than we do and can handle more than we can. Having the answers for today's struggle will not give us the answers for tomorrow's. However, seeing and personally experiencing who God is and how He works will take us through each and any hardship life throws at us.

God has shown you some part of Himself through your hardships. Have you taken the time to look at Him? What part of the Creator has been revealed to you? Don't take this new knowledge for granted. Build on this to become stronger and wiser. You have been hearing about God with your ears, but what have you seen with your eyes? Open them, and take Him in.

Bible Reading: Job 42:1–6, Ephesians 1:15–23

Day 4

After the Lord talked to Job, He said this to Eliphaz the Temanite:

> *"My wrath is kindled against you and against your two friends, because you have not spoken of Me what is right as My servant Job has. Now therefore, take for yourselves seven bulls and seven rams, and go to My servant Job, and offer up a burnt offering for yourselves, and My servant Job will pray for you. For I will accept him so that I may not do with you according to your folly, because you have not spoken of Me what is right, as My servant Job has." So Eliphaz the Temanite and Bildad the Shuhite and Zophar the Naamathite went and did as the LORD told them; and the LORD accepted Job.*
>
> —Job 42:7–9

At this point, Job had finally heard from God, but he was still physically sick with no possessions, livelihood, or children. Slowly God was restoring order to his life. First, God gave Job the sound of His voice and the knowledge of His presence. Next, God defended Job's honor to his friends. Along with the Lord's defense of Job and anger at his unjust friends, God required an astounding thing. He wanted Job to pray for his friends—the friends who had accused him, who said Job deserved his hardships because he had sinned. They were the friends who had mocked and condemned him and then had to humble themselves and apologize in front of Job. But Job had to ask God to forgive them.

Could you do that? God asks the same thing of us. When our friends or family members come to us to apologize and humbly tell us they were wrong, God wants us to forgive them. In an open and tangible way, we are to prove that we forgive them by praying for them to be forgiven and restored to God.

The fifth chapter of James explains to us that we must be patient for God's timing and plan to show themselves, and we must be patient with other believers who are struggling.

> *You too be patient; strengthen your hearts, for the coming of the Lord is near. Do not complain, brethren, against one another, so that you yourselves may not be judged; behold, the Judge is*

standing right at the door. As an example, brethren, of suffering and patience, take the prophets who spoke in the name of the Lord. We count those blessed who endured. You have heard of the endurance of Job and have seen the outcome of the Lord's dealings, that the Lord is full of compassion and is merciful. Therefore, confess your sins to one another, and pray for one another so that you may be healed. The effective prayer of a righteous man can accomplish much.

—James 5:8–11, 16

Part of our healing process is stepping outside of ourselves, outside of our hurt feelings and justified anger, and taking up the cause of a weaker believer. That's an enormous task when that weaker person is the one who has hurt us. Yet at no other time will we look more like Jesus. He carried your sins in His perfect heart on the cross. Because of my sins, He was beaten and nailed to that cross. While hanging on the cross, Jesus prayed to the Father and said, "Father, forgive them; for they do not know what they are doing" (Luke 23:34).

Job shows us that God does not remain silent forever. At just the right moment, He speaks to us and reveals more of Himself. Our Father is also our Defender, and He will set our accusers straight. And this God who knows us so well, who sees that our lives are like gold, will expect much of us. He will expect us to forgive as we are forgiven and to pray for those who've hurt us. Our Lord will hear and accept our prayers. Be ready to finish like Job.

Bible Reading: **Job 42:1–9, Matthew 5:43–48**

Day 5

The Lord restored the fortunes of Job when he prayed for his friends, and the Lord increased all that Job had twofold. Then all his brothers and all his sisters and all who had known him before came to him, and they ate bread with him in his house; and they consoled him and comforted him for all the adversities that the Lord had brought on him. And each one gave him one piece of money, and each a ring of gold. The Lord blessed the latter days *of Job more than his beginning; and he had 14,000 sheep and 6,000 camels and 1,000 yoke of oxen and 1,000 female donkeys. He had seven sons and three daughters. He named the first Jemimah, and the second Keziah, and the third Keren-happuch. In all the land no women were found so fair as Job's daughters; and their father gave them inheritance among their brothers. After this, Job lived 140 years, and saw his sons and his grandsons, four generations. And Job died, an old man and full of days.*

—Job 42:10–17

This, my friends, is grace—unearned, undeserved favor, benefits, and pleasure. In Job chapter 3, Job cursed the day he was born. Yet God's response at the end of this ordeal was to give him twice as much as he had previously possessed. Every animal was doubled. Job had seven sons and three daughters that he would see again in glory, and God gave him seven sons and three daughters once again to raise and love on earth. We see that even Job's health was restored as he lived to an old age. All that Job had was twice blessed by God. The precious gifts God gave Job were far more than wealth.

Job chose to live with integrity. He did the hard thing and prayed for the friends who had hurt him, and God was well pleased. There were times in Job's life when his thoughts and words were not in line with God. What a wonderful thing to realize that we are not expected to be perfect. Our Father is a God of second and third chances. Job's humble and repentant heart allowed him to learn from his mistakes, and that pleased the Lord.

He has removed my brothers far from me, and my acquaintances are completely estranged from me. My relatives have failed, and my intimate friends have forgotten me. Those who live in my house and my maids consider me a stranger. I am a foreigner in their sight. I call to my servant, but he does not answer; I have to implore him with my mouth. My breath is offensive to my wife, and I am loathsome to my own brothers. Even young children despise me; I rise up and they speak against me. All my associates abhor me, and those I love have turned against me.

—Job 19:13–19

God can repair and rebuild relationships. We may be completely abandoned by people for a time, but Job shows us that with God's grace, our family and friends can be restored to us. Not only will they come back to us, but we will be glad to be reconnected with them. Job's heart had been prepared for this reconciliation when God required him to pray for his friends. The same will hold true for us. When we forgive and pray for the people in our lives, God will flood us with an unbelievable amount of love and support.

Above all, Job received a new and intimate knowledge of the Creator of the universe. God revealed Himself to be all-powerful, all-knowing, far-sighted, and personally and thoroughly involved in Job's life. God showed that He was Job's defender, supporter, guardian, and protector. Joyfully Job could declare, "My ears had heard of You, but now my eyes have seen You."

Bible Reading: **Job 42**

Day 6

Reading the book of Job showed us some of the mind and purpose of God. We were given a rare glimpse into the work in heaven, the spiritual realm. Knowing that God is indeed sovereign and supreme, the absolute authority and Creator is important. It is a stabilizing truth that will keep our heads above water when others drown in the troubles and sorrows of life.

Who are we to criticize God and His timing? Can we even begin to imagine how all the world works separately yet together in perfect harmony? This is our assurance as well as our stumbling block. Pride and a desire to know tell us to demand answers from God. Our Father tells us we can't handle the truth, but He does want to reveal more of Himself to His children.

Job is like a miniseries on television. We have watched a portion of his life, and the drama and tragedy have alternately angered us, confused us, scared us, and brought us to tears. If the book of Job had stopped at chapter 41, we would have seen new things about God. Abundantly clear would have been the intricate mind of the Creator, the all-powerful force of His will, the ultimate authority that is God's, and the awesomeness of His abilities. But the Lord didn't end there. That is an incomplete picture of Him.

Herman Melville, the author of *Moby Dick*, wrote in a letter to his friend in 1851, "The reason the mass of men fear God, and *at bottom dislike* Him, is because they rather distrust His heart, and fancy Him all brain like a watch."[16] That is how we could feel if we didn't read the last chapter recorded in Job's saga.

Finally, our Father's heart was revealed, and it was stunningly forgiving, loving, and generous. Job said, "I have heard of You by the hearing of the ear; but now my eye sees You" (Job 42:5). The Master of the universe, the brain behind creation, showed Himself intimately to a mere man. God loves Job and you and me enough to make His mind, character, and heart visible to us. After revealing more of Himself, God confronted Job's friends and stood up for Job. That is love. God could have shrugged and brushed it off as unimportant, but He set the record straight. He was angry with the friends, but He still loved them. Showing even more of His heart, God told them how they could be forgiven. The Lord respected Job by making him the vehicle of their forgiveness. God showed His heart by pouring His grace on all the people involved in Job's life.

Finally, in a physical way, the Lord doubled all that had been taken from Job. The names Job gave his daughters reflect the extent of God's love and grace in his life. Jemimah means the light of day—God had brought Job into the light from deep darkness. Illustrating how fully sweet life was again, Job named one daughter Keziah, which means sweet cinnamon. Keren-happuch means eye cosmetic (like eye shadow). Her name would remind Job of the beautiful depth of God that he could see, as well as the Lord's gifts and grace that enhanced his life. Job shows us we should fear God with an awesome reverence, but there is no reason to distrust His heart. Our Lord cares in intimate detail about our lives. We cannot understand His ways or reasons, but we can know His love and will.

Bible Reading: **Psalm 27, Jeremiah 29:11–14**

Week 5

PETER

Day 1

Simon Peter is an apostle we all recognize. He was a man who experienced higher heights than most believers because of his willingness to risk all for the sake of his faith and his love of Jesus. Peter was also a man who experienced the deepest pit of fear, shame, and guilt because of his unwillingness to risk all for the sake of Christ. Through forgiveness, he was able to rise from his dark shame into victory again. Look with me at this fisherman whose encounter with the Son of God empowered him to impact many people in his time and even to this day.

In the first century AD, Hebrew children up to five years old were taught the Scriptures in their homes according to the charge of Deuteronomy 6:5-9. Boys and girls ages five through 10 attended primary school called Bet Sefer, or Bet Heder, which means "house of the book." Educating Hebrew children about God and their heritage was very important, so all Jewish children, regardless of family income and status, went to Bet Sefer. There, the boys and girls learned to read and write. Depending on their school, they either memorized the first five books of the Old Testament or learned Leviticus, which teaches about ritual purity and how to approach God by sacrifice. Some Bet Sefer schools focused on the Psalms and the nature of God.

After 10 years of age, most boys left school to learn their family's business, and all girls left to learn to keep a home. The boys who showed promise in their learning went on to Bet Midrash, or Bet Talmud, the house of interpretation or learning. Boys ages 13 to 18 learned the oral laws and the books of the judges and the prophets. By 18, the young men were expected to marry and carry on their family business, except for a few who felt God calling them to be rabbis (teachers). Those young men found a rabbi with whose teachings they most closely agreed and asked to follow and work with him until they became rabbis at around 30 years of age.[17]

Most of the apostles fell into the group who stopped their schooling at the age of 10, which is equivalent to our fourth or fifth grade. Simon Peter grew up as a fisherman with a heart that yearned for the Lord. Let's join him in his search for truth.

> *The next day John was standing with two of his disciples, and he looked at Jesus as He walked, and said, "Behold, the Lamb of God!" The two disciples heard him speak, and they followed Jesus. And Jesus turned and saw them following, and said to them, "What do you seek?" They said to Him, "Rabbi (which translated means Teacher), where are You staying?" He said to them, "Come, and you will see." So they came and saw where He was staying; and they stayed with Him that day, for it was about the tenth hour. One of the two who heard John speak and followed Him, was Andrew, Simon Peter's brother. He found first his own brother Simon and said to him, "We have found the Messiah" (which translated means Christ). He brought him to Jesus. Jesus looked at him and said, "You are Simon the son of John; you shall be called Cephas" (which is translated Peter).*
>
> —John 1:35–42

Jesus is asking each of us, "What do you seek?" If it is just feel-good religion we want, Jesus is not the Rabbi for us. Peter had learned the truths of God's Word, and he wanted to experience walking with the Son of God. Real knowledge, authentic faith, and knowing God's love for you results in a willingness to take risks and follow Jesus. If we are honestly and sincerely seeking God, He will reveal Himself and empower us, like Peter, to impact lives for eternity.

Bible Reading: John 1:12–51

Day 2

Now it happened that while the crowd was pressing around Him and listening to the word of God, He was standing by the lake of Gennesaret; and He saw two boats lying at the edge of the lake; but the fishermen had gotten out of them and were washing their nets. And He got into one of the boats, which was Simon's, and asked him to put out a little way from the land. And He sat down and began teaching the people from the boat. When He had finished speaking, He said to Simon, "Put out into the deep water and let down your nets for a catch." Simon answered and said, "Master, we worked hard all night and caught nothing, but I will do as You say and let down the nets." When they had done this, they enclosed a great quantity of fish, and their nets began to break; so they signaled to their partners in the other boat for them to come and help them. And they came and filled both of the boats, so that they began to sink. But when Simon Peter saw that, he fell down at Jesus' feet, saying, "Go away from me Lord, for I am a sinful man!" For amazement had seized him and all his companions because of the catch of fish which they had taken; and so also were James and John, sons of Zebedee, who were partners with Simon. And Jesus said to Simon, "Do not fear, from now on you will be catching men." When they had brought their boats to land, they left everything and followed Him.

—Luke 5:1-11

We see into the heart of Simon Peter here. A generous man, he was willing to have his schedule and work interrupted by Jesus and willing to share his possessions. Fishermen generally fished at night, casting out and hauling in heavy nets weighted down with water and, hopefully, fish. These men were probably tired and frustrated from not catching any fish that past night. Yet when Jesus asked to use Peter's boat as a means to teach the crowd, Peter immediately stopped his work and rowed Jesus out from the shore.

Peter's faith and loyalty were not taken lightly. The Son of God, the Messiah, was the most important thing in his life, and he proved it by complying with Jesus's requests without expecting anything in return. Calling Jesus "Master," Peter used a word that meant boss or leader. Simon

Peter was not just offering lip service to God; he was offering all of himself—his time, his energy, his trust, his loyalty, his willingness to change his business practice when Jesus told him to, his control, his pride. He didn't try to keep some parts of his life as personal and some parts as business, and only his emotions as religious. Meeting Jesus caused Peter to hand over every part of himself to the Master of the universe. That attitude resulted in a fisherman with a fifth-grade education successfully teaching and leading men and women for more than 2,000 years by means of his life experiences with Christ and his inspired writings.

Notice that Jesus's grace and great blessing came before Peter humbled himself, left his business, and followed Jesus. Romans 2:4 tells us that the kindness of God leads us to repentance. The gift of overflowing fish led Peter to see himself honestly, as a person who sinned, and to see Jesus as holy. Jesus wanted more than Peter's works. His blessing caused Peter to give his heart.

That is the heart God wants in you and in me. He wants us to see the truth of who He is and who we are. The Lord wants us to receive His love and willingly love Him and follow Him, trusting Him when things look a little different from how we usually operate. God wants all of us to realize that when we humble ourselves, He will exalt us. He will take a fisherman, a student, a child, a parent, a doctor, a pastor, a reporter, or a gardener and enable them to change lives with the knowledge and power of the living God.

Bible Reading: Matthew 14:19–33, Mark 6:7–13, Romans 2:4

Day 3

Jesus taught, "Truly, truly, I say to you, he who believes has eternal life. I am the bread of life. Your fathers ate the manna in the wilderness, and they died. This is the bread which comes down out of heaven, so that one may eat of it and not die" (John 6:47–50). He was explaining that manna from heaven kept Israel from starving for the 40 years in the wilderness. Our spiritual manna, or bread, is Jesus. When we take Him in as we would eat bread—chew on His Word, digest every bit of Him so that all His nutrients become an intricate part of our cells and lives—we will never die but will have an abundant quality of life and eternal life.

Jesus said, "Truly, truly, I say to you, unless you eat the flesh of the Son of Man and drink His blood, you have no life in yourselves. He who eats My flesh and drinks My blood has eternal life, and I will raise him up on the last day" (John 6:53–54). Blood is known as the seat of life. Jesus used this allegory, or symbolic picture, to show us that He is the real and the eternal life that came from heaven. He would give His flesh and His blood for our salvation. We must take in His life-giving blood that was shed to cover our sins, and we must take in, or consume, the offering of His body for the payment of our debt of sin.

Eating is very personal. Hunger and thirst aren't satisfied by looking at food, watching others eat, or talking about it. The only way to satisfy our need for life-giving nourishment, to satisfy our desire for taste, to fill ourselves so we aren't hungry or thirsty is to eat and drink. The food and drink become part of us, intertwined with our very being to give us life. In order to have eternal life, we must consume Jesus in this complete and personal way.

"As a result of this many of His disciples withdrew and were not walking with Him anymore. So Jesus said to the twelve, 'You do not want to go away also, do you?' Simon Peter answered Him, 'Lord, to whom shall we go? You have words of eternal life. We have believed and have come to know that You are the Holy One of God'" (John 6:66–69).

Sometime after this Jesus asked His disciples, "'Who do people say that I am?' They told Him, saying, 'John the Baptist; and others *say* Elijah; but others, one of the prophets.' And He *continued* by questioning them, 'But who do you say that I am?' Peter answered and said to Him, 'You are the Christ'" (Mark 8:27–29).

One reason Simon was called Peter, which means Rock, was that Peter's knowledge that Jesus was the Son of God was the rock of his faith and life. When some people left, Peter wasn't shaken or confused. If some got angry and vicious, Peter's resolve to follow Christ didn't crumble. He knew to his very core that Jesus was the Christ, the Son of the living God. Without a doubt, Peter believed Jesus was eternal life, so no hardship, no surge of popularity or drop in it, no mistake on his part could break the foundation of his faith.

Hebrews 11:1 says, "Now faith is the assurance of *things* hoped for, the conviction of things not seen." That's what Peter had. He was sure of the eternal life Jesus promised. The evidence of the miracles Jesus performed, every way He fulfilled prophecies, and Jesus's knowledge and understanding of God's Word proved that Jesus was God. Peter had ingested all of Jesus, eaten and drunk His life, and knew Jesus was the Christ, the eternal life promised by the Father. His faith was in a rock-solid truth.

Bible Reading: John 6

Day 4

People have a knack for getting it right and being on the highest mountain of success, and then with the next step getting it wrong and sliding down that mountain into frustration and failure. Peter was a person. Right after declaring Jesus was the Christ, he took Jesus aside to scold Him for saying He was going to die. Jesus turned and said to Peter, "Get behind Me, Satan! You are a stumbling block to Me; for you are not setting your mind on God's interests, but man's" (Matt. 16:23). Peter regrouped and went on to contribute to Jesus's teachings and miracles.

Within weeks the disciples were sharing the Passover supper with Jesus.

> "Then Jesus said to them, "You will all fall away because of Me this night, for it is written, 'I WILL STRIKE THE SHEPHERD, AND THE SHEEP OF THE FLOCK SHALL BE SCATTERED.' But after I have been raised, I will go ahead of you to Galilee." But Peter said to Him, "Even though all may fall away because of You, I will never fall away." Jesus said to him, "Truly I say to you that this very night, before a rooster crows, you will deny Me three times."
>
> —Matt. 26:31–34

Jesus led the disciples to a garden and went in farther with Peter, James, and John to pray. Because Jesus was very anguished, He begged them to pray for Him, and three times they fell asleep, failing their friend. Jesus woke them as Judas and the soldiers were approaching to arrest Him. "Simon Peter then, having a sword, drew it and struck the high priest's slave, and cut off his right ear. So, Jesus said to Peter, 'Put the sword into the sheath; the cup which the Father has given Me, shall I not drink it?'" (John 18:10–11). Then Jesus healed the man's ear.

That very night as Jesus was being lied about in a mockery of a court trial and as He was being beaten and spit upon, Peter was in the courtyard. Three times people said Peter was one of Jesus's followers, and three times Peter angrily and fearfully denied knowing Jesus. "Immediately, while he was still speaking, a rooster crowed. The Lord turned and looked at Peter. And Peter remembered the word of the Lord, how He had told him, 'Before a rooster crows today, you will deny Me three times.' And he went out and wept bitterly" (Luke 22:60–62).

Slip into Peter's shoes for a time. The roller coaster of ups and downs Peter experienced in a few short weeks would be enough to make any of us throw up our hands in frustrated defeat and walk away. A flash of knowledge may have bolstered our confidence until pride caused us to say things we shouldn't. Back on track again, we next boasted that we'd never fall or make the mistakes everyone so easily does. But when a friend needed us, we failed them. When we should have prayed for them and ourselves, we didn't, and the big test came. Hardship smacked us, and we responded in fear and anger, failing at the very thing we had gotten right just days before. Have you ever run out and wept bitterly like Peter? Maybe no tears fell, but in your heart, bitter self-hatred caused your soul to cry out in harsh judgment of yourself. *I'm a loser. I hate myself. Why would God ever forgive me or want me? I don't deserve to be respected or forgiven.*

When Peter failed, Jesus prayed that Peter's faith would not fail. We all will fail, but if our faith is in the rock of Christ Jesus, our faith will hold us up. "Simon, Simon, behold, Satan has demanded *permission* to sift you like wheat; but I have prayed for you, that your faith may not fail; and you, when once you have turned again, strengthen your brothers" (Luke 22:31–32). Jesus believes in us and knows our hearts. We can turn again and strengthen others with our experience of bitter failure, knowing that our faith is strong because it's in the Rock, Jesus.

***Bible Reading*: Luke 22:31–51, 1 Peter 5:5–11**

Day 5

When Jesus is Lord of our lives, our failure and defeat will not define us. His forgiveness and restoration lift us from a pit of shame and embarrassment. Our life, like Peter's, will be defined by God's courage and integrity in us. It will be possible to go on with purpose, living boldly and wisely, impacting the lives of people for many generations.

Peter learned from his failures. The disciples were fishing one morning after Jesus had risen from the dead.

> *Jesus said to them, "Come and have breakfast." None of the disciples ventured to question Him, "Who are You?" knowing that it was the Lord. Jesus came and took the bread and gave it to*

> them, and the fish likewise. This is now the third time that Jesus was manifested to the disciples, after He was raised from the dead. So when they had finished breakfast, Jesus said to Simon Peter, "Simon, son of John, do you love Me more than these?" He said to Him, "Yes, Lord; You know that I love You." He said to him, "Tend My lambs."
>
> —John 21:12–15

Two times Jesus asked Peter if he loved Him. However, Jesus and Peter used different words for love. Jesus asked if Peter *agape* Him. Remember how selfless and strong *agape* love is? Yet Peter responded, "Yes Lord I *phileo* You." Honesty prompted Peter to tell Jesus he liked and approved of Him. He was fond of Jesus in friendship, but Peter realized he didn't dearly love Jesus the same way Jesus loved him. Simon Peter's denial of knowing Jesus had taught him that he loved himself more than his Lord. It was easy to say he'd die for his friend, but the humbling fact was that he wouldn't. Failure had given Peter a new perspective of himself and of true love.

Can we be that honest with ourselves and with God? Sometimes we know what words we're supposed to say, so we say them. We know the rituals; we know what certain people expect of us, and we pretend to think and feel that way. Or, like Peter, we believe we love Jesus enough to die for Him even though we've never been put to the test. Let's take a moment to ask God to show us our true hearts and minds. Do we *agape* Jesus, or do you and I *phileo* Him?

The third time, Jesus asked Peter if he *phileo* Him. "Peter was grieved because He said to him the third time, 'Do you love Me?' And he said to Him, 'Lord, You know all things; You know that I love [*phileo*] You.' Jesus said to him, 'Tend My sheep'" (John 21:17). Jesus wants our honesty. He will take us where we are and use us. We don't have to be perfect, fearless, and full of *agape* for God in order to tend His sheep. God's not impressed when we say all the right words, know Bible verses, and sound spiritual. He's impressed when our hearts are humble and sincere, when we want to serve Him, and when we're honest about our thoughts, motives, and emotions.

The Holy Spirit filled all the disciples after Jesus went to heaven, and they taught in every language of the people in Jerusalem. Peter taught how Jesus fulfilled Old Testament prophecy.

> *Now when they heard* this, *they were pierced to the heart, and said to Peter and the rest of the apostles, "Brethren, what shall we do?" Peter said to them, "Repent, and each of you be baptized in the name of Jesus Christ for the forgiveness of your sins; and you will receive the gift of the Holy Spirit." So then, those who had received his word were baptized; and that day there were added about three thousand souls.*
>
> —Acts 2:37–38, 41

When we learn and grow from our mistakes, failure becomes success. When we let go of our strength and reputation and live in God's, greater things than we can imagine will be accomplished through us and for His glory. And when God is glorified, we are exalted too.

Bible Reading: Acts 3

Day 6

Peter had a solid faith that Jesus was the Son of God, the Rock of our salvation, the cornerstone. Faith is what led Peter to the mountaintops of success and victory. And faith is what guided him out of his dark valley of guilt, shame, self-accusation, and defeat. Jesus said, "If you had faith like a mustard seed, you would say to this mulberry tree, 'Be uprooted and be planted in the sea'; and it would obey you" (Luke 17:6). A mustard seed is as big as the top of a pin.

You see, it's not about Peter's faith, my strong faith, or your faith. It only takes the size and strength of a mustard seed of faith to change us from ineffective, frightened people into God-fearing world-changers. What our faith is in makes all the difference.

Suppose you and I drive our car to a bridge that crosses a canyon. Whether our faith in that bridge's stability is big and solid or small and nervous doesn't really matter. It's the reliability and trustworthiness of the bridge that validates our faith. The size and strength of our faith are not as important as the strength of what our faith is in. Simon Peter's faith was in the Rock of our Salvation, Jesus Christ the Son of God. So no matter what was going on in the world around him, no matter if he excelled or failed, the foundation of his faith—Jesus Christ—stood strong.

Peter was willing to leave the business world of fishing to become a full-time worker for God because of his faith in Jesus. God doesn't always ask us to change jobs or live in poverty in order to serve Him. But He does want us to leave our love of and dependence on money, people, and prestige, and put Jesus first in our lives. That is a call every one of us has, and leaving our stuff takes faith that Jesus is the Son of God.

Jesus told Peter and each of us that His prayer for us is that when we fail, our faith will not fail; that when we fall and sin and totally blow it, we will land on the solid foundation of what our faith is in—Jesus Christ. He prayed that our faith may not fail, that we would still know God had forgiven us, would help us stand back up, and would restore us. And you, when once you have turned again (that's repentance), would strengthen your brothers and sisters by your example.

That is the picture of Peter's life—running the race, falling, getting back up, and finishing strong. In a letter toward the end of Peter's life, he wrote this:

> *Now for this very reason also, applying all diligence, in your faith supply moral excellence, and in* your *moral excellence, knowledge, and in* your *knowledge, self-control, and in* your *self-control, perseverance, and in* your *perseverance, godliness, and in* your *godliness, brotherly kindness, and in* your *brotherly kindness, love. For if these qualities are yours and are increasing, they render you neither useless nor unfruitful in the true knowledge of our Lord Jesus Christ. For he who lacks these* qualities *is blind or short-sighted, having forgotten* his *purification from his former sins. Therefore, brethren, be all the more diligent to make certain about His calling and choosing you; for as long as you practice these things, you will never stumble; for in this way the entrance into the eternal kingdom of our Lord and Savior Jesus Christ will be abundantly supplied to you. Therefore, I will always be ready to remind you of these things, even though you* already *know* them, *and have been established in the truth which is present with* you. *I consider it right, as long as I am in this* earthly *dwelling, to stir you up by way of reminder, knowing that the laying aside of my* earthly *dwelling is imminent, as also our Lord Jesus Christ has made clear to me. And I will*

also be diligent that at any time after my departure you will be able to call these things to mind.

—2 Pet. 1:5–15

Jesus said if you love me, tend my sheep, and that is what Peter the Rock did. It was not always a perfect love, not always a big or solid faith, but what Peter's faith was in made all the difference. Jesus is the Christ the Son of the living God, and He *agapes* us enough to die for us. Knowing Him will cause us to live well and finish strong.

Bible Reading: Matthew 7:21–29, Hebrews 10:35–39, 11:1–3

Week 6

EASTER

Day 1

What is the story of Easter? On a strictly fun and nonreligious level, we hunt for eggs full of candy hidden by the Easter Bunny. Baby bunnies, eggs and chicks, pastel colors of pink and yellow flowers, green leaves and light blue skies celebrate spring and the renewing of life after winter. To a believer in Jesus Christ, Easter is the remembrance and celebration of the crucifixion and resurrection of God's Son, Jesus. Christianity's entire existence and foundation is the Easter story.

Jews celebrate Passover at this time in spring. It is no coincidence that God—the Father, Son, and Holy Spirit—selected Passover as the time Christ Jesus would be made the sacrificial lamb. The symbolism in Christ's death and its effects on humanity closely relate to that time long ago when Moses led Israel in the first Passover.

A thousand years of prophecy was fulfilled in the life and death of Jesus Christ. We'll look at why that is important and what it means to you and me today. Rituals initiated by God for His people in the Old Testament are vivid pictures of what happened to Jesus in the week leading to His arrest, crucifixion, burial, and resurrection.

The Apostle Paul gave a simple explanation to the church in Rome. He showed how the Old Testament laws tied in with Christ's story. Every person can be God's child—Jews and Gentiles, rich and poor, men and women, children and adults, big sinners and "good" people.

> *By the works of the Law no flesh will be justified in His sight; for through the Law comes the knowledge of sin. But now apart from the Law the righteousness of God has been manifested, being witnessed by the Law and the Prophets, even the righteousness of God through faith in Jesus Christ for all those who believe; for there is no distinction; for all have sinned and fall short of the glory of God, being justified as a gift by His grace through the redemption which is in Christ Jesus; whom God displayed publicly as a propitiation in His blood through faith. This was to demonstrate His righteousness, because in the forbearance of God He passed over the sins previously committed; for the demonstration, I say, of His righteousness at the present time, so that He would be just and the justifier of the one who has faith in Jesus.*
>
> —Rom. 3:20–26

Jesus told a man this:

> *As Moses lifted up the serpent in the wilderness, even so must the Son of Man be lifted up; so that whoever believes will in Him have eternal life. For God so loved the world, that He gave His only begotten Son, that whoever believes in Him shall not perish, but have eternal life. For God did not send the Son into the world to judge the world, but that the world might be saved through Him.*
>
> —John 3:14–17

What is Easter? It is all of the above. Easter is a glorious and fun celebration of a physical and spiritual spring—new life after the cold deadness of winter and sin. The story of Jesus is symbolized by sweetness, soft blooming colors, and innocent new life. He fulfills prophecy in an astounding way and frees us from the consequences of trying to live by God's law and failing. Easter is the story of love and life—abundant life today as well as eternal life. Easter is Jesus.

Bible Reading: John 3:1–17, Romans 3:20–31

Day 2

Writers of the New Testament give these two proofs that Jesus of Nazareth is the Messiah: His fulfillment of prophecy and His resurrection. The Old Testament covers thousands of years and contains hundreds of prophecies of the Messiah. Jesus fulfilled them all.

His birth by a virgin woman from the line of David in Bethlehem fulfilled prophecies from Genesis, Numbers, 1 Chronicles, 2 Samuel, the Psalms, Proverbs, Isaiah, Jeremiah, and Micah. His childhood and adult ministry satisfied more prophecy, and the arrest through the resurrection of Jesus fulfills even more of what God foretold. That matters to us today because it provides solid foundational truth on which we build our faith and knowledge of God.

Peter Stoner in *Science Speaks* shows us that coincidence is ruled out in Jesus's fulfillment of prophecy by the science of probability. Consider just eight prophecies being fulfilled by one person. The chance that any man might have lived down to the present time and fulfilled all eight prophecies is 1 in 10^{17} (1 in 100,000,000,000,000,000). To illustrate this point, let's take 100 trillion silver dollars and lay them on the face of Texas; they would be two feet deep. We mark one of these silver dollars and stir the whole mass thoroughly all over the state. Now we'll blindfold a man and let him travel as far as he wishes, but he must pick only one silver dollar. What chance would he have of picking the marked one? The chance would be the same chance the prophets would have to write just eight of these prophecies and have them all come true for any one man—that is, if they had written them without God's inspiration.[18]

Palm Sunday's account of Christ entering Jerusalem on the back of a donkey was foretold in Zechariah 9:9. It happened 500 years later as told in Matthew 21 and Luke 19. Zechariah wrote in Zechariah 11-13 that Jesus would be betrayed by His friend Judas for 30 pieces of silver. Judas would throw the money in God's house, and it would later be used to buy the Potter's Field as a burial place for strangers, and all the disciples would forsake Jesus (Matt. 26-27, Mark 14).

It was prophesied that the Messiah would be falsely accused; stand quietly in response; be wounded, bruised, hit, spit on, and mocked; fall under the cross; have His hands and feet pierced; be crucified with thieves; pray for His persecutors; be rejected by His own people; and be hated without a cause. His friends stood far off, people shook their heads and stared, soldiers cast lots for His clothes, and Jesus was thirsty and given gall and vinegar. He cried out in forsakenness and then committed Himself to God. A psalm foretold that His bones would not be broken, and Zechariah said His side would be pierced, and that happened in John 19. Amos told of darkness over the land (Matt. 27), and Isaiah said Jesus would be buried in a rich man's tomb (Matt. 27). The Psalms and Hosea tell us that Jesus would rise from the grave—and He did, as seen in Matthew 28, Mark 16, Luke 24, John 20, and Acts 2. Christ Jesus is, beyond a doubt, the promised Messiah.

The Lord said, "I declared the former things long ago and they went forth from My mouth, and I proclaimed them. Suddenly I acted, and they came to pass. Therefore I declared *them* to you long ago, before they took place I proclaimed *them* to you, so that you could not say, 'My idol has done them, and my graven image and my molten image have commanded them'" (Isa. 48:3, 5).

Bible Reading: 1 Peter 1:1–21

Day 3

God sent a total of nine plagues upon Egypt so Pharaoh would let the Israelite slaves go with Moses to the Promised Land. Finally, God told Moses, "One more plague I will bring on Pharaoh and on Egypt; after that he will let you go from here. About midnight I am going out into the midst of Egypt, and all the firstborn in the land of Egypt shall die, from the firstborn of the Pharaoh who sits on his throne, even to the firstborn of the slave girl who is behind the millstones; all the firstborn of the cattle as well" (Exod. 11:1, 4–5).

Moses told the elders of Israel that God said to take a year-old, unblemished, male lamb and kill it. They were to drain the blood into a basin and apply some of the blood from the basin to the top and sides of the doorframe; and no one should go outside the door of their house until morning. The Lord was going to pass through the land and strike down the Egyptians. But when He saw the blood on the top and sides of the doorframe, He would pass over that home and not permit the Destroyer to enter and kill the firstborn. Then they were to roast and eat the lamb whose blood saved them from death. God said to observe this event forever. "When your children say to you, 'What does this rite mean to you?' you shall say, 'It is a Passover sacrifice to the Lord who passed over the houses of the sons of Israel in Egypt when he smote the Egyptians'" (Exod. 12:26–27).

Christ, the firstborn Son of God, is the unblemished, sinless Lamb of God (1 Pet. 1:19). Picture the door of your life and heart as the literal door to the house of those Israelite slaves in Egypt. The blood stains on the top of your heart's doorpost is from the Lamb of God where He was beaten, His beard was pulled out, and the crown of thorns was pressed in. As the nail was driven into Jesus's right hand, His blood dripped onto that side of your heart's doorframe and then flowed again onto the left as the nail was forced through His left hand into the cross.

Believing Jesus died for our sins means we are covered by His blood. So when the judgment of death comes, it will pass over each heart that has the blood of the Lamb on the doorframe of their lives. The literal lambs had no choice when they were sacrificed. Jesus, however, was a Lamb who chose to give up His life for those whom He loved. He said, "For this reason the Father loves Me, because I lay down My life so that I may take it again. No one has taken it away from Me, but I lay it down on My own initiative. I have authority to lay it down, and I have authority to take it up again. This commandment I received from My Father" (John 10:17-18).

I know some of this can be hard to take in. It seems a little bloodthirsty and gory. But you see, sin is a messy business. Just as Israel was enslaved, so we are enslaved to the emotions and thoughts even more than the physical actions of sin. The world tells us we're free to behave sexually any way we please, lie, get wasted, betray marriages, and cheat to get ahead. Then the world turns around and shames us for doing those very things. Satan and the world system drain the very lifeblood from us through lies about our rights, how unforgivable we are, and how unlovable and permanently stained we are. So the Lamb of God redeemed us with His blood. But you were washed, you were sanctified (set apart as holy), and you were justified in the name of the Lord Jesus Christ and by the Spirit of our God (1 Cor. 6:11).

Bible Reading: John 19:1-37

Day 4

Old Testament events drew vivid pictures of the Messiah. Moses and Israel were told by Edom that they could not pass through their land. Soon the Canaanites went out to fight Israel who asked God to give them victory over Canaan, and Israel completely destroyed them. Then they set out from

Mount Hor by way of the Red Sea to go around the land of Edom, and the people became impatient because of the journey.

> *The people spoke against God and Moses, "Why have you brought us up out of Egypt to die in the wilderness? For there is no food and no water, and we loathe this miserable food." The LORD sent fiery serpents among the people and they bit the people, so that many people of Israel died. So the people came to Moses and said, "We have sinned, because we have spoken against the LORD and you; intercede with the LORD, that He may remove the serpents from us." And Moses interceded for the people. Then the LORD said to Moses, "Make a fiery serpent, and set it on a standard; and it shall come about, that everyone who is bitten, when he looks at it, he will live." And Moses made a bronze serpent and set it on the standard; and it came about, that if a serpent bit any man, when he looked to the bronze serpent, he lived.*
>
> —Num. 21:5–9

When we got to know the Israelites in autumn, we noticed that they complained against Moses but didn't have the gall to openly grumble against God Himself. Now they have upped the offense and spoken directly against God and Moses. Not only did they complain about the long trek through the wilderness, but they complained about the food God sent from heaven, the manna. Fast forward 1,000 plus years. The religious leaders said this:

> *"Our forefathers ate the manna in the wilderness; as it is written, 'HE GAVE THEM BREAD OUT OF HEAVEN TO EAT.'" Jesus said to them, "Truly, truly, I say to you, it is not Moses who has given you the bread out of heaven, but it is My Father who gives you the true bread out of heaven. For the bread of God is that which comes down out of heaven, and gives life to the world." Then they said to Him, 'Lord, always give us this bread.' Jesus said to them, "I am the bread of life; he who comes to Me will not hunger, and he who believes in Me will never thirst."*
>
> —John 6:31–35

God's punishment of fiery, biting serpents was in response to His gift of life being rejected as well as His leadership. Serpents or snakes are a symbol of evil and sin, leading to death. That is always the punishment if we reject God's provision of life.

Yet He made a way out. Moses made a bronze serpent and put it on a pole. Colors and materials are very symbolic in the Bible. Bronze denotes judgment and cleansing. Jump forward to Jesus again. He said, "As Moses lifted up the serpent in the wilderness, even so must the Son of Man be lifted up; so that whoever believes in Him will have eternal life" (John 3:14–15).

The bronze serpent speaks of evil being judged—just as Jesus who knew no sin became sin for us on the cross; and our sin was judged and purified in Him (2 Cor. 5:21). A bronze serpent is a picture of sin judged and purged. Healing and life came from trust in God.

All we need to do is look to Jesus's death and resurrection to be saved from our sins and their consequence—death. The people weren't saved by doing anything, only by looking to the bronze serpent. They had to trust that an act as seemingly foolish as looking at a serpent on a pole was enough to save them. Surely they should do penance, give money, and help the poor. Don't we believe the same? We must work to get saved; we need some control in the process. "Turn to Me and be saved, all you ends of the earth; for I am God, and there is no other" (Isa. 45:22).

Bible Reading: John 3:14–17, John 6:31–40, 47–58

Day 5

A covenant is a promise, a pledge. God sealed His covenants with blood, the outpouring of one life for another. Moses offered burnt offerings and sacrificed young bulls as peace offerings to the Lord; he sprinkled half the blood on the altar and then read God's new laws from the book of the covenant God had given him on the mountain. Israel said they would follow and obey the Lord. So Moses sprinkled the blood on the people and said, "Behold the blood of the covenant, which the LORD has made with you in accordance with all these words" (Exod. 24:8).

Pointing toward the new covenant was the blood of the lamb on the top and sides of the doorframes and the feast of the Passover. In the wilderness, the people rejected God's manna from heaven, which depicted the Messiah coming from heaven to give eternal life. Now we'll sit with Jesus and His disciples as they celebrate the Passover feast before the crucifixion. While they were eating, Jesus took some bread, and after a blessing, He broke *it* and gave *it* to the disciples, and said, "Take, eat; this is My body." And when He had taken a cup and given thanks, He gave it to them, saying, "Drink from it, all of you; for this is My blood of the covenant, which is poured out for many for forgiveness of sins" (Matt. 26:26–28).

Communion, or the Lord's Supper, is a remembrance of the beginning of the new covenant of grace instead of the Law; it is between God and all people. Jesus is the bread of life. Part of the Passover celebration includes unleavened bread, bread without yeast. Leavened bread spoils much faster than bread without yeast. Even the smallest amount of yeast dough mixed with unleavened dough causes the whole mixture to rise and be full of the properties of the yeast. So it is with sin. The smallest sin in our lives causes us to be full of sin and dying because of it. Jesus took the unleavened bread to represent His body. He is without the spoiling properties of sin, and His body would be broken for the payment of our sin.

Three of the Gospels tell of the Lord's Supper, and in 1 Corinthians 11, Paul leads us in it and tells us to take the bread and the cup in remembrance of Jesus. The elements do not turn into His body and blood as we take them. In no way do they save us from our sins. They are only a tangible way for us to remember what Jesus did to give us the New Covenant with God. Paul said, "For as often as you eat this bread and drink the cup, you proclaim the Lord's death until He comes" (1 Cor. 11:26).

This beautiful and meaningful ceremony, or observance, gives us a clear picture of what we should be doing spiritually every day. Remember, Jesus told us that "he who eats My flesh and drinks My blood abides in Me, and I in him. As the living Father sent Me, and I live because of the Father, so he who eats Me, he also will live because of Me. This is the bread which came down out of heaven; not as the fathers ate and died; he who eats this bread will live forever" (John 6:56–58). Each moment of every day we should live with, abide with, and take in Jesus. Read His word, talk to Him through prayer, praise Him, cry with Him, know Him. Taking communion bread symbolizes ingesting the perfect body of Christ that He offered as a sacrifice to pay for our sins. Drinking the wine (or grape juice) illustrates absorbing His shed blood to seal the promise of forgiveness and eternal life. We do it in remembrance of Him.

Bible Reading: **1 Corinthians 5:6–8, 1 Corinthians 11:23–29**

Day 6

First, we will establish the fact that Christ Jesus did die on the cross. Hanging on a cross caused suffocation since the person could not breathe. He would push up from his feet in order to breathe in and out and could last for days before finally dying. To hurry the process, the Romans broke their legs so they could no longer move up and down, and death would then come more quickly.

> *He [Jesus] bowed His head and gave up His spirit. Then the Jews, because it was the day of preparation, so that the bodies would not remain on the cross on the Sabbath for that Sabbath was a high day), asked Pilate that their legs might be broken, and that they might be taken away. So the soldiers came, and broke the legs of the first man and of the other who was crucified with Him; but coming to Jesus, when they saw that He was already dead, they did not break His legs. But one of the soldiers pierced His side with a spear, and immediately blood and water came out.*
> —John 19:30–34

Roman soldiers knew death when they saw it. These men were trained to crucify criminals and saw death on the cross daily. Jesus was already dead when they determined they didn't need to break His legs. They pierced His side with a spear, and blood mixed with a water-like substance of serum flowed out, again a sign that death had just recently occurred. All this fulfilled the prophecies of Exodus 12:46, Numbers 9:12, and Psalm 34:20 that no bones would be broken. It fulfilled Zechariah 12:10 that they would pierce His side and Psalm 22:14 that His heart would be broken and melt within Him, causing the blood and water to flow.

Jesus was buried, as prophesied in Isaiah 53:9, in a rich man's unused tomb, and He rose from the dead three days later as Jesus Himself foretold. Mark 8:31 says, "And He [Jesus] began to teach them that the Son of Man must suffer many things and be rejected by the elders and the chief priests and the scribes, and be killed, and after three days rise again."

Paul wrote this:

> *For I delivered to you as of first importance what I also received, that Christ died for our sins according to the Scriptures, and that He was buried, and that He was raised on the third day*

according to the Scriptures, and that He appeared to Cephas [Simon Peter], then to the twelve. After that He appeared to more than five hundred brethren at one time, most of whom remain until now, but some have fallen asleep; then He appeared to James, then to all the apostles; and last of all, as to one untimely born, He appeared to me also.

—1 Cor. 15:3–8

The massive number of people who saw Jesus gives more than enough proof that He indeed rose from the grave and is alive. Previously fearful, the defeated apostles were emboldened by witnessing Christ's resurrection. Because of this truth, they had the courage to openly teach Christ and be imprisoned and persecuted for it without backing down. Religious leaders would have gained victory if they could produce His dead body, but they could not because Jesus was seen alive for 40 days after His resurrection, and then witnesses saw him go up to heaven. Why is this important to us?

Now if we have died with Christ, we believe that we shall also live with Him, knowing that Christ, having been raised from the dead, is never to die again; death no longer is master over Him. For the death that He died, He died to sin once for all; but the life that He lives, He lives to God. Even so consider yourselves to be dead to sin, but alive to God in Christ Jesus.

—Rom. 6:8–11

Bible Reading: Luke 24:1–49

Week 7

EASTER

Day 1

Last week we looked at Easter from the physical perspective, how it is validated and proved by science and history. Easter has even deeper meanings and messages. Jesus led us on a spiritual journey that plumbed the depths of His heart and broke free the chains of death. He took us to the battlefield of the spiritual war raging between Satan and God and crushed our enemy with His victory, dying for our sins once and for all and living for God for eternity.

"When they [Jesus and the soldiers] came to the place called The Skull, there they crucified Him and the criminals, one on the right and the other on the left. But Jesus was saying, 'Father, forgive them; for they do not know what they are doing'" (Luke 23:33–34). Remember the abuse Jesus had already endured—physically beaten and humiliated, emotionally betrayed and abandoned, mentally hated, and falsely accused. Yet the first words He spoke on the cross were "Father, forgive them; for they do not know what they are doing." Physically it was obvious what each person was doing. The big picture, however, was not so clear. All those people were whipped into a frenzy of hatred and dark emotions by God's sworn enemy, Satan. They were not just killing a man who would be forgotten after the next major news event. The deeds of those days shook and shaped all of creation on a physical, emotional, and spiritual level for all time. But the emotion of the moment was all that was real to them.

You and I function in the same fog of unawareness. Insecurities about our looks, brains, and purpose cause us to shy from acting and speaking as we really want to. Do we realize that when we believe that we are stupid or inept, too ugly or untalented to be useful or respected that we believe Satan's lies? God said He made us wonderfully and with a purpose. Believing we're worthless is calling God a liar. Living in fear of what people will think or say and manipulating situations and people to have things "work right" are based on our lack of faith in God. We really don't believe He can be trusted to keep us from hurt or pain. We list all the obvious wrongs and then search for what we don't see—but God does. That's what Jesus was talking about.

The Jews would also recognize a gift Jesus was giving. In Numbers 35 and Joshua 21, God set up six cities of refuge for people to flee to when they had accidentally killed someone. If it was proven that the person had not meant to kill, they could live with the high priest in their city, enjoying the best food, clothing, and shelter Israel gave to their priests. They were protected from the avenger of blood. Jesus's words put all of us into the category of people who could flee to God for protection from the death penalty. We who have fled to Him for refuge can have great confidence as we hold to the hope that lies before us where Jesus, who went before us, has entered on our behalf. He has become a high priest forever (Heb. 6:17–20).

Jesus's last words before His death are eye-opening. Listen carefully as He takes us from the obvious into the hidden. Our Savior looked at the people throughout time and forgave them in the middle of His pain because He saw deeper than the surface. We are being offered the same ability. Looking at ourselves and others and seeing the root of why we've done the things we've done will free us from bitterness, pain, and unforgiveness. Easter offers us the ability to pull sin out of our lives by the roots, freeing us from the obvious results of the problem as well as the deeper causes of it. It gives us a city of refuge to run to where we can be safe and forgiven, living in rich grace.

Bible Reading: Luke 23:33–49, Hebrews 6:17–20

Day 2

As passersby and the criminals hanging on either side of Jesus hurled insults at Him, one of the crucified thieves realized Jesus truly was the Son of God. He admitted his punishment was just and said, "'Jesus, remember me when You come in Your kingdom!' And He said to him, 'Truly I say to you, today you shall be with Me in Paradise'" (Luke 23:42–43).

Jesus's mother and some of her friends were standing at the bottom of the cross. "When Jesus then saw His mother, and the disciple whom He loved [John] standing nearby, He said to His mother, 'Woman, behold, your son!' Then He said to the disciple, 'Behold, your mother!' From that hour the disciple took her into his own *household*" (John 19:26–27).

This crucible proves Jesus truly is the innocent Son of God sent to be our Savior. A crucible is a place or set of circumstances where people or things are subjected to forces that test them and often make them change. Jesus stayed constant in His caring for others. Immediately He accepted the thief's faith in Him and gave the assurance of heaven that day to an unworthy man. Christ's words touch each of us today with the proof that whoever believes in God's only Son will not perish but have everlasting life in heaven with Jesus (John 3:16). If you are a "whoever," this promise is for you. If you believe Jesus is God's Son and can forgive your sins and make you clean, you've fulfilled God's conditions. Romans 10:9–10 says, "If you confess with your mouth Jesus *as* Lord, and believe in your heart that God raised Him from the dead, you will be saved; for with the heart a person believes, resulting in righteousness, and with the mouth he confesses, resulting in salvation."

Suffering and distress did not prevent Jesus from caring about His mother's physical well-being. While His spiritual mission was of greater importance than saving anyone from bodily harm or discomfort, Christ showed tender concern for people's hunger, health, feelings, and welfare. He loved His mother, Mary, and saw how devastated she was at the foot of His cross. So Jesus took His mind off His painful circumstances and made sure His mom would be loved and cared for after His death. Even though John had run away at first, Jesus gifted him with His trust by placing His mother in his care.

God does allow us to get beat up by this world, but He notices us and provides for us just as He provided for Mary. If we've blown it like John, God sees our hearts and still believes in us. In giving Mary and John into each other's care, Jesus gave a blessing and responsibility to them both. We need to look at the people in our lives and see them as the gifts God intends them to be. He is providing us with security, protection, encouragement, and purpose.

Even from the cross, Jesus was saying, "Cast all your cares on Me." His love for us is enormous and completely consuming. Forgiveness is offered, not because of who we are or what we've done but because of Who He is and what He has done. Comfort, security, and protection are offered to us spiritually as well as physically. "Greater love has no one than this, that one lay down his life for his friends" (John 15:13). Jesus didn't simply say those words; He lived and died them.

Easter's message is one of love, acceptance, forgiveness, and security. Jesus offers the peace and assurance of a secure home in heaven and on earth to you and to me.

Bible Reading: John 19:23–42, Ephesians 2:1–9

Day 3

At noon, as Jesus hung on the Roman cross, darkness fell across the whole land until 3:00 in the afternoon. At 3:00, Jesus called out with a loud voice, "'ELOI, ELOI, LAMA SABACHTHANI?' which is translated, 'MY GOD, MY GOD, WHY HAVE YOU FORSAKEN ME?'" (Mark:15:34). "After this, Jesus, knowing that all things had already been accomplished, to fulfill the Scripture, said, 'I am thirsty.' A jar full of sour wine was standing there; so they put a sponge full of the sour wine upon *a branch of* hyssop and brought it up to His mouth. Therefore when Jesus had received the sour wine, He said, "It is finished"' (John 19:28–30).

Let's put ourselves in the shoes of those standing at the foot of Jesus's cross. As they looked around, they saw that not much had changed. It had been eerily dark for the last three hours. Danger, hatred, and sinister feelings pulsed through the crowd as they had for days. The Man we believed to be God's Son and our Savior still hung as a battered mass of blood and torn flesh on the cross. When Jesus cried in anguish, asking God why He'd forsaken Him, the last of our hope shriveled and died. None of this looked like we thought it would. It was horrible, out of control, evil, and wrong. Then Jesus said, "It is finished." Still, nothing changed. What had finished? He still hung there. It was still dark. We'd still lost, and injustice had still won.

Physically, the situation looked hopeless and beyond redemption. The Roman government was too big to fight. Religious leaders had too much power over the people for Jesus's message to ever break through. Fear, laziness, and selfishness would always rule people's behavior. This situation looked impossible, even if God was involved.

However, spiritually the most significant event throughout eternity had taken place. An epic battle between the two most powerful forces of all time had climaxed with a bloody victory for God and a final defeat for Satan.

Second Corinthians 5:21 tells us that God made Jesus who knew no sin to be sin on our behalf so we might be made right with God through Christ. Every ugly, depraved sin for all time was placed on Jesus on that cross. Sin puts a barrier between God and the person with sin in their life. For the first time, Jesus experienced living with a wall between Him and His Father, and it crushed His heart. Not only was Christ's relationship with God broken but He also felt the full force of God's wrath for sin. In those hours when our eyes could see no change to our world, Jesus carried our sins.

He felt deep shame and guilt, acute embarrassment and humiliation, aloneness and worthlessness. Sin separated Him from the Father, causing Jesus to feel forsaken and abandoned, empty and isolated. The Light of the world was covered with the darkness of sin, and all creation was placed in an unnatural darkness for that time. Jesus said He was thirsty, and then it was finished. Finally, the debt was paid—paid in full. Nothing seemed to have changed. Jesus was still nailed to the cross, hanging onto life. But the sins of all who would believe in Jesus were now paid in full once and for all (Rom. 6:10).

The message for us is to realize that God is working. We may not see it, and we may not feel it, but the powerful hand of God is working things out behind the scenes. Greater is God who is in us than the evil one who is in the world. We have hope when the world around us seems to be chaotic and evil, unchanging, and hopeless. Easter is the absolute spiritual victory over evil.

Bible Reading: **Matthew 27:39–49, Romans 6:10, Deuteronomy 31:6**

Day 4

By this time, it was noon, and darkness fell across the whole land until 3:00 in the afternoon because the sun was covered, and the veil of the temple was torn in two. Jesus called out with a loud voice, "Father, INTO YOUR HANDS I COMMIT MY SPIRIT." When He had said this, He breathed His last (Luke 23:44–46).

Back in Exodus, God gave Moses the directions for the tabernacle, which translated to the temple. A veil or curtain that was four fingers thick hung between the Holy Place and the Holy of Holies, or Most Holy Place. The Ark of the Covenant was in the Most Holy Place, and that was where God met the High Priest once a year on the Day of Atonement. Before the High Priest could go in, he had to sacrifice sheep or oxen for the sins of himself and all Israel. After God accepted the blood sacrifice, the priest would then go through the veil into the Most Holy Place.

> *By this will we have been sanctified through the offering of the body of Jesus Christ once for all. But He [Jesus], having offered one sacrifice for sins for all time,* SAT DOWN AT THE RIGHT HAND OF GOD. *Therefore, brethren, since we have confidence to enter the holy place by the blood of Jesus, by a new and living way which He inaugurated for us through the veil [curtain], that is, His flesh, and since* we have *a great priest over the house of God, let us draw near to God with a sincere heart in full assurance of faith, having our hearts sprinkled clean from an evil conscience and our bodies washed with pure water.*
>
> —Heb. 10:10, 12, 19–22

Jesus was the veil between holy God the Father and all people. His blood sacrifice was more powerful than any animal sacrifice and only had to be given once. God tore the veil in the temple from top to bottom. This was not humans reaching up to make a way to God. The Father tore the barrier in two that had separated Him from us. Jesus's blood and broken body was God reaching down to you and me. Christ made the way for us to draw near to God with confidence—clean and with a pure conscience. When we believe Jesus is the Son of God who died for our sins and rose from the dead, His blood is sprinkled over us as Moses sprinkled blood over Israel to seal our promise forever. Our hearts are cleansed and our bodies washed with His pure water. Jesus is the torn veil. We can enter God's presence through Him and stand before the Father now in confidence.

And then, at just the right time Jesus gave His spirit into His Father's hands. The life and death of Jesus was His choice, done with a purpose and in God's sovereign control. To those standing at the foot of His cross, His death looked tragic and final, but Jesus's words should give us a boost of security. He gave His spirit to God. Jesus could have stayed alive longer or died sooner. It looked as if the Roman soldiers were in control, but it was God all the time.

Easter was God reaching down to us, tearing the veil that separated us. This beautiful and awful moment in time is the celebration of a love that was bigger than a life.

Bible Reading: Romans 5:1–11, 1 Peter 2:9–10

Day 5

As meaningful and significant as Jesus's crucifixion and death are, that was not the end.

> *But on the first day of the week, at early dawn, they came to the tomb bringing the spices which they had prepared. And they found the stone rolled away from the tomb, but when they entered, they did not find the body of the Lord Jesus. While they were perplexed about this, behold, two men suddenly stood near them in dazzling clothing; and as* the women *were terrified and bowed their faces to the ground,* the men *said to them, "Why do you seek the living One among the dead? He is not here, but He has risen. Remember how He spoke to you while He was still in Galilee, saying that the Son of Man must be delivered into the hands of sinful men, and be crucified, and the third day rise again." And they remembered His words, and returned from the tomb and reported all these things to the eleven and to all the rest. Now they were Mary Magdalene and Joanna and Mary the mother of James; also the other women with them were telling these things to the apostles.*
>
> —Luke 24:1–10

Why do we seek the living One among the dead? Why do we look for Jesus to be like us, a god after our own image, with our limitations—a god we can fully understand? Everything about Jesus fulfilling prophecy is beyond our comprehension and ability. The deep spiritual battle and victory He fought and won on the cross is beyond our physical sight. To His followers in those days, the world looked bleak, hopeless, and evil. They'd forgotten what Jesus had said. We live in harsh, hopeless, evil times too. The angel's message for us is to remember what Jesus said and did. Don't get caught up in the physical reality and forget there is also a spiritual reality. Death strikes terror in the hearts of so many. Jesus wants us to know that death is not the end. Stop looking for all of life to be lived out here among the dying. Look for the life that lasts forever. Look forward, past physical life and death, to heaven.

Jesus said, "I am the resurrection and the life; he who believes in Me will live even if he dies, and everyone who lives and believes in Me will never die. Do you believe this?" (John 11:25–26). What an amazing statement! What an amazing miracle! Jesus died on the cross and rose from the grave. Really, we could say this is not the land of the living but rather the land of the dying because the dying process starts at the moment the life process starts. Jesus conquered death, which is the consequence of sin. Because of His resurrection, when we believe Jesus, we will live spiritually even when our bodies die. Our bodies will also be raised to live in heaven.

Because God's children are human beings made of flesh and blood, Jesus also became flesh and blood by being born in human form. For only as a human being could He die, and only by dying could He break the power of the devil who had the power of death. Only as a human could He free those who all their lives were held in slavery by their fear of death (Heb. 2:14–15). When our perishable, earthly bodies have been transformed into heavenly bodies that will never die, then at last the Scriptures will come true: "DEATH IS SWALLOWED UP IN VICTORY. O DEATH, WHERE IS YOUR VICTORY? O DEATH, WHERE IS YOUR STING?" (1 Cor. 15:54–55).

Easter is the gift of life forever and God's victory over death. Do you believe that?

Bible Reading: John 20, Revelation 1:17–18

Day 6

Mary Magdalene stood outside Jesus's empty tomb sobbing, not believing He was alive. Then when she recognized Jesus, she hugged Him tightly. Jesus said to her, "Stop clinging to Me, for I have not yet ascended to the Father; but go to My brethren and say to them, 'I ascend to My Father and your Father, and My God and your God'" (John 20:17).

Mary's hug was not being rejected. Jesus didn't want her or any of us to cling to Him as a human being, His earthly body that we could recognize and understand. He was letting us know that we would be better off clinging to Him after He went to heaven, holding on to Him spiritually because He will never die. His next words were full of love and forgiveness. Tell everyone I ascend to My Father and your Father, and My God and your God. Tell one of my best friends who denied ever knowing me that I'm going to My

Father and his Father. I still consider us brothers. Tell all my followers who ran and abandoned Me that I am going to My God and their God. They are still accepted by Me and by God the Father.

> *Before His crucifixion, Jesus had said, "But I tell you the truth, it is to your advantage that I go away; for if I do not go away, the Helper will not come to you; but if I go, I will send Him to you. And He, when He comes, will convict the world concerning sin and righteousness and judgment; concerning sin, because they do not believe in Me; and concerning righteousness, because I go to the Father and you no longer see Me; and concerning judgment, because the ruler of this world [the devil] has been judged. I have many more things to say to you, but you cannot bear them now. But when He, the Spirit of truth, comes, He will guide you into all the truth; for He will not speak on His own initiative, but whatever He hears, He will speak; and He will disclose to you what is to come."*
>
> —John 16:7–13

Life was changing. No longer would Jesus be in human form walking with us. Christ lived for us, He died for us, and He rose from the dead in order to defeat Satan who had the power of death. And now Christ Jesus was going to go to heaven and send the Holy Spirit. The Holy Spirit is our Helper, our Comforter, our Teacher, our Guide, our Warranty, and our Promise.

> *In Him, you also, after listening to the message of truth, the gospel of your salvation—having also believed, you were sealed in Him with the Holy Spirit of promise, who is given as a pledge of our inheritance, with a view to the redemption of God's own possession, to the praise of His glory. For this reason I too, having heard of the faith in the Lord Jesus which exists among you and your love for all the saints, do not cease giving thanks for you, while making mention* of you *in my prayers; that the God of our Lord Jesus Christ, the Father of glory, may give to you a spirit of wisdom and of revelation in the knowledge of Him. I pray that the eyes of your heart may be enlightened, so that you will know what is the hope of His calling, what are the*

riches of the glory of His inheritance in the saints, and what is the surpassing greatness of His power toward us who believe. These are in accordance with the working of the strength of His might which He brought about in Christ, when He raised Him from the dead and seated Him at His right hand in the heavenly places.

—Eph. 1:13–20

Easter is Christ's death, resurrection, and ascension, and it offers us victory and new life.

***Bible Reading*: Matthew 28, Romans 8:14–17**

Week 8

DANIEL

Day 1

Most of us have heard of Daniel and the lion's den. Daniel's life story is fascinating, and we'll see similarities between our lives and his in many ways. Genuine honor grew boldly even as the world around Daniel fell apart. May we, like Daniel, choose integrity throughout our lives.

Israel had split in two and had a king for each new country. The north was named Israel, and the south was called Judah. Regardless of which section God's people lived in, they repeatedly left God and worshiped false gods, living in very sinful ways. And God repeatedly warned them through His prophets that He would take His protection and provision from them as punishment if they didn't repent and turn back to Him.

> *In the third year of the reign of Jehoiakim king of Judah, Nebuchadnezzar king of Babylon came to Jerusalem and besieged it. The Lord gave Jehoiakim king of Judah into his hand, along with some of the vessels of the house of God; and he brought them to the land of Shinar [Babylon], to the house of his god, and he brought the vessels into the treasury of his god. Then the king ordered Ashpenaz, the chief of his officials, to bring in some of the sons of Israel, including some of the royal family and of the nobles, youths in whom was no defect, who were good-looking, showing intelligence in every branch of wisdom, endowed with understanding and discerning knowledge, and who had ability for serving in the king's court; and he ordered him to teach them the literature and language of the Chaldeans.*
>
> —Dan. 1:1–4

God not only allowed Judah to be taken over, but God in His sovereignty—His absolute power and authority—gave Judah to their enemy. He had warned them for many years, and His children learned once again that God is faithful to keep His word. What the Lord promises He delivers—always, at just the right time. And God's warnings of punishments and natural consequences are always delivered when people ignore His words.

Babylon was similar to some of Europe and the United States in its wealth and abundance of food and things. Babylon's attitudes and values are mirrored by us today. Babylon's king wanted the strong, handsome, smart, gifted people from the "right" families. Their names were changed in an effort to erase their past and create Babylonian identities. Daniel and his countrymen were taken away into captivity, and for most of them, it was a friendly captivity.

Scholars believe Daniel and his three friends were around 15 years old. While largely all the people had fallen away from God, these four teenagers loved Him and determined to live with integrity and faithfulness for their Lord. They quickly learned that friendly captivity held more dangers to their moral fiber and honor than hostile slavery. Satan uses his powers in the world to beat us down at times, which highlights his darkness and evil. That can bolster our inner determination to fight the wrongs and turn to the light and goodness of God. But when the world's powers seduce us into the same dangerous captivity, so many of us follow without a thought. Daniel made up his mind that he wouldn't defile himself with the king's food. A life of integrity requires making a conscious choice. We don't accidently fall into honor and authentic integrity—every day each of us must choose to live right and honorably.

Bible Reading: Daniel 1, Proverbs 11:2–8

Day 2

By the world's standards, Daniel and his friends had every reason to be arrogant and self-important, yet they were humble. The book of Daniel says, "As for these four youths, God gave them knowledge and intelligence in every *branch* of literature and wisdom; Daniel even understood all *kinds of* visions and dreams" (Dan. 1:17). They recognized that God was the One who gave them their abilities and successes. Because these young men were God-reliant instead of self-reliant, they were in a position to succeed when others failed.

> *Now in the second year of the reign of Nebuchadnezzar, Nebuchadnezzar had dreams; and his spirit was troubled and his sleep left him. Then the king gave orders to call in the magicians, the conjurers, the sorcerers and the Chaldeans to tell the king his dreams. So they came in and stood before the king. The king said to them, "I had a dream and my spirit is anxious to understand the dream." Then the Chaldeans spoke to the king in Aramaic: "O king, live forever! Tell the dream to your servants, and we will declare the interpretation." The king replied to the Chaldeans, "The command from me is firm: if you do not make known to me the dream and its interpretation, you will be torn limb from limb and your houses will be made a rubbish heap. But if you declare the dream and its interpretation, you will receive from me gifts and a reward and great honor; therefore declare to me the dream and its interpretation." They answered a second time and said, "Let the king tell the dream to his servants, and we will declare the interpretation." The king replied, "I know for certain that you are bargaining for time, inasmuch as you have seen that the command from me is firm, that if you do not make the dream known to me, there is only one decree for you. For you have agreed together to speak lying and corrupt words before me until the situation is changed; therefore tell me the dream, that I may know that you can declare to me its interpretation." The Chaldeans answered the king and said, "There is not a man on earth who could declare the matter for the king, inasmuch as no great king or ruler has ever asked anything like this of any magician, conjurer or Chaldean. Moreover, the thing which the king demands is difficult, and there is no one else who could declare it to the king except gods, whose dwelling place is not with mortal flesh." Because of this the king became indignant and very furious and gave orders to destroy all the wise men of Babylon. So the decree went forth that the wise men should be slain; and they looked for Daniel and his friends to kill them.*
>
> —Dan. 2:1–13

These men held positions of great honor. They seemed superior to common people and enjoyed all the perks of the rich and famous. Nevertheless, they had no security. If they couldn't perform or meet all the needs and whims of the powers that be, they became expendable. Suddenly the tempting lure of this friendly captivity was showing its dark side.

We experience this today, don't we? Desperately we want to be popular, part of the "in crowd." Oh, to be a rock star, a movie star, or a professional athlete! All our troubles would disappear. We'd party, be cool, and have opinions the world would respect. No one would overlook us again because we'd be on top. But just like the king's advisors, the rugs can be pulled out from under us at the whim of someone else.

Yet even in the middle of Babylon—or America or Europe—there is a way to succeed with honor and proceed with confidence. Calmly, Daniel asked the king's commander with discretion and discernment what was going on—discretion and discernment, not reckless and thoughtless posturing. Because Daniel's focus had stayed on God, he was able to bravely go before the king and ask for time so he could help the king. Then came the most important step of all. Daniel went home and told his friends to pray. He urged them to plead for mercy from the God of heaven concerning this mystery so he and his friends might not be executed with the rest of the wise men of Babylon (Daniel 2:14–18). God revealed the mystery to Daniel because of His love for him and because of his friends and their humble and believing hearts.

To the world, we are all dispensable. To God, we are indispensable. No matter where we are or what talents we do or do not have, we are precious and valuable to God. He promises to meet us when we seek Him and answer us when we ask with sincere hearts.

Bible Reading: Daniel 2:1–28, Luke 11:1–10

Day 3

Power-posturing is old behavior. Important people bowing to our will or acknowledging us make us feel more significant than if Joe Public did. King Nebuchadnezzar made an image of gold that was 90 feet high and nine feet wide and set it up on the plain of Dura in the province of Babylon. Then he sent word to all the highest-ranking people in the land to come and fall down and worship the golden image. It was proclaimed that whoever did not fall down and worship it would immediately be cast into the midst of a furnace of blazing fire (Dan. 3:1-6).

For some 20 years, Daniel and his friends—Shadrach, Meshach, and Abednego—had lived in Babylon without allowing Babylon to live in them. That is a choice each of us must make today—to live where riches, beauty, power, and self are god and not allow those beliefs to become ours. Shadrach, Meshach, and Abednego were put to the ultimate test. They were able to stand firmly when threatened because they practiced integrity every day of their lives.

The king was enraged when he was told that the three Jews wouldn't bow to the image, and he called them to him. "Now bow," he said. "But if you do not worship, you will immediately be cast into the midst of a furnace of blazing fire; and what god is there who can deliver you out of my hands?" (Dan. 3:15). Pretty arrogant, wasn't he? How would you respond?

Shadrach, Meshach, and Abednego replied to the king, "O Nebuchadnezzar, we do not need to give you an answer concerning this matter. If it be *so*, our God whom we serve is able to deliver us from the furnace of blazing fire; and He will deliver us out of your hand, O king. But *even if He does* not, let it be known to you, O king, that we are not going to serve your gods or worship the golden image that you have set up" (Dan. 3:16-18). These men knew God offered them more than the king ever could. Jesus said, "What does it profit a man to gain the whole world, and forfeit his soul? For what will a man give in exchange for his soul?" (Mark 8:36-37).

Nebuchadnezzar was so furious that his face became distorted with rage. He commanded the furnace to be heated seven times hotter than usual. The men were tied up and thrown into the furnace, the heat killing those who threw them in. Then the king leaped to his feet in amazement and asked his advisors, "Weren't there three men that we tied up and threw into the fire? Look! I see four men walking around in the fire, unbound and unharmed, and the fourth looks like a son of the gods." Then he said, "Shadrach, Meshach, and Abednego, servants of the Most High God, come out! Come here!" So they stepped out of the fire. Not one part of them was burned nor did they smell like smoke. The king blessed their God and decreed that no one speak against their God or they would be torn limb from limb, and their houses crushed into heaps of rubble. "For there is no other god who can rescue like this!" (see Dan. 3:19-29).

No amount of talk will change the life choices for people of conviction. Our loyalty cannot be bought or bullied. So when a test comes, we won't need to think about our response. We will simply act with integrity and loyalty. We know God will be with us in the fire and will deliver us from the fire, through the fire, or by the fire. He stands with us—always.

Bible Reading: Daniel 3, 1 Chronicles 29:17–19

Day 4

Success is often more difficult to handle well than adversity. We start to feel entitled to praise and glory. Because not everyone achieves our level of success, it's easy to believe we are the only reason for our accomplishments. As we become more focused on our amazing selves, we stop seeing the needs around us.

The Hanging Gardens of Babylon is one of the ancient wonders of the world. King Nebuchadnezzar was a man of great vision, charisma, and achievement. He was also a man of great ego, self-centeredness, and arrogance. His identity was wrapped up in his success. Isaiah foretold Babylon's haughty arrogance and God's response. You say, "I will be a queen forever." In your heart you say, "I am, and there is no one besides me" (Isa. 47:7–8).

Let's look at ourselves and our nation. How often do we think, "I am, and there is no one besides me"? In what ways do we act on that? It's the *what-about-me* mindset. *I deserve this respect, promotion, acknowledgement, stuff.* Timidity and insecurity are the negative forms of self-absorption. Whether we boast with pride or shrink in anxiety, our focus is all on us. And along with that, we start ignoring the needs of others. Self-centeredness, positive or negative, seats us in God's place and causes those around us to become unimportant.

God gave Nebuchadnezzar a dream to warn him of what would happen if he kept exalting himself over God. Four God-fearing men worked for the king, and God showed Himself in many ways. Daniel interpreted the king's dream, saying if the king did not humble himself, God would. "You [will] be driven away from mankind and your dwelling place [will] be with the beasts of the field, and you [will] be given grass to eat like cattle and be drenched with the dew of heaven; and seven periods of time will pass over you, until you recognize that the Most High is ruler over the realm of mankind and bestows it on whomever He wishes" (Dan. 4:25).

Daniel continued, "Your kingdom will be assured to you after you recognize that *it is* Heaven *that* rules. Therefore, O king, may my advice be pleasing to you: break away now from your sins by *doing* righteousness and from your iniquities by showing mercy to *the* poor, in case there may be a prolonging of your prosperity" (Dan. 4:26–27). The king did not take Daniel's advice, and a year later he suffered a mental breakdown, fulfilling God's words. At the end of the time, Nebuchadnezzar raised his eyes to heaven, and his reason returned to him. He blessed the Most High and praised and honored God who lives forever, saying His dominion is an everlasting dominion, and His kingdom endures from generation to generation. God restored his glory and kingdom, and the king said, "Now I, Nebuchadnezzar, praise, exalt and honor the King of heaven, for all His works are true and His ways just, and He is able to humble those who walk in pride" (Dan. 4:37).

When our identity is wrapped up in God instead of our accomplishments or lack of them, God blesses us. At some point, God will humble us if we refuse to humble ourselves, but He will restore us when we recognize His sovereignty. God's aim is not to destroy us; His goal is to keep us from destroying ourselves and others.

Bible Reading: Daniel 4, Psalm 34:2–4

Day 5

Babylon was taken over by the Medes and Persians when Daniel was about 80 years old, and Darius became king. Daniel became one of three commissioners and distinguished himself by his exceptional qualities, so the king planned to set him over the whole kingdom. As happens to this day, Daniel's integrity and hard work stirred jealousy and hatred in his coworkers. They tried to find some charge against Daniel in his conduct of government affairs, but they couldn't. They found no corruption in him because he was trustworthy and neither corrupt nor negligent. Then these men said, "We will not find any ground of accusation against this Daniel unless we find it against him with regard to the law of his God" (Dan. 6:5).

Daniel is proof that we can live in the world without being corrupted by it. It's possible to be spiritually relevant and culturally relevant at the same time. And when we live effectively for God while making significant contributions to our society and jobs, people will resent us.

The other government officials went to the king and stroked his ego. They told him they thought he should make a law that for 30 days no one could pray to anyone but him. And the punishment for praying to anyone but the king was being thrown into the lion's den.

When Daniel knew the document was signed, he went home three times a day and kneeled, praying and giving thanks to his God as he had done previously. Daniel's enemies reported this to the king who was greatly distressed. He tried to think of a way to save Daniel and was reminded that no one could change the king's law. As they put Daniel into the lion's den, the king said, "Your God whom you constantly serve will Himself deliver you" (Dan. 6:16). A stone was placed over the mouth of the den, and the king and his nobles sealed it with their rings so Daniel's situation might not be changed. At dawn the king yelled down, "Daniel, servant of the living God, has your God, whom you constantly serve, been able to deliver you from the lions?" (Dan. 6:20). As they brought Daniel up, he told them an angel of God shut the lions' mouths, and he had not been harmed in any way because he trusted in his God.

We may argue that being set up, accused, and imprisoned with lions was not being protected. Yet repeatedly God has shown us that He's capable of working difficult, scary, and painful things for our good. God protected Daniel's mind, so instead of panic, he had calm. In his heart, he knew God had not deserted him, and in this case, God protected Daniel's body from harm.

Daniel and his friends lived with integrity and were willing to die to keep it. In God's sovereign grace and plan, they were protected from death in unexpected ways. After our two weeks of Easter, we know there are times when God allows evil people to kill our bodies. Each outcome shows that the living God endures forever and His kingdom will not be destroyed. When God is seen in our lives and glorified, no matter what the circumstances, we are respected too. We can be remarkable when we allow our extraordinary God absolute control of our lives. He who pursues righteousness and loyalty finds life, righteousness, and honor (Prov. 21:21).

Bible Reading: Daniel 6

Day 6

Daniel tells of the sovereign God who keeps His word, whether in promise or in warning. Each chapter of the book of Daniel reveals the absolute power, knowledge, and love of God. King Nebuchadnezzar remains to this day one of the most powerful and influential leaders of all time, yet God directed the events of his life and kingdom in order to fulfill His purposes. It was God who gave the nation of Judah into this king's hand, and it was God who humbled him when his arrogance grew too large.

God shows Himself to be the giver of all things, and He shows He is capable of taking all things away. Proverbs 21:1 says, "The king's heart is *like* channels of water in the hand of the LORD; he turns it wherever He wishes." What a comfort to know that every world leader, judge, and parent answers to our Lord. Their power is not absolute. Our lives are in the capable hands of the God of heaven. He sees us, He knows what is going on, and He cares.

Four godly teenagers grew into four men of integrity and courage. Their story of being taken from their homes is gut-wrenching. Self-pity and fear were never cultivated in their thinking. Instead, these young men realized they were in the hands of the supreme God. On purpose they chose to live lives of integrity, truth, boldness, and discretion.

There are some practical steps we can take to become people of integrity. Moses said this in Deuteronomy 6:1, 4–9:

> *Now this is the commandment, the statutes and the judgments which the LORD your God has commanded me to teach you . . . The LORD is our God, the LORD is one! You shall love the LORD your God with all your heart and with all your soul and with all your might. These words, which I am commanding you today, shall be on your heart. You shall teach them diligently to your sons and shall talk of them when you sit in your house and when you walk by the way and when you lie down and when you rise up. You shall bind them as a sign on your hand and they shall be as frontals on your forehead. You shall write them on the doorposts of your house and on your gates.*

You may not have grown up in a home that taught you God's truths, but you are being offered that opportunity now. Choose Him as your strength and guide. The reason it's vital to know God and His Word is because different options arise when a crisis strikes. We could panic and do the wrong thing, freeze in fear and do nothing, or, like Daniel, pray and respond in God's power and courage. There is no time to think when fiery furnaces and lions' dens come into our lives. Our true selves emerge in the heat of battle. The only way to be people of integrity and courage is to choose to live that way every day.

Daniel, Shadrach, Meshach, and Abednego were surrounded by Babylon and immersed in its selfishness and wealth. How did they live in that world without that world living in them? Paul taught us this:

> *Be anxious for nothing, but in everything by prayer and supplication with thanksgiving let your requests be made known to God. And the peace of God, which surpasses all comprehension, will guard your hearts and your minds in Christ Jesus. Finally, brethren, whatever is true, whatever is honorable, whatever is right, whatever is pure, whatever is lovely, whatever is of good repute, if there is any excellence and if anything worthy of praise, dwell on these things. The things you have learned and received and heard and seen in me, practice these things, and the God of peace will be with you.*
> —Phil. 4:6–9

Bible Reading: **Deuteronomy 5:32–33, 6:1–14, Philippians 4:4–13**

Week 9

HEBREWS

Day 1

Hebrews was a letter written to Hebrew (Jewish) followers of Christ in the late AD 60s. Following Christ Jesus had made life very difficult for these people. Their Jewish families and friends turned against them, refusing to do business with them, kicking them out of their families, and even openly threatening their safety or lives. Discouraged and tired, the Hebrew Christians wanted to slide back to the Jewish religious traditions. While still believing Jesus was the Messiah, they would go along with those who didn't believe in Him, compromising to stop their persecution.

The Bible doesn't tell us who the author of the book of Hebrews was, but they continually urged readers to grow up in their faith. The author also showed that the object of their faith is superior to any other. Jesus Christ is compared to Old Testament prophets and angels. He's compared to Israel's greatest political, religious, and military leaders such as Moses, the prophets, the kings, and the high priests and the priesthood (the religious establishment).

Jesus is compared to the tabernacle and the Law, sacred buildings, good works, and rules. In every way Jesus is supreme. The answer to immense pressure and hardship is not to go back to something inferior. It is to run with endurance the race set before us, eyes fixed on Jesus who had endured the same treatment and now rested in victory in heaven (Heb. 12:1–2).

Jesus is our encouragement, and here is why:

> *God, after He spoke long ago to the fathers in the prophets in many portions and in many ways, in these last days has spoken*

> *to us in His Son, whom He appointed heir of all things, through whom also He made the world. And He is the radiance of His glory and the exact representation of His nature, and upholds all things by the word of His power. When He had made purification of sins, He sat down at the right hand of the Majesty on high, having become as much better than the angels, as He has inherited a more excellent name than they.*
>
> —Heb. 1:1–4

Today we need to understand this message. Life is hard. Following Jesus can make us the target of ridicule. Just like those believers thousands of years ago, we can be faced with losing our family and friends and maybe even our jobs. We may be mocked and physically threatened. Do we bow to the "god of this world" for some comfort and ease now, or do we stand strong in the storm of loss and pain? Should we keep our knowledge of Jesus a secret in our hearts and just pretend to go back to our old ways to keep everyone happy? Should we whisper our allegiance to the Savior while we walk and talk like the people around us?

Hosea 6:3 says, "So let us know, let us press on to know the Lord. His going forth is as certain as the dawn; and He will come to us like the rain, like the spring rain watering the earth." So let us "know"—let us recognize and see Jesus by experience; let us understand and be skillful in living with Jesus Christ. God is certain and reliable. Press on in His strength.

The way to get through hard times is to grow up and mature. The way to grow up is not to go back to how we were as babies. It is to push on, take the next step, experience, learn, and get stronger. Jesus's kingdom cannot be shaken (Heb. 12:28). Know Him personally. Grow in Him daily. Press on through troubles and pain. Jesus is the same yesterday, today, and forever (Heb. 13:8). He leads us, strengthens us, and loves us. So go forward, never backward.

Bible Reading: Hebrews 3:1–6, 13:20–21

Day 2

Yesterday we learned that *knowing* Jesus Christ is superior to everything else and enables us to get through difficult and painful times with integrity. No other alternative would be as effective as Him.

As if knowing that Jesus is better than every other system, method, and person were not enough, the book of Hebrews offers another reason to turn to Him. We matter to God. He loves us and values us. When the angels followed Lucifer (Satan) and fell to sin (these are fallen angels, or demons), God didn't rescue them. But when people fell to sin, God sent Jesus to rescue us. His love for us is monumental. Why would we turn our backs on Someone who loves us and brings us into His family as His own children?

> *For both He who sanctifies and those who are sanctified are all from one* Father; *for which reason He is not ashamed to call them brethren, saying, "I WILL PROCLAIM YOUR NAME TO MY BRETHREN, IN THE MIDST OF THE CONGREGATION I WILL SING YOUR PRAISE." And again, "I WILL PUT MY TRUST IN HIM." And again, "BEHOLD, I AND THE CHILDREN WHOM GOD HAS GIVEN ME." Therefore, since the children share in flesh and blood, He Himself likewise also partook of the same, that through death He might render powerless him who had the power of death, that is, the devil, and might free those who through fear of death were subject to slavery all their lives. For assuredly He does not give help to angels, but He gives help to the descendant of Abraham. Therefore, He had to be made like His brethren in all things, so that He might become a merciful and faithful high priest in things pertaining to God, to make propitiation for the sins of the people. For since He Himself was tempted in that which He has suffered, He is able to come to the aid of those who are tempted.*
> —Heb. 2:11–18

God loves us more than any other part of His creation. Genesis 1:26–27 tells us that at creation, the triune God (the Trinity) made people in His own image and likeness. Jesus tells us in John 4:24 that God is Spirit. We were created to be like Him; we are the only part of creation that has a spirit. Sin—doing things our way instead of following God's directions—changed us. We no longer looked like God spiritually. So the Son of God decided to take on an earthly body and look like us in order to pay our sin-debt. When we believe in Jesus, our spirits are changed to what God intended at creation. We are made right with the Father and look like Him spiritually through Jesus Christ the Son. So Jesus isn't ashamed to say we're related to Him.

Another benefit of Jesus becoming a person is that He knows what it's like to be human. He is merciful to us because He understands our pain, weakness, and fears. Jesus has walked a mile in our shoes. Since He's gone through suffering and temptations, He's able to help us when we're being tempted.

Jesus loves you and me. His sacrifice on the cross enables us to be pure and holy and to be God's children. We are spiritually sisters and brothers of Jesus. When we are loved and surrounded by a strong family, we are secure. People can mistreat us; we can be in frightening situations yet press on toward the best solution because of our family support. That is what Jesus offers—to be in His family, have His Father's name, and be protected and covered by Him.

Bible Reading: 1 John 3

Day 3

I want to talk to you about rest. When we looked at Psalm 23, we saw that the Good Shepherd made it possible for His sheep to lie down and rest in green pastures by cool waters. The book of Hebrews also teaches about God's rest. From creation until today, rest has been important to God. After six days of creating all that is, God rested, and He has told us to follow His example. Our Father knows the importance of letting our bodies, minds, emotions, and spirits rest. It's a simple word yet incredibly difficult for us to do. Rest means a state or period of refreshing freedom from exertion and effort. Freedom from anxiety as well as a building up of peace and strength happens when we stop and lean on the Lord.

The Hebrew Christians were facing immense troubles and fearful threats, so the author reminded them of Israel in the wilderness. God promised them a land with plenty of food and shelter, a place where they could rest and be safe from their enemies. In order to get to this Promised Land, they needed to follow God, do things His way, and build up their trust in the Lord as they watched Him work. In all that, in fighting every enemy, they were supposed to rest in—lean on, depend upon, be supported by—God. Rest—in the middle of life—rest.

The only way to enter into His rest is to believe God is God. We need to accept that His words and actions are true and trust Him to protect and provide for us. We can trust Him by knowing what He did in the past and by knowing Him in a personal and intimate way now.

Hebrews tells us why the first generation of Israelites that Moses led out of slavery couldn't enter the Promised Land and into God's rest. "So we see that they were not able to enter because of unbelief" (Heb. 3:19).

> *Therefore, let us fear if, while a promise remains of entering His rest, any one of you may seem to have come short of it. For indeed we have had good news preached to us, just as they also; but the word they heard did not profit them, because it was not united by faith in those who heard. For we who have believed enter that rest, just as He has said,*
>
> *"As I swore in My wrath, They shall not enter My rest," although His works were finished from the foundation of the world.*
>
> —Heb. 4:1-3

Believing Jesus is the Son of God who died for our sins and lives in heaven now brings us into His family. That faith makes us children of God and joint heirs with Jesus (Rom. 8:16-17). But we must be careful our faith doesn't stop there. Every day—step-by-step through the good times and the painful scary times—we must trust God to be working out His good and perfect purpose in our lives. If the rug of family security is pulled out from under our feet, if the memories of past abuses haunt our thoughts and dreams, if there's barely enough to eat, we need to remember that God is bigger than our enemies. The way to enter into God's rest is to fix our eyes on Him—not our troubles, not our fears, not the most "logical" solution. Trust God.

Today we can rest in the Lord no matter what is going on around us. Rest from trying to be good enough for God to accept us. Jesus's work is enough. Rest in peace by leaning on God and trusting Him to be more powerful than our biggest enemy. Rest on the unshakable rock of personally knowing God and being His child. Jesus said, "Come to Me, all who are weary and heavy-laden, and I will give you rest" (Matt. 11:28).

***Bible Reading*: Hebrews 4**

Day 4

Being told to grow up is a bit offensive while at the same time good advice. The writer of Hebrews told the Jewish Christians to grow up for a number of reasons. When life got hard, they gave up and caved in to the pressure. To be fair, life was very painful and difficult for them. But instead of going toward the solution, they decided to take what looked like the easy way out and go along with the people around them. In school, life, our jobs, and our belief in God, we should grow and build on past knowledge and experience. That is natural and right. Yet when life got tough, these believers went back to being babies in their faith instead of growing stronger. Many of us do that today.

There were some lessons and useful applications from the Old Testament that the author wanted to give these hurting people. Hebrews 5:11–14 says this:

> *Concerning him we have much to say, and* it is *hard to explain, since you have become dull of hearing. For though by this time you ought to be teachers, you have need again for someone to teach you the elementary principles of the oracles of God, and you have come to need milk and not solid food. For everyone who partakes* only *of milk is not accustomed to the word of righteousness, for he is an infant. But solid food is for the mature, who because of practice have their senses trained to discern good and evil.*

Here's an easy picture. If a healthy, average teenage boy sat next to you at the table, took out a baby bottle and started sucking on it, you'd be horrified. While everyone else at the table ordered hamburgers, this kid opened a jar of strained mixed vegetables, handed you a little spoon, and asked you to feed him. How embarrassing and shocking. It's just not natural or right for people to choose to go backward physically. Let's not even wonder if he's wearing diapers!

It is just as illogical for a person to go back toward spiritual infancy. The knowledge of Jesus is pure, spiritual milk that grows us up in our salvation (1 Pet. 2:2). But we shouldn't stay there. There are some things about God that are solid food. They are a lot to chew on and take some time to digest, yet they are worth the effort. So here they are. We are in a spiritual battle.

We feel and see it physically in our lives—evil people hurting us, injustice, lies—but the cause of our physical hardships is the fight between Satan's forces and God's.

Hebrews 7 and 8 give us a grownup, mature picture of Jesus. He is compared to King Melchizedek in the Old Testament. Jesus is first a king of righteousness and then a king of peace. Integrity and virtue come before peace and prosperity. Jesus is instantly available. He meets us on the battlefield and stands between us and the enemy. Jesus offers us strength and a righteous way out of our trials. Not only is Jesus instantly available, He is permanently available to us—always, forever. He will never leave us or forsake us (Heb. 13:5). God gave us a promise that we can draw near to Him, that our hope of a confident, close, and loving relationship with our Father is sealed by Jesus. Christ is our peacemaker; He intercedes to the Father on our behalf. That means that when Satan goes to God and accuses us of blowing it, of being too bad or useless or immature to be loved and forgiven, Jesus stands up for us, claiming us as His own.

Our pain, injustice, loneliness, shame, and fears are the outward signs of the spiritual battles going on. "Be strong in the Lord and in the strength of His might. Put on the full armor of God, so that you will be able to stand firm against the schemes of the devil" (Eph. 6:10–11).

Bible Reading: **Ephesians 6:10–18, 2 Chronicles 20:8–18**

Day 5

Because we have Jesus, "let us draw near with a sincere heart in full assurance of faith, having our hearts sprinkled *clean* from an evil conscience and our bodies washed with pure water. Let us hold fast the confession of our hope without wavering, for He who promised is faithful" (Heb. 10:22–23). "Now faith is the assurance of *things* hoped for, the conviction of things not seen. For by it the men of old gained approval. By faith we understand that the worlds were prepared by the word of God, so that what is seen was not made out of things which are visible" (Heb. 11:1–3).

Remember, the people to whom this letter was first written were in a terrible way. They were rejected by their countrymen, their friends, and their families. No one would do business with them, which meant they had no money to buy food or pay their rent. Not merely ignored by their community, these Christ-followers were also ridiculed, beaten, and vandalized. Then they received this letter that encouraged them to be strong and keep growing up, moving forward, pressing on, choosing well. Jesus was what made their lives possible. Jesus was their strong foundation. Jesus was worthy of their faith.

You and I need to hold on to that today. We've learned a lot about God and His love for us, and hopefully we have decided to ask Him to be our Lord and Savior. But many of us could still have a hole in our hearts from the rejections we've experienced. We may still believe that only a parent's or friend's love can fill that hole. Perhaps we have anger that God allowed our worst fears to become reality, that no one protected us—not even God. The everyday hurts and injustices act like dripping water, wearing away at us until we want to lash out and solve things on our own, usually in an ineffective way.

Before turning back to what we remember . . . before giving up on God . . . before sinking into despair as we focus on our pain . . . look one more time at Jesus. Look at Jesus who has given us for the first time a clear and clean conscience and has taken away all our shame and guilt. Look at Jesus who has washed our bodies clean and pure using His own blood to cleanse us. Look at Jesus who has given us a solid foundation in this unstable world. Know that without wavering, we can hold tightly to the hope we have *in* Jesus and *from* Jesus. Christ Jesus who has promised us love, forgiveness, protection, care, freedom, and His name is faithful to keep His promises.

Break down Hebrews 11:1 with me. "Now faith is the assurance of *things hoped for*, the conviction of things not seen." *Faith*—is conviction of the truth of anything. Belief is the *assurance*—the substructure, foundation, that which has actual existence, confidence, firm trust—of *things hoped for* to wait for salvation with joy and full confidence, confident expectation, and anticipation. It is the *conviction*—the evidence and proof of *things not seen.*

Our firm conviction that Jesus is God and superior to everything is the real, existing foundation in our lives of the rescue and salvation we confidently expect and wait for. And the things our eyes can't see—like our clean consciences and lack of fear—are evidence and proof that our belief (faith) in Jesus is firm and true.

We can get through our hard times by remembering Jesus and keeping our eyes fixed on Him. He is real and trustworthy, our strength and firm foundation. God is a promise-keeper.

Bible Reading: Hebrews 11

Day 6

Through all the pain, fear, rage, and injustice we face in life, we have a hope. This week we've looked into the lives of a group of Jewish believers in Christ who were experiencing the worst that life had to offer. Tough love prompted the letter writer to push these people, and us, to grow up, suck it up, and move forward. That sounds a bit severe, yet we all know that when we are knocked down and about to be kicked, we need that kind of fire under us.

As we straighten our shoulders, put on the full armor of God, and get ready to stand firm, let's remember our hope. God has given us both His promise and His oath. These two things are unchangeable because it is impossible for God to lie. We who have fled to Him for refuge can take new courage, for we can hold on to His promise with confidence. This hope is like a strong and trustworthy anchor for our souls. It leads us through the curtain of heaven into God's inner sanctuary (Heb. 6:18–19).

Because of God's oath, it is Jesus who guarantees the effectiveness of this better covenant. Therefore, He is able, once and forever, to save everyone who comes to God through Him. He lives forever to plead with God on their behalf. He is the kind of High Priest we need because He is holy and blameless, unstained by sin. He has now been set apart from sinners, and He has been given the highest place of honor in heaven. He does not need to offer sacrifices every day. But Jesus did this once for all when He sacrificed Himself on the cross (Heb. 7:22–27).

Our hope . . . the thing that will keep our heads up in the storm . . . the one thing that will anchor us securely . . . is Jesus Christ. He is it. It seems too simple. We're so used to plotting and working and fighting that believing Jesus is God can seem inadequate, like we should do more. But the truth is that Jesus is our hope. God loves you and me just as He loved the Hebrew believers years ago. He doesn't always take us out of our hard circumstances, but He always—always—is our anchor in them.

"Therefore, since we receive a kingdom which cannot be shaken, let us show gratitude, by which we may offer to God an acceptable service with reverence and awe. For our God is a consuming fire" (Heb. 12:28–29). Today, wherever we live, our worlds can be shaken. The justice system can fail, our families can fall apart, our faith in our friends or ourselves can be shattered. Why on earth would any of us look to this breaking world as our place of safety? Why would we go back to old beliefs? We have been offered a kingdom of grace that cannot be shaken. God has provided us His own Son to anchor us to His unshakable kingdom when the spiritual and physical battles rage around us.

This week we have seen that Jesus is superior to anyone or anything. You and I have been offered the greatest gift that could ever be given. Jesus has walked in our shoes and knows how difficult life is. With tears He went to the cross because He loved His Father, and He loved you and me. If Jesus had stared at that terrible event, that painful cross, He wouldn't have been able to go through with His plan. But for the joy set before Him, Jesus endured the cross, despising the shame, and has sat down at the right hand of the throne of God. The matchless, ultimate, greatest gift ever given is our hope in time of trouble. Don't look at life; look to Jesus.

Bible Reading: Hebrews 12

Week 10

ACTS

Day 1

The book of Acts tells the story of the beginning of the church. Each new spurt of growth and spreading came after traumatic and painful events. We know that God is completely holy, good, loving, and righteous. He did not cause anything sinful that happened, but He did and does allow people's bad choices to touch others. Paul said in Romans 8:28, "And we know that God causes all things to work together for good to those who love God, to those who are called according to *His* purpose."

The fact that we are quoting Paul is a testimony to this. We will look at his story and see how a patient and loving Father pursued and forgave a murderous, religious fanatic. Not only was Paul forgiven, he was changed into a new person who loved God more than his religion, risked his life to teach others about Jesus, and spread God's good news to all the known world.

But we're jumping ahead of ourselves. Remember how justifiably afraid Jesus's disciples were when Jesus was arrested? They ran and hid, and Peter denied ever knowing Jesus as the fear of torture and death oppressed the nation. After Jesus rose from the grave and then ascended to heaven, the promised Holy Spirit came. After being filled with the Spirit, that group of barely educated, frightened men turned the world upside down with their wisdom and boldness.

The church in Jerusalem grew, but Jesus had said to go into all the world. Just as we need a push (or gentle kick) today to move out of our comfort zone, God allowed something Satan meant for harm to push His church out of one city and into the world. It all began when God the Holy Spirit baptized ordinary people and filled them with His power.

> When the day of Pentecost had come, they [the believers in Jesus] were all together in one place. And suddenly there came from heaven a noise like a violent rushing wind, and it filled the whole house where they were sitting. And there appeared to them tongues as of fire distributing themselves, and they rested on each one of them. And they were all filled with the Holy Spirit and began to speak with other tongues [languages], as the Spirit was giving them utterance.
>
> —Acts 2:1–4

People of many nations were in the city and were amazed to hear these men speaking in their own languages, teaching them about Jesus Christ. Peter told the crowd to repent and be saved. "So then, those who had received his word were baptized; and that day there were added about three thousand souls. They were continually devoting themselves to the apostles' teaching and to fellowship, to the breaking of bread and to prayer. Everyone kept feeling a sense of awe, and many wonders and signs were taking place through the apostles" (Acts 2:41–43).

Know this for yourself today. What other people have done to hurt you, God can and will change into good. Quoting Romans 8:28 to someone won't comfort them in the middle of a trauma, but knowing it is true will get them through it. It is God's work, not ours. He produces good out of every bad, painful, and hard thing when we love Him. Believe in Jesus, recognize your sin, and repent—turn from your old way of living, and turn to God. Love Him the way He loves you and me. Love Him with all our heart, and know that God causes all things to work together for good to those who love Him, to those who are called according to His purpose.

Jesus proved to us that there is a love that is greater than life. The Holy Spirit now proved to us that there is a love that is greater than our enemy and our limitations.

Bible Reading: Acts 1 and 2

Day 2

Peter and John went to the temple one afternoon to take part in the 3:00 prayer service. A man who had been lame since birth was being carried into the gates to beg. Seeing Peter and John, he asked them for money. But Peter said, "I have no silver and gold, but what I do have I give to you. In the name of Jesus Christ of Nazareth, rise up and walk!" Helping him up by the right hand, the man's feet and ankles became strong. Leaping up, he stood and began to walk and entered the temple with them, walking and leaping and praising God. All the people watching were amazed, and Peter asked them why; then he told them the miracle was done in the power of Jesus of Nazareth. He went on to teach about Christ to everyone in the temple (Acts 3).

This caused the religious leaders to become very disturbed. They arrested Peter and John and put them in jail until the next day. But around 5,000 people who had seen and heard them believed in Jesus. Intending to find Peter and John guilty of some wrong, the leaders asked them by whose power they healed and taught. Peter said, "By the name of Jesus Christ the Nazarene, whom you crucified and God raised from the dead. And there is salvation in no one else; for there is no other name under heaven that has been given among men by which we must be saved" (Acts 4:1-12).

Then an odd thing happened. Acts 4:13 says, "Now as they observed the confidence of Peter and John and understood that they were uneducated and untrained men, they were amazed, and *began* to recognize them as having been with Jesus." The Holy Spirit's power, wisdom, and courage will be recognized in you and me today just as it was in the first century AD. People will look at us when we speak God's wisdom and truth and be amazed because they know how difficult school was for us or how nervous we were to speak publicly. Or perhaps we thought we were too smart to believe in God. They will see us boldly stand up for others, for justice and rightness, and be surprised because they remember the old us. We used to be fearful and bitter; we used to use our temper and angry words to fight instead of the peaceful and powerful words of God. Instead of giving in and giving up, we now stand firm and step up. God in us is just as astonishing as the God who was in Peter and John.

The religious leaders threatened Peter and John and told them to stop teaching about Jesus. Peter and John, bold in the Spirit, said, "Whether it is right in the sight of God to give heed to you rather than to God, you be the judge; for we cannot stop speaking about what we have seen and heard" (Acts 4:19-20). After being released, they went to their friends and told them of the threats. All the believers prayed over the situation. The prayers ended like this:

> *"Now, Lord, take note of their threats, and grant that Your bond-servants may speak Your word with all confidence, while You extend Your hand to heal, and signs and wonders take place through the name of Your holy servant Jesus." And when they had prayed, the place where they had gathered together was shaken, and they were all filled with the Holy Spirit and* began *to speak the word of God with boldness.*
> —Acts 4:29-31

When people or laws tell us to go against God's Word, we must respectfully stand firm in our convictions and actions. Is it scary? Yes. Are the threats real? They are. But equally real and more persuasive is the power of God in us. Opposition highlights God's power and effectiveness.

Bible Reading: Acts 3–4

Day 3

Peter is by now an old friend of ours. He's impulsive, loud, passionate, gutsy, boastful, fearful, repentant, honest, and bold. But he is also an unfolding man of God. Do you remember that he told Jesus that all the other apostles may leave Him but he never would? After Jesus rose from the grave, Peter's bitter failure of denying ever knowing Jesus changed him. He was surprisingly cautious in declaring his love for Jesus because he'd learned from his failure. Two times Jesus asked Simon Peter if he loved (*agape*—godly love) Him, and Peter answered that He did love (*phileō*—friendship) Him. The third time Jesus asked Peter if he *phileō* Him, Peter was upset and said, "Lord you know I do." Each time Jesus said, "Tend my sheep" (John 21:15-17).

The Holy Spirit came upon the believers, and Peter started walking in God's power instead of his own. From the moment he was filled with the Spirit, Peter started to tend and care for Jesus's sheep. Fear and intimidation had once affected him, but now they rolled off his shoulders as he boldly stood before crowds and told them of Christ Jesus. Along with the other believers, Peter performed miraculous healings. When the ultimate test came, facing the religious and political leaders and guards, Peter was a rock. Recalling his past failure did not lure him back to living in fear. Their threats no longer controlled his behavior. His focus was on the spiritual. The physical was short-lived; the spiritual was eternal. He realized that the biggest, strongest part of him was now the Spirit of God living in Him, not his body, emotions, or thoughts.

Peter traveled from Jerusalem to Joppa where a woman named Tabitha served and loved God. She became sick and died, and some of the disciples called for Peter. He sent them all out of the room and then got down on his knees and prayed. Turning toward the dead woman, he said, "Tabitha, get up." She opened her eyes, and seeing Peter, she sat up. It became known all over Joppa, and many believed in the Lord (Acts 9:32–43).

About that time, King Herod Agrippa began to persecute some believers in the church. He had the apostle James, John's brother, killed with a sword. When Herod saw how much this pleased the Jewish leaders, he arrested Peter during the Passover celebration. Peter was kept in prison, but the church was earnestly praying to God for him. The night before Peter was to be placed on trial, he was asleep, chained between two soldiers with others standing guard at the prison gate.

Suddenly an angel of the Lord appeared, and a light shone in the cell. He struck Peter on the side and woke him up. "Quick! Get up!" he said, and the chains fell off Peter's wrists. Then the angel told him, "Get dressed, and put on your sandals." And he did. "Now put on your coat, and follow me," the angel ordered. Peter followed him but thought it was just a dream. When he got outside the prison, the angel left and Peter went to a friend's house where many believers were praying for him. When the servant girl answered his knock, she recognized Peter's voice. Overjoyed, she ran back without opening the door and exclaimed, "Peter is at the door!" Finally, they let him in, and he told of God's deliverance. He told them to tell everyone and then left. And the word of the Lord continued to grow and multiply (Acts 12).

Peter tended Jesus's sheep. He led them to a deeper knowledge of God and cared for them in sorrow and in trouble. Boldly and with *agape* love, Peter sacrificed his safety and comfort for the sake of God's children. Only God can change a person like Peter (or you and me) into a shepherd like Jesus.

Bible Reading: Acts 12, 1 Peter 1:3–9

Day 4

As thousands were added to the church, it became impossible for the apostles to handle all the ministries and business, as well as teach. They decided to select from among them seven men of good reputation, full of the Spirit and of wisdom, who could be put in charge of the tasks. Stephen, a man full of faith and of the Holy Spirit, was one of the men chosen.

Stephen, full of grace and power, was performing great wonders and signs among the people. Some well-educated men argued with him, but they were unable to cope with the wisdom and the Spirit with which he was speaking. So they persuaded some men to lie about Stephen, saying, "We heard him blaspheme Moses, and even God." They stirred the people up and dragged him before the Council and had false witnesses say he spoke against the holy places and the Law. And gazing at him, all who sat in the council saw that his face was like the face of an angel (Acts 6).

Stephen then taught Old Testament history and showed how God's chosen people had always resisted God and His leaders. Bringing it full circle, Stephen boldly said, "You stiff-necked people, with uncircumcised hearts and ears! You are just like your fathers. You always resist the Holy Spirit! Was there ever a prophet your fathers did not persecute? They even killed those who predicted the coming of the Righteous One. And now you have betrayed and murdered Him, you who received the law as delivered by angels and did not keep it."

When they heard this, they were furious and gnashed their teeth at him. But he, full of the Holy Spirit, gazed into heaven and saw the glory of God and Jesus standing at the right hand of God. "Look," he said, "I see heaven open and the Son of Man standing at the right hand of God." At this they covered their ears, and yelling at the top of their voices, they all rushed at him, dragged him out of the city, and began to stone him. Meanwhile, the witnesses laid their clothes at the feet of a young man named Saul. They went on stoning Stephen as he called on the Lord and said, "Lord Jesus, receive my spirit!" Then he fell on his knees and cried out, "Lord, do not hold this sin against them." When he had said this, he fell asleep (died) (Acts 7).

Saul approved of Stephen's death. On that day, a great persecution broke out against the church at Jerusalem, and all except the apostles were scattered throughout Judea and Samaria. Godly men buried Stephen and mourned deeply for him. But Saul began to destroy the church. Going from house to house, he dragged off men and women and put them in prison. But the believers who had fled Jerusalem went everywhere preaching the Good News about Jesus (Acts 8:1–4).

We see again how God takes the winter of death, cold-hearted hatred, and evil, and uses them for the good of people at that time and into the future. As he was slowly dying, Stephen recognized the spring that was coming. God in him, the Holy Spirit, filled Stephen with His perspective. From the physical, Stephen felt pain, probably some fear, and knew injustice. Spiritually Stephen saw His goal—Jesus by the throne in heaven. He understood that when he died, he would truly be falling asleep physically and coming fully, completely awake for the first time spiritually.

The Christ-followers who had stayed comfortably in Jerusalem were now forced to run for their lives. But they took the Holy Spirit with them, teaching God's good news of Jesus Christ to all the world. Satan had intended to kill and intimidate God's Word into silence. God used Satan's tactics to do just the opposite. Jesus spread like wildfire by the very plot of His enemy.

Bible Reading: Acts 7, 8:1–4, Genesis 50:19–21

Day 5

Now Saul, still breathing threats and murder against the disciples of the Lord, went to the high priest, and asked for letters from him to the synagogues at Damascus, so that if he found any belonging to the Way, both men and women, he might bring them bound to Jerusalem. As he was traveling, it happened that he was approaching Damascus, and suddenly a light from heaven flashed around him; and he fell to the ground and heard a voice saying to him, "Saul, Saul, why are you persecuting Me?" And he said, "Who are You, Lord?" And He said, "I am Jesus whom you are persecuting, but get up and enter the city, and it will be told you what you must do." The men who traveled with him stood speechless, hearing the voice but seeing no one. Saul got up from the ground, and though his eyes were open, he could see nothing; and leading him by the hand, they brought him into Damascus. And he was three days without sight, and neither ate nor drank.

—Acts 9:1–9

The Lord called a disciple named Ananias in a vision and told him to look for a man from Tarsus named Saul who was praying. God told Ananias to lay hands on him so Saul would regain his sight. "But Lord," exclaimed Ananias, "I've heard about the terrible things this man has done to the believers in Jerusalem! We hear that he is authorized to arrest every believer in Damascus." But the Lord said to him, "Go, for he is a chosen instrument of Mine, to bear My name before the Gentiles and kings and the sons of Israel; for I will show him how much he must suffer for My name's sake." So, Ananias went and did as God had told him (Acts 9:10–18).

Ananias—his courage, trust, and obedience were amazing. If God directed you to go to a dangerous person to pray for him, what would you think? Would you go? I love the fact that Ananias talked with God and made sure he was hearing correctly. God's explanation gave insight into how big His love, forgiveness, and purpose are. No one was out of reach of God's love, too evil for God to forgive, or unusable. Trusting God, Ananias went to Saul, laid hands on him, and prayed. Courage is acting even when you're afraid. Filled with God's courage, Ananias obeyed and became part of a missionary's legacy that changed the world.

Saul kept increasing in strength and confusing the Jews who lived at Damascus by proving that Jesus is the Christ. Soon the Jews were plotting to kill Saul, so his fellow believers helped him escape the city. He fled to Jerusalem, and after the disciples finally accepted him, he taught about Jesus until his life was threatened. Fleeing again, this previous killer of Christ-followers continued to teach boldly about Jesus. Then the church throughout Judea, Galilee, and Samaria enjoyed a time of peace. It was strengthened and encouraged by the Holy Spirit, and it grew in numbers, living in the fear of the Lord (Acts 9:22–31).

Saul, also known as Paul, was filled with the Holy Spirit. He brought the good news of Jesus Christ to the uttermost parts of the world. Everywhere he taught, many people came to know Jesus as their Lord and Savior. Paul knew God intimately. He was also imprisoned, beaten, whipped, stoned, shipwrecked, and lost at sea. He was in danger from robbers, his countrymen, and the Gentiles in the city, the wilderness, on the sea, and among false brothers. He was hungry, thirsty, and cold; he worked hard and had no shelter (2 Cor. 11:23–28). Killing, justified by religious fervor, transformed into service motivated by love. Paul lived in eager expectation and hope that he would never do anything that caused him shame but that he would always be bold for Christ as he had been in the past, and that his life would always honor Christ. He said, "For to me, to live is Christ and to die is gain" (Phil. 1:20-21).

***Bible Reading*: Acts 9, 13:9, 2 Corinthians 11:22-28, 12:7-10**

Day 6

The complete title given to the book of Acts by second-century scholars is "The Acts of the Apostles." But that is a bit misleading. Acts is sandwiched between the Gospels and Paul's letters. At the end of the four Gospels—Matthew, Mark, Luke, and John—we see a small group of Jewish Christ-followers trying to recover from the trauma of Jesus's crucifixion and resurrection. Romans, the book that follows Acts, tells about Jesus being taught to the Gentile world. What happened between the small band of traumatized believers and the spreading of the good news to the world? Well, it was "The Acts of the Holy Spirit."

You and I are living in the "church age" today, and the acts of the Holy Spirit are still being written in our hearts and lives. Romans 6:23 tells us, "For the wages of sin is death, but the free gift of God is eternal life in Christ Jesus our Lord." Romans 10:9 says, "If you confess with your mouth Jesus *as* Lord, and believe in your heart that God raised Him from the dead, you will be saved." It is by believing in your heart that you are made right with God, and it is by confessing with your mouth that you are saved. You were also included in Christ when you heard the word of truth, the gospel of your salvation. Having believed, you were marked in Him with a seal, the promised Holy Spirit (Eph. 1:13). It is God who makes both us and you stand firm in Christ. He anointed us, set His seal of ownership on us, and put His Spirit in our hearts as a deposit, guaranteeing what is to come (2 Cor. 1:21-22).

Remember all the remarkable things Jesus did in His life on earth? He changed water into wine; healed blind, deaf, and mute people; cast out demons; made the lame walk; and raised people from the dead. Jesus knew what people were thinking, and He understood the Scriptures better than scholars with years of study, and He could teach difficult truths in a way anyone could understand. Thousands were fed with a few loaves of bread and fish, and He walked on top of a stormy sea and helped Peter do the same. He calmed a storm and cured diseases, and He gave the promise of His future death and resurrection for our salvation. Christ Jesus was tempted in every way but didn't cave in and sin, He was terrified and distressed about the cross yet still obeyed His Father's plan. Never has there been a résumé like that. Yet listen to what Jesus tells us.

> *Believe Me that I am in the Father and the Father is in Me; otherwise believe because of the works themselves. Truly, truly, I say to you, he who believes in Me, the works that I do, he will do also; and greater works than these he will do; because I go to the Father. Whatever you ask in My name, that will I do, so that the Father may be glorified in the Son. If you ask Me anything in My name, I will do it. If you love Me, you will keep My commandments. I will ask the Father, and He will give you another Helper, that He may be with you forever; that is the Spirit of truth, whom the world cannot receive, because it does not see Him or know Him, but you know Him because He abides with you and will be in you.*
>
> —John 14:11–17

Jesus was fully and completely human and fully God. God in Him gave Him the ability to live the life He lived. He promised us we'd be filled with the Holy Spirit. God in us will enable us to do even greater works than Jesus did and offer the hope of His finished redemption. When our life is about God—loving, trusting, and obeying God—anything we ask will be according to His will and to further His purpose. God will give us whatever we ask. We can live the effective, miraculous lives of Jesus and the apostles, all because of "The Acts of the Holy Spirit."

Bible Reading: **John 14:11–31, Acts 2:33–39**

Week 11

KINGS

Day 1

Samuel was a prophet in Israel who worshiped and served God with all his heart. The elders came to him when he was old and said, "You are old, and your sons do not walk in your ways; now appoint a king to lead us, such as all the other nations have." Samuel was very upset with their request and went to the Lord for advice. And the Lord told him, "Listen to all that the people are saying to you; it is not you they have rejected, but they have rejected Me as their king" (1 Sam. 8:1–7). God told Samuel to tell the people they could have their king but to be warned. The king would tax them heavily and expect their sons and daughters to serve him however he wished. He would take the best of all they worked for, and when he made war, the king would make their sons fight it for him. Despite the fact that a king would be an inferior ruler to God, building his own earthly kingdom instead of God's, Israel wanted to be like the other nations. They rejected God as their leader, and the Lord let them go (1 Samuel 8).

Samuel anointed Saul as the first king of Israel. After 40 years of his unfaithful and corrupt rule, David became king. Forty years later, David's son Solomon became king of Israel and also reigned for 40 years. King David was a man after God's own heart and loved the Lord's laws and words. His son Solomon started out loving the Lord, and God granted him more wisdom and wealth than any man has ever had to this day. Gradually, Solomon started serving himself instead of God. He taxed the people heavily and put them into forced labor in order to construct grand buildings and other possessions.

When King Solomon died, his son Rehoboam was set to take over the throne. The people asked him to lighten their taxes and forced labor and they would follow him. Rehoboam requested three days to think about it and then asked the elders who had served with his father what they thought. The older counselors replied, "If you are willing to serve the people today and give them a favorable answer, they will always be your loyal subjects." But he rejected the advice the elders gave him and consulted the young men who had grown up with him and were serving him. They told him to be even harsher than his father had been. Rehoboam did as his young friends told him, and the people rebelled. The 10 tribes from the north split off and anointed Jeroboam as their king. King Rehoboam was left with the two tribes of Judah in the south (1 Kings 12:1–24).

Before Rehoboam consulted the younger men, he rejected the advice of the elders. With a total lack of open-mindedness, honesty, and wisdom, Rehoboam sought to find someone who agreed with what he wanted. To some extent, we have probably all done that. We know what we want and what we believe is our right, and we are not willing to listen to any other views. Our only goal is to find someone who backs our way of thinking—right or wrong. Don't tell us of possible consequences, and don't put any responsibility on us; just tell us what we want to hear.

Notice, too, that Rehoboam never went to God for wisdom and counsel. When Solomon was walking with the Lord, he wrote, "The proverbs of Solomon the son of David, king of Israel: to know wisdom and instruction, to discern the sayings of understanding, to receive instruction in wise behavior, righteousness, justice and equity; to give prudence to the naive, to the youth knowledge and discretion, a wise man will hear and increase in learning, and a man of understanding will acquire wise counsel" (Prov. 1:1–5). Be warned: walking away from God and godly advice has a high cost.

Bible Reading: 1 Kings 12:1–24, Proverbs 1:7–19

Day 2

Israel divided into two separate countries. The 10 northern tribes retained the name Israel, while the two southern tribes became known as Judah. The nation was split for the remainder of biblical history. Israel's king became Jeroboam who built up the city of Shechem in the hill country of Ephraim, and it became his capital. Jeroboam thought to himself, "Unless I am careful, the kingdom will return to the dynasty of David. When they go to Jerusalem to offer sacrifices at the temple of the Lord, they will again give their allegiance to King Rehoboam of Judah. They will kill me and make him their king instead." So on the advice of his counselors, the king made two gold calves. He said to the people, "It is too much trouble for you to worship in Jerusalem. Look, Israel, these are the gods who brought you out of Egypt!" King Jeroboam and the people of Israel worshiped the idols and made feasts like the ones in Judah to celebrate their false gods. And this thing became a sin (1 Kings 12:25–33 NLT).

We can draw a great deal of lessons from these tragic events. Surrounding ourselves with "yes men" is risky and unwise. Jeroboam was no different from King Rehoboam, seeking people who would tell him what he wanted to hear and advisors who would back his behavior no matter how damaging and foolish it was. The athletic, entertainment, and political industries today give us vivid pictures of popular, powerful people who live the same way. Their "friends" and consultants enable them as they destroy their lives with drugs, alcohol, sex, and abuse of others. It is possible for each of us to choose weak friends and foolish mentors too. As we've seen from these two kings, the damage ripples out to many people and generations.

Proverbs 12:15 reads, "The way of a fool is right in his own eyes, but a wise man is he who listens to counsel." Proverbs 19:20–21 says, "Listen to counsel and accept discipline, that you may be wise the rest of your days. Many plans are in a man's heart, but the counsel of the LORD will stand." "The fear [awe and reverence] of the LORD is the beginning of wisdom; a good understanding have all those who do *His commandments*; His praise endures forever" (Ps. 111:10). "I, wisdom, dwell with prudence, and I find knowledge *and* discretion. The fear of the LORD is to hate evil; pride and arrogance and the evil way and the perverted mouth, I hate. Counsel is mine and sound wisdom; I am understanding, power is mine" (Prov. 8:12–14).

The people of Israel shared responsibility with their king. Like today, they willingly believed lies about where their freedom and power came from. They pushed God out of their government when they demanded a king. Then they pushed Him out of their churches, worshiping fake, man-made images that were fashionable and convenient. Those decisions were the outward results of each person's heart. Long before falling at the feet of human rulers, long before worshiping false gods, the people in Israel rejected God in their personal lives.

Our country's fight to take God out of our government, our schools, and even our homes is the same outward sign. Each of us individually should respond to God's love by making Him the sovereign King of our lives. The Lord said, "If I shut up the heavens so that there is no rain, or if I command the locust to devour the land, or if I send pestilence among My people, and My people who are called by My name humble themselves and pray and seek My face and turn from their wicked ways, then I will hear from heaven, will forgive their sin and will heal their land" (2 Chron. 7:13–14). Wise counsel says to know God's love and love Him in return.

Bible Reading: **Proverbs 8, James 4:10**

Day 3

From the time the 10 northern tribes became a separate nation until they were taken captive by Assyria, all of Israel's 19 kings were considered evil in God's sight. They worshiped other gods and led their people to do the same, which was why God allowed them to be defeated by their enemy. Judah to the south had a total of 20 kings before they were defeated by Babylon. Eight of Judah's kings loved God and led their people according to His Word, and God protected and grew them in astonishing ways.

Jehoshaphat was the fourth king of Judah and served God as his father, King Asa, had. He allied himself with Israel's king for a time during some wars, but unlike Israel, Judah listened to and obeyed the Word of God.

After Jehoshaphat led Judah in worshiping the Lord, the armies of the Moabites, Ammonites, and some of the Meunites declared war on Jehoshaphat, who was afraid and turned his attention to seek the Lord. He proclaimed a fast throughout all Judah. He prayed before all of Judah and said, "O Lord, the God of our fathers, are You not God in the heavens? And are You not ruler over all the kingdoms of the nations? Power and might are in Your hand so that no one can stand against You." He listed his fears and dilemmas and then prayed, "O our God, will You not judge them? For we are powerless before this great multitude who are coming against us; nor do we know what to do, but our eyes are on You" (2 Chron. 20:6, 12).

When the powerful ruler of a nation humbles himself and admits he really doesn't have supreme power and control, God rewards him. The Spirit of the Lord spoke through one of the men of Judah and said, "'Do not fear or be dismayed because of this great multitude, for the battle is not yours but God's. You *need* not fight in this *battle*; station yourselves, stand and see the salvation of the LORD on your behalf, O Judah and Jerusalem. Do not fear or be dismayed; tomorrow go out to face them, for the LORD is with you.' Jehoshaphat bowed his head with *his* face to the ground, and all Judah and the inhabitants of Jerusalem fell down before the LORD, worshiping the LORD" (2 Chron. 20:15, 17–18). The next morning Judah went out trusting and praising God. As they started singing praise to the Lord, He set up an ambush for all Judah's enemies, and they destroyed themselves.

How can this interesting history be applied in our lives today? Note that obeying God does not keep our enemies from attacking us. In fact, sometimes our greatest battles come because we are living right with God. That is not what the devil wants, and he will try to distract us with fear, pain, and overwhelming conflicts. Also remember that the physical enemies and battles are usually outward signs of what is going on spiritually. And no one is more qualified to fight and win a spiritual war than God. Like King Jehoshaphat, we must gather those around us, drop our faces to the ground, and give up all our ideas and control for how to fight and win. When we ask the God of the universe to lead us and give us wisdom, He will tell us to not be afraid or dismayed. The battle is His, and we can trust Him to fight it in His might and with His divine weapons. We also see that when we humble ourselves before the Lord, we are not humiliated or demeaned. In God's economy, the way to be exalted is to be truthfully humble. His victory brings glory to Him and to us. We win more than the war when we give ourselves over to the Lord.

Bible Reading: 2 Chronicles 20:19-37, 2 Corinthians 10:3-7, Ephesians 6:10-12

Day 4

One of the best kings to reign in Judah was Hezekiah. Although his father had been an extremely wicked king, Hezekiah loved God. During his reign, Assyria was the most powerful nation in the world. They swept through the land, destroying every country in their path. Assyria crushed Israel and took them captive. Setting up a stronghold in Samaria, which was directly between Israel and Judah, Assyria continued its attacks. Although Judah and its king followed God faithfully, Assyria eventually took over all the fortified cities of Judah except Jerusalem.

Without consulting the Lord, King Hezekiah offered to pay the king of Assyria, hoping to win his favor. After that, Assyria engaged in classic psychological warfare. The field commander said to them, "Tell Hezekiah that this is what the great king of Assyria says: 'On what are you basing this confidence of yours? You say you have strategy and military strength, but you speak only empty words. On whom are you depending that you rebel against me? If you say you trust in the Lord, I'll tell you the Lord told me to come take you over.'" Judah's leaders said, "Speak in Aramaic, for we understand it; and don't speak Judean in the hearing of the people who are on the wall." Then Rabshakeh yelled in Judean, saying, "Hear the word of the great king of Assyria. Don't let Hezekiah deceive you that the Lord will deliver you. Has any one of the gods of the nations delivered his land from the king of Assyria?" (see 2 Kings 18).

When King Hezekiah heard this, he tore his clothes, put on sackcloth, and went into the temple of the Lord. He sent for the prophet Isaiah who told him that the Lord said, "Do not be afraid because of the words that you have heard." God caused a rumor to send the military leaders back to Assyria's homeland. Rabshakeh sent a message to Hezekiah, saying, "Do not let your God in whom you trust deceive you saying, 'Jerusalem will not be given into the hand of the king of Assyria.' You've heard what we've done to other lands and no other god could stop us."

Satan's lies and methods of demoralization haven't changed over time. At some point, most of us will feel as if we're surrounded by our enemies. Once we are isolated, the lies start. Pitting each person against the other, our enemy tells us that God can't be trusted and neither can any person we know. Our enemy points out all the times they have won and all the ways it appears God has failed. Above all, our enemy wants us to believe that no one has more power than he does. He wants us to think that standing against him is hopeless and foolish and that our defeat is inevitable.

We should follow King Hezekiah's example. He took the letter from Assyria to God and prayed, "You are the God, You alone, of all the kingdoms of the earth. You have made heaven and earth. Listen, and see what our enemy is saying. It's true the enemy has defeated many. Now, O Lord our God, deliver us from his hand so that all kingdoms on earth may know that you alone, O Lord, are God" (see 2 Kings 19).

A wise person doesn't bother answering the threats of a godless bully. Hezekiah found out that no amount of money could bribe them, and they definitely could not be reasoned with. We must take our problem to God, remember His past protections, know His power, and trust His love for us to be good and perfect. It is true that "the king's heart is *like* channels of water in the hand of the Lord; He turns it wherever He wishes" (Prov. 21:1). Don't listen to the lies of your adversary. God is able to defeat any enemy, so stay focused on Him and His truth.

Bible Reading: 2 Kings 19:6–19, 34–36

Day 5

Josiah was the 16th king of Judah and the last good one. His father and grandfather were two of the most wicked kings in Judah's history. Anointed king at the age of eight years old, Josiah reigned 31 years in Jerusalem. He did what was right in the eyes of the Lord and walked in all the ways of his ancestor David, not turning aside to the right or to the left (2 King 22:1–2).

That is amazing. How would an eight-year-old child be able to overcome the horrible influence of his father and have the wisdom, confidence, and ability to lead an army, economy, and nation of people? That shows us once again that each of us has control over our own minds and hearts. Our parents can give us the tools to make good decisions, or they can make it extremely difficult to make the right choices. But we answer for ourselves. It is to our credit when we choose well, and it will be our responsibility if we choose poorly.

King Josiah had all the places of the false gods destroyed and repaired the temple of the Lord in Jerusalem. The book of the Law was found when the temple was cleaned out. It was read to the king, and he tore his clothes (2 Kings 22). All the people of Judah gathered, and the king read the book of the Law to them. Then he made a covenant before the Lord, to walk after the Lord and to keep His commandments, His testimonies, and His statutes with all his heart and soul, to carry out the words of this covenant that were written in this book. And all the people entered into the covenant (2 Kings 23:1–3). King Josiah then issued this order to all the people: "Celebrate the Passover to the Lord your God as it is written in this book of the covenant" (2 Kings 23:21). Josiah also got rid of the mediums and psychics, the household gods, and every other kind of idol worship both in Jerusalem and throughout the land of Judah. He did this in obedience to all the laws written in the scroll found in the Lord's temple (2 Kings 23:21–24).

We can learn invaluable lessons from young King Josiah. He responded to God's promises and love by wanting to love and follow God with all his heart and soul. It was no halfhearted, Sunday-only kind of relationship. This relationship was based on God. He loves us with all His heart, soul, strength, and mind. That kind of love will lead and empower us to live according to God's ways, loving Him as He loves us.

Josiah not only celebrated God and put His laws into practice but he got rid of the things that were bad. We would never consider putting new clothes on top of our old, torn, dirty clothing. Similarly, God doesn't want to put His new life into our old, dirty souls. Paul wrote about this:

> *Therefore if you have been raised up with Christ, keep seeking the things above, where Christ is, seated at the right hand of God. Set your mind on the things above, not on the things that are on earth. For you have died and your life is hidden with Christ in God. When Christ, who is our life, is revealed, then you also will be revealed with Him in glory. Therefore consider the members of your earthly body as dead to immorality, impurity, passion, evil desire, and greed, which amounts to idolatry. For it is because of these things that the wrath of God will come upon the sons of disobedience, and in them you also once walked, when you were living in them. But now you also, put them all aside: anger, wrath, malice, slander, and abusive speech from your mouth. Do not lie to one another, since you laid aside the old self with its evil practices, and have put on the new self who is being renewed to a true knowledge according to the image of the One who created him—a renewal in which there is no distinction between Greek and Jew, circumcised and uncircumcised, barbarian, Scythian, slave and freeman, but Christ is all, and in all. So, as those who have been chosen of God, holy and beloved, put on a heart of compassion, kindness, humility, gentleness and patience.*
>
> —Col. 3:1–12

***Bible Reading*: Ephesians 4:22–32, 5:1–12**

Day 6

Studying the kings has caused me to think of all the different forms leadership takes. We will all be called to be leaders in some capacity—in our relationships, the classroom, a sports team, our job, family, church, club, military unit, or government. Our first two days showed us the importance of choosing strong, wise friends and advisors and surrounding ourselves with people who truly love us and who are honorable and care for others. They are people who will be bold enough to hold us accountable and sensitive enough to build us up when we feel we are in over our heads. They will be someone who points to God and His Word, the kind of person we should have in our corner.

The duty of listening and hearing the words our advisors give is all on us. Rehoboam asked for advice with his mind already made up. At times we all do that. We listen until the sound of the voice stops, and then we move on. Yet we did not hear one word spoken. Numerous times Jesus said, "He who has ears to hear, let him hear." Whoever has the ability and common sense to understand and know, to get the picture with their mind, let them consider what has been said. As leaders, we must want to have ears to hear. We must listen to God and to others and get the picture in our minds of all that is said and meant. Only then will we be able to make good and wise decisions.

Humble leadership is the strongest leadership. Days three through five showed us the kings who fell on their faces before God in front of their people, admitting they were powerless and didn't know what to do. That demonstrated strength, not weakness. It takes courage, resolve, and guts to say those things. When we humble ourselves before God and give the situation to Him, we will . . . eventually but definitely . . . be respected and exalted. For a good leader, more important than glory is a victorious and beneficial outcome for the people they are leading.

Each good king acted on their faith, even when it took radical change. Leaders must be willing to clean out dangerous, damaging people and things, and then replace them with new and godly people and things. Again, this should be done with God as the head and wise advisors and friends as the support. Excellent leaders never stand alone.

All the kings God counted as good made some bad choices in their lives. How often we beat ourselves up and judge others as failures because of the mistakes we made. When God told Samuel to find the second king of

Israel (David), He said, "Do not look at his appearance or at the height of his stature, because I have rejected him [the oldest brother]; for God *sees* not as man sees, for man looks at the outward appearance, but the LORD looks at the heart" (1 Sam. 16:7). How very reassuring that is. God doesn't look at the outward appearance of our bodies or our accomplishments. He doesn't look at our performance, count the failures with more weight than the successes, or grade us on a negative curve. Our Father looks at our hearts. Remember, Jesus prayed that when Peter failed, his faith would not fail, and when he turned back, he'd strengthen his brothers (Luke 22:31–32).

God does not expect perfection from us. He expects us to be human. The Lord does not treat us as our sins deserve or repay us according to our iniquities. As a father has compassion on his children, so the Lord has compassion on those who fear Him. He knows how we are formed, and He remembers that we are dust (Ps. 103:10–14). He's the gracious and good King.

***Bible Reading*: Psalm 25**

Week 12

JONAH

Day 1

Think about obeying God. By now we know a lot about Him. Our Father is completely loving and good. He is always pure, just, and righteous. The Lord is all-knowing, all-powerful, and everywhere all the time. God's eyes see things we can't; He sees the big picture and into eternity. We have experienced His patience and kindness waiting for as many people as possible to turn to Him. His joy is in saving us and having a relationship with us, not in punishing us. Our Savior is more powerful than Satan or any enemy we'll ever encounter, and He shares His power with us. He is faithful. So God is someone worthy of our obedience. Doing things His way is all good.

Suppose there was a city that stood for every evil thing you've ever feared or lived through. The people of this city treated children in horrible ways, abused anyone too weak to defend themselves, and found pleasure in hurting others. When certain people attacked you or your family, they would run to this city as a safe haven, knowing they would never have to answer for illegal behavior while there. This place was the original "Sin City." How would you feel if God told you to go to that city and tell them He was angry with them? Knowing God as we do, we know He would want us to tell others about Him so they'd turn to Him. And if they turned to Him, we know He'd forgive them. Again, these aren't just petty thieves or recreational drug users who tell white lies. These are murdering child abusers, gang bangers, and drug lords.

Suddenly, the very things we know to be true about God are why it becomes difficult to obey Him. Theoretically, we agree that all have sinned—including us—and all people have fallen short of God's glory (Rom. 3:23). But we may feel that some people have crossed lines and that we should never forgive them. When we focus on those people, on the things they've done, the pain they've caused, and the lives they've destroyed, the only justice we can see for them is hell.

Jonah, an Old Testament prophet, found himself in the same predicament. "The word of the Lord came to Jonah . . . saying, 'Arise, go to Nineveh the great city and cry against it, for their wickedness has come up before Me.' But Jonah rose up to flee to Tarshish from the presence of the Lord. So he went down to Joppa, found a ship which was going to Tarshish, paid the fare and went down into it to go with them to Tarshish from the presence of the Lord" (Jon. 1:1–3).

The story of Jonah and the whale is familiar to most of us, and we even smile at him for thinking he could run away from God. Yet how often do we run from God spiritually, emotionally, or intellectually? We may never leave home, but we go the opposite direction. From our viewpoint, from the world's perspective, we seem to be in the right. It's crazy to forgive the person who killed our parent. God would never expect us to tell our ex-abuser about Him—that's simply too much to ask of someone. How is it just for that person to go to heaven after living their lifestyle? Sometimes God's compassion makes us feel as if a person got away with murder.

Forgiveness is hard and requires God's perspective. He was not asking Jonah to excuse Nineveh's violence and evil. God was asking him to let go of his hatred and bitterness toward them and tell them His message. The Lord loves justice, and He will not forsake His saints. They are preserved forever, but the children of the wicked shall be cut off (Isa. 37:28). God said vengeance was His to repay (Rom. 12:19, Heb. 10:30). Trusting His justice frees us of the chains that bind us to our enemy and allows us to experience God's grace and healing.

Bible Reading: Jonah 1–4

Day 2

Imagine being Jonah. Think of God asking something of us we totally disagree with on every level. If He'd asked us to tell Northern Israel His words, we'd do it. They worshiped false gods and practiced human sacrifice and some of the other disgusting things of Nineveh, but they're our own people. While we weren't happy with them, we did want them to straighten out their lives. And we weren't snobby. We would have gone to the Gentile, blue-collar fishermen of Joppa if God asked us to. But Nineveh? It's like asking a Jewish person to go to Berlin, Germany, during World War II to tell the Nazis that God saw their evil and was angry. No. We won't do it. It's traitorous.

So we run to the coast, pay the fee, and go to the bottom of the boat that's heading to the farthest destination in the opposite direction. Suddenly we're being shaken awake by the captain as the ship rocks and cracks in the midst of a great storm, and we know that God knows where we are and wants our obedience. Seeing the cargo the men had already thrown overboard makes us realize that our rebellion has damaged people we've never even met before. They cast lots, and of course, the hand of God causes the rocks to fall in our direction. The men ask, "What have you done to bring this awful storm down on us? Who are you?" Our answer is this: "I am a Hebrew, and I fear the Lord God of heaven who made the sea and the dry land, and I am running away from Him." That statement strikes us as ridiculous even though it's true. Although we're mad at God right now, we really do still love and revere Him.

Slipping back into the present day, we see a little Jonah in each of us. We understand that we don't deserve to experience God's mercy and grace. Honesty causes us to admit our faults and sins. But we're not serial killers. As long as we're being honest, let's admit that we feel comfortable judging and condemning certain people (such as serial killers). Making illegal behavior deserving of legal punishment is different from saying they don't deserve God's love. That judgment is a slippery slope. Once we start saying that specific people don't deserve God's grace because their sin (missing the mark) is too horrible, we start comparing sin to sin. The mark or target we're missing is not a small sin. The target is God's pure holiness. That means any and every fault and sin misses God's perfect holiness. If we believed that, we could not have a Jonah heart.

Jesus said this in Matthew 7:1–5:

> *Do not judge so that you will not be judged. For in the way you judge, you will be judged; and by your standard of measure, it will be measured to you. Why do you look at the speck that is in your brother's eye, but do not notice the log that is in your own eye? Or how can you say to your brother, "Let me take the speck out of your eye," and behold, the log is in your own eye? You hypocrite, first take the log out of your own eye, and then you will see clearly to take the speck out of your brother's eye.*

We're repeating the message from yesterday because it's so important and so difficult. If we want to be free of bitterness and resentment, we must trust God in His desire to have a relationship with everyone, even our worst enemy. Trust Him to deal justly as well as graciously with them. Resisting God's call to share His truth will hurt us and others. That log of rebellion and resentment in our eyes blinds us to the truth that Jesus loved and died for the whole world. The grace that saves us is the same grace that will save our enemies. It belongs to God, and He can give it to whoever He pleases. God so loved the world that He gave us Jesus.

Bible Reading: **Romans 5:6–10, 1 Peter 3:18**

Day 3

God showed Himself in the middle of Jonah's rebellion. We've seen God move powerful kings to work out His plans. He's worked through foreign countries, enemies, and devoted followers. Thankfully, God is also willing and able to do His good will through His children who disobey, have attitude problems, and are self-serving. Once again, we see our performance is not the key to the world's salvation or problem-solving.

The seamen from Joppa did not know the Lord. Like many people today, they were spiritual, believing in a higher power but wanting it to be merely a bigger version of themselves. Open to any person's god, they thought all roads led to the same place—the most powerful god. When trouble hit, they started calling out to any and every god they could think of. Not surprisingly, the gods of their imaginations didn't do a thing.

Enter the rebellious, disobedient child of the true God. When Jonah told the men that he served the Lord God of heaven who made the sea and the dry land and that he was running away from his God, the men were stunned and frightened. "So they said to him, 'What should we do to you that the sea may become calm for us?'—for the sea was becoming increasingly stormy. He said to them, 'Pick me up and throw me into the sea. Then the sea will become calm for you, for I know that on account of me this great storm *has come* upon you.' However, the men rowed *desperately* to return to land but they could not, for the sea was becoming *even* stormier against them" (Jon. 1:11–13).

This shows a couple things about these men. They were decent people; murdering to save their own skin wasn't an option they wanted to explore.

Also, they thought they could work hard enough to get out of their terrible predicament. Jonah's story points to Christ's salvation. Like many of us, the seamen, parents, or kids, or . . . rowed harder, worked harder, tried to be better. Our salvation has to be within our power and control. Finally, they cried out to God, "'We earnestly pray, O Lord, do not let us perish on account of this man's life and do not put innocent blood on us; for You, O Lord, have done as You have pleased.' So they picked up Jonah, threw him into the sea, and the sea stopped its raging. Then the men feared the Lord greatly, and they offered a sacrifice to the Lord and made vows (Jon. 1:14–16).

Seeing the power and deliverance of God changes people. If the person bringing the message of God messes up, God can still be seen. When you and I look at the church today, we can see hypocrites and people we know are just like the rest of the world. But we can also see God. Because He loves us, He uses our broken and sometimes rebellious lives to spread His perfect and holy message. God knows we'll mess up. He knows we'll be selfish, hurt others, hold back in fear or anger, and be unsure and insecure. And still He chooses to let us be part of a mission vital to the survival of all, which affects people into eternity. Our Father is so brilliant and powerful that He can be seen beyond our bumbling attempts and in spite of them.

So there are no excuses. God has shown Himself to us. Just because some people in the church are cracked and broken doesn't mean God is. Our response should be to God, not to people who are just like us. If you are His child, He wants to use you to show Himself to others. Let God do the work, and allow the Spirit to be in control of how others respond. Our job is to live and speak the truth of Christ even through our failures. God will be seen. He will change lives.

***Bible Reading*: Deuteronomy 10:12–22, Jonah 1**

Day 4

Everything about Jonah's life seemed to be as it should; however, God knew there were some heart issues that needed His touch. So God told Jonah to go to Nineveh, but Jonah refused and ran. The storm emphasized that he couldn't hide from God; the sailors threw him overboard; sea water surged over, through, and into him; a huge fish swallowed him; and he huddled, twisted in seaweed, being slowly digested in the fish's stomach. And Jonah's heart was moved.

Then Jonah prayed to his God from the belly of the fish. This is what he prayed:

> *Then Jonah prayed to the Lord* his God from the stomach of the fish, *and he said, "I called out of my distress to the* L*ord*, *and He answered me. I cried for help from the depth of Sheol; You heard my voice. For You had cast me into the deep, into the heart of the seas, and the current engulfed me. All Your breakers and billows passed over me. So I said, 'I have been expelled from Your sight. Nevertheless I will look again toward Your holy temple.' Water encompassed me to the point of death. The great deep engulfed me, weeds were wrapped around my head. I descended to the roots of the mountains. The earth with its bars* was *around me forever, but You have brought up my life from the pit, O* L*ord* my God. While I was fainting away, I remembered the Lord, and my prayer came to You, into Your holy temple. Those who regard vain idols forsake their faithfulness, but I will sacrifice to You with the voice of thanksgiving. That which I have vowed I will pay. Salvation is from the* L*ord.*"
>
> —Jon. 2:1–9

When you and I have a relationship with God and then reject Him, our rebellion breaks our hearts as well as His. David said, "How blessed is he whose transgression is forgiven, whose sin is covered! How blessed is the man to whom the Lord does not impute iniquity, and in whose spirit there is no deceit! When I kept silent *about my sin*, my body wasted away through my groaning all day long. For day and night Your hand was heavy upon me; my vitality was drained away *as* with the fever heat of summer" (Ps. 32:2–4).

Have you felt like Jonah and David? Maybe you're too new in your relationship with the heavenly Father, or maybe you don't have one with Him yet. But we can experience that in our relationships with other people too. Walking away from someone, rejecting everything they are and stand for, rebelling against their arms holding us in our lives causes us to feel desolate. Our choice leaves us feeling alone as the consequences threaten to drown us. Heavy darkness presses us down into despair, depression, and dejection.

There's a way out though. Both Jonah and David knew God well enough to know that the very One they rejected, the One they disobeyed, was the only One who could revive them. The Lord's discipline shows us that He is still present and involved. It shows us His love. Jonah said that when his life was slipping away, he remembered God who heard his prayer and answered him, even from the pit of the whale's stomach in the depth of the ocean. There is no depth we can sink to where God cannot hear us and reach us. David agreed. "I acknowledged my sin to You, and my iniquity I did not hide; I said, 'I will confess my transgressions to the LORD'; and You forgave the guilt of my sin" (Ps. 32:5).

Getting back into the relationship we left just takes turning around to face God (repenting), admitting what we did wrong (confessing), and accepting God's forgiveness and restored relationship (reconciling). Nothing can separate us from the love of God.

Bible Reading: **Psalm 51**

Day 5

God's response to Jonah's prayer was immediate and clear. "Then the Lord commanded the fish, and it vomited Jonah up onto the dry land. Now the word of the LORD came to Jonah the second time, saying, 'Arise, go to Nineveh the great city and proclaim to it the proclamation which I am going to tell you'" (Jon. 2:10, 3:1-2). Our Father doesn't cave in to temper tantrums or emotional blackmail, does He? Jonah had endured quite a traumatic experience. God had disciplined, protected, and rescued him, but He didn't change His purpose for Jonah. One of God's objectives was for Jonah to go to the city of Nineveh and look at the people there. Enemies can become faceless shells to us. We strip them of the feelings, thoughts, fears, and needs that make them like us as we focus only on their actions. It's so easy for us to lump people into groups of gender, ethnicity, or behavior and not see them as individual creations of God.

You and I can use this lesson too. If we've been abused by a man or a woman, the tendency would be to lump all men or all women into that bad category. Mistrusting all adults, law enforcement, or skin colors flows naturally from our experiences of pain and betrayal. We even paint the face of our dads or moms onto the face of God and distrust Him because of their behavior. Our heavenly Father wants to free us from these lies and limitations. He wants us to see ourselves and the individuals in our world with His eyes. So He tells all of us to get up and go—don't stay in your little bubble where you only see the results of some people's horrible actions. Go into the world and see the children, the men, the women, the elderly, the animals, and tell them what God says. The Lord is angry with injustice, violence, and immorality; and He has made a way out of those lifestyles. He loves and forgives and renews.

Jesus lived this. He ate with the tax collectors and sinners. He forgave prostitutes, touched diseased people to heal them, and drank water in a hated community with an immoral woman. Christ healed Roman soldiers' families and children, and He healed old people. He taught religious leaders, Jews, foreigners, rich, poor, orphans, and widows. Society and His experiences said to fear and dislike some of them, to be repulsed by various conditions and too important for some ages and social statuses. But all of those things are labels, and God doesn't deal with labels. He works with people. God wanted Jonah—He wants us—to work with people too.

Jonah wasn't told to go to the city of people who victimized Israel and become best friends with them. Nor was he told to gloss over their wickedness and say it didn't matter. God told Jonah to tell them He was about to rain down the consequences of their appalling lifestyle. Their sins were never listed by God or by Jonah because the people knew that what they were doing was wrong. The king of Nineveh said, "Let everyone turn from his evil way and from the violence that is in his hands." Each person is created in God's image, and part of us knows that violence and immorality is wrong. Without knowing God personally, these people knew their choices were bad and harmful. When God finally called them out and warned them of the coming penalty, they knew exactly why.

Our lesson is simple. With our eyes fixed on our Father, we need to be willing to see our enemies with His perspective. Pulling our focus off our experiences, we should go and see and speak God's truth. Their response is up to them and God. Let it go. God's heart is for us to be free of hatred, full of His love and peace, and willing to trust His plan.

Bible Reading: Colossians 3:3–17

Day 6

God's grace and Jonah's story can be seen in a parable Jesus told in Matthew 20:1–15.

> *For the kingdom of heaven is like a landowner who went out early in the morning to hire laborers for his vineyard. When he had agreed with the laborers for a denarius for the day, he sent them into his vineyard. And he went out about the third hour and saw others standing idle in the market place; and to those he said, "You also go into the vineyard, and whatever is right I will give you." And so they went. Again he went out about the sixth and the ninth hour, and did the same thing. And about the eleventh hour he went out and found others standing around; and he said to them, "Why have you been standing here idle all day long?" They said to him, "Because no one hired us." He said to them, "You go into the vineyard too." When evening came, the owner of the vineyard said to his foreman, "Call the laborers and pay them their wages, beginning with the last group to the first." When those hired about the eleventh hour came, each one received a denarius. When those hired first came, they thought that they would receive more; but each of them also received a denarius. When they received it, they grumbled at the landowner, saying, "These last men have worked only one hour, and you have made them equal to us who have borne the burden and the scorching heat of the day." But he answered and said to one of them, "Friend, I am doing you no wrong; did you not agree with me for a denarius? Take what is yours and go, but I wish to give to this last man the same as to you. Is it not lawful for me to do what I wish with what is my own? Or is your eye envious because I am generous?"*

This is the essence of God's grace. He rewards and blesses us according to His will and pleasure, not according to what we deserve. At first thought, we believe it is only fair that each person get what they deserve—good or bad. The violent people of Nineveh and in our lives should get what's coming to them. Conversely, the nonviolent, socially accepted people should get rewards. However, the Lord gives His grace in ways that are beyond our comprehension. God deals with us according to who He is, not according to who we are or what we do.

The landowner in the parable was never unfair; he was simply more generous with some people than with others. Here's another illustration. I have never murdered, robbed, or beaten anyone. I've never taken drugs or gotten drunk. However, I have missed God's mark of perfect holiness (sinned). I chose to accept Jesus as my Lord and Savior, I repented of my sins, and I have a wonderful, peaceful, and joy-filled relationship with God. Someday when I die, I know I will live in heaven forever with Him. Additionally, my body has been spared the ravages of drugs or other abuses, and my memories are guilt-free, not filled with horrible actions and regrets.

There's a man who beat a woman to death in a robbery when he was high on drugs and drunk. His body bears the marks of his choices, and he is serving time in prison for his crimes. He missed the mark of God's perfect holiness (sinned), yet he later chose to accept Jesus as his Lord and Savior. He repented of his sins and has a wonderful, peace-filled relationship with God. When he dies, he knows he'll live in heaven forever with Him. The Lord was generous to both me and this man. God was more generous with the man because he came to God later than I did and had caused more harm and damage than I ever had. Those scars, memories, and consequences will be with the man the rest of his life. Yet both of us are now God's children.

Grace has nothing to do with what we deserve. It is God giving to us out of the abundance of His goodness, completely apart from what we earn. Receive it, and give it.

Bible Reading: Ephesians 2

Week 13

JONAH

Day 1

After experiencing God's discipline, being vomited out of the large fish's stomach, and being told once again to go to Nineveh, Jonah did what God wanted and went to Nineveh. It was a very important city, a three-day journey across. On the first day, Jonah entered the city. He proclaimed, "Forty more days, and Nineveh will be overturned." The people of Nineveh believed in God, called a fast, and humbled themselves before Him, and when the king heard, he did the same. God relented concerning the calamity He had declared when He saw their hearts and actions (Jon. 3). But it greatly displeased Jonah, and he became angry (Jon. 4:1).

It is possible to do the right thing for the wrong reason, to do what someone wants with a resentful attitude, to obey God while disagreeing with Him and harboring aggravation and disapproval. Knowing and loving God moves us through disobedience and selfishness into obedience. Knowing how God works can move us from a bad attitude into a soft-hearted, joyful, and peace-filled attitude.

God was not focused solely on having Nineveh know Him and repent. We've seen before that His purposes are vast as well as individual for today as well as for the future. This job was for the benefit of Jonah, the benefit of Israel, and the benefit of Nineveh and the other nations who interacted with them. And it was for the benefit of us today and people in the future. Jonah needed to get his mind off himself and his feelings and onto his Lord and his Lord's perspective. God wanted to grow Jonah, to give him a more intimate understanding of His heart and mind and open Jonah's eyes to the spiritual war being waged and the people being ravaged by it. The Lord wanted Jonah to realize that killing an enemy may slow the evil in the world. But changing an enemy's heart would stop their evil, satisfy God's love for them, and train their next generation.

Can you and I fully realize this lesson in our own lives? When God asks us to let go of our hatred and unforgiveness, it's because He loves us and wants to grow and free us. He also loves and wants to grow and free our enemy. God asks us to go to our adversary and tell them how He's changed our lives or some truth from His Word. There are people around us who will also be affected by God in the life of our opponent. Think of it. Israel was not the only victim of Nineveh's violence and immorality. Other nations were rescued by God's life-changing presence in Nineveh. Many saw God's power and grace when people who were "too bad" and "too powerful" to ever change did change.

Do you know what God wanted from Jonah? It's the same thing He wants from us. God told Israel in Deuteronomy 6:5, "You shall love the LORD your God with all your heart and with all your soul and with all your might." Jesus said that was the greatest commandment and the second was that "You shall love your neighbor as yourself" (Matt. 22:39). Having a relationship with God is the only way we will be able to obey our Father when He asks the hard things from us. Loving Him will motivate us to forgive, reach out, teach, and accept the unlovables in our lives. Jesus's love for us and for our neighbors (next door, next state, another country or continent) will change our attitude as well as our behavior. God's looking to do a mighty work in our lives and our adversary's lives, as well as the lives of a watching world. Love Him, and let Him.

Bible Reading: **Luke 10:25–37, 2 Timothy 3:14–17**

Day 2

Nineveh was a tough crowd. Today's news tells of obscene violence in countries where drug cartels run the cities, political powers crush opponents by genocide, religious fanatics kill en masse, and children are sold for sex and labor. Prisons in our own country are full of violence and abuse as daily occurrences. All these places are hopeless. No one can change them. Who would even dare try? Listing all the problems and which ones should be addressed stops most people from even attempting to intervene. The types of people who live like that are hard-core bad, beyond reaching.

Yet God steps up and says, "Go and tell them about Me. Tell them who I am. Tell them I love them. Tell them I hate violence and abuse. Tell them I've made a way out." It's not just the important cities God wants to reach; it's you too. If your lips are thinned into a hard line and your heart is burning with anger for all the pain you've had to endure at the hands of another person, God is stepping toward you. Life may have caused you to cover up with a tough shell. Maybe you've allowed your heart to become rock-hard and unfeeling. You don't care anymore. Your motto is to do unto others before they can do it unto you. Some may say you're a lost cause, hopeless, and there is no way you can change.

With great confidence I am telling you that none of that is true. Jeremiah 32:17 says, "'Ah Lord GOD! Behold, You have made the heavens and the earth by Your great power and by Your outstretched arm! Nothing is too difficult for You." *That* is what is true. The Lord of all creation loves you just as He loved the people of Nineveh. You are not too difficult for Him. The things you need to overcome are not too difficult for God. There is no person, no group of people, no cities or countries that are too difficult for God to reach and change.

The people of Nineveh and their king believed God's message, and from the greatest to the least, they decided to go without food and wear sackcloth to show their sorrow. Then the king and his nobles sent this decree throughout the city: "Do not let man, beast, herd, or flock taste a thing. Do not let them eat or drink water. But both man and beast must be covered with sackcloth; and let men call on God earnestly that each may turn from his wicked way and from the violence which is in his hands. Who knows, God may turn and relent and withdraw His burning anger so that we will not perish" (Jon. 3:7–9).

If you're reading this, it's because God wants you to hear His message. He's reaching out to you. Listen. Humble yourself, and be full of sorrow for the mess you've made. Pray earnestly to God, and turn from your evil ways. His Word promises He will not destroy you if you repent. Consequences for choices won't disappear, but His perfect love for you takes away all fear of condemnation and hell (1 John 4:18). Dr. Richard D. Dobbins said, "Until the pain of remaining the same hurts more than the pain of change, most people prefer to remain the same." Jesus is offering change—to take your pain and your shame, to heal you, and to make you clean.

Perhaps you are a Jonah, and God is starting to impress upon you to go share His words with some hard-core people. Don't be afraid. Let go of your opinions and judgments against the people, and trust God to do the work. Teaching about salvation, Jesus told His disciples, "With people it is impossible, but not with God; all things are possible with God" (Mark 10:27). Now the God of peace equip you in every good thing to do His will (Heb. 13:20–21).

Bible Reading: Hebrews 13:20–21, 1 John 4:9–21

Day 3

When God saw what Nineveh did and how they turned from their evil ways, He had compassion and didn't bring upon them the ruin He'd threatened. But it greatly displeased Jonah, and he became angry. He prayed to the Lord, "O Lord, is this not what I said when I was still at home? That's why I was so quick to flee to Tarshish. I knew You are a gracious and compassionate God, slow to anger and rich in love, a God who relents from sending calamity. Now, Lord, take away my life, for it is better for me to die than to live." The Lord said, "Do you have good reason to be angry?" Jonah went out and sat down at a place east of the city. There he made himself a shelter, sat in its shade, and waited to see what would happen to the city. Then the Lord provided a vine and made it grow up over Jonah to give shade and ease his discomfort, and Jonah was very happy about the vine. But at dawn the next day, God provided a worm, which chewed the vine so it withered. When the sun rose, God provided a scorching east wind, and the sun blazed on Jonah's head so he grew faint. He wanted to die, and said, "It would be better for me to die than to live." But the Lord said, "You've been concerned about this vine, though you did not tend it or make it grow. It sprang up overnight and died overnight. But Nineveh has more than 120,000 people who cannot tell their right hand from their left, and many cattle as well. Should I not be concerned about that great city?" (Jon. 4).

Before we become too critical of Jonah, let's consider his past couple of months. They'd been pretty tough. God was taking him through a process that revealed some ugliness in his heart. Jonah was learning the lesson of total surrender to God. He'd just spent 40 days with a group of people he never wanted to know or like, looking them in the eyes, seeing their children, and hearing them call out to God. Can we be honest with ourselves? It would be emotionally draining to change our opinions of a person or group of people we've always disliked, distrusted, and been hurt by. Resisting the whole experience would be normal. Every thought and belief would shift for us as God exposed the truths in our hearts, in His heart, and in our enemy's hearts.

Jonah may have seemed a bit dramatic saying, "Just kill me now!" but we all know that feeling. Life's just too hard. We're done. We don't want to deal with people anymore. It's total discouragement and disillusionment. The world isn't working the way we thought it should, and neither is God. "So, Lord, since You don't want to do anything my way, take my life because it's better for me to die than to live with everything going the opposite of how I want."

Jonah chapter 4 shows us that God was satisfied with Nineveh, but not with Jonah. God loved Jonah and was determined to show that man the truth of his heart as well as the truth of God's heart. Physically growing can be painful at times as our bones and muscles stretch and baby teeth come in and then fall out. Growing pains are a natural part of life. Jonah was experiencing spiritual growing pains. His ideas of who were redeemable and how God's justice worked were being stretched. God wanted Jonah to lose the childish notions of putting his comfort and "rights" as a top priority and replace them with the mature and sacrificial love of God.

Spiritual growing up doesn't happen any faster than the physical process. We need to allow ourselves and others the time for maturing. Along with time, we need to recognize that growing up is painful. Being critical of a growing boy or girl doesn't speed up the process. Our Father is patient and committed to our growth. He loves us each step of the way.

***Bible Reading*: Ephesians 4:11-16, 1 Peter 2:1-3**

Day 4

At the end of the forewarned 40 days, Jonah went east of Nineveh to watch what would happen. Perhaps he thought that once the people saw God had forgiven them and not destroyed them, they would go back to their old ways—and then finally God would zap them. So Jonah built a shelter to shade him from the sun and waited. During this time, he had a conversation with the Lord, and God asked him twice, "Do you have good reason to be angry?"

We've covered pretty thoroughly that God asked Jonah to do a hard thing and that it was indeed difficult to let go of Nineveh's past mistreatment of Israel, as well as their gross immorality and violence. But God's question went a little deeper than that. Remember in Luke 15 where the oldest son was angry when his father welcomed and rejoiced over his prodigal younger brother coming home? Or think back to God's conversation with Cain after He rejected his gift but accepted Abel's. Jonah, the prodigal's eldest brother, and Cain were all angry with God for doing things His way, for showing mercy and grace to whoever He wanted.

These men didn't get their own way, and God didn't change His plans to please them. Then the Father asked them some questions so they'd start thinking about their behavior and attitude. "Why are you so angry? Do you have a good reason to be angry? Have you made good choices? Is your heart right? Are you doing what you're doing for the right reasons? Do you realize you've always had an opportunity to have a relationship with me, that I'm not walking away from you? Why do you want to do things your way instead of My way?"

Without thinking, we can slip into the theory that God should always please us. The root of most sin is that we want to be number one, in control, doing things our way. That can even be true after we've given up our will and obeyed God, like Jonah did. Because *then* we want our own way . . . we want to feel a certain sensation, have other people respond the way we want. We want God to give us what we desire since we did what He wanted. We want to be God, at least for all the control. We want Him to do things our way. We want God to please us with His actions, rewards, and plans.

Jonah's focus zoomed in on himself. He didn't see God in all His glory, justness, and righteousness. He didn't see the people in Nineveh, even the children and animals. He truly didn't see Israel or any other victims of Nineveh. Jonah saw Jonah.

Proverbs 14:12 and 16:25 both say, "There is a way *which* seems right to a man, but its end is the way of death." Jonah's way seemed right to him. His reasons seemed logical and reasonable. But his heart was leading him to death and destruction. Have you experienced that—the utter destruction and damage of your emotions because you could not let go of your anger, your bitterness, and your desire for retribution? Have you experienced not being able to think clearly because your mind was so consumed with your swirling, raging feelings over a situation?

Answer God's questions. Do you have a good reason to be angry? Do you feel the righteous indignation Jesus had when others were hurt or the

Father was disrespected? Or was your anger self-serving and vengeful? Was God unjust in His actions? Was He wrong in His patience and grace? Allow God's questions to draw you to Him and free you from your anger.

Bible Reading: **Deuteronomy 10:12–21, Ephesians 4:24–27**

Day 5

Class was still in session for the reluctant servant of the Lord. God used a volatile storm to reach Jonah. Being thrown into the sea wasn't the only solution to save the ship. Perhaps if Jonah had told them to turn back to Joppa so he could obey, the storm would have stopped. But Jonah had early on determined that if he couldn't do things his way, he may as well die. To save the sailors' lives and relieve himself of God's call, he told the sailors to throw him overboard.

Object lesson number two: God used a huge fish to swallow Jonah whole. Within three days, Jonah admitted that the Lord was in control and a good God. The fish vomited him up, and Jonah went on his way to do God's will. Like many of us unenthusiastic, stubborn, grumbling children, Jonah still needed an attitude adjustment. So the Lord God provided a vine and made it grow up over Jonah to give shade for his head and ease his discomfort, and Jonah was very happy about the vine. But at dawn the next day, God provided a worm that chewed the vine so it withered. When the sun rose, God provided a scorching east wind, and the sun blazed on Jonah's head so he grew faint. He wanted to die and said, "It would be better for me to die than to live." Then God said to Jonah, "Do you have good reason to be angry about the plant?" Jonah said, "I do, and I am angry enough to die." But the Lord said, "You have been concerned about this vine, though you did not tend it or make it grow. It sprang up overnight and died overnight. Nineveh has more than a 120,000 people who cannot tell their right hand from their left, and many cattle as well. Should I not be concerned about that great city?" (see Jon. 4:6–11).

What was God's point? He was saying, "Jonah, this plant that I made became important and valuable to you in such a short time. You loved it and grieved its death. Why is it so hard for you to love the people I made? Do you seriously not understand My love for the people of Nineveh? Would you not grieve their death? Can you really see value in one plant but not in 120,000 innocent children and animals? Why is it so easy for you to attach yourself and find value in the meaningless things in life but so difficult for you to give Me and My purposes the right place in your heart?"

Self-centeredness and short-sightedness stand out in Jonah's attitude. Those meaningless things of life make us comfortable and feel good. The plant shaded Jonah; the education, clothes, and cars give us status, and they don't require more of us than we're willing to give. Jonah's concern for the plant was selfish; he was sorry for its destruction because it served his personal comfort. Our perception is that physical distress requires more immediate attention than spiritual trouble. We tend to give more care to what makes us physically comfortable than what gives us spiritual comfort and security. Narrow-minded selfishness causes our attitude problems.

God's concern for people is unselfish. He seeks to give spiritual and physical comfort instead of take it. We, like Jonah, have caused God great discomfort, even the pain of the cross. Still, He wants a relationship with us. We have no right to question or resent the outpouring of God's love in saving people from sin and the destruction of sin. Romans 5:15 says, "But the free gift is not like the transgression. For if by the transgression of the one the many died, much more did the grace of God and the gift by the grace of the one Man, Jesus Christ, abound to the many." Christ's selfless love is greater than any person's sin. Instead of anger, sharing that truth should bring us great joy.

Bible Reading: 2 Corinthians 5:14–21

Day 6

Jonah is a story of spring, of God offering life after death. The decent, hard-working sailors from Joppa did not know the one and true God. They had no relationship with Him and worshiped any god they could think up. Yet the Lord who created the dry land and the sea stepped into their lives and showed Himself. Near physical death led them to spiritual life.

There was nothing decent about the people of Nineveh. Wicked, violent, depraved, and immoral describes them better. While they had no way to know the finer, more detailed aspects of living well, they were fully aware how offensive most of their behavior was. What they didn't know was that God cared. He cared about their wicked lifestyles, and He cared about them personally. The Lord wanted better for them. He'd created them for a good purpose, for life instead of the constant darkness and death they lived in. Realizing they fully deserved the destruction Jonah said God would bring on them, they repented and stopped their sinful ways. Humbly they waited to see if God would be gracious and spare them the ultimate punishment they deserved. And God's mercy and grace abounded. Ezekiel 18:30–32 tells us this:

> *"Therefore I will judge you, O house of Israel, each according to his conduct," declares the Lord God. "Repent and turn away from all your transgressions, so that iniquity may not become a stumbling block to you. Cast away from you all your transgressions which you have committed and make yourselves a new heart and a new spirit! For why will you die, O house of Israel? For I have no pleasure in the death of anyone who dies," declares the Lord God. "Therefore, repent and live."*

And then there's Jonah. As a prophet of the Lord, Jonah thought he feared and loved God, but when he was put to the test, his life became a whirlwind of despair. This man had a faith crisis—anger at his Lord, disillusionment, utter fatigue, and complete confusion. To any of us who've been there, we can relate to how hard that place is. At first, Jonah's reluctance to go to Nineveh was probably innocent—he couldn't possibly have heard God correctly. Once God made His plan clear, Jonah's confusion turned to rebellion, and the death of his peace reverberated throughout his entire life. It's as if we have a civil war within ourselves when we are God's children and fight against Him, vehemently resisting what God wants for us. Jonah's emotions swung crazily from wanting to die because he was so angry and frustrated to loving a plant and being exceedingly happy with it. The life of joy, peace, and contentment that God has promised to all who love Him had turned dark.

But God was no less patient with Jonah than He was with Nineveh. He wanted Jonah to get past the stumbling block of his own ideas of right and wrong. The Father wanted Jonah to join Him in His place of love and grace. God wants us to know that if we can trust Him, if we can get past our desire for control, if we can agree with His view of people and situations, our world will right itself. Paul said we've died, and our life is hidden with Christ in God.

So, as those who have been chosen of God, holy and beloved, put on a heart of compassion, kindness, humility, gentleness and patience; bearing with one another, and forgiving each other, whoever has a complaint against anyone; just as the Lord forgave you, so also should you. Beyond all these things put on *love, which is the perfect bond of unity. Let the peace of Christ rule in your hearts, to which indeed you were called in one body; and be thankful.*

—Col. 3:3, 12–15

Bible Reading: Romans 15:1–14

Special Holiday
MOTHER'S DAY

When I was growing up, Matthew 23:37 was one of my favorite Bible verses. Jesus was so passionate when He spoke those words, and the picture He created was poignantly beautiful. This verse is one of the few times God relates Himself as a mother. And the picture He gives will erase any negative or damaging images our own mothers may have lived out in our lives.

Jesus was going into Jerusalem for the final time. He knew the time had come for the plan to be fulfilled, for Him to die on the cross. He had spent the last three years of His life personally teaching and performing miracles for His chosen people. Throughout the Old Testament and into Jesus's life at the beginning of the New Testament, God desperately reached out to His children, loving them, drawing them, and teaching them. And for the most part, they continually rejected Him. Jesus looked out over the city and said, "Jerusalem, Jerusalem, who kills the prophets and stones those who are sent to her! How often I wanted to gather your children together, the way a hen gathers her chicks under her wings, and you were unwilling" (Matt. 23:37).

A hen is a mother chicken. When there is a fire or predators, a hen will gather her chicks and nestle them under her wings. In fire, the down feathers insulate her babies from the heat and destruction of the blaze. Once the fire burns out, the charred remains of the hen are left standing. Slowly, the little chicks emerge from under their mom's burned wings, unharmed. A mother hen instinctively and willingly gives up her life to save her children. She endures immense pain in order to protect them. Nothing about a mother hen is selfish. Her chicks are her love, and their safety and well-being drive her actions.

Some people have not experienced the love of a mother. Neglect, abuse, rejection, and abandonment by moms happen every day. Jesus wanted us to know that He has the perfect heart of a mother. God is what a mom should look like. The members of the Trinity—Father, Son, and Holy Spirit—have the heart of a loving, protective hen. They created you. They were in the womb with you, knitting you together (Ps. 139:13–16). God is our mama. Jesus said that as our mommy, He wants to gather you and me and hold us close. When danger comes, our God wants to hide us close to His mama heart, covered by His wings. Our mommy was willing to die for us, withstanding horrific pain so we would not have to.

Mother's Day can be a lonely and aggravating Sunday for anyone whose memories are seared with pain and anger. Looking at the woman who gave us life but never loved us can twist our hearts. This Mother's Day, let's celebrate the mama's heart of our Lord. Let's completely wipe the face of our physical mom off what we think God looks like; let's refuse to put our mom's selfishness and unlovingness onto Jesus. Instead, Jesus invites you and me to nestle under His wing, press our cheeks in close, and listen to the heartbeat of an adoring mom. Tears can trickle down, and we can weep. We can laugh or sleep or hum—because we're safe. And we're loved. Looking into our eyes, Jesus marvels at how much He loves us and how beautiful He finds us. Jesus is whispering into our ears, "How often I wanted to gather you children together the way a hen gathers her chicks under her wings."

Celebrate today. We are in the hands of Jesus whose mother love is soft and endless.

Bible Reading: Isaiah 66:12–13, Ephesians 2:10

Special Holiday
FATHER'S DAY

Father's Day is today, and for a lot of people, this is a day we turn on our acting skills and fake our feelings. Some of us don't even try to fake it. The word *dad* brings to mind cruelty, punishment, constant criticism, rejection, and abuse. Yet that was not God's plan for fatherhood. In fact, He thought being a dad was so important that He chose to relate to us as and call Himself our Father. Let's open up His photo album and see the way our heavenly Father loves His kids.

Romans 8:15 says, "For you have not received a spirit of slavery leading to fear again, but you have received a spirit of adoption as sons by which we cry out, 'Abba! Father!'" So you should not be like cowering, fearful slaves. You should behave instead like God's very own children, adopted into His family, calling Him "Daddy, Father." God is a Daddy who chooses to take us in and give us His name. He's our loving Daddy and reliable Father. Because He has adopted us, we have no fear of losing our place in His family. We are beyond a doubt His children. Nothing we could ever do will make Him love us less.

First John 3:1–2 tells us, "See how great a love the Father has bestowed on us, that we would be called children of God; and *such*

we are.... We know that when He appears, we will be like Him, because we will see Him just as He is." Not only has our Father given us His family and His name, but we will also look like Him. No one will wonder whose kid we are. When Jesus comes back, we will look like we belong in His family. Listen to God's own words.

> *When Israel* was *a youth I loved him, and out of Egypt I called My son. The more they called them, the more they went from them;* ... *Yet it is I who taught Ephraim to walk, I took them in My arms; but they did not know that I healed them. I led them with cords of a man, with bonds of love, and I became to them as one who lifts the yoke from their jaws; and I bent down* and *fed them.*
>
> —Hos. 11:1–4

What touching images. Our Daddy is the one who taught His children how to walk. That's Him in the picture gently lifting us to stand up, steadying us and then allowing us to grab His finger as we toddled around. Do you see the joy and pride on Abba's face as we take our first steps by ourselves? And when we fall and get hurt, that's Dad who's healing us. He's not angry we got hurt; he's not yelling and rough. When we reach our little arms up to our Daddy with teary eyes and say, "Carry me," He picks us up and cradles us in His strong arms. Feeling so loved and secure that our bodies melt into our Father, we snuggle our faces into the crook of His neck.

Look at the next pictures. Dad is leading us with cords of love like they do in preschool. He is loosely holding on to one end of a soft rope as each of us grabs hold and lines up, waiting for Abba to lead us on a great adventure. We're not chained to Him or driven to follow Him out of fear of harsh punishment. We're led with ties of love and kindness. Our Dad lifted the heavy yoke or burden of expectations we could never live up to—the yoke of working so hard to gain His approval and love—and then Father provided food for us. He bent down to feed us. The massively big Warrior and Creator squatted down to cut our food into bites we wouldn't choke on, to help us hold our cup, and to make sure we didn't go hungry.

These pictures prove we have a reason to celebrate Father's Day. See how great a love the Father has for us that we would be called children of God. His love is tender and constant.

***Bible Reading*: Psalm 68:5–6, 103:8–18**

SUMMER

INTRODUCTION

Slowly the new life of spring is growing stronger and fuller. Summer is here, long sunny days leading into glorious, balmy nights. Sunlight is what marks this season. God's light is shining down on His creation, warming the earth, growing the plants, filling us with a sense of happiness.

Traditionally, school is out, and we all breathe a huge sigh of release from the pressures and schedules that constrained us. We're free! The possibilities for adventure and fun are endless. Backyard barbecues, picnics, swimming, camping, and gardening fill our calendars. Summer is relaxing, invigorating, and fun.

Of course, the phrase "dog days of summer" was coined for a reason. They're the sweltering hot days, days with no breeze, just blazing sun for hours and hours. Unexpectedly, our long days of freedom turn to boredom because it's just too hot to do anything. Sunshine that gave us joy and grew our flowers and vegetables now wilts and burns them. We find yet again how difficult it is to be content. Sun, long days, free time . . . too much of a good thing can be hard to endure. The constant light begins to expose the flaws as well as the brilliance of our lives.

Pour a glass of lemonade, and sit under the shade of a tree with me as we discover the mysteries that only God's light can reveal. Our God—the Father, Son, and Holy Spirit—show Themselves in this summer season. God is the light of the world, shining into our dark and scary caverns, highlighting the beauty in us and in creation, illuminating truth and lies, guiding the lost in this dark and dangerous world.

From heaven's perspective, both sides of summer are for our good. The unfolding of God's words gives light, and His light gives us eternal life.

Week 1

JESUS

Day 1

"In the beginning was the Word, and the Word was with God, and the Word was God. He was in the beginning with God. All things came into being through Him, and apart from Him nothing came into being that has come into being. In Him was life, and the life was the Light of men. The Light shines in the darkness, and the darkness did not comprehend it" (John 1:1-5). "Then Jesus again spoke to them, saying, 'I am the Light of the world; he who follows Me will not walk in the darkness, but will have the Light of life'" (John 8:12).

Jesus, the Son of God, is the Word. He is Life, and Jesus is Light. In those first verses of the Gospel of John, the deity of Jesus is declared in no uncertain terms. Jesus is God. Genesis 1 starts with the same words as John's Gospel: "In the beginning"—in the beginning of time when God decided to create our world and universe—the eternal, already-there Trinity spoke. The words spoken by God the Father, God the Son, and God the Holy Spirit created life in every form. Everything is completely wrapped up in Christ Jesus. Jesus is the Word. When He spoke, His Word, Life, and Light created the existence of our world and universe and was clearly seen in it.

Jewish rabbis referred to God as "the word of God." God and His words were one—what He said was true, holy, just, and right. Greeks saw "the word," or *logos*, as the power that puts sense and order into the world instead of chaos. Logos was the "Ultimate Reason," the "Ultimate Logic," or the "Ultimate Underlying Principle" that controlled all things. John was introducing both the Jews and the Greeks—indeed, all the world—to who "the Word" really was.

Then we are told this:

> *What was from the beginning, what we have heard, what we have seen with our eyes, what we have looked at and touched with our hands, concerning the Word of Life—and the life was manifested, and we have seen and testify and proclaim to you the eternal life, which was with the Father and was manifested to us—This is the message we have heard from Him and announce to you, that God is Light, and in Him there is no darkness at all.*
> —1 John 1:1-2, 5

God Himself, the Word of God, is Jesus, who is the "Ultimate Intelligence" who created and controls the universe and our individual lives. That means the Word gave all Life. He gave all physical life and all spiritual life. And when the Word and the Life gave Himself—He also gave eternal life. Christ Jesus is God; He is the Word, and He is Life—and He is Light. His words (or Jesus Himself) open our eyes to truth and pureness and show us the lies and darkness of sin. Jesus enlightens our minds and spirits. Christ is a physical light reflecting the glory of the Father (Heb. 1:3), and Jesus is the light that guides us through our lives and shines on His Word (and Himself) so we can understand what to do and how to live.

Do you feel like we're going in circles? This is what knowing these truths mean to you and to me. "Every good thing given and every perfect gift is from above, coming down from the Father of lights" (James 1:17). When our world is full of chaos and darkness and the death of our relationships, reputations, or bodies, we need to know Jesus. He is our hope. His words are true and orderly and give direction and purpose. Christ is our night-light when we're scared, our bright and shining light of wisdom and understanding. Jesus gives us an abundantly good and full life as well as eternal life. Our world needs to know Jesus. He is the Word, the Life, and the Light.

***Bible Reading*: John 1:9-14, 1 John 1:1-7**

Day 2

Christ Jesus is the Word. Let's not make this more complicated than it is. Jesus is God, and as God, His word (what He says) is the final and ultimate authority; is always correct, right, wise, and true. His word is pure, holy, and harmonious. His word gives life, light, and love. His word is living, active, and effectual. God's word is everything that He is. That's why the Bible tells us Jesus is the Word. So let's open it up and learn how to live victoriously.

The Lord compares His words to fire and a hammer. Jeremiah was His prophet who continually tried to get Israel to change their wicked ways and turn back to God. He honestly spoke God's words to them, telling the people what was good in God's sight and what was evil and that God would eventually punish those who chose evil.

Some men started telling Israel what they wanted to hear, that God would give them peace no matter what they did. God's response to the false prophets was strong. "But if they had stood in My council, then they would have announced My words to My people, and would have turned them back from their evil way and from the evil of their deeds" (Jer. 23:22). "'The prophet who has a dream may relate *his* dream, but let him who has My word speak My word in truth. What does straw have *in common* with grain?' declares the LORD. 'Is not My word like fire,' declares the LORD, 'and like a hammer which shatters a rock'" (Jer. 23:28–29)?

Jesus – the Word – is a fire that burns through the lies of Satan and the world system. He is a hammer that shatters false beliefs and teaching. Ephesians 6 tells us to put on the full armor of God in order to fight the spiritual battles we live through. One of our weapons is the true Word of God, which is called the sword of the Spirit. The Word is the ultimate weapon of warfare against the enemy of our souls and the world.

Ah, but God is not one-dimensional. The Word that destroys evil and lies also heals and frees. Psalm 107:19–20 tells us that God's children cried out to the Lord in their trouble, and He saved them out of their distresses. He sent His Word and healed them, and delivered them from their destructions. In John 8:31–32, "Jesus was saying to those Jews who had believed Him, 'If you continue in My word, *then* you are truly disciples of Mine; and you will know the truth, and the truth will make you free.'"

What will heal us of the destructive forces of bitterness, hatred, and jealousy? God's Word. Who and what will free us from the lies that we've failed too often and too badly to ever be forgiven in order to be useful, clean, and whole? Jesus the Word. The Word tells us that "God demonstrates His own love toward us, in that while we were yet sinners, Christ died for us. Much more then, having now been justified by His blood, we shall be saved from the wrath *of God* through Him" (Rom. 5:8–9).

The Word burns up the lies and frees us at the same time. Through Christ we are clean, not by our own works but because of His. We're useful, valuable, and beautiful, and we're His masterpiece. Galatians 5:1 says it is for freedom Christ set us free. We're not chained up to rules and people's expectations; we're free in Christ to live His way because of His love. We're free of the chains of fear, anxiety, performance, bitterness, and rage . . . we're free! So keep standing firm, believing the truth, knowing God does condemn immorality, violence, lies—all sin—and knowing God does forgive any and all people who believe in Jesus as the Son who died for our sins and rose from the grave. The Word fights for us and gives truth and life.

Bible Reading: **Psalm 119:97–106, John 8:31–36**

Day 3

Genesis 1 and John 1 show us that Jesus is the source of all life, every kind of life. John 3 tells us how to have spiritual life.

> *Now there was a man of the Pharisees, named Nicodemus, a ruler of the Jews; this man came to Jesus by night and said to Him, "Rabbi, we know that You have come from God as a teacher; for no one can do these signs that You do unless God is with him." Jesus answered and said to him, "Truly, truly, I say to you, unless one is born again he cannot see the kingdom of God." Nicodemus said to Him, "How can a man be born when he is old? He cannot enter a second time into his mother's womb and be born, can he?" Jesus answered, "Truly, truly, I say to you, unless one is born of water and the Spirit he cannot enter into the kingdom of God. That which is born of the flesh is flesh, and that which is born of the Spirit is spirit. Do not be amazed that I said to you, 'You must be born again.' The wind blows where it wishes and you hear the sound of it, but do not know where it comes from and where it is going; so is everyone who is born of the Spirit." Nicodemus said to Him, "How can these things be?"*
>
> —John 3:1–9

Jesus answered, "As Moses lifted up the serpent in the wilderness, even so must the Son of Man be lifted up; so that whoever believes will in Him have eternal life. For God so loved the world, that He gave His only begotten Son, that whoever believes in Him shall not perish, but have eternal life" (John 3:14–16).

Nicodemus was trying to grasp a spiritual truth with only a physical understanding. He understood how we were given life physically, but Jesus wanted him to know how to get life spiritually. You and I have been born physically and are living in the physical world. We can be born again spiritually and given life in the kingdom of God that is partially seen here on earth now and will be fully seen for eternity in heaven.

How do we gain entrance into the kingdom of God, which has abundant and eternal life? The Word tells us we have to be born spiritually. Understanding this is like understanding the wind. God's ways are not our ways; His thoughts are so much bigger and beyond our understanding and comprehension. So instead of trying to understand how it all works, just trust and do what God says. Because He loves us, He gave Jesus to die as the punishment and payment for our sins. Do you believe that? If you do, you will have eternal life. Your physical body will die, but you—your spirit—will not perish but have eternal life.

This new spiritual life we have is an abundant life. Jesus said, "The thief comes only to steal and kill and destroy; I came that they may have life, and have it abundantly" (John 10:10). Satan and those who believe his lies are here to steal our peace, our effectiveness, and our hope. They want to kill and destroy us spiritually and physically by taking us out of Jesus's protected flock of sheep. Our adversary tells us we can do what we want sexually, that we have the right to take what we want or force our will on others. If we go with the "thief" and believe what he says, our lives eventually spiral into the fear of betrayal and rejection, constant fighting for our "rights," and shame, guilt, regret, and self-reproach.

Jesus offers us a full life—a life where we don't have to cave in to every feeling and desire we have, even if they're destructive. Paul said we want to do good, and then we mess up; we end up doing the things we don't want to do. But who will set us free from this body of death? Jesus! And there is no condemnation for those who are in Christ Jesus because the law of the Spirit of life in Jesus has set us free from the law of sin and death (Romans 7–8). Jesus is everything that is life.

Bible Reading: John 14:6, Romans 7:14–25, 8:1–4, 1 John 5:20

Day 4

"In the beginning was the Word, and the Word was with God, and the Word was God. He was in the beginning with God. All things came into being through Him, and apart from Him nothing came into being that has come into being. In Him was life, and the life was the Light of men. The Light shines in the darkness, and the darkness did not comprehend it" (John 1:1–5).

This word *Light* that is Jesus is a big word. Jesus is the Eternal Light; He was never kindled and will never be quenched. The Apostle John talked about John the Baptist in the first chapter of John, and in verse 8, he said that John the Baptist was not the Light but that he came to tell about the Light (Jesus). We often say when we mourn someone who has died that they were a candle that burned brightly for the short time they were with us. That is the contrast between Jesus's light and ours. A person's light is kindled or lit by Someone else (God) and is enjoyed by others for a time, but eventually that light is extinguished. Jesus is eternal; no one ignited His light, and His light cannot be snuffed out.

We need this assurance. Life can be intimidating and dark, and we have so many things threatening our safety and welfare. But for those of us who are God's children, we have the reality of Jesus's eternal, never-ending light. Satan can't put Jesus's light out. No enemy, no false religion, no government, and no court system—nothing—can extinguish the Light of Life. David wrote this description of God:

> *O Lord, You have searched me and known me. You know when I sit down and when I rise up; You understand my thought from afar. You scrutinize my path and my lying down, and are intimately acquainted with all my ways. Even before there is a word on my tongue, behold, O Lord, You know it all. You have enclosed me behind and before, and laid Your hand upon me. Such knowledge is too wonderful for me; it is too high, I cannot attain to it. Where can I go from Your Spirit? Or where can I flee from Your presence? If I ascend to heaven, You are there; if I make my bed in Sheol [the grave], behold, You are there. If I take the wings of the dawn, if I dwell in the remotest part of the sea, even there Your hand will lead me, and Your right hand will lay hold of me. If I say, "Surely the darkness will*

overwhelm me, and the light around me will be night," even the darkness is not dark to You, and the night is as bright as the day. Darkness and light are alike to You.

—Ps. 139:1–12

God's light has always been and will always be. It wraps around us in a protective blanket, comforting us and assuring us. There will be times in life when we feel lost in the dark, surrounded by the enemy or wallowing in a pit of our mistakes. We may run in shame or exist in the "shadow of death" of depression, but Jesus always sees us. Always. His light shines brightly. He sees things we may not want Him to see, but the Light also shines on the path out of that place of rebellion or misery. Christ's light shines hope into our misery and hopelessness. It's our beacon when we're afraid, our guide when we're lost, our constant reminder of God's presence.

The light of God is perfect for whatever situation we are in. Remember how He led Israel through the wilderness as a cloud by day and a fire by night? Jesus is always bright enough for us to see and gentle enough to not blind us. His goal is for His light to teach and enlighten us, guide and accompany us, comfort and assure us, reveal the good and the bad in us, draw us, and attract others. Jesus is the true Light who, coming into the world, enlightens every person.

Bible Reading: John 1:1–17

Day 5

Let's talk about darkness and light. There's no real definition of what dark is. It isn't a tangible thing or idea. Darkness is the *absence* of light, or having little or no light—a dark room or dark night. The Dark Ages was a time when people were unenlightened, meaning they had an absence of learning and understanding. So a person who's in the dark about something has no information, can't figure something out, or is unaware of the information. The darkness that means evil and bad behavior is defined by the lack of something—an absence of goodness and light.

On the other hand, light is a tangible, concrete, actual thing or idea. Light is the energy that produces a sensation of brightness that illuminates (clarifies, lights up) something or someone. We've learned that Jesus is the

Light of men (all humans). His light is extremely delicate, subtle, pure, and brilliant in quality. That is a beautiful description of Jesus. In His 30-some years living on earth, Jesus was brilliantly pure in His holiness and love of all people. He called sin "sin" but shined His light on the people living in sin in a delicate and subtle way.

John 8:1–12 tells the story of a bunch of men who wanted to trick Jesus and weaken His teachings. They brought a woman who'd been caught doing something immoral to Jesus and quoted Moses's Law, which said she should be stoned. Refusing to answer their accusations, He bent down and started writing on the ground. And as they continued to ask Him, He stood up and said to them, "Let him who is without sin among you be the first to throw a stone at her." When they heard that, they left one by one, and Jesus was left alone with the woman in the center of the court. Jesus said to her, "Woman, where are they? Did no one condemn you?" She said, "No one, Lord." And Jesus said, "I do not condemn you, either. Go. From now on sin no more." Then Jesus again spoke to them, saying, "I am the Light of the world; he who follows Me will not walk in the darkness, but will have the Light of life."

Between what Jesus wrote on the ground and His saying, "Let him without sin cast the first stone," some light was shed on the motives and actions of the woman's accusers. The darkness of their hearts—evil intentions—were exposed in Christ's subtle and pure light. That same light, brilliant in its delicate purity, shined on the woman. His light didn't condemn her to death; it caused her to want to change to a new life.

That is God's offer. Look at the Light of the world, and follow Him. You and I will not walk in darkness. We won't walk—live each step of our days and lives—in sin, shame, or lack of knowledge of Jesus. When we follow Christ Jesus, we will have the Light of life.

Jesus the Light is truth, and truth's knowledge, together with the spiritual purity associated with it, exposes everything. A few verses down, Jesus said, "If you continue in My word, *then* you are truly disciples of Mine; and you will know the truth, and the truth will make you free" (John 8:31–32). Each accusing man saw a truth that revealed some sin in their life. That enlightenment had the power to set them free. The woman's sin had been physically exposed for all to see, but what Jesus spoke and wrote also enlightened her, and she chose to let that truth set her free. What He said to those men was meant for her too. Motives mattered, attitudes counted, and actions were significant.

Each of us is enslaved by the darkness of our sins. Realize that Jesus doesn't shine His light on those areas to condemn us but so we can clearly see what we need to leave at His feet as we "go and sin no more." His light is meant to release us from sin's control.

Bible Reading: John 8:1–12, 31–36

Day 6

How astounding our Savior Jesus Christ is. He is the Word, the "ultimate reason" that continually causes our universe to function with order. Jesus says what He means and means what He says. Added to that, Jesus is what He says. And what He said in the beginning were the words that spoke creation into being—the words of Life and the words of Light.

Now that we have the reminder that Jesus was more than a man, that He is God in every way, we can move into a deeper appreciation of all He brought to us when He came down from heaven to live among us. Christ Jesus brought the very words from the Father's mouth to us, not only for the intellect of God's thought or deep theology of His Spirit. Jesus's words are full of life and light. A few years ago, God impressed upon my heart that His words in the Bible were everything any person would ever need in order to get through life. Believing that opened my eyes as I read Scripture. Applying some of the passages to my life today or to things I've read in history was easy. There were other times when it seemed as if a deeper knowledge of God was all I could see, without any practical daily application or significance.

In the books John wrote, he gave the Word some perspective. "In the beginning was the Word, and the Word was with God, and the Word was God. He was in the beginning with God. All things came into being through Him, and apart from Him nothing came into being that has come into being. In Him was life, and the life was the Light of men. The Light shines in the darkness, and the darkness did not comprehend it" (John 1:1–5).

When you and I walk through life—the highs of life and the lowest times of life—Jesus is the One with the answers. He breathes new life into our existence when we're tired and depressed and don't want to go on. The way to be successful with integrity and live in pain with dignity was shown to us in His words and actions. Jesus is the Light of this world. We've all seen and experienced Satan's darkness, but we aren't swallowed up by it. Learning the truth about Jesus being the eternal Light exposes the truth of our situation. No matter how dark our lives have been, we know God's light is still here. By definition, darkness is the absence of light. That is the spiritual war we're in—lies of darkness holding us captive in fear, rage, selfishness—living as a constant victim in sadness . . . whatever darkness we're in. Knowing the truth of the Word, knowing the eternal Light and complete Life of Jesus allows us to destroy imaginations and "every lofty thing raised up against the knowledge of God, and *we are* taking every thought captive to the obedience of Christ" (2 Cor. 10:5).

Job taught us that coming away with a deeper knowledge of God's attributes is very beneficial to us. When the odds are against us and our enemy is more powerful, it is a good thing to know who God is. If God is for us, who can be against us? (Rom. 8:31). I mean really . . . He spoke this world into being from nothing. Before He made the sun, moon, and stars, He created light, and He is light. God is the giver of life, the breath of life, and eternal life. And He is for us. So the truth is . . . who are the courts when they're against us? Who is an abusive parent, guardian or friend? Who is the government—or even Satan—when it is against us? This is who they are. They're powerful and painful, but they are weaker than the Word, the Light, and the Life. Knowing Jesus is practical. His Word, Light, and Life get us through each moment of every day with perspective and confidence. Greater is He who is in us than he who is in the world (1 John 4:4).

Bible Reading: John 1:1–17, 2 Corinthians 10:3–7

Week 2

NOAH

Day 1

God's love is shown in many ways. Patience is one expression of our Father's love. Second Peter 3:9 says, "The Lord is not slow about His promise, as some count slowness, but is patient toward you, not wishing for any to perish but for all to come to repentance." Our Father protects those He loves. He told Joshua and Israel, "Have I not commanded you? Be strong and courageous! Do not tremble or be dismayed, for the LORD your God is with you wherever you go" (Josh. 1:9).

God's love also gives us justice. Paul reminded us in Galatians 6:7–9, "Do not be deceived, God is not mocked; for whatever a man sows, this he will also reap. For the one who sows to his own flesh will from the flesh reap corruption, but the one who sows to the Spirit will from the Spirit reap eternal life. Let us not lose heart in doing good, for in due time we will reap if we do not grow weary."

Noah, the ark, and the flood reveal God's love to us in an unforgettable way. Our challenge will be to look beyond the story we all think we know and into the hearts of the people and our Lord. Things really aren't so different now from that time thousands of years ago.

Genesis 5 is a list of men, how many years they lived, and who their sons were. Basically, it's like walking through a cemetery and reading the headstones. What it tells us is that these people existed and mattered, and that they died. They died because death is one of the consequences of sin. The last father introduced was Noah. His story hinges on the fact that for hundreds, even thousands, of years God was in conflict with people because of their terrible sinfulness.

> *Then the L*ORD *saw that the wickedness of man was great on the earth, and that every intent of the thoughts of his heart was only evil continually. The L*ORD *was sorry that He had made man on the earth, and He was grieved in His heart. The L*ORD *said, "I will blot out man whom I have created from the face of the land, from man to animals to creeping things and to birds of the sky; for I am sorry that I have made them." But Noah found favor in the eyes of the L*ORD.
>
> —Gen. 6:5–8

Our actions may fool some of the people some of the time, and they may fool some of the people all of the time, but they cannot fool God. His eyes see what we do, and His ears hear what we say, and beyond that God sees the intents of our thoughts—and not just our thoughts but our *intentions*, our objectives, our plans, and our goals. People during Noah's time were extremely wicked. God said that *every* (not some or most, but all) intent of their thoughts was *only* (alone, no other reason) evil *continually* (repeatedly and constantly). Their chosen lifestyle and character were evil.

In the present day, it isn't politically correct to call people's choices bad. It's as if immoral, corrupt, dishonest, and vulgar aren't words anymore, because if they had meaning, they could then be attached to the actions that matched their meaning, and that wouldn't be nice. So we tolerate dishonorable and sinful behavior for fear of being judgmental, uncool, and some kind of a phobic label. But God will not put up with this forever. He's not stupid, and He's not blind. Seeing into our hearts, God sees our intents just as He saw the people in Noah's time. When our every intention is only evil all the time, we will have to face the consequences for our choices. Believers in Christ have found favor in God's eyes. As modern-day Noahs, we need to live for God and tell of His patient love, truth, justice, and saving grace.

***Bible Reading*: Genesis 6:1–14, Psalm 139:23–24**

Day 2

The beginning of Genesis 6 creates a lot of speculation.

> *Now it came about, when men began to multiply on the face of the land, and daughters were born to them, that the sons of*

> *God saw that the daughters of men were beautiful; and they took wives for themselves, whomever they chose. Then the* Lord *said, "My Spirit shall not strive with man forever, because he also is flesh; nevertheless his days shall be one hundred and twenty years." The Nephilim were on the earth in those days, and also afterward, when the sons of God came in to the daughters of men, and they bore* children *to them. Those were the mighty men who* were *of old, men of renown. Then the* Lord *saw that the wickedness of man was great on the earth, and that every intent of the thoughts of his heart was only evil continually.*
>
> —Gen. 6:1–5

The term *sons of God* is used for angels in the Bible. God told Satan in Genesis 3:15 that the woman's seed would crush his head. Many think Satan tried to contaminate the human race so that could never happen. He attempted it by having demons (fallen angels) have children with women. That could also mean that men who loved and followed God married or had children with women who did not love and follow God. Because it is not clear, we'll focus on what is. People participated in sexual sin at that time, as well as every other form of wickedness and violence.

We've learned that sin is missing the mark of God's perfect holy pureness. Anything that misses His standard of rightness is sin. However, not all sins are equal. Sexual sin is personal and against our bodies. Paul said this to believers:

> *Do you not know that your bodies are members of Christ? Shall I then take away the members of Christ and make them members of a prostitute? May it never be! Or do you not know that the one who joins himself to a prostitute is one body* with *her? For He says, "*The two shall become one flesh.*" But the one who joins himself to the Lord is one spirit* with *Him. Flee immorality. Every* other *sin that a man commits is outside the body, but the immoral man sins against his own body. Or do you not know that your body is a temple of the Holy Spirit who is in you, whom you have from God, and that you are not your own? For you have been bought with a price: therefore glorify God in your body.*
>
> —1 Cor. 6:15–20

A prostitute here refers to a person who has sex for gain or for monetary or lustful fulfillment. Promiscuous or loose morals and prostitution are said to be victimless behaviors that we should overlook. God has an entirely different opinion. Societies that sin often and in countless ways become calloused. Gradually the people defile their own bodies in more and more degrading ways. Open sexual immorality is a sign of long-standing, deep-seated sin. As in Sodom and Gomorrah, it's an indication that a person or group of people has walked a long way from God for a long period of time.

God was very clear that He created sex and that it is good—when it is done the way He intended. One man and one woman are to marry and be faithful to each other in every way (Gen. 2:24, Heb. 13:4). Every form of sexuality outside of God's created relationship is wrong, not because sex is wrong but because the connection of the two people is a picture of God's pure, spiritual union with us. The desire of God's heart is for us to know His love and the love of our husband or wife completely. Love and lust (sexual hunger) are two different things. Love gives and cares for the other person. Lust is selfish and wants only to be fulfilled. Our Father wants to protect us from breaking our bodies and hearts in pieces by uniting with multiple people. He wants us to understand the beauty of being one with Him, dearly intimate and safe.

Bible Reading: **Romans 13:12–14, 1 Corinthians 6:9–11, 1 Thessalonians 4:3–5**

Day 3

For generations God had pled with and made a great effort to convince people to listen to Him and follow His way of living. Finally, He'd had enough. The Lord was sorry He had made mankind, and His heart was filled with pain and grief over their destructive choices and rejection of Him. So the Lord said, "I will completely wipe out this human race that I have created. Yes, and I will destroy all the animals and birds, too. I am sorry I ever made them."

As Creator, God has the right to erase whatever He wants to from His creation. But He isn't like the Greek gods we learn about in mythology who wielded their power because they were bored or mean-spirited. The Bible said God was heartbroken because His children chose to destroy themselves, other people, and the rest of creation with their immoral, corrupt, violent, and depraved ways. Our perfectly loving Father had strived and appealed with His children for thousands of years to follow Him instead of Satan. There came a time, however, when God said that enough was enough. No more talking, no more slaps on the wrist—God declared His judgment.

Out of all the people, Noah was the only one who loved the Lord and obeyed Him. Noah wasn't a perfect man, but he had a relationship with God. So God told Noah He was going to destroy the world with a flood and that Noah needed to build an ark for protection.

Building a boat for a flood took a lot of faith because it had never rained before. Mist used to rise from the earth, but no rain had fallen, and the seawaters had stayed in their boundaries (Gen. 2:5–6). Imagine the ridicule and mockery Noah and his family endured as they obeyed God in this strange act. The only thing they knew for sure was God—the Creator; the Father; the Truth; the Protector; the all-knowing, ever-present, all-powerful Ruler of the universe. They believed in God. We're asked to live by that same kind of faith today.

Maybe you've never experienced love from another person, only betrayal, manipulation, greediness, or abuse. Now you hear that God wants to have a relationship with you and that He loves you. Do you have faith like Noah? You've never seen love like he'd never seen floodwaters. People around you may tell you you're weak or believing a lie. What each of us should do is take that first step toward God, knowing He loves us because we can see it in the intricate details that make up our bodies and minds. God's love whispers to us in our darkest despair to hold on to Him because He'll never leave nor forsake us. Our faith is wise because history proves repeatedly that He is all-powerful and involved and good. With that knowledge tucked into our hearts we can say, "For this moment, for today, I will trust You, Lord. Fill me with Your love, and show Yourself to me." Before we know it, days will have passed, and our faith will reveal Jesus's "ark" that will save us from judgment and give refuge to us during life's storms.

Patient love and second (and third and . . .) chances were given to the entire human race during the time it took for Noah to build the ark. The Bible doesn't definitively say how long it took, but it was probably between 100 and 120 years (Gen. 5:32, 6:3, 7:6). However long, it was an opportunity for repentance. Watching wild animals go to Noah and enter the ark in pairs was even more reason to believe in God. Remember, God does not rejoice when men die. He loves us and wants us to willingly turn to Him because we love Him too. Each step of building the ark was an opportunity for someone to ask why and turn from their evil ways and turn to God. We have that opportunity today.

Bible Reading: **Genesis 6:13-22, 7:1-10; Ezekiel 33:11**

Day 4

Here are some things I love about God. In the midst of thousands of years of wicked people, He still looked at each individual person. My heart swells with affection because His plans are minutely detailed even though not completely revealed. I love that the Lord provides for more than our obvious needs.

God observed the extent of the people's wickedness and was sorry He had ever made them. His heart was broken by His rebellious and disloyal children. But Noah found favor with the Lord. This is the history of Noah and his family. Noah was a righteous man, the only blameless man living on earth at the time. He consistently followed God's will and enjoyed a close relationship with Him (Gen. 6:9).

Our tendency would be to write off everyone as a lost cause. In our own lives that would seem the safest and wisest thing to do. How much hurt and betrayal does it take before we stop trusting everyone? God's example pushes us beyond our comfort zone. It requires us to risk being hurt but also take a chance on finding the love and loyalty of a good person. Life is precious, and each of us has value. Because of that, God doesn't lump us into groups and labels. Each of us has a choice to make for how we will live today and into the future. The Father wants a relationship with all of us and will not reject us because of other people's sins. With His strength and wisdom, we can be open to a relationship with Him and other people, even if we've been surrounded by mostly harmful and unsafe people before. What a gift His example can be to us!

Detailed instructions on the size, materials, and structure of the ark had to be enough information for Noah. What questions would we want answered before we started the job? Why? What will I tell other people? How long will it take? How will all the animals get in, live, and behave? When will we need this? For how long? How will it work? Instead of asking those questions, let's you and I take a page from Noah's book and gain confidence from the details God does give. As important as the big picture is, so are the little microscopic details of our life. God is involved in all of it. Knowing the Creator is involved in our life and circumstance should be sufficient encouragement to move forward and do what we know to do. We can't control tomorrow, but we can do the next thing and live how God has asked us to live.

God told Noah the whole earth would be flooded, but God swore to take care of him. The Lord sent all the animals to Noah and told him, "Take for yourself some of all food which is edible, and gather *it* to yourself; and it shall be for food for you and for them" (Gen. 6:21). Seriously, how do you plan for that? What would be enough food? How many days were you going to have to feed the animals and your family? None of those things were Noah's problems. None of those things are my problem or your problem. God is in charge of His plans. He provides all we need. Jesus said not to worry about what we'll eat, what we'll wear, or where we'll live because if God clothes the flowers and grasses of the fields, how much more will He take care of you? (Matt. 6:27–34). Mark 13:11 says, "When they arrest you and hand you over, do not worry beforehand about what you are to say, but say whatever is given you in that hour; for it is not you who speak, but *it is* the Holy Spirit." Our Lord gives us exactly what we need for each moment.

I love God for searching us out and loving us, for being sufficient and in control.

Bible Reading: **Proverbs 3:5–7, Isaiah 55:6–13, Luke 12:22–32**

Day 5

As one person in the middle of this huge planet of humanity . . . as a solitary individual surrounded by a world gone crazy with violence and immorality . . . how could you or I be noticed by God as being different? How did Noah find favor with the Lord when surrounded by filth, corruption, and violence?

Noah was a righteous man, blameless in his time; Noah walked with God (Gen. 6:9). That says it all. We need to be righteous people. In the Hebrew, the word *righteous* means "just and right in one's cause and in conduct and character"—correct and lawful. Society may yell to save the cop killer, lighten up on drug enforcement, spend more money than we have and then claim bankruptcy. It may say abort inconvenient babies, use unethical money practices, twist words, disrespect authority, ignore the needs of the young or ugly or invisible. The cry is for free sexual expression and restricted religious expression. Righteous people stand opposite all of that. Walking with God enables us to live differently than the world's standards. Speak the truth about God's way of love, pureness, rightness, and justice. Conduct ourselves with integrity all the time—when people are looking and when no one sees.

You and I can be blameless in our time. Blameless in Genesis 6:9 is to be complete and sound, to be unimpaired (not weakened) and upright ethically. Righteousness is not an act; it's who we are. No matter what door is opened in our life, the complete picture of us shows our desire to be just and live with integrity. When we blow it and sin, that is not where we stay and live. We turn back to God, to justness and rightness. Stumbling and falling is guaranteed, but Noahs are ethically upright. Staying down in the mess of the world is not an option.

Jesus said in John 15 that we should abide in Him like He abides in the Father. Abide means to live in Jesus, walk each step of every day with God, stay with and spend time with the Father. Our Lord wants a relationship with us, just like He had with Noah. In a crowd we can always find the person we love and live with. That's why Noah stood out in the midst of his world. His love relationship with the Father made him clearly noticeable and enabled him to live righteously and blamelessly.

Here's what David wrote:

> O Lord, who may abide in Your tent? Who may dwell on Your holy hill? He who walks with integrity, and works righteousness, and speaks truth in his heart. He does not slander with his tongue, nor does evil to his neighbor, nor takes up a reproach against his friend; in whose eyes a reprobate is despised, but who honors those who fear the Lord; he swears to his own hurt and does not change; he does not put out his money at interest, nor does he take a bribe against the innocent. He who does these things will never be shaken.
> —Ps. 15:1–5

> Do not let kindness and truth leave you; bind them around your neck, write them on the tablet of your heart. So you will find favor and good repute in the sight of God and man. Trust in the Lord with all your heart and do not lean on your own

understanding. In all your ways acknowledge Him, and He will make your paths straight. Do not be wise in your own eyes; fear the LORD and turn away from evil.

—Prov. 3:3–7

Finding favor with God is as simple as having a relationship with Him. He is the One who enables us to stand upright with consistent integrity in our sinful world.

Bible Reading: John 15:4–14

Day 6

We've spent a week in Genesis 6 gaining a better understanding of God's heart and mind. This is an important chapter because it shows that it wasn't on a whim that God killed most of the animals and all but eight of the human race. Flooding the world was the last resort of a heartbroken and grieved Father. Those aren't just words. Anyone who's experienced having their love thrown back in their face knows the pain of heartbreak. If you've watched people you love destroy their lives as well as others' lives, you know the aching sorrow. We also realize that someone needs to protect others from such destructive choices. There was suffering and grief involved in the emotions God endured for thousands of years because of people's life choices.

However, He has an undying love for us, a love that would not give up. In the righteous anger that accompanied His grief, God wished He'd never created us. Righteous anger is the key here. Sinful behavior deserves anger, but righteousness does not allow us to act out in revenge. So instead of writing us all off, God remembered the one man who walked with Him every day, one man and seven members of his family out of the entire world. No one is overlooked by God. One person matters. Though violence and immorality dominated the society, Noah stood apart. He refused to blend in or buy the "everybody's doing it or times have changed" excuses for compromising. Integrity and righteousness are consistent, and Noah knew the only way to stay consistent was to walk with God every day.

For you and me today, Noah's story brings home the truth that it matters how we choose to live. Our lives affect people around us. Each of us individually shapes our entire society by the choices we make. Beyond that is the fact that Jesus loved us enough to come and die to pay for our sins. The Father made a great sacrifice when He sent His Son for that purpose. And the sacrifice Jesus gave being tortured and slowly killed on the cross was enormous.

For those of us who are like Noah, who have a personal relationship with God because we believe Jesus is God who died and rose from the dead, we are reminded that our bodies are where the Holy Spirit lives. First Corinthians 6:19–20 says, "Do you not know that your body is a temple of the Holy Spirit who is in you, whom you have from God, and that you are not your own? For you have been bought with a price; therefore glorify God in your body."

We were bought with a price. That's why it matters how we think, what we watch on TV, what we read, what language we use, how we treat others, and how we handle our anger. The price Jesus paid for us was high, so it's important that we stay sexually pure, that we are honest with money, and that we are truthful, fair, and kind.

If you have not yet accepted Jesus Christ as your Savior, you need to know that you are still one of the people He loves. "God demonstrates His own love toward us, in that while we were yet sinners, Christ died for us" (Rom. 5:8). Jesus paid a high price to rescue you. Just as God pleaded with the people in Genesis 6, He is pleading with you. He truly loves you with a patient and protective love. But He is just. Anyone who dies without believing in Jesus experiences the same judgment as the people of the flood. So don't reject God's offer of love and forgiveness. He wants a relationship with you, to walk with you every day, and to teach you how to live in integrity. Believe in Jesus, and enter into the "ark" of His saving forgiveness and love.

Bible Reading: **John 3:16–21, 2 Peter 3:5–18**

Week 3

NOAH

Day 1

> *Then the LORD said to Noah, "Enter the ark, you and all your household, for you alone I have seen to be righteous before Me in this time. For after seven more days, I will send rain on the earth forty days and forty nights; and I will blot out from the face of the land every living thing that I have made." Noah did according to all that the LORD had commanded him. So they went into the ark to Noah, by twos of all flesh in which was the breath of life. Those that entered, male and female of all flesh, entered as God had commanded him; and the LORD closed it behind him.*
> —Gen. 7:1, 4–5, 15–16

Noah and the animals were in the ark, and God shut the door as the rain began to fall and the waters of the deep broke open. No person on the outside of the ark could get in. Salvation had been offered. The invitation to have a relationship with the Lord God had been given repeatedly for years. Until the last minute, the door to the saving protection of the ark was open. Noah had spoken God's words loudly, and he had completed God's work for all to see. Everyone watched miracles happen as pairs of every living animal came to Noah in an orderly way. Grace was there for the taking. Forgiveness and a new relationship were offered from God's open heart. Along with the generous love and salvation God had promised, He had also given His word about the punishment He would finally give to any who rejected Him. God is faithful. His words are true. At just the right time, the Lord fulfills all His promises.

The door to the ark was shut by the hand of God, and no one could open it. It's important to note that only God can close the door on salvation. You or I may want to say a certain person is beyond saving; we may believe we are too broken or terrible to be rescued and forgiven. But we don't have the power to close that door—on ourselves or on anyone else. Revelation 3:7 says, "To the angel of the church in Philadelphia write: He who is holy, who is true, who has the key of David, who opens and no one will shut, and who shuts and no one opens."

Our job is to be like Noah, to do according to all the Lord commands us (Gen. 7:5). We are to confess with our mouth Jesus as Lord and believe in our heart that God raised Him from the dead, and we will be saved (Rom. 10:9). God's Word tells us to love the Lord our God with all our heart, and with all our soul, with all our strength, and with all our mind; and love our neighbor as ourself (Luke 10:27). Jesus commanded us to "go therefore and make disciples of all the nations, baptizing them in the name of the Father and the Son and the Holy Spirit, teaching them to observe all that I commanded you" (Matt. 28:19–20). We're to be on our guard, stand firm in the faith, be men and women of courage, be strong, and let all we do be done in love (1 Cor. 16:13–14). All of this is what we know to do each step of our every day. With complete relief and confidence, we can release the responsibility of closing the door to the One who knows best when to do that.

"'Yet even now,' declares the Lord, 'return to Me with all your heart, and with fasting, weeping and mourning; and rend your heart and not your garments.' Now return to the Lord your God, for He is gracious and compassionate, slow to anger, abounding in lovingkindness and relenting of evil" (Joel 2:12–13).

***Bible Reading*: Genesis 7, Nahum 1:3–7**

Day 2

Genesis chapters 6 and 7 show God's judgment. Now we are moving into God's redemption story. Genesis 7 ends this way: "The water prevailed upon the earth one hundred and fifty days." Then Genesis 8:1–3 says, "But God remembered Noah and all the beasts and all the cattle that were with him in the ark; and God caused a wind to pass over the earth, and the water subsided. Also the fountains of the deep and the floodgates of the sky were closed, and the rain from the sky was restrained; and the water receded steadily from the earth, and at the end of one hundred and fifty days the water decreased."

When the Bible says God remembered someone, it's not indicating they had slipped His mind and then He suddenly recalled them. The Lord had not forgotten Noah and the inhabitants of the ark. For God, remembering is an action word. He expresses concern and acts with loving care and protection for the one He remembers. When we forget about the people living in poverty and oppression who have touched our hearts and then recall them, we need to act on that remembrance. God remembers or is mindful of us. He considers and keeps in mind what we're going through, and He acts on that.

If we were Noah's family, do you think we would feel lost in the turmoil of the storm and destruction? Torrents of rain had fallen for 40 days and 40 nights. When the rain stopped, the ark was still tossed about in a world covered in water for 150 days, and there was no word from God. Some of us have lived like this for a long time. Because God has remained silent through the craziness and devastation in our lives, we feel forgotten. The truth is that God remembers you, just as He remembered Noah. God is mindful of your situation, pain, and fear. In His perfect time, He will show Himself in a physical way. He is already acting on His remembrance—guaranteed.

Hang on to these promises when you feel as if the Lord has forgotten you. He told Joshua, "No man will *be able to* stand before you all the days of your life. Just as I have been with Moses, I will be with you; I will not fail you or forsake you" (Josh. 1:5). And David said to his son Solomon, "Be strong and courageous, and act; do not fear nor be dismayed, for the Lord God, my God, is with you. He will not fail you nor forsake you until all the work for the service of the house of the Lord is finished" (1 Chron. 28:20).

Jesus said in Matthew 28:20, "And lo, I am with you always, even to the end of the age." In John 14:16–18, Jesus said, "I will ask the Father, and He will give you another Helper, that He may be with you forever; *that is* the Spirit of truth, whom the world cannot receive, because it does not see Him or know Him, *but* you know Him because He abides with you and will be in you. I will not leave you as orphans; I will come to you."

The beginning of God's new life, of His redemptive, saving freedom and recovery is the realization that He is with us and working. The Lord remembered Noah and all the wild animals and the livestock that were with him in the ark. He remembers you in your life. And God caused a wind to pass over the earth, and the water subsided. The word *wind* is the same word used in Genesis 1:2 for the Spirit. The earth was formless and void, and darkness was over the surface of the deep, and the Spirit of God was moving over the surface of the waters. God sends His breath of life to move over our destroyed worlds. When we have a relationship with Him as Noah did, we will have new life. The process may be long. We may feel alone and forgotten. Cling to His truth. You are in His heart, and He is preparing new life for you.

Bible Reading: John 14:15–31

Day 3

Noah and his family, along with all the animals, had been in the ark for a long time. Depending on which calendar system we use, the days spent in the ark were between 370 and 375 (Gen. 7:11–13, 8:14–15). That was more than one of our American years that they were shut up in the large ship with only one long window—safe but isolated, free of judgment but confined physically to a restricted space.

A series of birds were sent out to test if the land was dry. Finally, Noah removed the covering of the ark and looked, and the surface of the ground was dried up. Then God spoke to Noah, saying, "'Go out of the ark, you and your wife and your sons and your sons' wives with you. Bring out with you every living thing of all flesh that is with you, birds and animals and every creeping thing that creeps on the earth, that they may breed abundantly on the earth, and be fruitful and multiply on the earth.' So Noah went out" (Gen. 8:16–18).

Let's put ourselves in those people's lives. God had protected them from the terrible chaos and destruction going on all around them. As reassuring as it is to be held tightly and kept safe, after a while it's irritating. A year in an ark is way past most of our comfort zones. Yet when God finally releases us to go out into the new world, a little apprehension can creep in. We could find ourselves wanting to stay in the ark, the place where we knew how things worked, where we felt comfortable with the sameness, the safe haven where we were sheltered from all outside threats, where our responsibilities as well as our freedoms were limited.

We saw this in autumn with the Israelites. They hated their slavery in Egypt, but their freedom was also overwhelming and difficult. The truth is that God never wants us to stop moving forward in life. During the heart-wrenching times of injustice and evil, through the sweet and quiet times in God's protective covering, and into the challenging times of rebuilding and transforming our lives and the world around us, the Lord wants us to go and to act and to grow. We must remember to be strong and courageous, and to act. Do not fear nor be dismayed, for the Lord God is with us. He will not fail us nor forsake us during all the work that's to be done.

What an extraordinary example Noah gives us to follow. He obeyed God in the middle of evil, corruption, and violence. God says in Hosea 6:6, "For I delight in loyalty rather than sacrifice, and in the knowledge of God rather than burnt offerings." Noah went into the ark to live for an undetermined amount of time and waited many months before leaving after the rain had stopped. Without leaping ahead of God's schedule, which may have seemed logical since the rain had ended, Noah waited on God and lived every day in the ark without complaint. David said, "*I would have despaired* unless I had believed that I would see the goodness of the Lord in the land of the living. Wait for the Lord; be strong and let your heart take courage; yes, wait for the Lord" (Ps. 27:13–14). Finally, Noah honored God by leaving the familiarity and safety of the ark when God told him to. Then he made an altar and worshiped the Lord his God.

In response to Noah's faithfulness, God promised to never again destroy every living thing with water, even though the intention of man's heart is evil from childhood. God knows we will still sin. But His plan is to rescue us by the death and resurrection of Jesus His Son, which the ark so beautifully pictured. Like Noah we can walk through the open door to our new life in Christ where the old has passed away and the new has come (2 Cor. 5:17).

Bible Reading: **Genesis 8, 2 Corinthians 5:17–21**

Day 4

And God blessed Noah and his sons and said to them, "Be fruitful and multiply, and fill the earth. The fear of you and the terror of you will be on every beast of the earth and on every bird of the sky; with everything that creeps on the ground, and all the fish of the sea, into your hand they are given. Every moving thing that is alive shall be food for you; I give all to you, as I gave the green plant. Only you shall not eat flesh with its life, that is, its blood. Surely I will require your lifeblood; from every beast I will require it. And from every man, from every man's brother I will require the life of man. Whoever sheds man's blood, by man his blood shall be shed, for in the image of God He made man. As for you, be fruitful and multiply; populate the earth abundantly and multiply in it."

—Gen. 9:1-7

The sanctity of life was established in no uncertain terms by the Creator of life. One might think that after God wiped out all living people and animals that He didn't value life. So to set the record straight, from the moment Noah and his family stepped into the new, cleansed world, God said that no animal or person could take a person's life. Remember that God had not flooded the world and caused the death of all the people on an impulse. He valued each life, and during the thousands of years He'd warned them of the consequences of their actions, He had also begged them to turn to Him in order to save their lives.

But the Lord knew we humans could easily get the wrong impression because of His judgment on the sinful world. For that reason, He made Himself perfectly clear. If an animal killed a person, the animal was to be put down because every single person's life is important. People are made in God's image; animals are not. And because of that, the life of a person is more precious than the life of an animal. God said when one person murdered another person, the murderer was to be put to death—again, because human life is extremely valuable and sacred.

At the time of Cain and Abel as well as with Noah, God was the head and authority, the ruler who governed society. As more people populated the earth, God set up leaders and gave them His cloak of authority, and they were the ones who put to death a person convicted of murder. Romans 13:1-2 says, "Every person is to be in subjection to the governing authorities. For there is no authority except from God, and those which exist are established by God. Therefore, whoever resists authority has opposed the ordinance of God; and they who have opposed will receive condemnation upon themselves." The life of an accused murderer had as much value as a victim, but once it was established that a person did, in fact, commit murder, according to God's words to Noah, they were to be put to death by the ruling authorities.

Animals were given to us as food. Yet in that sentence they were also protected from abuse. They were not given to us to kill as sport or abuse in any way. God told us we had permission to eat animals, although we could also eat vegetation. But the reason we could kill an animal was to eat it or because it had killed a person. To protect the animals, God gave them a fear of mankind so they would naturally hide and run from us and not be easy prey.

As precious as we are physically (our bodies and breath of life), our spiritual life is treasured even more. God protected us from physical murder with laws, and He has protected us from sin's murderous power by His grace. "For the wages of sin is death, but the free gift of God is eternal life in Christ Jesus our Lord" (Rom. 6:23). We are, indeed, precious in His sight.

Bible Reading: Genesis 9:1-17, John 11:25-26

Day 5

Then God made a covenant with Noah and all people forever and with all the animals that He would never again destroy the world with a flood. Here's what God said:

> *This is the sign of the covenant which I am making between Me and you and every living creature that is with you, for all successive generations; I have set My bow in the clouds, and it shall be for a sign of a covenant between Me and the earth. It shall come about, when I bring a cloud over the earth, that the bow will be seen in the cloud, and I will remember My covenant, which is between Me and you and every living creature of all flesh; and never again shall the water become a flood to destroy all flesh. When the bow is in the cloud, then I will look upon it, to remember the everlasting covenant between God and every living creature of all flesh that is on the earth.*
>
> —Gen. 9:12-16

A rainbow is an arc of light separated into bands of color that appear when the sun's rays are refracted and reflected by drops of mist or rain. The colors of the rainbow are the full spectrum of colors that make up the sun's white light. Refraction means (quite simply) the change of direction of a ray of light when passing through something else.

What beautiful symbolism God gives us with His promise shown in a rainbow. He is light—pure, delicate, and bright. When His light shines on us through the storms of life or through God's discipline and cleansing rain, we see a more detailed aspect of His light than ever before. Noah and his family knew God intimately because they had lived through the flood. Job knew more about God because he'd lived through the ravaging storm in his life. We may know God is light, but it takes experiencing great hardship or discipline to see the fullness of His light.

We are reminded of God's pledge to never again destroy all life with a flood. When we read the book of Esther, we talked about the importance of making a memorial to traumatic and significant events in our lives. God looks at the memorial of the rainbow and keeps in mind that man's complete wickedness is nothing new and that His promise to not flood the world and destroy all life is good. His rainbow reminds us of His purging justice as well as His patient grace. It is a promise born from a punishment, a restoration generated by God's finished work.

Noah's story ends in a surprising way. He became a farmer and planted a vineyard. One day he became drunk on some wine he had made and lay naked in his tent. His son Ham, the father of Canaan, saw that his father was naked and went outside and told his two brothers. Shem and Japheth took a robe, held it over their shoulders, walked backward into the tent, and covered their father's naked body. As they did this, they looked the other way so they wouldn't see him naked. Noah woke up and knew what Ham had done. So he cursed Ham for his disrespect and blessed Shem and Japheth (Gen. 9:20–29). Ham didn't just catch an unplanned glimpse of his dad; he stared at him and told others instead of protecting Noah's reputation with silence.

Even someone as honorable as Noah will make mistakes. He sinned in getting drunk (Eph. 5:18), but it's never right to expose and ridicule a person when they fall in sin. Love means we cover and protect them from the contempt of other people because of their bad choices (1 Cor. 13:4–8). First Peter 4:8 tells us, "Above all, keep fervent in your love for one another, because love covers a multitude of sins." Lying is not required to protect someone's reputation. Discrete tactfulness will show our love and respect, and it will reflect God's covering of our sinful states as well.

Bible Reading: **Genesis 9:12–29, Isaiah 54:7–17**

Day 6

Noah is a story of human rebellion and hard-heartedness. It is the story of one man standing alone in integrity, obeying and trusting in God. And its story tells part of the true nature and character of the Lord God. It is a shadow of the real and lasting saving work of Jesus.

To the rebellious world, the Bible says, "Do not be deceived, God is not mocked; for whatever a man sows, this he will also reap. For the one who sows to his own flesh will from the flesh reap corruption, but the one who sows to the Spirit will from the Spirit reap eternal life" (Gal. 6:7–8). First Corinthians 6:9–10 reads, "Do you not know that the unrighteous will not inherit the kingdom of God? Do not be deceived; neither fornicators, nor idolaters, nor adulterers, nor effeminate, nor homosexuals, nor thieves, nor *the* covetous, nor drunkards, nor revilers, nor swindlers, will inherit the kingdom of God."

While we live without Christ in a wicked lifestyle with a wrong and wicked heart, we are doomed to the judgment the people of Noah's day faced. But it is not God's desire that we die in judgment. He wants us to inherit His kingdom as His children. First Corinthians 6 continues on in verse 11, "Such were some of you; but you were washed, but you were sanctified, but you were justified in the name of the Lord Jesus Christ and in the Spirit of our God." We can all put our sinful ways behind us by the power of Jesus. God is striving with us, telling us to be careful with our choices and not be deceived—we will reap (harvest, bring in) what we sow (plant, live).

Those of us who have chosen to believe in Christ Jesus and live for Him know how alone Noah must have felt. The Bible encourages us in Galatians 6:9, "Let us not lose heart in doing good, for in due time we will reap if we do not grow weary." For more than 100 years Noah built an ark on dry land with no prior experience of flooding. You know that discouragement hit him. But he persevered, keeping his eyes on God—not the people around him, not the passing time or lack of rain or other circumstances. We can experience this with Noah. "Yet those who wait for the Lord will gain new strength; they will mount up *with* wings like eagles, they will run and not get tired, they will walk and not become weary" (Isa. 40:31).

God's absolute justice and righteousness were shown to us along with His complete love and patience. If we reject salvation by rejecting God's gift of Jesus and His death and resurrection, we will face the wrath of God. The wages of sin is death. Sin enslaves us now with its deadly chains of cravings, shame, fear, insecurity, anger, guilt, unforgiveness, and bitterness. When we physically die without telling God we accept His gift of cleansing, saving love—His gift of Jesus who willingly died to pay the debt of our sin—we will face God's wrath. Jesus said, "Do not fear those who kill the body but are unable to kill the soul; but rather fear Him who is able to destroy both soul and body in hell" (Matt. 10:28).

"The Lord is not slow about His promise, as some count slowness, but is patient toward you, not wishing for any to perish but for all to come to repentance" (2 Pet. 3:9). The time that was agonizingly slow for Noah was the time of grace God was giving to a lost and dying people. Romans 5:8–9 says, "But God demonstrates His own love toward us, in that while we were yet sinners, Christ died for us. Much more then, having now been justified by His blood, we shall be saved from the wrath *of God* through Him."

Bible Reading: Galatians 6:1–10, 2 Peter 3:3–15

Week 4

ISAIAH 11

Day 1

Isaiah was a prophet of Israel at a time when Judah (Southern Kingdom) was living in sin, completely apart from God's will. God showed Himself in heaven surrounded by angels, and Isaiah realized how unclean he was, specifically his language. He confessed, and God forgave him. Isaiah wrote, "'Then I heard the voice of the Lord, saying, 'Whom shall I send, and who will go for Us?' Then I said, 'Here am I. Send me!' He said, 'Go, and tell this people . . .'" (Isa. 6:8–9). So that is what the prophet did. He went where God sent him and spoke the Lord's words—words of truth to convict the nation so they would return to God; words of love to encourage the nation as they lived through God's discipline; words of prophecy telling of judgment yet to come and the promised Messiah.

Comparing Israel to a tree and a forest, God said He would lop off the boughs with a terrible crash and cut down the thickets in the forest (Isa. 10). But He also promised life after that punishment, hope found in the Messiah.

> *Then a shoot will spring from the stem of Jesse, and a branch from his roots will bear fruit. The Spirit of the LORD will rest on Him, the spirit of wisdom and understanding, the spirit of counsel and strength, the spirit of knowledge and the fear of the LORD. And He will delight in the fear of the LORD, and He will not judge by what His eyes see, nor make a decision*

ISAIAH 11

> *by what His ears hear; but with righteousness He will judge the poor, and decide with fairness for the afflicted of the earth; and He will strike the earth with the rod of His mouth, and with the breath of His lips He will slay the wicked. Also righteousness will be the belt about His loins, and faithfulness the belt about His waist.*
>
> —Isa. 11:1–5

Christ Jesus is the Branch, born into the family line of King David (Luke 1:32), and anointed by the Holy Spirit (Luke 3:22, 4:1). One of the first clues that the Messiah was not meant to be a political savior as most people wanted (and still want) was the fact that God said in Isaiah that He would spring from the stem of Jesse, not from the stem of King David. David was in Jesus's ancestry, but Isaiah introduced the family a generation before the warrior king who secured and expanded his kingdom with military strength. The Messiah was coming from the stem of a hard-working father and sheep owner, an unknown man of humble and peaceful beginnings.

We will spend this week looking at the fruit this Branch produced. Not only is this a clear picture of the character and person of Jesus, but it is a clear picture of who we as His body (the church) are to be. Every believer of Christ Jesus is sealed by the Holy Spirit and can be filled with the Spirit. The spirit of wisdom and understanding, the spirit of counsel and strength, the spirit of knowledge and fear of the Lord are to be evident in our lives. Our reverence and respect of God should be our delight, and we should not judge others by only what we see and hear but should look to their hearts and see the true persons and circumstances as God does. God's church should wear and live righteousness and faithfulness.

Isaiah said the Messiah will judge the poor and decide with fairness for the afflicted of the earth. Usually the world steps on or ignores the poor unless it benefits them to defend their cause. God's wisdom says if the poor and the weak are given justice, then all will be given justice. Jesus sees each foster child, each broken person, each misused and abused man and woman. He is just and righteous and good. He is our Disciplinarian, our Defender, our Redeemer, and our Savior.

***Bible Reading*: Isaiah 11:1–5, Ephesians 1:15–23**

Day 2

When the Son of God came to live among us as a man named Jesus, He was fully God and fully human. I don't think that is something we can completely comprehend, but it is something that God is very capable of. Because Jesus wanted to experience life completely as a human, He chose to not utilize His divine powers throughout most of His life. So the way Jesus taught, the way He lived, and the miracles He performed were done through the power of the Holy Spirit that filled Him. This is the exact same Holy Spirit and power we have in us when we are followers of Christ (Acts 10:45, Rom. 8:11).

Matthew 3:16 tells us, "After being baptized, Jesus came up immediately from the water; and behold, the heavens were opened, and he saw the Spirit of God descending as a dove *and* lighting on Him." Luke 4:1 says, "Jesus, full of the Holy Spirit, returned from the Jordan and was led around by the Spirit in the wilderness." Christ Jesus the man was filled with the Holy Spirit, who led Him where the Father wanted Him to go. That is precisely what the Holy Spirit does in our lives. He rests on us and fills us and speaks to our spirits—teaching us, leading us, energizing us, and empowering us to do God's will.

The Holy Spirit gave Jesus the spirit of wisdom and understanding. *Wisdom* in the Hebrew language means skill in war, wise leadership and organization, ethical and religious practical sense, discretion and insightfulness. *Understanding* means to discern, perceive, know with the mind, consider, observe.

Matthew 17 tells an account where Jesus exhibited the spirit of wisdom and understanding in His life. A man came to Him and begged Jesus to heal his son who was a lunatic and very sick. Although the disciples had tried to heal his son, they had failed. Jesus cast a demon out of the boy and healed him. The disciples asked why they hadn't been able to do that. "And He said to them, 'Because of the littleness of your faith; for truly I say to you, if you have faith the size of a mustard seed, you will say to this mountain, "Move from here to there," and it will move; and nothing will be impossible to you. [But this kind does not go out except by prayer and fasting']" (Matt. 17:20–21).

Jesus was skilled in spiritual warfare. Wisdom told Him this was not a physical battle, even though the boy was mentally and physically sick. "For our struggle is not against flesh and blood, but against the rulers, against the powers, against the world forces of this darkness, against the spiritual *forces* of wickedness in the heavenly places" (Eph. 6:12). "Though we walk in the flesh, we do not war according to the flesh, for the weapons of our warfare

are not of the flesh, but divinely powerful for the destruction of fortresses" (2 Cor. 10:3–4).

Understanding gave Jesus the ability to observe the situation and quickly see beyond the obvious. Not all illness is connected with spiritual warfare, but discernment revealed it was that time. Jesus was ready for any battle that came up because He spent time praying and fasting as a regular part of His lifestyle. When a fight comes to us, we can't say, "Time out, I need to pray and skip a meal." The power and wisdom that comes from prayer and fasting are with us as we live a God-centered life. Divinely powerful weapons are at our disposal as the body of Christ. Filling us with wisdom and understanding, the Holy Spirit lets us know when and how to use them.

***Bible Reading*: Psalm 35:13, Matthew 17:14–21, Acts 13:1–4**

Day 3

Isaiah 11:2 says of the promised Messiah, "The Spirit of the Lord will rest on Him, the spirit of wisdom and understanding, the spirit of counsel and strength." We've seen that Christ had the spirit of wisdom. He was an organized, skilled, and insightful leader in ethics, religion, and warfare. Added to wisdom, Christ Jesus had understanding. He discerned or separated truth from lies and the hidden from the obvious; He had His Father's perspective and considered situations and people before acting.

Furthermore, the spirit of counsel guided Jesus. This is advice, God's purpose, the ability of forming plans with prudence (carefulness) and wisdom. At no time was Jesus the man a rogue agent going it alone and trying to solve the world's problems by Himself. The Son of God prayed at His baptism, before selecting His disciples, at His transfiguration, in secret, early in the morning, with others, alone, on the mountain, and in the Garden of Gethsemane before His arrest. Before living every day, before making decisions, before choosing friends and coworkers, when being personally glorified, before doing the hardest thing in His life—Jesus sought wise counsel.

Of course, the wisest counsel we can receive is from God Himself. This comes to us from His Word, the Bible, and from prayer. But we can also receive intelligent counsel from wise and God-centered people. Proverbs 1:5 tells us, "A wise man will hear and increase in learning, and a man of understanding will acquire wise counsel." Then Proverbs 12:15 says, "The way of a fool is right in his own eyes, but a wise man is he who listens to counsel." And in Proverbs 13:10 we're told, "Through insolence [arrogance, disrespect] comes nothing but strife, but wisdom is with those who receive counsel."

Figuring out how to get wise counsel and really taking it can be difficult. Remember when we studied the kings, we saw people who surrounded themselves with "yes men." When they sought counsel, it was just for show. They expressed the idea they wanted people to approve, knowing that the counsel they got back would agree with them every time. That is not wise counsel. One of the reasons wisdom and understanding are listed before counsel is so we will use them to filter the advice we get from other people.

Jesus was also given the spirit of strength, which is power, valor, bravery, and mighty deeds of God. Sometimes the world portrays Jesus and Christians as milk toast, timid little wimps. Because Jesus said to turn the other cheek when someone slaps us, we are seen as intimidated and fearful. In reality, it takes great strength and power to hold our emotions in check and not retaliate to every insult or improper action thrown at us. The strength Jesus—and His followers—have been given is a strength of character as well as inner courage to live contrary to the world; to stand alone for justice, honor, and purity; and to act when we know it is right. In addition, we carry within us the power of God to do the same miraculous teachings and healings Christ Jesus did. Jesus meant it when He said, "Truly, truly, I say to you, he who believes in Me, the works that I do, he will do also; and greater *works* than these he will do; because I go to the Father" (John 14:12).

The Holy Spirit empowers us with the spirit of wisdom and understanding, the spirit of counsel and strength. It is through Him that we can live wisely, productively, and victoriously.

Bible Reading: **Psalm 33:10–11, Ephesians 6:10–11, James 3:13–18**

Day 4

The spirit of knowledge and the fear of the Lord rested in the Messiah, Jesus Christ. The spirit of knowledge may seem a lot like wisdom and even understanding, but it does have a little different twist to it. It means to find out, to know by experience, to recognize, to be skillful in, to be revealed. Do you recall learning about Adam and Eve? Eve wanted knowledge. She wanted to know what the tree of the knowledge of good and evil would tell her, but... she did not use wisdom in gaining that knowledge. We can make the same mistake, wanting to know for the sake of knowing and being smart and informed. Perhaps we want to know by experience, so we try drugs or sex or something else so we can have a knowledge that can't be gained by reading a book.

Wisdom, understanding, counsel, and strength are valuable tools in our quest for knowledge. Consider Eve again. Her desire to know about that tree in the center of the garden was not wrong. If she had been wise in gaining her knowledge, she would have been better off. Eve should have asked God what good and evil were and what the tree was all about. She could have asked about the serpent and discussed their conversation in order to gain the knowledge she wanted. True, it would have taken strength to push off the desire for instant gratification and wait for God. But slowing down and taking a step back—thinking, considering, pulling on the power of her self-control, and seeking God's advice—would have garnered her all the knowledge with none of the painful consequences. But Eve grabbed for knowledge without using wisdom. She didn't just gain an understanding of evil and its consequence of death, she experienced it.

Jesus had the spirit of knowledge surrounded by all the other attributes of the Holy Spirit. Without sinning, He gained knowledge of what it was like to live as a person in this fallen and painful world. The reason He was able to live with the Holy Spirit's guidance as His priority is because Christ delighted in the fear of the Lord. He had an awe-filled respect and reverence for God. Awe, respect, and reverence are all positive, but the word *fear* also means "terror."

Knowing God—truly knowing Him—and knowing that He is love and that He is completely and thoroughly good, patient, righteous, pure, just, wise, all-knowing, all-powerful, timeless, and everywhere is awe-inspiring. Any one of those things deserves respect. Living with our God causes reverence or feelings of deep respect and devotion but also a healthy dose of fear. This is a God who says what He means and means what He says. And He has the power to back up every single word. Fear of the Lord comes with the whole package we've learned about. We're in awe of and respect God, and yes, we are even afraid of Him based on the wisdom, understanding, counsel, strength, and knowledge the Holy Spirit has given us.

When we put everything the Bible tells us about God together, we know beyond a shadow of a doubt that the only reason bad guys look like they're getting away with sin is because God is patient and loving. But we also know that He's just. Believers pray for the unsaved with the fear of the Lord, knowing that rejecting Jesus results in eternal separation from Him in hell. It is a terrifying thing to fall into the hands of the living God (Heb. 10:13).

The fear of an abusive parent is different because it's based on the person's negative, temporary power that is selfish, defective, and inconsistent—and wrapped in malice. Real knowledge of God results in life-changing reverence and fear of Him based on His love, justice, and righteousness.

Bible Reading: Psalm 19:7–14, Proverbs 2:1–12

Day 5

Isaiah said this:

> *Then a shoot will spring from the stem of Jesse, and a branch from his roots will bear fruit. The Spirit of the* Lord *will rest on Him, the spirit of wisdom and understanding, the spirit of counsel and strength, the spirit of knowledge and the fear of the* Lord. *And He will delight in the fear of the* Lord, *and He will not judge by what His eyes see, nor make a decision by what His ears hear; but with righteousness He will judge the poor, and decide with fairness for the afflicted of the earth; and He will strike the earth with the rod of His mouth, and with the breath of His lips He will slay the wicked. Also righteousness will be the belt about His loins, and faithfulness the belt about His waist.*
> —Isa. 11:1–5

The Messiah will never judge by appearance, false evidence, or hearsay. Jesus sees past a person's bank account and clothes, beyond their possessions or where they live, and makes accurate judgments of the person's character and life. He also doesn't make a decision based solely on what He hears. In Matthew 7:21-23 Jesus said, "Not everyone who says to Me, 'Lord, Lord,' will enter the kingdom of heaven, but he who does the will of My Father who is in heaven *will enter*. Many will say to Me on that day, 'Lord, Lord, did we not prophesy in Your name, and in Your name cast out demons, and in Your name perform many miracles?' And then I will declare to them, 'I never knew you; depart from Me you who practice lawlessness.'"

For most of us, it is difficult to distinguish when a person is sincere with their words or just giving us lip service. As believers in Christ, we have the same powers as Jesus to hear the words of praise, admiration, and loyalty, and discern if they are true. In essence, Jesus said actions speak louder than words. Don't just call me "Lord"; live it in every way every day. Don't only do the showy religious acts that also draw attention to you; do the will of the Father. The Father's will is that everyone who sees the Son believes in Him and receives eternal life (John 6:40).

The poor and afflicted in our world don't have a voice. When they tell of their situations or unfair treatment, most people listen with a jaded ear. It's too painful to either hear or see; we think they should try to help themselves or that they deserve it. Isaiah told us that Christ Jesus would hear and see the poor. Jesus proved it by walking among them, touching them, eating with them, healing them, listening to them, and teaching them. What matters to Jesus is each person's heart more than each person's physical circumstance. When He looks at you and me, when He listens to us, it is our hearts and intentions that Jesus notices.

Righteousness will be the belt about His loins and faithfulness the belt about His waist. Every day, Jesus got dressed and secured His clothes with the belts of righteousness and faithfulness. Psalm 119:137–138 says, "Righteous are You, O Lord, and upright are Your judgments. You have commanded Your testimonies in righteousness and exceeding faithfulness." Christ is and wears righteousness—He is right, just, and honest. He is and wears faithfulness—He is firm, trustworthy, and steady.

This is a God we can count on. He can't be fooled by fancy things or words. The love He feels for us has nothing to do with how much we have or don't have. Who He is, every fiber of His being, is honest and just and trustworthy. Evil and wickedness are defined by Him and His standard. Goodness and righteousness are also defined by Him. He judges us all honestly.

Bible Reading: **Matthew 7**

Day 6

God told Moses exactly how to build the tabernacle (traveling temple) for the people of Israel when they wandered in the wilderness on their way to the Promised Land. Every piece of furniture and utensil had a specific design that held precious and holy significance and function to God and His children. There was only one light in the entire tabernacle—the golden lampstand.

> *Then you shall make a lampstand of pure gold. The lampstand and its base and its shaft are to be made of hammered work; its cups, its bulbs and its flowers shall be of one piece* with it. *Six branches shall go out from its sides; three branches of the lampstand from its one side and three branches of the lampstand from its other side. Three cups* shall be *shaped like almond* blossoms *in the one branch, a bulb and a flower, and three cups shaped like almond* blossoms *in the other branch, a bulb and a flower—so for six branches going out from the lampstand; and in the lampstand four cups shaped like almond* blossoms, *its bulbs and its flowers. Their bulbs and their branches* shall be of one piece *with it; all of it shall be one piece of hammered work of pure gold. Then you shall make its lamps seven* in number; *and they shall mount its lamps so as to shed light on the space in front of it.*
>
> —Exod. 25:31–34, 36–37

Revelation is the last book of the Bible and a revelation or disclosure from God about the end of God's plan and Jesus's return. The Apostle John wrote this:

> *Then I turned to see the voice that was speaking with me. And having turned I saw seven golden lampstands; and in the middle of the lampstands* I saw *one like a son of man . . . [who said], "As for the mystery of the seven stars which you saw in My right hand, and the seven golden lampstands: the seven stars are the angels of the seven churches, and the seven lampstands are the seven churches."*
>
> —Rev. 1:12–13, 20

Isaiah told us a shoot will spring from the stem of Jesse, and a branch from his roots will bear fruit. The Spirit of the Lord will rest on Him, the spirit of wisdom and understanding, the spirit of counsel and strength, the spirit of knowledge and the fear of the Lord. Seven lights shine in God's

Isaiah 11

temple from one lampstand, lighting up the space in front of it. We've seen how illuminating are the spirit of wisdom and understanding, the spirit of counsel and strength, and the spirit of knowledge and fear of the Lord. In the center of those six branches is the base that is the Holy Spirit—the seventh light.

This all makes for fascinating Bible knowledge, but what does it do for us today? That's where Revelation 1 comes in. The churches are the lampstands; they are the lights of this world. Colossians 1 tells us the body of Christ is the church, so believers in Christ Jesus together make up the church. Also, each of us as individuals is a church because the Holy Spirit is in us (1 Cor. 3, 6). So you and I, once we've said we believe in Jesus as the Son of God and our Savior—are lampstands. The Holy Spirit is our base or center shaft that keeps us standing firmly and shines one of the seven lights. You and I have the spirit of wisdom and understanding shining in our lives. We have the spirit of counsel and strength and knowledge and fear of the Lord. It is possible for us to look like our Savior. That's what God wants. Paul told us to be "imitators of God, as beloved children; and walk in love, just as Christ also loved you" (Eph. 5:1–2).

Isaiah told of Jesus's coming as the world's Savior, clothed in righteousness and faithfulness, standing up for the poor and afflicted and judging honestly. We should imitate Him.

Bible Reading: Matthew 5:13–16, 1 Corinthians 3:11–17

Week 5
TOUCHED BY JESUS

Day 1

During the three years of Jesus's ministry, He walked countless miles teaching, healing, and making friends. Many people were touched by Jesus—physically, emotionally, intellectually, and spiritually. Today as we study His life, His desire is to touch us, too, in just the same way. His physical touch mainly comes through Jesus's body, the church, reaching out to hug a sorrow-filled person, putting a gentle and compassionate hand on someone's shoulder as we pray for them or help them with their needs. Jesus still walks countless miles with each of us today. He promised to never leave us nor forsake us. So though we don't see Him in a physical body, He is most definitely with us in Spirit. As we pick out a few accounts when Jesus interacted with the people around Him, let's see how their experiences speak to us right now.

The disciples and Jesus went to the region of Judea and beyond the Jordan, and crowds gathered around Jesus again. According to His custom, He once more began to teach them. Some Pharisees came up to Jesus, testing Him (Mark 10:1–2). People were bringing little children to Jesus to have Him touch them, but the disciples rebuked them. When Jesus saw this, He was indignant. He said to them, "'Permit the children to come to Me; do not hinder them; for the kingdom of God belongs to such as these. Truly I say to you, whoever does not receive the kingdom of God like a child will not enter it *at all*.' And He took them in His arms and *began* blessing them, laying His hands on them" (Mark 10:13–16).

Jesus loves children. Many people in the first century felt as some adults do today that children were to be seen but not heard. At that time, children were at the bottom of the list of important and valuable people, with women just above them. Men were valued most, and no one would dare interrupt or get in front of men with money and religious or political power. But Jesus didn't see others by the world's standards. Children were people, and God loved their hearts and faith. Not only did Jesus take time from teaching the powerful to love and bless kids, but He protected them too.

The disciples were arguing about who was most important, and Jesus said this:

> *Truly I say to you, unless you are converted and become like children, you will not enter the kingdom of heaven. Whoever then humbles himself as this child, he is the greatest in the kingdom of heaven. And whoever receives one such child in My name receives Me; but whoever causes one of these little ones who believe in Me to stumble, it would be better for him to have a heavy millstone hung around his neck, and to be drowned in the depth of the sea. See that you do not despise one of these little ones, for I say to you that their angels in heaven continually see the face of My Father who is in heaven. So it is* not *the will of your Father who is in heaven that one of these little ones perish.*
>
> —Matt. 18:3–6, 10, 14

Jesus loves children. God knew little kids would be vulnerable and need protection, so He gave them parents. He also knew not all parents and adults would want to protect and cherish the gift of a child and that, in fact, they would want to harm them. So God gave every child angels to watch over them and report to the Father each day. Because of the great abuse and pain many children face, that may not seem true, but we've seen before that God allows us all to choose how we live, even when our choices hurt others. In God's perfect timing, He steps in and rescues us. He is already working to heal His little ones' spirits, hearts, minds, and bodies, and to grow them strong in Him. The Lord's judgment will come down extremely harsh on child abusers.

Bible Reading: Matthew 18:1–14, Psalm 127:3–5

Day 2

John the Baptist was Jesus's cousin. King Herod had John killed, and when Jesus heard the news, He went away by Himself. When the people heard where Jesus was, they walked to be with Him. Even though Jesus was grieving the death of His cousin, He had compassion on the crowd and began to heal the sick.

> *When it was evening, the disciples came to Him and said, "This place is desolate and the hour is already late; so send the crowds away, that they may go into the villages and buy food for themselves." But Jesus said to them, "They do not need to go away; you give them something to eat!" They said to Him, "We have here only five loaves and two fish." And He said, "Bring them here to Me." Ordering the people to sit down on the grass, He took the five loaves and the two fish, and looking up toward heaven, He blessed the food, and breaking the loaves He gave them to the disciples, and the disciples gave them to the crowds, and they all ate and were satisfied. They picked up what was left over of the broken pieces, twelve full baskets. There were about five thousand men who ate, besides women and children.*
> —Matt. 14:15–21

Jesus was completely human, and as a man He was surely upset about His cousin being killed and the corruption in the government that led to John the Baptist's death. At some point, grief demands some alone time, time to cry and think and remember, and even be angry. So Jesus went away by Himself. Yet even in His personal grief, He saw other people and put their needs before His own. Stepping outside of ourselves has a healing balm to it. Our situations don't change, and whatever caused our grief still remains, but our perspective gets jarred back into line with the Father's perspective. It is not wrong to grieve; it is just a healthy and godly thing to still be actively involved in the world around us while we grieve.

As always, Jesus pushed His followers to think bigger than what seemed possible. They were healing the sick and casting out demons right alongside Jesus, but when it came time for dinner, they couldn't imagine how those thousands of people could get fed. I think each of us has this same view of God. We've experienced Him in very real ways. The release of guilt and shame, physical or mental healing, the provision of money or a home when needed, everything about nature speaking of God's power . . . the list goes on. But then the next big need or disaster hits, and we can't imagine how God can fix it. It's just too big. We list all the logical ways to address the situation, but God doesn't move on any of them. Jesus wants us to look for the miracle.

The disciples found a boy with five loaves of bread and two fish and gave them to Jesus. Sometimes that's what He wants of us—to give our meager resources and trust Him to do the rest. He thanked the Father for the food and proceeded to feed 5,000 men plus women and children until they all had enough to eat. And there were 12 full baskets of leftovers. This overflowing grace is how God wants to feed us too.

> *[I pray] that He [the Father] would grant you, according to the riches of His glory, to be strengthened with power through His Spirit in the inner man, so that Christ may dwell in your hearts through faith; and that you, being rooted and grounded in love, may be able to comprehend with all the saints what is the breadth and length and height and depth, and to know the love of Christ which surpasses knowledge, that you may be filled up to all the fullness of God. Now to Him who is able to do far more abundantly beyond all that we ask or think, according to the power that works within us, to Him be the glory in the church and in Christ Jesus to all generations forever and ever. Amen.*
>
> —Eph. 3:16–21

Bible Reading: Matthew 14:10–21, Ephesians 3:13–21

Day 3

They came to the other side of the sea, into the country of the Gerasenes. When He got out of the boat, immediately a man from the tombs with an unclean spirit met Him, and he had his dwelling among the tombs. And no one was able to bind him anymore, even with a chain; because he had often been bound with shackles and chains, and the chains had been torn apart by him and the shackles broken in pieces, and no one was

> *strong enough to subdue him. Constantly, night and day, he was screaming among the tombs and in the mountains, and gashing himself with stones. Seeing Jesus from a distance, he ran up and bowed down before Him; and shouting with a loud voice, he said, "What business do we have with each other, Jesus, Son of the Most High God? I implore You by God, do not torment me!" For He had been saying to him, "Come out of the man, you unclean spirit!" And He was asking him, "What is your name?" And he said to Him, "My name is Legion; for we are many." And he began to implore Him earnestly not to send them out of the country. Now there was a large herd of swine feeding nearby on the mountain. The demons implored Him, saying, "Send us into the swine so that we may enter them." Jesus gave them permission. And coming out, the unclean spirits entered the swine; and the herd rushed down the steep bank into the sea, about two thousand of them; and they were drowned in the sea. Their herdsmen ran away and reported it in the city and in the country. And the people came to see what it was that had happened. They came to Jesus and observed the man who had been demon-possessed sitting down, clothed and in his right mind, the very man who had had the "legion"; and they became frightened.*
>
> —Mark 5:1–15

Spiritual warfare is not new to us, and we see here Jesus casting out a legion of demons from one man. The moment Jesus got out of the boat, the battle was on. For us, talking with God needs to be like breathing, and we should read His words from the Bible daily. Then, like Jesus, we will be prepared for whatever comes our way.

This man who lived in the tombs cut himself with stones. Does it surprise you that people were cutting 2,000 years ago? Self-mutilation usually begins in the early teens and can continue into a person's 20s. There are different reasons a person cuts themselves, but at the bottom of it is a deep sense of emotional pain and hopelessness. Suicide is not the goal, and neither is attention. Some say they cut to dull the pain from abuse or deep feelings of worthlessness and insecurity. Others do it as if for that moment they have control because they are the ones choosing to inflict the pain and choosing to stop.

In the case of the man from Gerasenes, he was demon-possessed. Demons are either working in or on a person who is cutting. Their goal is to destroy humans who are made in God's image. So Satan stirs up misery and anger, lying about our being worthless and unlovable. Feeling no emotion or deep despair spurs some to self-mutilate. The truth is that you and I are fearfully (awesomely) and wonderfully made (Ps. 139:14). "For we are His workmanship, created in Christ Jesus for good works, which God prepared beforehand so that we would walk in them" (Eph. 2:10). God created us very lovable, and we have great value.

Physical, emotional, or sexual abuse is so damaging. The person who has endured this life will never heal by hiding the truth and their feelings. After Jesus cast the demons out of the young man, He clothed him and sat down and talked with him. It's necessary to seek wise counsel. It helps to talk with a professional who knows God's Word and has the Holy Spirit, who is wise and understanding, who receives and gives godly counsel and strength, who has knowledge and fear of the Lord. They should be someone who sees beyond the scars and hears what is said and what is not said. Jesus wasn't repulsed with this man, He loved him and cared that he was in such pain and misery. Christ listened and heard what the man had to say, and He also spoke the truth to Him.

***Bible Reading*: Mark 5:1–20, Psalm 139:1–16**

Day 4

Let's stand with the disciples and Jesus on the shore at Gerasenes. What would we see? First of all, it was an amazing fact that the demons knew Jesus. Not only did they know who He was and what He could do, but they talked to Him. Actually, they prayed, "I beg You, do not torment me." That shows we can know who Jesus is and still not surrender to Him; we can pray to Him without giving our lives over to His will and direction. Talking religious, knowing some facts, and speaking to God are not what makes us part of His family. Life-changing belief that Jesus is God's Son and taking the gift of His death and resurrection are. That faith saves us from death and gives us abundant and eternal life with Him. Our response to salvation causes us to confess our sins and turn away from them and toward God, giving Him control of our life and choices.

Also noticeable was how Jesus responded to a crazy, filthy man filled with a legion of demons. He had no fear and was calm. This was not a movie version of *The Exorcist*. It isn't violent acts, religious artifacts, or yelling that defeats Satan's forces. It is the power of God. With complete composure, Jesus told the demons to come out of the man. We would say those words in Jesus's name because He is the One with the power (Matt. 10:1, Luke 10:17).

After the pigs drowned, their herdsmen ran away and reported it. People came to see what had happened and saw the man who had been demon-possessed sitting down, clothed, and in his right mind. Becoming frightened, they begged Jesus to leave the region . . . really? They didn't beg Him to heal them or teach them how to do what He did? They were more afraid of Jesus than a crazy man they couldn't keep chained down? Perhaps having their preconceived ideas turned upside down caused this reaction. By all rights, the demons should have been stronger than Jesus. Jesus broke long-held superstitions, and people like the status quo; it's comfortable even if it's not good, not to mention the money lost when all those pigs drowned. No one seemed to care that Satan's forces had proved their intentions were to completely destroy—man or animal didn't matter, just destruction. That's why Jesus said, "The thief comes only to steal and kill and destroy; I came that they may have life, and have it abundantly" (John 10:10). Good and evil were unmistakable that day but unimportant to those people.

A sad lesson learned from this reaction is that some people don't want the truth and freedom. They don't want whole lives. What they want is to do things their way or the way it's always been done. So Jesus got back in the boat to leave. He is a gentleman and will not force Himself on anyone, no matter how much He loves them, no matter how much someone needs Him.

The healed man begged to go with Him. But Jesus told him, "Go home to your people and report to them what great things the Lord has done for you, and *how* He had mercy on you" (Mark 5:19). Again we see that part of the healing process is to serve others. This man's problems were not all solved that day. He had no job and many broken relationships, but he was grateful for what God had done in his life. We can't ignore the blessings and gifts God has given us if we want to grow stronger. Without knowing who he would help with his testimony, he gave it willingly, allowing God's glory and power to do the work. Focusing on God and others was the next step in restoring this man to an abundantly full and good life.

Bible Reading: Luke 8:26–39, Luke 10:17–20, James 2:18–26

Day 5

So many times when Jesus saw a person or a group of people, He felt compassion for them. That compassion caused Him to act and teach and pray. The dictionary defines *compassion* as "sympathy for the suffering of others, often including a desire to help." In the Bible, the word also has a passionate emotion attached to it. It means to be moved in one's bowels—that is, guts or inner organs. Greeks and Romans believed the bowels were the seat of the more violent passions such as anger and love; but the Hebrews saw it as the seat of more tender feelings such as kindness, compassion, and love.

When Jesus saw the condition of a sick or demon-possessed person, when He witnessed injustice, abuse, and grief, it was gut-wrenching to Him. From the depths of His gut, He felt sorrow and caring, love and anger for the plight of the people. It's the emotion that causes a moan to rise from deep in our stomach, through our hearts, and out our mouths. Compassion causes action.

Luke tells of a time when Jesus's compassion for one woman changed her life and the lives of the people in the crowd, and glorified the Father.

> *He went to a city called Nain; and His disciples were going along with Him, accompanied by a large crowd. Now as He approached the gate of the city, a dead man was being carried out, the only son of his mother, and she was a widow; and a sizeable crowd from the city was with her. When the Lord saw her, He felt compassion for her, and said to her, "Do not weep." And He came up and touched the coffin; and the bearers came to a halt. And He said, "Young man, I say to you, arise!" The dead man sat up and began to speak. And Jesus gave him back to his mother. Fear gripped them all, and they began glorifying God, saying, "A great prophet has arisen among us!" and, "God has visited His people!" This report concerning Him went out all over Judea and in all the surrounding district.*
> —Luke 7:11–17

Jesus saw the tragedy of this woman's life and grieved along with her. Losing a child to death is said to be one of the most painful events to endure. This woman's pain was on top of the ache of having lost her husband. In those days, a woman without a husband or son had no means to support herself. The grieving mother had not only lost the family she loved, but she had lost her security, her protectors, and her future. Deep grief was wrapped in fear and hopelessness. When Jesus saw her, He saw all of that—and from deep within His body and heart, He cared enough to do something about it.

Touching the coffin, Jesus told the young man to arise, and he did. God alone is able to do this. Romans 4:17 says, "God, who gives life to the dead and calls into being that which does not exist." Physical life—heart beating, brain functioning, and lungs breathing—had ceased to exist, but the Creator of life is able to call into being that which does not exist, to give new life.

Eventually the young man would die again. But Jesus hates death; it is the enemy and the result of sin. He came to conquer death once and for all so that all who believe in Him will be resurrected to eternal life. God's great compassion for each person caused Him to groan from deep within His gut, up through His heart, and out of His mouth. Our Father moaned with love and grief over our lost and dying state, which caused Him to act. He sent His Son to take our punishment for us so we could be healed and resurrected to eternal life with Him in heaven. Jesus is God's compassion.

Bible Reading: **Romans 6:4–11, 1 Corinthians 15:50–58**

Day 6

Samaria was a territory in Palestine between northern Israel and the southern portion known as Judah. Many of Israel's enemies had lived in that land. When Babylon took Judah captive, they left the poorest and least socially acceptable Jews behind. Those Jews intermarried with the foreigners and enemies of Israel and lived in Samaria. Israelites hated Samaritans and would walk miles out of their way to avoid going through their country.

Jesus, however, went through Samaria on His travels. There was a well there called Jacob's well, and Jesus, tired from the long walk, sat wearily beside the well about noontime.

> *There came a woman of Samaria to draw water. Jesus said to her, "Give Me a drink." For His disciples had gone away into the city to buy food. Therefore the Samaritan woman said to Him, "How is it that You, being a Jew, ask me for a drink since*

I am a Samaritan woman?" (For Jews have no dealings with Samaritans.) Jesus answered and said to her, "If you knew the gift of God, and who it is who says to you, 'Give Me a drink,' you would have asked Him, and He would have given you living water." She said to Him, "Sir, You have nothing to draw with and the well is deep; where then do You get that living water? You are not greater than our father Jacob, are You, who gave us the well, and drank of it himself and his sons and his cattle?" Jesus answered and said to her, "Everyone who drinks of this water will thirst again; but whoever drinks of the water that I will give him shall never thirst; but the water that I will give him will become in him a well of water springing up to eternal life." The woman said to Him, "Sir, give me this water, so I will not be thirsty nor come all the way here to draw." He said to her, "Go, call your husband and come here." The woman answered and said, "I have no husband." Jesus said to her, "You have correctly said, 'I have no husband'; for you have had five husbands, and the one whom you now have is not your husband; this you have said truly."

—John 4:7–18

Have you ever talked with a person about one subject only to realize they were responding and thinking you were talking about something different? It happened to Jesus all the time. People tend to take everything on a physical level. Even when it's God who's speaking, we think He's just talking about our physical comfort, health, attitude, and situation. Jesus used the natural, tangible things of life to teach us about the spiritual. He wanted this woman and us to know that the things of this world that fill us up and give us comfort and health physically only last a short time. God offers an everlasting, spiritual supply of everything we need. To drive home the point that He could deliver the spring of eternal life, Jesus told her about her life. He knew things about her she had not told Him. God truly does know each of us, too, the hidden parts as well as the open. And no matter how badly we've lived, He offers eternal life to us all.

Then Jesus did an amazing thing. He revealed His true identity and purpose to a woman—not just any woman, but a hated Samaritan woman; and not just any Samaritan woman, but an immoral and shunned Samaritan woman. Peter said, "I most certainly understand *now* that God is not one to show partiality, but in every nation the man who fears Him and does what is right is welcome to Him" (Acts 10:35). Salvation is offered to you and to me, regardless of our past.

Jesus said, "'God is Spirit, and those who worship Him must worship in spirit and truth.' The woman said to Him, 'I know that Messiah is coming (He who is called Christ); when that One comes, He will declare all things to us.' Jesus said to her, 'I who speak to you am *He*'" (John 4:24–26).

Bible Reading: John 4:1–42

Week 6

ELISHA

Day 1

Elijah was a prophet of God. Courageously he stood alone in God's strength in a country led by evil kings and queens, filled with people who didn't love God or care that their society was deteriorating. The Lord revealed to Elijah that there were others who loved God. While hiding in a cave in fear and utter exhaustion, God encouraged Elijah and told him He would appoint another man to take Elijah's responsibilities. He allowed Elijah to be involved in finding his replacement.

> *So he [Elijah] departed from there and found Elisha the son of Shaphat, while he was plowing with twelve pairs of oxen before him, and he with the twelfth. And Elijah passed over to him and threw his mantle on him. He left the oxen and ran after Elijah and said, "Please let me kiss my father and my mother, then I will follow you." And he said to him, "Go back again, for what have I done to you?" So he returned from following him, and took the pair of oxen and sacrificed them and boiled their flesh with the implements of the oxen, and gave it to the people and they ate. Then he arose and followed Elijah and ministered to him.*
>
> —1 Kings 19:19–21

> *And it came about when the* LORD *was about to take up Elijah by a whirlwind to heaven, that Elijah went with Elisha from Gilgal. Elijah took his mantle and folded it together and struck the waters, and they were divided here and there, so that the two*

of them crossed over on dry ground. When they had crossed over, Elijah said to Elisha, "Ask what I shall do for you before I am taken from you." And Elisha said, "Please, let a double portion of your spirit be upon me." He said, "You have asked a hard thing. Nevertheless, if you see me when I am taken from you, it shall be so for you; but if not, it shall not be so." As they were going along and talking, behold, there appeared *a chariot of fire and horses of fire which separated the two of them. And Elijah went up by a whirlwind to heaven. Elisha saw* it *and cried out, "My father, my father, the chariots of Israel and its horsemen!" And he saw Elijah no more. Then he took hold of his own clothes and tore them in two pieces. He also took up the mantle of Elijah that fell from him and returned and stood by the bank of the Jordan. He took the mantle of Elijah that fell from him and struck the waters and said, "Where is the* Lord, *the God of Elijah?" And when he also had struck the waters, they were divided here and there; and Elisha crossed over.*

—2 Kings 2:1, 8–14

It would appear that this was the grand beginnings of the prophet Elisha. But in reality, his ministry started long before we met him. Elisha was a man marked by his humbleness and servant's heart. God saw him to be a noble and righteous man. We first saw him plowing his field along with his servants. Second Kings 3:11 says, "Elisha the son of Shaphat is here, who used to pour water on the hands of Elijah." The people knew Elisha as the servant of the great prophet Elijah. How that would have chafed if Elisha were not confident in himself and God's purpose for him.

No other person in the Bible except Jesus performed more miracles than Elisha. Pride, self-promotion, and image-building were not part of this man's character. Elisha knew he was God's chosen man. The miracles he performed, the courage he had when faced with kings and soldiers, the knowledge he possessed, and the truths he was able to teach were all because the Lord was working in his life. Elisha lived a life of distinction because he knew no one was greater than God. His remarkable life began with his humble heart. He did extraordinary things because he was willing to be the servant of his extraordinary God.

Bible Reading: 2 Kings 2

Day 2

Early in Elisha's role as a prophet of the Lord, Israel (led by an evil king) asked Judah (led by a godly king) to go with them and the king of Edom to fight against the advancing army of Moab. The armies and kings traveled for seven days across the desert of Edom without any water for the soldiers or their animals. Then king Jehoram of Israel said, "What? Has the Lord brought the three of us here to let the king of Moab defeat us?" (2 Kings 3:1–10).

Truly there is nothing new in our world, is there? King Jehoram's attitude can be seen in many people today. He believed there was "a god," but he didn't believe in and follow the true God. Like his parents, Israel's king worshiped many false gods. His decision to go fight was not because he'd asked God and then obeyed; it was something he did on his own initiative. Yet when the going got tough and looked hopeless, he blamed God. When natural disasters or acts of terrorism strike us, we yell out in pain and ask how a good God could let this happen. After pushing God out of our lives and government and schools and saying there is more than one god, we shake our fist at the one true God when life hurts. No one yells at fake gods in a crisis.

> *But Jehoshaphat [Judah's king] said, "Is there not a prophet of the LORD here, that we may inquire of the LORD by him?" And one of the king of Israel's servants answered and said, "Elisha the son of Shaphat is here, who used to pour water on the hands of Elijah." Jehoshaphat said, "The word of the LORD is with him." So the king of Israel and Jehoshaphat and the king of Edom went down to him. Now Elisha said to the king of Israel, "What do I have to do with you? Go to the prophets of your father and to the prophets of your mother." And the king of Israel said to him, "No, for the LORD has called these three kings together to give them into the hand of Moab." Elisha said, "As the LORD of hosts lives, before whom I stand, were it not that I regard the presence of Jehoshaphat the king of Judah, I would not look at you nor see you."*
>
> —2 Kings 3:11–14

Elisha had the courage of the Lord as well as His perspective. Kings and men of wealth and power did not impress him. Loyalty to God, integrity, honesty, and sincere faith did. He saw through Israel's religious words, and he didn't pretend to not see how they lived every day. Because Judah's king loved and followed God, the other kings would share in his blessing. The Lord's protection of His children also covered the people with them who rejected Him, not because they deserved it but because God is a God of mercy and love, a God who offers second chances.

The kings came wanting water, but God was going to give them so much more. He told them to dig trenches in the desert, and without them seeing a rainstorm, He would send water. What a humbling task—digging ditches—for mighty warriors. What a difficult task—shoveling sand—in the hot desert for the thirsty men. We all have a part to play in God's plan, and when we do it, God's blessings go beyond our expectations. The next morning, about the time for offering the sacrifice, there it was—water flowing from the direction of Edom! And the land was filled with water. The Moabites saw the sunrise reflected off the water and thought it was blood, so they raced down to take the spoils of their enemies. When they came into the camp of Israel, they were turned back and destroyed (2 Kings 3:16–25).

The amount of water available to the thirsty men was directly linked to how faithful they were to dig ditches—many and big. Though essential to the blessing and the victory, the ditches meant nothing without the miraculous blessing of God. We, too, must believe and obey in order to receive.

Bible Reading: 2 Kings 3:1–25, Matthew 9:28–29, Hebrews 11:6

Day 3

A prominent woman from Shunem and her husband asked Elisha to stay with them and eat whenever he traveled through their land. Eventually they built a room for him on the roof of their home. In gratitude, Elisha asked her what he could do for her, but she needed nothing. Elisha's servant Gehazi told him the woman didn't have a son, and her husband was very old. They called the woman back up to them and Elisha said, "About this time next year you will hold a son in your arms." "No, my lord," she objected. "Don't mislead your servant, O man of God!" Then the woman had a son just as Elisha had promised (see 2 Kings 4:8–17).

When the child was old enough to help his dad in the fields, he got sick and went home to his mom. Within hours he died, and his mom placed him on Elisha's bed and closed the door. Without telling her husband their son had died, she told him she was going to find Elisha. Gehazi ran out to meet her, but she would not tell him about her son. She fell at Elisha's feet in great sorrow and asked him why God would take the son He had given as a special gift. Elisha told Gehazi to run with his staff and lay it on the boy's face, but the mother would not leave without Elisha. The servant laid Elisha's staff on the boy's face, and nothing happened, so he ran to meet them and tell them. When Elisha got to his room, the boy was dead, so he went in and shut the door to his room and prayed to the Lord. Then he lay on the child, and the boys flesh became warm. Elisha walked around and then lay on him again; the child sneezed seven times and opened his eyes. His mother came in and fell at Elisha's feet in thankfulness (2 Kings 4:18–37).

This woman was generous, giving to and serving the prophet of the Lord without being asked. She didn't just make a sandwich or count exactly 10 percent of her income; she gave lavishly of all she possessed. In turn, the Lord blessed her beyond material things. So when the gift that was her son died, she couldn't understand why. When we don't know why things happen, we can still know who to run to. This mother ran to the man of God. We can run directly to our Father and also to people who know God deeply with our sorrows and questions.

Her faith in God was so great that she let no one in her household know of her son's death. She didn't want grieving and funeral planning, she didn't want to waste time calming others, and she didn't want to give emotions a foothold. Quickly she stepped out in faith to make the situation right. This was a woman of strength as well as generosity and faith. Emotions and explanations could be dealt with later. Her son needed her faith in action.

I find what happened with Elisha comforting. He didn't hear from God; he didn't know why the woman was there or what to do. Sometimes the strongest believers experience God's silence. We should start with prayer and then act in faith. Elisha knew God would do the raising from the dead, and he knew his servant was much faster than he, so he sent Gehazi with one of his possessions, not because the staff was magical but to give Gehazi a physical tool. Elisha believed God could work in that way—and He could. But God didn't. Today we can act with that same faith and regroup when our first idea doesn't work as we thought. No one understands the plans and mind of the Lord all the time. As with Elisha, plan B should begin with prayer. After listening as well as talking to God, we should then act, no matter how odd the action may seem. Elisha saw a young boy raised from the dead. He wasn't embarrassed by his first attempt; he was tenacious, trusting God's power and love. Everyone saw it was God and not Elisha in control.

Bible Reading: **2 Kings 4:8–37, Jeremiah 32:17, 27**

Day 4

A little Israeli girl had been taken captive by the Arameans (Syria) and made the servant of a commander of the army's wife. Aram's king found Commander Naaman to be great and honorable because by him the Lord had given them victory. He was a mighty man of valor, but he had leprosy. The little girl said to her mistress, "If only my master would see the prophet who is in Samaria, he would cure him of his leprosy." Naaman's king sent a letter to the king of Israel and sent Naaman to find the prophet with gifts of 750 pounds of silver, 150 pounds of gold, and 10 sets of clothing. Israel's king was greatly upset and tore his clothes because he knew he could not cure leprosy, and he thought this was a setup to attack him. When Elisha heard about it, he sent word to his king, saying, "Why have you torn your clothes? Now let him come to me, and he shall know that there is a prophet in Israel."

With his horses and chariots, Naaman came and stood at the doorway of the house of Elisha, who sent his servant to tell Naaman to wash in the Jordan River seven times and he'd be healed. The mighty commander was furious because Elisha hadn't come to meet him and wave his hand over him in a grand gesture of healing. The Jordan was a dirty, muddy river, and Naaman refused to step foot into it when there were beautiful rivers in his own country. As he left in a rage, his servants said, "If the prophet had told you to do some great thing, wouldn't you have done it? How much more, then, when he tells you, 'Wash and be cleansed'!" So Naaman dipped seven times in the Jordan, and his flesh was restored like a little child's, and he was clean. Naaman went back to Elisha saying, "Now I know that there is no God in all the world except in Israel. Please accept now a gift from your servant." But Elisha refused to take any gifts (2 Kings 5:1–16).

First, let's learn from the captured little girl. Torn from her family and given no choice but to work as a servant in her enemy's house, this child showed immense faith, love, strength, and courage. There's a corny saying— "bloom where you're planted"—that comes to mind. Can you relate to her, in a place not of your choosing, so much of your life out of your control? This child saw the good in the people around her even though there was also some bad. She cared about her master. They must have been kind because she felt comfortable speaking up and offering advice. Most impressive to me is that although God had allowed her to be taken and made a servant, she still believed Him to be good and able to heal.

This young girl illustrates the mysterious ways God works. Her tragedy set off a chain of events that accomplished a greater good in many people's lives, including hers. You and I need to lay our gut reactions and emotions down and really digest this. What we want and what seems to be the nicest, easiest, best thing to us—and in the mind of our society—may be good, but God wants the best for us. We don't always know what the absolute best of God is until He unfolds it in our lives. Difficulty and pain are not always bad. Remember what Joseph said as second in command in Egypt years after his brothers sold him into slavery: "As for you, you meant evil against me, *but* God meant it for good in order to bring about this present result, to preserve many people alive" (Gen. 50:20).

Wherever we are right now, however others have hurt us, God is with us. His best is working out in our lives. Let's have the courage and faith of this little girl and live victoriously.

***Bible Reading*: 2 Kings 5:1–16, Romans 8:24–31**

Day 5

In addition to the servant girl's example, Naaman and the two kings have many lessons to teach us. It's estimated in today's currency that Naaman took more than $1.2 million with him to Israel. Not only does that show how desperate his condition was, but it shows how much his king cared for him and wanted to help. So it's understandable why King Jehoram of Israel was afraid of the whole situation.

Remember, King Jehoram did not worship or love God nor did he have any sort of a relationship with God's prophet Elisha. Syria's king just assumed he did because who wouldn't be close to someone who could heal an incurable and deadly disease? Who wouldn't believe in the God who heals and performs miracles? We have seen God's power and love in many astounding ways, but many of us still choose to stay at a distance from the

Lord. Like Jehoram, we want God to jump when we need Him, but we have no desire for a relationship with Him.

Obviously, Naaman was a man used to being recognized and treated with admiration. People were impressed with him. From the start, Elisha treated him with respect but did not play up to his ego. And from the beginning, that bothered the commander. Instead of going to the important man, Elisha told Naaman to come to him. Naaman wanted to be healed, so he went. Instead of going out to meet the captain, Elisha sent his servant with a message of how to be healed. Instead of a showy and dignified method of healing, Elisha said to dunk seven times in a dirty river. And Naaman was furious. In that moment, his wounded ego outweighed his desperate need for healing. He had imagined just how God would work, and when God didn't perform with all the pomp and pageantry he wanted, Naaman walked.

It is so easy to get sidetracked, isn't it? We go to God or to church wanting to find an answer to take away our fear or pain or loneliness or insecurities. But if God tells us the process of healing takes repenting or forgiving, we often react like Naaman. We think our pain or victimization should be validated, our hard circumstance should be held in respect, our brave handling of life should be acknowledged. Sometimes, like Naaman, we walk away from help and healing because we take our eyes off our original goal.

Naaman's men wanted the best for him and boldly readjusted his attitude. "If the prophet had told you to do some great thing, wouldn't you have done it? So, you should certainly obey him when he says simply to go and wash and be cured!" Elisha wasn't trying to humiliate Naaman, but Naaman would have to humble himself in order to be cured. When the leprosy disappeared, Elisha wanted everyone to know it was not because of what Naaman did or who he was—it was an act of God.

God would never humiliate us, but He does want us to know that salvation can only come with our surrender. Nothing we do can cleanse us of our sin. No amount of money or popularity, no act of bravery or sacrifice can save us from the consequence of sin. Laying aside our pride, we must confess Jesus as Lord. That will lead to our admitting we are sinners in need of Jesus's cleansing blood. You'd take heaven and a healthy life now if God asked you to do some great thing, wouldn't you? So you should certainly obey Him when He simply says to wash in His Son's blood to be cleansed. Be willing to give God the glory and be restored to life.

Bible Reading: **Zechariah 4:6, Romans 3:21–28**

Day 6

Elisha left his oxen and ran after Elijah. "Let me kiss my father and mother goodbye," he said, "and then I will come with you." Elijah said, "Go back. What have I done to you?" Elijah told Elisha to count the cost and carefully consider what God was calling him to do. Following and serving God has a price. Don't believe it will always be a feel-good life, blessed with easy days. There were times Elijah wanted to die as he tried to reach a nation of people with God's truth. So consider the facts, and count the cost. Paul said this:

> *Do nothing from selfishness or empty conceit, but with humility of mind regard one another as more important than yourselves; do not merely look out for your own personal interests, but also for the interests of others. Have this attitude in yourselves which was also in Christ Jesus, who, although He existed in the form of God, did not regard equality with God a thing to be grasped, but emptied Himself, taking the form of a bond-servant, and being made in the likeness of men. Being found in appearance as a man, He humbled Himself by becoming obedient to the point of death, even death on a cross.*
>
> —Phil. 2:3–8

Elijah wanted his replacement to stick with his calling no matter how hard life got, so he was honest and blunt. That will cost you and be difficult, but it will reward you and be joyous too. Elisha went back and burned his plows in order to roast his slaughtered oxen. As a symbol as well as a pledge, he destroyed any way he would have to go back to his old life. There would be no turning back—Elisha was sold out to God.

The soldiers in the desert discovered they would receive as much water as they believed God would give. If they had not dug the ditches, the water He sent would have run off and soaked into the earth. Had they only dug a few shallow trenches, they would have gained only a little water, probably not enough for all the animals and men. But if they put their pride as warriors aside and dug many deep ditches, they would have more than enough water. And God gave more than water; He gave them victory over their enemy because of their obedience of Him.

Day three taught us that Elisha heard from God and lived for Him in extraordinary ways. He told the Shunamite woman that she'd have a son in a year despite the couple's age, and she did. Prior to that he had performed miracles and heard from the Lord. But when the woman came to him because her son died, God told him nothing. Silence. It doesn't say he prayed, but we know he lived a life of prayer and relationship with God, so in that spirit he told his servant to lay his staff on the boy. Again, nothing. Silence. He went into the room and prayed and lay on the boy. The child got warmer, but there was still no breath or heartbeat. Nothing. Silence. Elisha walked around and prayed and lay on the boy again, and then God raised him from the dead.

If we were in Elisha's place, our faith could be shaken. Did we do something wrong or misread the situation? Each person in this situation needed to be reminded that Elisha was not God—God was. His silence keeps us on our knees. His stillness keeps us searching. Jesus promised, "Ask, and it will be given to you; seek, and you will find; knock, and it will be opened to you" (Luke 11:9). He wants us to be God-reliant, not self-reliant. That is the way we will always be successful.

Finally, we saw an unnamed slave girl who had strength, courage, and faith. She lived like she understood that God's plans were not just good; they were the best. Her master, a mighty army captain, learned he must not go to God with a list of expectations; he must go in humility in order to be healed.

Humbling ourselves does not mean demeaning ourselves. It means we don't seek to place ourselves as first and most important. Putting God there results in life and healing and wholeness.

Bible Reading: **Proverbs 29:23, Psalm 34**

Week 7

ELISHA

Day 1

Naaman's story isn't finished.

> *When he returned to the man of God with all his company, and came and stood before him, he said, "Behold now, I know that there is no God in all the earth, but in Israel; so please take a present from your servant now." But he said, "As the* LORD *lives, before whom I stand, I will take nothing." And he urged him to take it, but he refused. But Gehazi, the servant of Elisha the man of God, thought, "Behold, my master has spared this Naaman the Aramean, by not receiving from his hands what he brought. As the* LORD *lives, I will run after him and take something from him." So Gehazi pursued Naaman. When Naaman saw one running after him, he came down from the chariot to meet him and said, "Is all well?" He said, "All is well. My master has sent me, saying, 'Behold, just now two young men of the sons of the prophets have come to me from the hill country of Ephraim. Please give them a talent of silver and two changes of clothes.'" Naaman said, "Be pleased to take two talents." And he urged him, and bound two talents of silver in two bags with two changes of clothes and gave them to two of his servants; and they carried them before him. When he came to the hill, he took them from their hand and deposited them in the house, and he sent the men away, and they departed. But he went in and stood before his master. And Elisha said to him, "Where have you been, Gehazi?"*

And he said, "Your servant went nowhere." Then he said to him, "Did not my heart go with you, when the man turned from his chariot to meet you? Is it a time to receive money and to receive clothes and olive groves and vineyards and sheep and oxen and male and female servants? Therefore, the leprosy of Naaman shall cling to you and to your descendants forever." So he went out from his presence a leper as white *as snow.*

2 Kings 5:15–16, 20–27

We see greed here in many ways. First, Gehazi coveted the silver and gold Naaman had. Elisha wasn't always opposed to earning a living for doing the Lord's work, but in this case, God had nudged him to show this rich and powerful foreigner that he couldn't buy or earn God's healing grace—it was a free gift. God, healing, and salvation were of no concern to Gehazi; money was. First Timothy 6:10 says, "The love of money is a root of all sorts of evil, and some by longing for it have wandered away from the faith and pierced themselves with many griefs." It's the *love* of money, not money. Love for God had been replaced by the love for money, and Gehazi turned into a lying, sneaking, disloyal man for a fraction of what Naaman had offered Elisha.

Elisha listed what could be bought with Gehazi's money—all good things. Yet because those good things meant more to him than loyalty to God and honor, obtaining them became bad. Gehazi held Elisha in contempt. Bitterness and disrespect filled him, and he blamed Elisha for refusing Naaman's present. He thought him foolish for not taking gold and envied and resented him for giving God's kindness to an enemy. Revealing God was of no importance, only physical compensation. He also envied his master's position and authority. When he met up with the commander, he dropped Elisha's name to make himself more important, to live in his limelight and success. Naaman knew who Gehazi was, so lying about who sent him wasn't necessary, but he greedily wanted Elisha's respect, honor, and authority.

At times I think each of us can find ourselves in Gehazi to some extent—wanting what others have; feeling entitled to awards, rewards, and gratitude; name-dropping; begrudging the popular, powerful, and talented because they don't seem to appreciate all they could get in their position; resenting those we're called to assist and support; greed fed by discontentment.

We can combat those feelings and actions by keeping God first in our lives. This is a spiritual battle. Confess discontentment, greed, and envy, and be filled to overflowing with God's good gifts—spiritual and physical. Daily choose to love and trust God more than anything else.

Bible Reading: 1 Timothy 6:6–19, Titus 3:4–7, Hebrews 13:5–6

Day 2

A couple of interesting and unusual verses are found in the middle of this story. After Naaman was healed of his leprosy and all his attendants went back to the man of God, he stood before him and said this:

> *"Now I know that there is no God in all the earth but in Israel . . . please let your servant at least be given two mules' load of earth; for your servant will no longer offer burnt offering nor will he sacrifice to other gods, but to the* Lord*. In this matter may the* Lord *pardon your servant: when my master goes into the house of Rimmon to worship there, and he leans on my hand and I bow myself in the house of Rimmon, when I bow myself in the house of Rimmon, the* Lord *pardon your servant in this matter." He said to him, "Go in peace." So he departed from him some distance.*
> —2 Kings 5:15, 17–19

A superstition at that time and held by some today was that taking holy soil or rocks back home would help a person better worship the God of Israel (or whatever god they chose). Superstitions are false notions, irrational, and often quasi-religious beliefs in and reverence for the magical effects of some actions and rituals or the magical powers of some objects. Clearly, superstition is not from the Lord God. God did not live in Israel's dirt, and the soil held no magical power. The Bible says, "Behold, to the Lord your God belong heaven and the highest heavens, the earth and all that is in it" (Deut. 10:14). We can worship God anywhere because this is His creation, and He lives in His believers and is with us wherever we go.

This sounds a bit confusing and shocking. After learning about Daniel, Shadrach, Meshach, and Abednego who refused to even appear to bow to a false god when threatened with a tortuous death, why was Naaman allowed to do it? God plainly tells us many times that we should never bow to idols and fake gods.

Elisha, through God's wisdom and discernment, understood that Naaman was only hours old in his faith and knowledge of the one true God. Daniel and his friends were years into a mature relationship with the Lord. "Naaman's faith was yet untaught; and with his personal need to follow publicly the state cults, Elisha may have felt that available Israelite soil may have afforded Naaman with some tangible reminder of his cleansing and new relationship to God."[19]

A baby is not ready to stand firmly or fight as a seasoned warrior. God gives new believers grace as they learn how to live for Him and obey His Word. Elisha did not say it was good or all right for Naaman to go and be his king's right-hand man into an idol's temple and bow physically even when not bowing spiritually. But realizing Naaman was a new believer without any support in his own country, Elisha told him to go in peace. He trusted God to teach and lead Naaman into what was right. Elisha's job had been to show God to Naaman and offer His cleansing and healing, as well as God's grace, and he accepted no gifts or pay. Then Elisha let go and allowed God to do the job of growing, convicting, and strengthening the man.

God's expectations of us are gentle. He knows how much we understand and how young or mature we are in Him. Loving us deeply, He gives us grace as He grows us stronger.

Bible Reading: 2 Kings 5, Psalm 103:8–17

Day 3

Now the king of Aram was warring against Israel; and he counseled with his servants saying, "In such and such a place shall be my camp." The man of God sent word to the king of Israel saying, "Beware that you do not pass this place, for the Arameans are coming down there." The king of Israel sent to the place about which the man of God had told him; thus he warned him, so that he guarded himself there, more than once or twice. Now the heart of the king of Aram was enraged over this thing; and he called his servants and said to them, "Will you tell me which of us is for the king of Israel?" One of his servants said, "No, my lord, O king; but Elisha, the prophet who is in Israel, tells the king of Israel the words that you speak in your bedroom." So

> he said, "Go and see where he is, that I may send and take him." And it was told him, saying, "Behold, he is in Dothan." He sent horses and chariots and a great army there, and they came by night and surrounded the city. Now when the attendant of the man of God had risen early and gone out, behold, an army with horses and chariots was circling the city. And his servant said to him, "Alas, my master! What shall we do?" So he answered, "Do not fear, for those who are with us are more than those who are with them." Then Elisha prayed and said, "O Lord, I pray, open his eyes that he may see." And the Lord opened the servant's eyes and he saw; and behold, the mountain was full of horses and chariots of fire all around Elisha.
>
> —2 Kings 6:8–17

There is a spiritual world that is as real as the physical world. We believe there is a microscopic world of organisms and chemicals that is as real as the bigger things we can see and feel because through scientific technology microscopic objects have been revealed. In many ways God has revealed to mankind that the spiritual world of angels and demons and God's divine power is real too.

Surrounded and outnumbered by a strong enemy, Elisha's servant was afraid. You and I would be too. That fear is natural and even healthy since it would keep us from living as if there were no real threats and enemies. However, being paralyzed or panicked and living in fear is not pleasing to God. Telling his servant not to fear, Elisha gave him a reason to not be frightened. He didn't offer empty hope or clichés. There was a real reason for confidence, even if the servant couldn't see it. Elisha prayed, not that the situation would change but that his servant would see the reality of the situation. It's important to note that only God can reveal a spiritual reality when someone's eyes are closed to it. We can say the true words—"You are from God, little children, and have overcome them; because greater is He who is in you than he who is in the world" (1 John 4:4), but only the "microscope" of the Holy Spirit can facilitate our spiritual eyes and reveal that truth as real in each of our lives.

The servant's eyes were opened, and he saw the greater number and weaponry of God's forces that had always been there. People not believing in God or spiritual warfare because they don't see it doesn't mean it isn't real. Faith is never the imagining of unreal things. It is understanding or perceiving things that can't be demonstrated to the senses but are real. The horses and chariots of fire were really there when the servant didn't see them and when he did. His perception did not change the facts.

Sometimes we magnify our circumstances—our enemies, our pain, whatever causes us fear. That is when we should clear our vision and remember what is true, even if invisible. If God is for us, who is against us? (Rom. 8:31). The bad people and things in our world are real but are also a tangible expression of the unseen spiritual war going on. Stand firm, and use the divinely powerful weapons of God's Word and Jesus's victory of the cross and His resurrection.

Bible Reading: 2 Kings 6:8–17, 2 Corinthians 10:3–7

Day 4

As we've touched just a few points of interest in Elisha's life, we've been able to observe the character of this man of God. In fact, when reading about Elisha, we see that he is more often called "the man of God" than his given name. At the beginning of his ministry, a servant said, "Elisha the son of Shaphat is here, who used to pour water on the hands of Elijah" (2 Kings 3:11). Elisha's character was marked by humbleness and a desire to serve the Lord and others. That resulted in his life being outwardly powerful, impressive, and effective.

First, let's be clear on what God does not want. He is not looking for a bunch of "mini-Me's." God made people in His image, but He definitely does not want puppets without personality or individual strengths and talents. Romans 12:4–8 says this:

> *For just as we have many members in one body and all the members do not have the same function, so we, who are many, are one body in Christ, and individually members one of another. Since we have gifts that differ according to the grace given to us, each of us is to exercise them accordingly: if prophecy, according to the proportion of his faith; if service, in his serving; or he who teaches, in his teaching; or he who exhorts, in his exhortation; he who gives, with liberality; he who leads, with diligence; he who shows mercy, with cheerfulness.*

First Corinthians 12:4–6 tells us, "Now there are varieties of gifts, but the same Spirit. And there are varieties of ministries, and the same Lord.

There are varieties of effects, but the same God who works all things in all *persons*." Many things about Elisha's life looked like his mentor's—his boldness in speaking out against disloyal and godless kings; many of his miracles; and his close, personal relationship with the Lord. Yet he was his own person, the person God uniquely made Elisha to be.

We've talked before that humility does not mean demeaning or shaming. It means we rejoice in the gifts God has given us and use them to show Him to others and bring glory to Him. Paul helps us get this in a couple different ways. In Ephesians 4:1-3, he tells us to "walk in a manner worthy of the calling with which you have been called, with all humility and gentleness, with patience, showing tolerance for one another in love, being diligent to preserve the unity of the Spirit in the bond of peace." The next step you and I take—and each step after that—should be with an attitude of humility, gently and patiently loving others and teaching them Christ by our words and lifestyle. Each step should preserve the unity, wholeness, and peace of our body. Think of our physical bodies. If our eyes weaken, we patiently restore them and take care of them as opposed to hitting at them in anger and frustration. We want our physical body to work together as a whole body. Jesus wants the same for His body, the church.

Paul gives us another picture in Colossians 3:12-13. "As those who have been chosen of God, holy and beloved, put on a heart of compassion, kindness, humility, gentleness and patience; bearing with one another, and forgiving each other, whoever has a complaint against anyone; just as the Lord forgave you, so also should you." We're getting dressed with these items of clothing. None of us would step out of our house naked, and we should not be spiritually naked either. This is how Elisha dressed and walked throughout his days and his life. Amazingly, God elevates us with respect and praise when we willingly lay down our desire for that.

Bible Reading: 1 Corinthians 12

Day 5

"When Elisha became sick with the illness of which he was to die, Joash the king of Israel came down to him and wept over him and said, 'My father, my father, the chariots of Israel and its horsemen!'" (2 Kings 13:14). Those were the words Elisha said of Elijah when the Lord took him to heaven. Years later, a king who only pretended to love God recognized what Elisha had meant to the nation of Israel. He was saying that Elisha had offered more protection and strength to Israel than all the military and their arsenals. The true power of Israel was in the presence of the prophet of God.

Let's understand this. Satan can do us damage. Using people and manipulating situations in the world, he has the power to hurt individuals and nations, tear them down, weaken them, and even destroy them. Yet one person who loves the Lord, humbly lives for Him, and speaks for Him has the ability to strengthen, preserve, and protect an individual and nation.

I want this to be said of me, that the strength of my family and community came from the presence of a woman who lived in the power of the Lord, who stood firm in God's authority, lived with His integrity, spoke His words of wisdom and conviction, and served for His purpose and glory. These are the things that make a family and nation strong. Throughout history, mighty armies have fallen and ceased to exist, but God and His people have persevered. It is true that we can overcome the lies and destruction of the world because greater is He who is in you and me as followers of Christ than he who is in the world (1 John 4:4).

In response to King Josah's mourning and fearing the loss of true strength in his nation, Elisha said to him, "Take a bow and arrows, open the windows to the east, put your hand on the bow, and shoot." Elisha put his hand over the king's on the bow as the king shot an arrow out the window. Syria (Aram) was to the east and Israel's greatest enemy. A custom of that time was to shoot an arrow or throw a spear into the country that an army intended to invade. It showed the commencement of hostilities. Elisha was letting the king know that God was still there to fight for Israel. The power and protection had not come from Elisha as a person but from his faith in God. He gave the king—and us—an illustration of the fact that we have the tools we need. We can shoot our arrow of faith into enemy territory. Whether or not our mentor or parent, pastor or friend is with us, the Lord's deliverance is still with us. Moses said, "Be strong and courageous, do not be afraid or tremble at them, for the Lord your God is the one who goes with you. He will not fail you or forsake you. The Lord is the one who goes ahead of you; He will be with you. He will not fail you or forsake you. Do not fear or be dismayed" (Deut. 31:6, 8).

Elisha is the picture of a good leader. He didn't want his people dependent on him and unable to function without leaning on his wisdom and control. Men and woman worth following strengthen and enable their people to stand firmly without them. They aren't afraid that wisdom and power will weaken their influence because they aren't leading for themselves—they're humbly leading others to know, fight, and glorify God, and be strong enough to live without them.

Choose well who you follow. Make certain their goals are to strengthen you, not keep you in a place of needing them. Choose to be a leader like Elisha. Humbly be the father, chariot, and horseman of your family, school, community, and nation.

***Bible Reading*: 2 Kings 13:14–25, Joshua 1:1–9**

Day 6

Elisha's life has challenged and encouraged us. He was a man who listened to the Lord. When God told him to heal the commander of the longtime, on-again-off-again enemy of Israel, Elisha did. The Lord told him not to take any of the gifts Naaman offered, and Elisha obeyed. God wanted to show Naaman and his king that He was different from the heathen gods and prophets whose leaders desired wealth and power. Israel's God healed and restored because He is good and full of grace, not because we have something to offer Him.

Naaman was told to go home in peace after asking if God would pardon him when he went and bowed with his king to their false god. Jesus taught about this in Luke 12. Peter asked Him if what He'd been teaching was for everyone or only His followers, and Jesus said He was speaking to His faithful servants. The example Jesus gave was a master going away and telling His servant to feed and care for His family and possessions. But if the servant abused the other servants, partied and got drunk, and the master came home and found out, the servant would be severely punished. Luke 12:47–48 says, "That slave who knew his master's will and did not get ready or act in accord with his will, will receive many lashes, but the one who did not know *it*, and committed deeds worthy of a flogging, will receive but few. From everyone who has been given much, much will be required; and to whom they entrusted much, of him they will ask all the more."

Sometimes we only want to think of that in light of being given money or talent, but Jesus also meant that to whom much spiritual wisdom and knowledge are given, much is required. Naaman had indeed been given the knowledge that the God of Elisha was the only true God. As a soldier, he knew a person could not be loyal to two different leaders. But Naaman was also going back to his pagan land and king with the discernment, wisdom, knowledge, strength, counsel, and fear of the Lord that a baby would have. Elisha gave God's grace and peace to Naaman, knowing that the Lord would be the One to teach him how to live a godly lifestyle.

Jesus also told us, "Do not judge, and you will not be judged; and do not condemn, and you will not be condemned; pardon, and you will be pardoned" (Luke 6:37). We don't know every part of another person's story. So we must be careful in our opinions of how they are living. There are things God has clearly said we are to do and not do (like not bowing to idols), but each of us is at a different level of Christian maturity. It is God's prerogative to convict one area of life in a person even when we see other problems. Elisha did not judge Naaman, and we should not judge others. Definitely speak and teach God's true and whole Word, but listen to God as we do it. As with Elisha, it may not be our job to convict and grow a certain person. In that case, we should be able to say to them, "Go in peace."

The spiritual world and its warfare were obvious to this man of God. His humble heart dictated that instead of preaching that to his fearful servant, Elisha prayed and asked God to reveal His angels standing ready to fight. That was the mark of Elisha—humble yet wise and powerful. At the end of his life, believers and nonbelievers recognized him as the best part of their nation. Peasants and kings mourned him. He had been a father to the people of Israel, not letting them get by with bad behavior and choices but loving and teaching them through it all. A young king wept over him and said, "My father, my father, the chariots of Israel and its horsemen!" (2 Kings 13:14). Elisha's faith had provided protection and strength for his people.

Bible Reading: Luke 12:41–48, Deuteronomy 31:6–8

Week 8

THE CHURCH

Day 1

Church. What do you think of when you hear that word? Some people say in a slightly cynical voice that they don't believe in organized religion. Others love the idea of spirituality and want to make sure their families go on special occasions. Throughout history, the church has been credited with many good things and discredited with scandal and abuse of power. Let's take a look at God's plan for the church, which He also calls the body of Christ.

Being described as the body tells us that organization is inherent to this thing called church. I don't know of anyone who wants a disorganized body where body parts operate randomly and sporadically, where there is not a head or brain to guide and coordinate each system. That's how God feels about His Son's body, the church. Ephesians 1:22–23 tells us, "And He put all things in subjection under His feet, and gave Him as head over all things to the church, which is His body, the fullness of Him who fills all in all." First Corinthians 11:3 says, "But I want you to understand that Christ is the head of every man, and the man is the head of a woman, and God is the head of Christ." This describes the basic organization and structure of the body of Christ, the church. God the Father is over Christ Jesus the Son, who is the head of the body. Jesus is over the entire body; He is over men, who are over women. The Bible transitions from describing the church as a body into a marriage.

> *Speaking to the church Paul said, "And be subject to one another in the fear of Christ. Wives,* be subject *to your own husbands, as to the Lord. For the husband is the head of the wife, as Christ also is the head of the church, He Himself* being *the Savior of the body. But as the church is subject to Christ, so also the wives* ought to be

> *to their husbands in everything. Husbands, love your wives, just as Christ also loved the church and gave Himself up for her, so that He might sanctify her, having cleansed her by the washing of water with the word, that He might present to Himself the church in all her glory, having no spot or wrinkle or any such thing; but that she would be holy and blameless. So husbands ought also to love their own wives as their own bodies. He who loves his own wife loves himself; for no one ever hated his own flesh, but nourishes and cherishes it, just as Christ also* does *the church."*
>
> —Eph. 5:21–29

We're first told that each of us, men and women, must submit to each other. Men submit to the women of the church, and women submit to the men of the church. *Submission* in the Greek means "a voluntary attitude of giving in, cooperating, assuming responsibility, and carrying a burden." One root word means "to mutually agree upon." God clearly wants His church and all marriages to be organized and have leadership. He wants discussion and conversation to take place. It is not possible to mutually agree with and voluntarily cooperate with someone we haven't talked with. Everything about this picture displays respect, kindness, wisdom, and sacrificial love.

When the church functions as a body, when men and women, boys and girls who believe in Jesus love Him, we are a beautiful thing. The church is a group of people who listen to God by reading the Bible and praying. We listen to our other body parts—each other—and show respect, care, and love for each other. In fact, each member of the body of Christ should be willing to give up their lives for each other. We may not be called to die physically, but we will need to give up our desire to have our own way—die to self. Church is unity and love.

Bible Reading: Romans 12:3–21

Day 2

Jesus said to His followers, "You are the salt of the earth; but if the salt has become tasteless, how can it be made salty *again*? It is no longer good for anything, except to be thrown out and trampled under foot by men" (Matt. 5:13). He said this directly after teaching what we now call the Beatitudes, which are all the "blessed are the . . . ." In order for the church to be the salt of the earth, we must be poor in spirit (realize our need for Jesus). We ought to mourn our sinful state and that of the world's and be gentle, which is mild and meek (power under constraint). The church will be salty if it hungers and thirsts for righteousness, is merciful, pure in heart, and filled with peacemakers. Those who have been persecuted for the sake of righteousness, who are insulted and falsely accused because of Christ Jesus, should be full of joy knowing that their reward is in heaven (Matt. 5:3–12).

People who live with these attitudes and actions act as a dash of salt being sprinkled onto a piece of meat or some vegetables. Believers in Christ season our world. Some say a situation was hard to swallow or it left a bitter taste in their mouths. The church should come alongside others with the salt of Jesus's promise. When we follow God's directions on living, we won't dump too much salt, which would taste bad and destroy. God's way of living enables us to add zest to life and seasoning to the hard times, making others hungry for more of Him.

Jesus was talking to a mostly Jewish crowd who knew that God had told them in Leviticus 2:13, "Every grain offering of yours, moreover, you shall season with salt, so that the salt of the covenant of your God shall not be lacking from your grain offering; with all your offerings you shall offer salt." Salt was important for multiple reasons. It was expensive and valuable. Living our lives for God is an offering that will cost us; it won't come cheaply. This life is not about us—getting our own way, making ourselves look good, stirring up conflict when we feel we have the right, condemning, shaking our fist at God when we're treated poorly. Those things please us for a moment but make our salt old and tasteless, useless to everyone. It costs a lot to live a selfless life, but the results to others and to us are worth the price.

In the Old Testament, salt spoke of purity because it stays pure as a chemical compound. God's covenant is pure, and our sacrifices will be pure when seasoned with the salt of a Christ-filled lifestyle. Salt is also used as a preservative. Curing meat with salt prevents the normal decay and spoiling process. Beef jerky is an example of meat that doesn't need to be refrigerated because it's cured with salt. Spiritually, there's a clear connection. God's covenant, which Jesus fulfilled on the cross, and His church stop the moral decay and death sin causes in this world.

We are the salt of the earth. Our lives are new in Christ, who is unchangeable, incorruptible, enduring, and pure. As the body of Christ, our presence in the world is a blessing. Have you and I been living as the salt of the earth? Do we show each other and a dying world the pure and incorruptible promises of the Lord?

Jesus said that not only will others be protected from dying and decaying, but we will be blessed. The kingdom of heaven will be ours; we'll be comforted and satisfied; we'll inherit the earth and receive mercy. We'll see God and be called His sons and daughters; our reward will be great, and the kingdom of heaven will be ours. God's salt is worth the price.

Bible Reading: Matthew 5:1–13, Ephesians 6:23–24

Day 3

Immediately after telling His followers to be the salt of the earth, Jesus said, "You are the light of the world. A city set on a hill cannot be hidden; nor does *anyone* light a lamp and put it under a basket, but on the lampstand, and it gives light to all who are in the house. Let your light shine before men in such a way that they may see your good works, and glorify your Father who is in heaven" (Matt. 5:14–16).

Individually and corporately, together as the body, the church is like a lighted city at night. Remember Isaiah 11 and the seven lights Jesus and His followers would have? The Holy Spirit shines brightly as the center of us; the spirit of wisdom and understanding, counsel, and strength; the spirit of knowledge and the fear of the Lord. Jesus just added to our brightness by telling us to live as if we needed Him, mourning sin, gentle and hungry for righteousness. He said we'd be like a lighted city on a hill when we are merciful, pure in heart, and peacemakers, and when we respond to persecution by looking joyously toward our goal in heaven.

It would be completely dark if we were traveling through an empty, uninhabited land at night. Even with the headlights of a car, visibility would only be a few feet in front of us. But when city lights suddenly radiate in the distance, we wouldn't feel so alone. Getting closer, the once-bright mass of light would show up as individual lights working together to illuminate the night. Up close or from a distance, the lighted city on a hill offers so much. We realize that once we reach the city, we will find food and water, a place to rest, and any services needed. Protection can be found in this city simply because there is light, and whatever caused fear or concern is now visible, and there are also people there whose job it is to protect.

Jesus was giving a physical picture to the crowd who understood the dangers of robbers and highwaymen when they walked or rode their donkeys from one city to the next. His picture was for His church to be a physical safe haven for others. Most definitely we are to meet the physical needs around us for food, shelter, and protection from harm. But Jesus was also talking about our spiritual lights. When people who are walking in the darkness of sin and brokenness see the church, its light will be a beacon of safety, truth, support, and love.

Every person Jesus taught in the crowd, as well as today, had some brokenness and hurt in their lives, even believers in Christ. Others have hurt us and treated us unfairly; corruption has seeped into governing groups; and we have hardened our hearts and resisted God. There are many reasons for the darkness around us, but at the root of it all is sin. Jesus knew the church would not be perfect and completely free of sin, but He wanted our daily goals to be living God's way. When we fail, our lights will flicker and dim. So He gave us guidelines to keep our lights shining brightly. Love God, and recognize that it is only by His grace and love that we are saved. Grieve the sin in our lives so we will turn from it and go back to Jesus. Mourn how sin shackles us to lies, failure, and darkness. Gently lead other broken and sinful people to God's truth, and feed them His bread of life. Mercifully forgive because we've been forgiven. With pure motives, make peace with ourselves and others, and offer the knowledge of that peace to the world around us. And when we are treated wrongly and purposefully hurt, stand firm in our faith; possess the joy of the Lord and the peace that passes all understanding, even through our tears. Living like this is a radiant light on a hill that will draw people to God's pure, delicate, and brilliant truth.

***Bible Reading*: Philippians 3:12–21, Philippians 4:1–4**

Day 4

Paul told this to the church in Thessalonica:

> *For you yourselves know full well that the day of the Lord [the end times] will come just like a thief in the night. But you, brethren, are not in darkness, that the day would overtake you like a thief; for you are all sons of light and sons of day. We*

> *are not of night nor of darkness; so then let us not sleep as others do, but let us be alert and sober. For those who sleep do their sleeping at night, and those who get drunk get drunk at night. But since we are of the day, let us be sober, having put on the breastplate of faith and love, and as a helmet, the hope of salvation. For God has not destined us for wrath, but for obtaining salvation through our Lord Jesus Christ, who died for us, so that whether we are awake [alive] or asleep [physically dead], we will live together with Him.*
>
> —1 Thess. 5:2, 4–10

The church is light, and we follow the God of light. James tells us that the Father of lights has no variation or shifting shadow; there is no darkness in Him. As such, the church is in a position to be constantly alert and clear-headed; we are not to fall asleep on the job. Christ's body has a purpose, which is to tell everyone we aren't intended to face God's wrath and final judgment of hell. Because we don't live in the darkness of night like the unsaved world does but rather in the daylight with the light of the Son of God, we can see things people in the dark can't see. God wants us to tell them that His desire is for all to have salvation through our Lord Jesus Christ.

> *But we request of you, brethren, that you appreciate those who diligently labor among you, and have charge over you in the Lord and give you instruction, and that you esteem them very highly in love because of their work. Live in peace with one another. We urge you, brethren, admonish the unruly, encourage the fainthearted, help the weak, be patient with everyone. See that no one repays another with evil for evil, but always seek after that which is good for one another and for all people. Rejoice always; pray without ceasing; in everything give thanks; for this is God's will for you in Christ Jesus. Do not quench the Spirit; do not despise prophetic utterances. But examine everything carefully; hold fast to that which is good; abstain from every form of evil. Now may the God of peace Himself sanctify you entirely; and may your spirit and soul and body be preserved complete, without blame at the coming of our Lord Jesus Christ.*
>
> —1 Thess. 5:11–23

When we treat the people in our church family with love and respect, it will be appealing to others. Living God's way speaks louder than any words we say. Paul told the church to encourage and build up each other. The opposite of that is to discourage, criticize, condemn, and tear down each other. We're to honor and respect our church leaders and lovingly appreciate all they do for us. Live in peace with everyone—our friends, that really irritating person who always rubs us the wrong way, our competition. Admonish, encourage, and help each other, and be patient as God grows and perfects each member of His body in His own way and time. Since we are to admonish others, we should also receive the warnings and reproofs given to us in love by someone in the church.

Paul told us to not quench the Holy Spirit. Do not stifle or put out the Spirit's fire. The Holy Spirit is supernatural and enables us to use all the gifts God has given to His body. We shouldn't be afraid of them or push them aside because they're uncomfortable. Christ's body will enlighten the world only when we allow the Holy Spirit to rule in our lives and lead us.

Bible Reading: James 1:17–27

Day 5

Ephesians was a letter written by Paul to the church, telling them how to live effectively and function as a unified body. He urged them to live a life worthy of the calling they have received, with all humility and gentleness, with patience, showing tolerance for one another in love. Always keep yourselves united in the Holy Spirit, and bind yourselves together with peace. We are all one body, we have the same Spirit, and we have all been called to the same glorious future; one Lord, one faith, one baptism, one God and Father of all who is over all and through all and in all (Eph. 4:1–6).

God does not let up on teaching us to be humble, gentle, patient, peaceful, and loving. It's what makes us look like Jesus. It's what makes us stand out as different from the rest of the world. And it's what makes Christ's body work together as one unified, interconnected, cohesive and organized church. We're told to always keep ourselves united in the Holy Spirit. That's important. On our own we'd easily become impatient and intolerant of people who keep making the same mistakes or mature at a slow pace. Nothing is more foreign to our nature than to put our needs and wants behind someone else's as a continuous way of living.

So the church is reminded constantly to remember the Holy Spirit. His power enables the life we're called to live. His wisdom and discernment make possible a life of forgiveness and patience. Being one with the Holy Spirit will connect each part of the body of Christ like ligaments and muscles connect the bones of our body. Even though we're all different with unique purposes and gifts, we are still all connected by the one Holy Spirit and one Father for one purpose. The Holy Spirit is the air we all breathe in the body where my eyes discern, my hands serve, someone else's mouth teaches, knees pray, and feet spread God's Word. We're all distinct yet united as one in Christ, empowered by His Spirit.

Then we will no longer be like children, forever changing our minds about what we believe because someone has told us something different or because someone has cleverly lied to us and made the lie sound like the truth. Instead, speaking the truth in love, we will in all things grow up into Him who is the Head; that is, Christ. Under His direction, the whole body is fitted together perfectly. As each part does its own special work, it helps the other parts grow so the whole body is healthy and growing and full of love. With the Lord's authority, let me say this: live no longer as the Gentiles (ungodly) do, for they are hopelessly confused. They are darkened in their understanding and separated from the life of God because of the ignorance that is in them due to the hardening of their hearts. Throw off your old, evil nature and your former way of life, which is rotten through and through, full of lust and deception. Be made new in the attitude of your minds, and put on the new self, which in the likeness of God has been created in righteousness and holiness of the truth. Therefore each of you must put off falsehood and speak truthfully to his neighbor, for we are all members of one body. Be angry and do not sin; do not let the sun go down on your anger; give no opportunity to the devil. Do not grieve the Holy Spirit of God by whom you were sealed for the day of redemption. Get rid of all bitterness, rage and anger, brawling and slander, along with every form of malice. Be kind to one another, tender-hearted, forgiving each other, just as God in Christ also has forgiven you (Eph. 4:14–32).

Christ's body is beautifully complicated and elaborate, yet it operates simply in His love. His Spirit moves us to light up the world that is lost in darkness.

Bible Reading: Ephesians 4

Day 6

All of us as part of Christ's body, the church, are supposed to look different from people who are not followers of Christ. Church is a stark contrast to the world because the head of the church is the complete opposite of the head of the world. Jesus is good and pure, righteous and just, caring and loving. Satan, the ruler of this world, is a murderer, a liar, a destroyer, an accuser, and a deceiver, and he is evil.

> *Therefore if you have been raised up with Christ, keep seeking the things above, where Christ is, seated at the right hand of God. Set your mind on the things above, not on the things that are on earth. For you have died and your life is hidden with Christ in God. When Christ, who is our life, is revealed, then you also will be revealed with Him in glory.*

> *Therefore consider the members of your earthly body as dead to immorality, impurity, passion, evil desire, and greed, which amounts to idolatry. For it is because of these things that the wrath of God will come upon the sons of disobedience, and in them you also once walked, when you were living in them. But now you also, put them all aside: anger, wrath, malice, slander,* and *abusive speech from your mouth. Do not lie to one another, since you laid aside the old self with its* evil *practices, and have put on the new self who is being renewed to a true knowledge according to the image of the One who created him—a renewal in which there is no distinction between Greek and Jew, circumcised and uncircumcised, barbarian, Scythian, slave and freeman, but Christ is all, and in all.*

> *So, as those who have been chosen of God, holy and beloved, put on a heart of compassion, kindness, humility, gentleness and patience; bearing with one another, and forgiving each other, whoever has a complaint against anyone; just as the Lord forgave you, so also should you. Beyond all these things put on love, which is the perfect bond of unity. Beyond all these things put on love, which is the perfect bond of unity. Let the peace of Christ rule in your hearts, to which indeed you were called in*

one body; and be thankful. Let the word of Christ richly dwell within you, with all wisdom teaching and admonishing one another with psalms and hymns and spiritual songs, singing with thankfulness in your hearts to God. Whatever you do in word or deed, do all in the name of the Lord Jesus, giving thanks through Him to God the Father.

—Col. 3:1–17

We've spent a week with God's vision for the church. He wants His Son's body to look like Him. All that is good and pure and honest and loving is to be what characterizes us. It's interesting to note that Jesus was everything the church is to be—and He was hated for it. Yet we've been told that living God's way will give us peace. As we stand out as different from the world and as our light reveals the filth and wrongness in the world, we will be resented and hated too. But greater is He who lives in us than he who is in the world. Through the Holy Spirit's presence and work in our lives, the church will live in peace and joy, even while being despised and falsely accused. And we will be able to love the unlovely as well as forgive and give grace to those who have hurt us.

In God's church, truth is always spoken, even when it's difficult. Our Father loves us just as we are, but He loves us too much to leave us as we are. So His church is to speak the truth in love—reprove, warn, teach, and reprimand. We're to love the Lord our God with all our heart, with all our soul, with all our mind, with all our strength, and love our neighbor as ourselves.

Bible Reading: 1 Peter 2:9–25

Week 9

JOSHUA

Day 1

Joshua reminds me of Moses, David, and Elisha because he served with a humble heart. As with most great leaders in the Bible, Joshua started as a hardworking man in the background and believed God could do great things. He was among the Israelites who Moses led out of Egypt, and he faithfully and willingly assisted Moses as a servant, chief of his family, and military leader.

Recollect with me what happened after Israel crossed the Red Sea on dry land as they fled from their Egyptian slave drivers. After watching their enemy drown as the sea closed over their chariots, Israel started on their way to the Promised Land of Canaan. But along the way, God did not do things the way they wanted, and Israel rebelled. Moses faithfully led the complaining nation as God directed, and many miracles from the Lord were seen on their behalf. Behind the scenes, Moses had the loyal and trustworthy assistance of young Joshua.

Finally, the nation of Israel reached the border of Canaan. Then the Lord spoke to Moses and said, "Send men to spy out the land of Canaan, which I am giving to the people of Israel. From each tribe you shall send a man, each one a chief among them." So Moses sent 12 men, one from each of the 12 tribes of Israel, to spy on the land of Canaan. Their names were Shammua, Shaphat, Caleb, Igal, Joshua, Palti, Gaddiel, Gaddi, Ammiel, Sethur, Nahbi, and Geuel (Num. 13:1–16). These 12 men had the potential to be remembered for their great faith, courage, and leadership. All of them bravely slipped into the land of unknown dangers, enemies, and bountiful goodness. But only two of them had the courage to believe that since it was the land God had promised them, all obstacles could be overcome.

After 40 days, the spies returned with a clump of grapes so large that two men had to carry it between them on a pole. Here's what they said:

> "We went in to the land where you sent us; and it certainly does flow with milk and honey, and this is its fruit. Nevertheless, the people who live in the land are strong, and the cities are fortified and *very large*; and moreover, we saw the descendants of Anak there. Amalek is living in the land of the Negev and the Hittites and the Jebusites and the Amorites are living in the hill country, and the Canaanites are living by the sea and by the side of the Jordan." Then Caleb quieted the people before Moses and said, "We should by all means go up and take possession of it, for we will surely overcome it." But the men who had gone up with him said, "We are not able to go up against the people, for they are too strong for us."
>
> —Num. 13:27–31

The people grumbled against Moses and said this:

> "Would that we had died in the land of Egypt! Or would that we had died in this wilderness! Why is the Lord bringing us into this land, to fall by the sword? Our wives and our little ones will become plunder; would it not be better for us to return to Egypt?" So they said to one another, "Let us appoint a leader and return to Egypt." Then Moses and Aaron fell on their faces in the presence of all the assembly of the congregation of the sons of Israel. Joshua the son of Nun and Caleb the son of Jephunneh, of those who had spied out the land, tore their clothes; and they spoke to all the congregation of the sons of Israel, saying, "The land which we passed through to spy out is an exceedingly good land. If the Lord is pleased with us, then He will bring us into this land and give it to us—a land which flows with milk and honey. Only do not rebel against the Lord; and do not fear the people of the land, for they will be our prey. Their protection has been removed from them, and the Lord is with us; do not fear them."
>
> —Num. 14:2–9

Twelve men saw the Promised Land. Two kept their eyes on God and believed He was capable of giving what He had promised. Ten men saw only the obstacles. Which group do you fall into? Do you know the Lord is with you and will do what He said? Don't fear others; trust God.

Bible Reading: Numbers 13

Day 2

Caleb and Joshua understood some very important truths. They said, "If the Lord is pleased with us, then He will bring us into this land and give it to us. Only do not rebel against the Lord; and do not fear the people of the land." These men heard the people's words and saw their fear, and realized there was a deeper spiritual reason for Israel's reaction. Israel doubted God—His capability, His goodness, His promises. They didn't believe Him, fearing He'd lied or misled them. And they didn't believe in Him, that God truly is real, all-powerful, and sovereign. Doubt and unbelief took over until all they could see were the dangers, the problems, and the work—which led to Israel's fear.

Truthfully, the giants were intimidating, the fortified cities were challenging, and the task was daunting. Yet those who trusted God understood that God was up to the task. They remembered everything God had done in the past and His promises, and they trusted the Lord completely, even without understanding how He would accomplish His goal.

Instead of gently validating the people's fears and doubts, Caleb and Joshua called it sin. They told the people not to rebel against the Lord. Seeing the situation and being hit with fear, doubt, unbelief, and distrust was Satan tempting them. And choosing to live in and respond to those things was rebelling against God. And that is sin.

We need to recognize that in our lives. We need to boil down what we're feeling and saying to the basic cause and see it the way God sees it. If another believer like Joshua or Caleb tells us they see some form of sin as the cause of our fears, anger, or poor choices, we should pay attention. They are not condemning us; they're offering truths that can free us so we can enter into God's promised land of rest and abundant provisions. That is one of the church's jobs.

If we say we don't want to take what God has promised us because we think the price is too high or it is physically impossible, we are rebelling against God. I had to think about this for a while. Refusing God's gifts and promises is rebellion. No matter what reasons we have for refusing them, our action is a rejection of the Lord, and it is rebellion. Ultimately, man's greatest rebellion is not believing in Jesus, God's promised gift of salvation, and receiving His blessing and rest.

God's response to the people was stern. "You shall not come into the land in which I swore to settle you, except Caleb the son of Jephunneh and Joshua the son of Nun. Your children, however, whom you said would become a prey—I will bring them in, and they will know the land which you have rejected. But as for you, your corpses will fall in this wilderness" (Num. 14:30–32).

Joshua and Caleb saw the physical truths in front of them and believed there was a spiritual answer. They'd matured to the point where their spirits were as real to them as their minds and bodies. Those two men knew their God was bigger and stronger than their circumstances. They were military leaders who understood what it was to pick up a weapon and fight. And they were spiritual leaders who understood what it was to trust in God's unseen weapons and power, to follow His lead, and fight in ways that seemed physically unusual.

Choose to live like Joshua and Caleb. Reject the fear and doubt that Satan is presenting to you, and take what the Lord has promised to us all—salvation, freedom, victory, and rest.

Bible Reading: Numbers 14

Day 3

After 40 years of wandering in the wilderness, Moses and Israel were at the border of the Promised Land once again. One time Moses had rebelled against God and did not treat Him as holy before Israel, and God told him he wouldn't be allowed to enter the Promised Land. God told Moses to stand on the mountain and look into Canaan, and then it would be time for him to die. Moses said, "O Lord, the God of the spirits of all living things, please appoint a new leader for the community. Give them someone who will lead them into battle so the people of the Lord will not be like sheep without a shepherd." The Lord replied, "Take Joshua, who has the Spirit in him, and lay your hands on him. Present him to Eleazar the priest before the whole community, and publicly commission him with the responsibility of leading the people. Transfer your authority to him so the whole community of Israel will obey him" (Num. 27:12–20).

Moses died, and Israel wept and mourned for him 30 days. Joshua was filled with the spirit of wisdom, for Moses had laid his hands on him; and the sons of Israel listened to him and did as the Lord had commanded Moses. Since that time, no prophet has risen in Israel like Moses, whom the Lord knew face to face (Deut. 34:7–12). "Now it came about after the death of Moses the servant of the Lord, that the Lord spoke to Joshua the son of Nun, Moses' servant, saying, 'Moses My servant is dead; now therefore arise, cross this Jordan, you and all this people, to the land which I am giving to them, to the sons of Israel'" (Josh. 1:1–2).

What made Moses the greatest prophet and leader of all time for the nation of Israel? It was the fact that he was the servant of the Lord. That was how God saw Moses, as His humble, willing servant. Once again, we see that when we put God in control and do His will for His glory with humble and true hearts, God elevates us. With the true God of the Bible, glorifying Him does not take debasing and degrading us. We simply take a step back in order to have the Lord in front, and His great power and miraculous works glorify Him and the people who serve Him.

Telling Joshua to finally take Israel into the Promised Land, God said this:

> *No man will be able to stand before you all the days of your life. Just as I have been with Moses, I will be with you; I will not fail you or forsake you. Be strong and courageous, for you shall give this people possession of the land which I swore to their fathers to give them. Only be strong and very courageous; be careful to do according to all the law which Moses My servant commanded you; do not turn from it to the right or to the left, so that you may have success wherever you go. This book of the law shall not depart from your mouth, but you shall meditate on it day and night, so that you may be careful to do according to all that is written in it; for then you will make your way prosperous, and then you will have success. Have I not commanded you? Be strong and courageous! Do not tremble or be dismayed, for the* LORD *your God is with you wherever you go.*
>
> —Josh. 1:5–9

Words spoken to Joshua thousands of years ago are spoken to you and me today. Whatever our purpose, wherever we are right now, we can know that the Lord is with us. He will not fail us nor forsake us. But we will have wars to fight, and they will be bloody and difficult and painful—so be strong and very courageous. In war we may lose some of the battles, but in order to win the war, in order to succeed in the entire mission of our life, we must do according to all of God's Word. Don't turn from it to the right or to the left. Know God intimately, experience Him, and believe Him. Be strong and courageous; don't tremble or be dismayed. God is with us.

Bible Reading: Joshua 1, Acts 13:15, 32–39

Day 4

The time had arrived for Israel to cross the Jordan River and go into the Promised Land of Canaan. God parted the Jordan for Joshua so all of Israel could cross over on dry land (Josh. 3). "Now it came about when all the kings of the Amorites beyond the Jordan to the west, and all the kings of the Canaanites by the sea, heard how the Lord had dried the Jordan for Israel to cross, their hearts melted, and there was no spirit in them any longer" (Josh. 5:1).

Here's a lesson to remember as we move forward with God. While He makes our next step possible, He is also showing His power and purpose to the people around us, even our enemies. We should not become so focused on where we're walking that we don't see God's work being accomplished in other places. Looking at God's big picture will help us be strong and courageous and not tremble or be dismayed.

After stopping in obedience to God, it was time to face the first fortified city in Canaan.

> Now it came about when Joshua was by Jericho, that he lifted up his eyes and looked, and behold, a man was standing opposite him with his sword drawn in his hand, and Joshua went to him and said to him, "Are you for us or for our adversaries?" He said, "No; rather I indeed come now *as captain of the host of the* Lord." *And Joshua fell on his face to the earth, and bowed down,*

> *and said to him, "What has my lord to say to his servant?" The captain of the L*ORD*'s host said to Joshua, "Remove your sandals from your feet, for the place where you are standing is holy." And Joshua did so.*
>
> —Josh. 5:13–15

This was probably one of the times Jesus showed Himself in the Old Testament because Joshua bowed down. No angel of God would allow himself to be worshiped. Also, the ground was holy ground, which was only said in the Bible when God (not angels) was present.

What an important lesson we need to learn from this. So many times as we get ready to fight for justice and rightness and good, we say that God is on our side and against our opponent. We want God to fight with us and for us. Joshua asked, "Are you for us or for our enemy?" God's answer set Israel, Joshua, and us in our places. It is not that God is on our side; it is that we are on His side. Joshua was supposed to be fighting where God called him to fight, not God fighting where we see the need for Him to fight. This is subtle but crucial. Arrogance silently slips into our thinking when we say we prayed and asked God to help us or bless us instead of asking God where He wants us to work and fight. We are taking control instead of letting God control; we want God to get with our program instead of being engaged in His plan.

There are many good causes, but it's imperative that we remember we are not the Commander in Chief—God is. He is the One who will tell us when to fight and where, and He is the One who will lead us into the battle. Joshua was a military leader, a spiritual and political leader. Remember the organization of the church? Jesus is the head, and the Father is over Him. Joshua was reminded to keep God as the leader and heaven's army as part of the battle plan.

I believe with all my heart that God's desire is to prepare each of us to do great things. When God allows tests and refining with the hardships we have endured, it is because He is creating men and woman of valor, precious gems who can withstand the heat and stand firm. Take Joshua's lessons to heart. God is calling you and me to follow Him as we lead others. He wants us to be on His side, fighting where He's fighting, following His lead.

Bible Reading: Joshua 4, Joshua 5

Day 5

With the proper Commander, weapons, and battlefield in focus, Joshua fought the battle of Jericho.

> *Now Jericho was tightly shut because of the sons of Israel; no one went out and no one came in. The* L*ord* *said to Joshua, "See, I have given Jericho into your hand, with its king and the valiant warriors. You shall march around the city, all the men of war circling the city once. You shall do so for six days. Also seven priests shall carry seven trumpets of rams' horns before the ark; then on the seventh day you shall march around the city seven times, and the priests shall blow the trumpets. It shall be that when they make a long blast with the ram's horn, and when you hear the sound of the trumpet, all the people shall shout with a great shout; and the wall of the city will fall down flat, and the people will go up every man straight ahead."*
>
> —Josh. 6:1–5

Forty years earlier, Joshua told his people that the Lord would give them the Promised Land and to not fear the enemy because the Lord was with them. Now Joshua was given the chance to prove that he really did believe in God and believe His promises. God's military plan was unconventional. Israel's soldiers and priests would be completely vulnerable as they marched around the fortified city of Jericho. Total dependence on God was required. Great faith was demanded from Joshua in order for him to explain the plan to the nation. And Israel needed faith in both God and Joshua in order to follow the plan.

May we be like this group of Israelites. They'd learned from watching their parents fail. Instead of resenting God for making them wander in the wilderness for 40 years, they chose to trust Him, His plans, and His chosen leaders. This is a good lesson for those of us who've had less-than-perfect parents. We don't have to follow in their footsteps. It is within our power to look at how they lived, learn from their mistakes, and live differently.

On the seventh day, they marched, blew the trumpets, and shouted. And the walls fell down flat so the people could go into the city, every man straight before him, and they captured the city (Josh. 6:3–20). God does things differently than we do. Over and over we've seen Him do the impossible in an abnormal way. The situations in Canaan and in our own lives may be similar. Large numbers of giant enemies lived in cities that were strongly fortified. Israel was outarmed and outnumbered. Our problems can look just as hopeless and overwhelming. Perhaps doing things the usual way has been ineffective; going through proper channels or getting the right lawyer or documents has been unsuccessful. Joshua and Israel trusted God in an unusual plan because they understood that the Creator and Sovereign Lord had the power to overcome any difficulty, overturn any decree, overrun any adversary, and overpower any stronghold.

God told them to utterly destroy the city. His patient judgment had finally come due for the Canaanites, and it was harsh. Deuteronomy 18:9–14 tells us that the Canaanites sacrificed their children, practiced witchcraft and sorcery, conjured spells, practiced as mediums, and called up the dead. And all who do these things are an abomination to the Lord. God did not want His children to be contaminated in any way by the occult, so God destroyed everything that could hurt them. Romans 1:19–20 says that the truth about God is known to people instinctively. God has put this knowledge in their hearts. From the time the world was created, people have seen the earth and sky and all that God made. They can clearly see His invisible qualities—His eternal power and divine nature. So they have no excuse whatsoever for not knowing God. The people of Canaan knew they were sinning, but they didn't care, and God wouldn't allow them to mix with His children.

Bible Reading: Joshua 6, Isaiah 54:17

Day 6

At the end of Joshua's life, the Promised Land had been conquered, divided, and given to each of the 12 tribes of Israel, and they lived in peace and prosperity. We've talked before that it is more difficult to live with intentional honor and loyalty to God in good times than in bad times. Success tends to make us spiritually lazy. Speaking through Joshua, God reminded Israel of their history and all He had done for them and given them.

Joshua said this to the people:

> *Now, therefore fear the* Lord *and serve Him in sincerity and truth; put away the gods which your fathers served beyond the River and in Egypt, and serve the* Lord. *If it is disagreeable in*

> *your sight to serve the* Lord, *then choose for yourselves today whom you will serve: whether the gods which your fathers served which were beyond the River, or the gods of the Amorites in whose land you are living; but as for me and my house, we will serve the* Lord.
>
> —Josh. 24:14–15

There's an important principle in those words. If we *don't* choose to serve God or if we choose *not to* serve God, we are choosing to serve someone else. Joshua wanted Israel to be very purposeful and honest with their choice. He listed God's attributes and history and said that's who they should select to honor and serve. But if they wanted to walk away from God, he said to be honest about the name of His replacement. If not the Lord, then who is it?

Jesus said, "He who is not with Me is against Me; and he who does not gather with Me scatters" (Matt. 12:30). In Revelation 3:15–16 God says, "I know your deeds, that you are neither cold nor hot; I wish that you were cold or hot. So because you are lukewarm, and neither hot nor cold, I will spit you out of My mouth." By not making a choice, we are making a choice. Jesus gave all of Himself for us, and He wants us to give all of ourselves to Him. In fact, He will settle for nothing less. Choose the Lord God of the Bible, or honestly state who you are choosing.

Joshua pushed the point so they wouldn't make a light commitment. God isn't seeker-friendly to those seeking feel-good religion. He wants us to count the cost and then choose to love and serve Him with our eyes wide open. We are never tricked by God into thinking His way is all blessings and no battles. Joshua said to the people, "You will not be able to serve the Lord, for He is a holy God. He is a jealous [not accepting any rival] God; He will not forgive your transgression or your sins. If you forsake the Lord and serve foreign gods, then He will turn and do you harm and consume you after He has done good to you" (Josh. 24:19–20). Our message is clear. Jesus did good for us in dying and rising from the grave. He is the only way to the Father. If we rebel and reject this gift, God will not forgive us. But believing in Jesus enables us to serve and obey Him.

"The people said to Joshua, 'We will serve the Lord our God and we will obey His voice.' It came about after these things that Joshua the son of Nun, the servant of the Lord, died, being one hundred and ten years old" (Josh. 24:24, 29). This strong, faithful, powerful, wise military and political leader started out as a servant and finished as the servant of the Lord. God had also called Moses, Israel's greatest leader, the servant of the Lord. What an honor that God saw Joshua in the same way.

"As for me and my house, we will serve the Lord" were the words Joshua lived by. When a nation rebelled against God, Joshua and Caleb believed and served. Stepping up to fill Moses's role in battle, in peace, in public, and in private, Joshua excelled because he served the Lord.

***Bible Reading*: Joshua 24, Acts 13:38–52**

Week 10
FRUIT OF THE SPIRIT

Day 1

How we live—the way we think, speak, treat ourselves and others, the choices we make—is the result of who we follow. God's Word teaches that we either live for the flesh, which means the natural physical world run by Satan, or we live for the Lord. To this point, Paul wrote this:

> *But I say, walk by the Spirit, and you will not carry out the desire of the flesh. For the flesh sets its desire against the Spirit, and the Spirit against the flesh; for these are in opposition to one another, so that you may not do the things that you please. But if you are led by the Spirit, you are not under the Law. Now the deeds of the flesh are evident, which are: immorality, impurity, sensuality, idolatry, sorcery, enmities, strife, jealousy, outbursts of anger, disputes, dissensions, factions, envying, drunkenness, carousing, and things like these, of which I forewarn you, just as I have forewarned you, that those who practice such things will not inherit the kingdom of God.*
> —Gal. 5:16–21

One way the Bible describes this list is the "fruit" of the flesh, or the results of choosing to live by the world system. Just as we'd know a tree was an apple tree by looking at its fruit, we know how a person believes by looking at their fruit.

Paul went on: "But the fruit of the Spirit is love, joy, peace, patience, kindness, goodness, faithfulness, gentleness, self-control; against such things there is no law. Now those who belong to Christ Jesus have crucified the flesh with its passions and desires. If we live by the Spirit, let us also walk by the Spirit" (Gal. 5:22–25).

Someone had told the Galatian church that in order to look like believers, they needed to follow some religious practices and rules such as circumcision. Paul told them that following the Law was not necessary or impressive. Living like Jesus and in His grace was. The Holy Spirit gives us life and also His fruit. Christian character is produced by the Holy Spirit, not by the strict moral discipline of trying to live by the Law. "It was for freedom that Christ has set us free; therefore keep standing firm and do not be subject again to a yoke of slavery [to rules]" (Gal. 5:1).

Two things have the power to enslave us: (1) the world system with all its harsh expectations, addictive behaviors, and guilt-inducing activities and (2) religious rituals and rules. In both of these situations, we are required to work, strive, and prove ourselves, and we're only as good as our last success or performance. Because these are not of God, they are of Satan, and he is our accuser. Besides continuous working and trying to impress and stay on top, we fight the accusations in our minds or from others when we fail or someone outdoes us.

"For by grace you have been saved through faith; and that not of yourselves, *it is* the gift of God; not as a result of works, so that no one may boast" (Eph. 2:8–9). Jesus Christ's work on the cross is what saves us and frees us, not following laws, doing rituals, or performing well. In Christ, you also, when you heard the word of truth, the gospel of your salvation, and believed in Him, were sealed with the promised Holy Spirit (Eph. 1:13).

The Holy Spirit seals us forever as God's children, and He enables us to live like we are the fruit on God's tree. Every believer in Jesus is given love, joy, peace, patience, kindness, goodness, faithfulness, gentleness, and self-control. There is no way we should be mistaken for someone of the world. Let's carefully cultivate God's fruit in our lives.

Bible Reading: Ephesians 5

Day 2

The fruit of the Spirit is love, joy, peace, patience, kindness, goodness, faithfulness, gentleness, and self-control. In the Greek, *fruit* can be translated "the work of the Spirit or the advantage of the Spirit." One of the results of the Spirit is love, which is *agape*. Think back to when we learned in great detail how very strong and purposeful *agape* is. You and I will choose to love our families, friends, church, and even the world around us as a result of having the Holy Spirit in our lives. Every part of *agape* is selfless. "Love is patient, love is kind *and* is not jealous; love does not brag *and* is not arrogant, does not act unbecomingly; it does not seek its own, is not provoked, does not take into account a wrong *suffered*, does not rejoice in unrighteousness, but rejoices with the truth; bears [protects] all things, believes all things, hopes all things, endures all things. Love never fails" (1 Cor. 13:4–8).

Joy is also a product of the Holy Spirit. That means to rejoice exceedingly, thrive, and have gladness. Jesus taught this:

> *I am the true vine, and My Father is the vinedresser. Every branch in Me that does not bear fruit, He takes away; and every branch that bears fruit, He prunes it so that it may bear more fruit. You are already clean because of the word which I have spoken to you. Abide in Me, and I in you. As the branch cannot bear fruit of itself unless it abides in the vine, so neither can you unless you abide in Me. I am the vine, you are the branches; he who abides in Me and I in him, he bears much fruit, for apart from Me you can do nothing. If anyone does not abide in Me, he is thrown away as a branch and dries up; and they gather them, and cast them into the fire and they are burned. If you abide in Me, and My words abide in you, ask whatever you wish, and it will be done for you. My Father is glorified by this, that you bear much fruit, and so prove to be My disciples. Just as the Father has loved Me, I have also loved you; abide in My love. If you keep My commandments, you will abide in My love; just as I have kept My Father's commandments and abide in His love. These things I have spoken to you so that My joy may be in you, and that your joy may be made full.*
>
> —John 15:1–11

Our relationship with Jesus generates joy; it's what makes us thrive and live an abundantly full and glad life. We see that living for Christ moves us beyond our circumstances and into a lasting, undying joy. Jesus knew how difficult life was. He experienced the pain of family ridicule, loss of friendships, death, fear, unfairness, anger, corruption, and violence.

But He lived totally connected to His Father like a branch is connected to a vine. Jesus was filled with the Holy Spirit and also chose to live by the Spirit (Gal. 5:25).

What does this look like for us? In the middle of our worst nightmare, our character will show. While we walk through the uninteresting daily routines or soar in our most successful times, who we really are will appear in our feelings, thoughts, actions, and words. The fruit of the Spirit is not an act we put on for certain people's benefits. It's not saying the words we know the church wants to hear. *Agape* and joy are part of our Christian DNA. Circumstances can't take away our blood type, and they can't take away any part of our new life in Christ. "If anyone is in Christ, *he* is a new creature; the old things passed away; behold, new things have come" (2 Cor. 5:17). The advantage of the Spirit in our lives is unwavering love and joy.

Love and joy aren't always giddy and bubbly feelings. They are the deep and strong knowledge of God. His triumph over sin and death constantly fuels our lives with *agape* and joy.

***Bible Reading*: 2 Corinthians 5:14–17, Colossians 1:2–14**

Day 3

Peace is the fruit of the Holy Spirit in a life. That is pretty easy for us to grasp at first glance. Here, peace means tranquility of heart, which comes from believing that our times are in the hands of God. When we lose our job or get sick, most Christians can honestly say, "I don't like this, but God is in control. I feel a peace about it." Sure, there's a little anxiety, but overall there is peace because we know God is big. Where this gets hard is when we haven't found a job two years later, when the cancer returns aggressively, when the courts take us from our home without listening to us, or when we are the victim of a violent crime. In the long term, excessively severe trials test our faith in God's goodness and ability to right wrongs, heal, and protect us.

The fruit of our experience is fear, anxiety, and doubt. It's time to remember some truths. We may not feel God or hear Him, but He is with us. He promised to never leave us or forsake us (Josh. 1:5). God does not cause sin and is never happy when a person sins, but He will use people's choices for good because He is good and sovereign (Ps. 5:4–5, Gen. 50:20). After beatings and imprisonment for preaching Jesus, Paul said, "Don't worry about anything; instead, pray about everything. Tell God what you need, and thank Him for all He has done. If you do this, you will experience God's peace, which is far more wonderful than the human mind can understand. His peace will guard your hearts and minds as you live in Christ Jesus. Now, dear brothers and sisters, let me say one more thing. Fix your thoughts on what is true and honorable and right. Think about things that are pure and lovely and admirable. Think about things that are excellent and worthy of praise. Keep putting into practice all you learned from me and heard from me and saw me doing, and the God of peace will be with you" (Phil. 4:6–9).

Christians automatically have God's peace, but in order for it to thrive, we must actively cultivate its growth. Take our thoughts captive—don't allow ourselves to worry about the future and imagine horrible things (2 Cor. 2:5). Tell God what we need, and truly trust Him. His peace will guard our hearts and minds so fear, anxiety, and doubt cannot come in. Our job is to pray and trust as we live for Christ. God's job is to guard us, defeat our enemies, heal us, and prosper us. Peace is the advantage we have when the Holy Spirit works in our lives.

Patience or long-suffering is what enables a person to bear adversity, injury, criticism, injustice, and pain. Knowing God and being His child makes it possible to patiently wait for the improvement of our circumstances. When the devil finds that he can't overcome us by force, he tries to overcome us with long, drawn-out warfare. We must patiently wait on the Lord for His perfect timing.

Another aspect of patience is in dealing with other people. There is not a person alive who is easy to live with all the time, and there are some people who are downright difficult to live with. Love, joy, peace, and long-suffering will enable us to treat each other with kindness and respect, even when we're irritated or disheartened.

Galatians 5:25 says in the New Living Translation, "Since we are living by the Spirit, let us follow the Holy Spirit's leading in every part of our lives." If we've asked Jesus into our lives, we have eternal life, and we sealed by the Spirit. But living like Jesus—using the provisions and tools the Holy Spirit gives us—is our choice. Choose to live in peace and with patience.

Bible Reading: Colossians 3:1–17

Day 4

Kindness, goodness, and faithfulness are the fruit of the Spirit. *Kindness* in the Greek means "moral goodness, integrity, gentleness, and caring." The root word means useful, mild, and pleasant as opposed to harsh, hard, sharp, or bitter. At first glance, love and kindness could be one and the same, and in fact, the Bible repeatedly tells us of God's lovingkindness. The dictionary says being kind means "being helpful," while the Greek calls kindness "useful." Loving others calls us to action, to good, gentle, pleasant, useful deeds. Practically, this is you and me volunteering to do the dishes, take out the trash, or help someone with their heavy grocery bags.

Let's take this to the next level. Kindness is the opposite of harsh words, dirty looks, hard hearts, or sharp and bitter retorts or thoughts. In the context of Galatians 5, kindness means we shouldn't criticize people who don't live life according to our expectations. We might believe that drinking alcohol or dressing a certain way is wrong. We might believe that doing harvest parties is better than Halloween parties. The Jews believed men must be circumcised to be acceptable, even though Jesus had delivered us from following the Law. We have all sorts of rules about what makes someone acceptable and worthy of our respect. Paul said that in Christ Jesus, neither circumcision nor uncircumcision (or any other rule or ritual) has any value. The only thing that counts is faith expressing itself through love. In the church, we should think kindly of each other, give our opinions with mild words, and care for each other's feelings and insecurities. Speak the truth in love (Eph. 4:15). People respond to kind and caring truth more positively than to harsh negative criticism.

Goodness is the definition of kindness with excellent, distinguished, and honorable added in. Simply put, goodness is doing the right thing for the right reason in the right way. Second Thessalonians 1:11–12 says, "To this end also we pray for you always, that our God will count you worthy of your calling, and fulfill every desire for goodness and the work of faith with power, so that the name of our Lord Jesus will be glorified in you, and you in Him, according to the grace of our God and *the* Lord Jesus Christ."

Faithfulness is the character of one who can be relied on, someone we can trust and have confidence in. That can be played out in such simple things. If we say we will go to someone's event, we should be faithful and go. When we say we will pray for someone, we should pray for them. If we say we'll call, we should call. Having a relationship of any kind with a person means they should be able to rely on us to put them first in love, to be patient and kind with them. We should be trustworthy with their personal information. They should feel confident that we have their backs and will keep our promises.

The fruit of the Spirit is such an obvious part of who God is. First John 1:9 tells us, "If we confess our sins, He is faithful and righteous to forgive us our sins and to cleanse us from all unrighteousness." God's kindness is seen in His forgiveness and gentle expectations of us. His goodness shines as He forgives and cleanses us simply because He loves us. And our Lord keeps His promises. No matter how many times we need to confess, He is faithful to forgive us and restore us to a relationship with Him. As we cultivate the fruit of His Spirit, we will look more like our Father every day.

Bible Reading: **Titus 3:1–9, Proverbs 15:1**

Day 5

Gentleness and self-control are the last two parts of the fruit of the Spirit. There are two different words in the New Testament for *gentleness*. In Galatians 5:23, gentleness is "mildness of disposition, gentleness of spirit, meekness." Tender, quiet thoughtfulness comes to mind when we think of how the Holy Spirit shows up in our lives. Peter said this:

> *To sum up, all of you be harmonious, sympathetic, brotherly, kindhearted, and humble in spirit; not returning evil for evil or insult for insult, but giving a blessing instead; for you were called for the very purpose that you might inherit a blessing. but sanctify Christ as Lord in your hearts, always being ready to make a defense to everyone who asks you to give an account for the hope that is in you, yet with gentleness and reverence; and keep a good conscience so that in the thing in which you are slandered, those who revile your good behavior in Christ will be put to shame.*
> —1 Pet. 3:8–9, 15–16

Our gentleness keeps us from cramming our knowledge of God down other people's throats, screaming condemnations on sidewalk corners, or publicly embarrassing someone who lives in open sin. Meekly (modestly and softly) we should live the truth and be prepared to give an answer to everyone who asks—*everyone* who asks—for the reason we have hope in this sad and painful world.

The Holy Spirit also ignites our self-control. Self-control is the virtue of one who masters his desires and passions. This is especially talking about our sensual passions but also every desire and passion we may have. First Timothy 4:4–5 says, "For everything created by God is good, and nothing is to be rejected if it is received with gratitude; for it is sanctified by means of the word of God and prayer." Everything God made is good—people, animals, plants, chemicals, sex, food, relationships, emotions, anger, religion, rest, work—it's all good. However, we are called to employ self-control in all things. Sensual passions were created by God to be between a man and the woman who are married. That is good. Yet there are so many temptations to look at sexy men and women and desire them, to flirt and tease and touch in ways that aren't pure and lead to more sensual thoughts and behavior. Food is good, but overeating, closet-eating, and binge-eating show a lack of self-control. Even the eating disorders are because of Satan's distorting the goodness of food and self-control. If any of the good things God made control us, we are out of line with God's perfect plan and in danger of great damage and pain.

Notice this is not called God-control but rather self-control. We're not His puppets. He made us with brains and hearts and a will. His good and perfect plan is for us to choose to love Him and obey Him, and to choose to control our desires and passions.

The fruit of the Spirit is love, joy, peace, patience, kindness, goodness, faithfulness, gentleness, self-control, against such things there is no law. What Paul was saying to those who came into the church in order to impose all their rules and rituals so people would be acceptable was that when we exhibit the fruit of the Spirit, there is no conflict with the law. We wouldn't even need a law if everyone actively operated in the fruit of the Spirit, which is why Paul added, "If we live by the Spirit, let us also walk by the Spirit. Let us not become boastful, challenging one another, envying one another" (Gal. 5:25). Our fruit is at different stages of growth. Don't be envious of someone whose love is greater than yours or boast because your kindness is stronger than another's. Just walk in the Spirit. As we do that, our fruit will mature and be ready for use.

Bible Reading: Galatians 5

Day 6

Having clearly stated the work and advantage of the Holy Spirit in our lives, Paul got down to explaining how to live it practically.

> *Brethren, even if anyone is caught in any trespass, you who are spiritual, restore such a one in a spirit of gentleness;* each one looking to yourself, so that you too will not be tempted. Bear one another's burdens, and thereby fulfill the law of Christ. For if anyone thinks he is something when he is nothing, he deceives himself. But each one must examine his own work, and then he will have *reason for boasting in regard to himself alone, and not in regard to another. For each one will bear his own load.*
>
> *The one who is taught the word is to share all good things with the one who teaches* him. *Do not be deceived, God is not mocked; for whatever a man sows, this he will also reap. For the one who sows to his own flesh will from the flesh reap corruption, but the one who sows to the Spirit will from the Spirit reap eternal life. Let us not lose heart in doing good, for in due time we will reap if we do not grow weary. So then, while we have opportunity, let us do good to all people, and especially to those who are of the household of the faith.*
>
> *See with what large letters I am writing to you with my own hand. Those who desire to make a good showing in the flesh try to compel you to be circumcised, simply so that they will not be persecuted for the cross of Christ. For those who are circumcised do not even keep the Law themselves, but they desire to have you circumcised so that they may boast in your flesh. But may it never be that I would boast, except in the cross of our Lord Jesus Christ, through which the world has been crucified to me, and I to the world. For neither is circumcision anything, nor uncircumcision, but a new creation. And those who will walk by this rule, peace and mercy be upon them, and upon the Israel of God. From now on let no one cause trouble for me, for I bear on my body the brand-marks of Jesus. The grace of our Lord Jesus Christ be with your spirit, brethren. Amen.*
>
> —Gal. 6:1–18

Fruit of the Spirit

Every relationship we have calls for us to walk in the Spirit with His fruit working in us. Each situation we get into, every problem, all our successes need the fruit of the Spirit. And each person who has asked Jesus to be the Lord of their lives has the fruit of the Spirit. This is different from the gifts God tells us He gives in 1 Corinthians 12. No one is given every gift; God distributes them to us individually as He wants. But His fruit is in all of us. It is part of the Holy Spirit who abides with us forever.

I am God's child, and I have love, joy, peace, patience, kindness, goodness, faithfulness, gentleness, and self-control. If you are God's child, you have love, joy, peace, patience, kindness, goodness, faithfulness, gentleness, and self-control also. So let's walk in the Spirit. Let's live loving others. Let's be joyful regardless of our circumstances, full of peace and at peace with others, patiently kind, doing good, faithful and trustworthy, gentle, and with self-control in all situations.

If we live this way, people will ask. They'll want to know how we can do it when that person was so awful, that job so hard, that situation so unfair, that circumstance so damaging, that pain so great. And we will be prepared to give an answer to everyone who asks the reason for the hope that we have. It is Christ Jesus and the power of His Spirit living in us.

***Bible Reading*: John 15**

Week 11
REVELATION 20–22

Day 1

Would you like to take a peek at the end of the story? Or more accurately, would you like to see the end of this chapter of life as we know it and the beginning of the rest of the story of life? Turn with me to the last three chapters of the book of Revelation. The Apostle John had been banished to the deserted island of Patmos as punishment for preaching Jesus Christ. While there, he was taken in the spirit to heaven to see and hear how God would end this brokenness and begin the rest of eternity.

> *Then I saw an angel coming down from heaven, holding the key of the abyss and a great chain in his hand. And he laid hold of the dragon, the serpent of old, who is the devil and Satan, and bound him for a thousand years; and he threw him into the abyss, and shut* it *and sealed* it *over him, so that he would not deceive the nations any longer, until the thousand years were completed; after these things he must be released for a short time.*
> —Rev. 20:1–3

The angel that will subdue Satan is nameless. It isn't Jesus nor is it Michael or Gabriel, the two named and high-ranking angels we've been told about. We also see that Satan is not God's opposite or equal in power because it is not the Father who deals with him or Christ Jesus, but only an unnamed angel empowered by God.

Seizing the devil and locking him into the abyss, the angel accomplished what Satan himself tried to do to Jesus. Satan always copies and counterfeits God, pretending it is he who is lord of all. He tried to imprison Jesus in a tomb but failed. God will imprison Satan for 1,000 years and then for eternity.

The devil is restrained so he would not deceive the nations any longer. Satan is a liar and a deceiver. Jesus said in John 8:44 to those who did not believe Him and called Him evil, "You are of *your* father the devil, and you want to do the desires of your father. He was a murderer from the beginning, and does not stand in the truth because there is no truth in him. Whenever he speaks a lie, he speaks from his own *nature*, for he is a liar and the father of lies."

This reveals Satan's chief method of attack: lies and deceit. What an astounding revelation! When we think of Satan's work, we think of horrendous physical tortures and sadistic behaviors and thoughts. But the way he gets people to do those things is by lying to them and deceiving them. Even followers of Christ believe some of Satan's lies—that we're unlovable, not as important as a well-known person, unforgivable; that grace frees us to sin instead of to live rightly; that we're incapable of living victoriously; that we're not allowed to state God's Word about what's right and what's wrong. The church is sometimes deceived into thinking there is not a spiritual world, spiritual gifts, or spiritual warfare—even though God's Word tells us there is. With very little effort, the devil can render God's children ineffective with his lies.

The weapon to use against the father of lies is the truth. John 8:31–32 says, "If you continue in My word, *then* you are truly disciples of Mine; and you will know the truth, and the truth will make you free." Put away falsehood; let each one of you speak the truth with his neighbor (Eph. 4:25). Stand firm, having girded your waist with truth (Eph. 6:14). We're to accurately handle the word of truth, which is the sword of the Spirit (2 Tim. 2:15, Eph. 6:17). Jesus Christ is the Truth and victorious over the father of lies.

Bible Reading: Revelation 20

Day 2

After the thousand-year reign of Christ known as the Millennium, Satan will be released from his prison and will come out to deceive the nations again. They will march across the breadth of the earth and surround the camp of God's people, the city He loves. But John saw fire come down from heaven and devour them. And the devil, who deceived them was thrown into the lake of fire and brimstone, where the beast and the false prophet are also; and they will be tormented day and night forever and ever (Rev. 20:4–10). Then John said this:

> *Then I saw a great white throne and Him who sat upon it, from whose presence earth and heaven fled away, and no place was found for them. And I saw the dead [spiritually], the great and the small, standing before the throne, and books were opened; and another book was opened, which is* the book *of life; and the dead were judged from the things which were written in the books, according to their deeds. And the sea gave up the dead which were in it, and death and Hades gave up the dead which were in them; and they were judged, every one of them according to their deeds. Then death and Hades were thrown into the lake of fire. This is the second death, the lake of fire. And if anyone's name was not found written in the book of life, he was thrown into the lake of fire.*
>
> —Rev. 20:11–15

For all of us who would argue that it would have been better if God had never allowed Satan to tempt Eve, that then all of humanity with its free will would have chosen to always follow God, we now see differently. Satan was imprisoned for 1,000 years, and Jesus reigned in complete truth, goodness, and righteousness that entire time. Yet when Satan was released, some of the people born during that time believed Satan's lies and chose to follow him. They'd had an intimate personal look at God, spoken with Him, seen how wonderful and painless and safe His way of life was. Yet still some of them rebelled against Jesus and followed the devil.

Our rebellion and evil ways are not because God hasn't shown enough of Himself to us or because He didn't perform enough miracles. We rebel because we choose to. God and truth stand before us with Satan and deceitfulness across from Him. We compare the two and choose what we want. The lies are beautiful and fun and carefree on the outside, and to a person focused on themselves and immediate gratification, that's all it takes. After a millennium of living like Adam and Eve in the Garden of Eden before the fall, some still chose to walk away.

Most scholars agree that Christians will not appear before this great white throne. We are spared from this throne of judgment because our sins are already judged in Jesus at the cross. Believers in Christ don't escape God's judgment; we satisfy it in Jesus. Everyone not in the book of life will be cast into the lake of fire with death and Hades (the grave, hell). The last effects of sin will be abolished. Death is the result of sin, and Hades is the result of death, and finally they are done away with forever. Sin's unlawful domination will be destroyed for eternity.

So how do we get into the book of life? "For God so loved the world, that He gave His only begotten Son, that whoever believes in Him shall not perish, but have eternal life. For God did not send the Son into the world to judge the world, but that the world might be saved through Him. He who believes in Him is not judged; he who does not believe has been judged already, because he has not believed in the name of the only begotten Son of God" (John 3:16-18).

Bible Reading: Malachi 3:16-18, Luke 10:17-20

Day 3

From the smoke and heat and anguish of the fires of judgment, we now get a glimpse of the clarity and beauty of the eternal morning of heaven.

> *Then I saw a new heaven and a new earth; for the first heaven and the first earth passed away, and there is no longer any sea. And I saw the holy city, new Jerusalem, coming down out of heaven from God, made ready as a bride adorned for her husband. And I heard a loud voice from the throne, saying, "Behold, the tabernacle of God is among men, and He will dwell among them, and they shall be His people, and God Himself will be among them, and He will wipe away every tear from their eyes; and there will no longer be any death; there will no longer be any mourning, or crying, or pain; the first things have passed away." And He who sits on the throne said, "Behold, I am making all things new." And He said, "Write, for these words are faithful and true." Then He said to me, "It is done. I am the Alpha and the Omega, the beginning and the end. I will give to the one who thirsts from*

the spring of the water of life without cost. He who overcomes will inherit these things, and I will be his God and he will be My son."
—Rev. 21:1–7

We may think of innocence or the inability to choose wrong as the perfect situation for people; but God views a knowledgeable, redeemed and new person as perfect. The truth is that we gain more in Jesus than we ever lost in Adam. If we'd been made puppets or robots, we'd have no feelings or will. Satan's lies wouldn't have tempted us, and we'd never have sinned, but we also would never know God's love or love Him in return. We can experience joy, love, success, and peace only because of our ability to choose. True, we can also feel the negative emotions, but they have the potential to lead us to a greater appreciation of all that God is. When all things are made new, each of us who has chosen Christ will be in heaven, experiencing the splendor and completed love of the Father.

The new Jerusalem is called the bride, the wife of the Lamb—and she is stunning. We're given a beautiful description of this actual city and told that the 12 gates were 12 pearls; each one of the gates was a single pearl (Rev. 21:21). This, I think, is significant. Jesus said in John 10:9, "I am the door; if anyone enters through Me, he will be saved, and will go in and out and find pasture." This new Jerusalem was made of precious and exquisite gems. The gates of pearls are Jesus. Pearls are the only precious stones made by pain and suffering being covered by the "blood" (oyster's nacre) of a living thing. Oh, what a breathtaking and wonderful Savior we have!

John continued. "I saw no temple in it, for the Lord God the Almighty and the Lamb are its temple. And the city has no need of the sun or of the moon to shine on it, for the glory of God has illumined it, and its lamp is the Lamb. The nations will walk by its light, and the kings of the earth will bring their glory into it. In the daytime (for there will be no night there) its gates will never be closed" (Rev. 21:22–25).

This is the joy that was set before Jesus as He endured the cross (Heb. 12:2). Heaven is what gives us hope, the incentive to endure the hard times, the motivation to persevere and stand firm through the daily routines and the heartrending sorrows. Paul said, "For I consider that the sufferings of this present time are not worthy to be compared with the glory that is to be revealed to us" (Rom. 8:18).

Bible Reading: Revelation 21

Day 4

Let's look again at creation.

> *The LORD God planted a garden toward the east, in Eden; and there He placed the man whom He had formed. Out of the ground the LORD God caused to grow every tree that is pleasing to the sight and good for food; the tree of life also in the midst of the garden, and the tree of the knowledge of good and evil. Now a river flowed out of Eden to water the garden; and from there it divided and became four rivers. Then the LORD God took the man and put him into the garden of Eden to cultivate it and keep it. The LORD God commanded the man, saying, "From any tree of the garden you may eat freely; but from the tree of the knowledge of good and evil you shall not eat, for in the day that you eat from it you will surely die."*
> —Gen. 2:8–10, 15–17

After Adam and Eve ate from the tree of the knowledge of good and evil, God stated His punishment of a curse on them, Satan, and creation.

> *Then the LORD God said, "Behold, the man has become like one of Us, knowing good and evil; and now, he might stretch out his hand, and take also from the tree of life, and eat, and live forever"—therefore the LORD God sent him out from the garden of Eden, to cultivate the ground from which he was taken. So He drove the man out; and at the east of the garden of Eden He stationed the cherubim and the flaming sword which turned every direction to guard the way to the tree of life.*
> —Gen. 3:22–24

Back to John's revelation.

> *Then he showed me a river of the water of life, clear as crystal, coming from the throne of God and of the Lamb, in the middle of its street. On either side of the river was the tree of life, bearing twelve kinds of fruit, yielding its fruit every month; and the leaves of the tree were for the healing of the nations. There will no longer be any curse; and the throne of God and of the Lamb*

will be in it, and His bond-servants will serve Him; they will see His face, and His name will be on their foreheads.

—Rev. 22:1–4

God has restored to mankind all that had been lost when sin entered the world. That is what He does. He forgives and restores and reunites us with our Father. It was a great mercy that God protected Adam and Eve from eating from the tree of life in the Garden of Eden. That would have meant having to live forever as sinners, separated from God. Instead, He offered His Son as the way to eternal life, a life of forgiveness and restoration. And when we accept Jesus's eternal life, we will once again live by the river of the water of life and the tree of life.

The leaves of the tree of life were for the healing of the nations. Isn't that interesting? In heaven the leaves will give therapeutic, restorative healing to many people. Healing also means to serve. "Nations" here means a group of people, the human family. The tree of life will enable all the different people who are God's children, yet from different backgrounds, to serve each other in a way that restores relationships, to finally love our neighbor as we love ourselves.

This river of the water of life is everything God is—pure and clean and life-giving. Psalm 46:4–5 says, "There is a river whose streams make glad the city of God, the holy dwelling places of the Most High. God is in the midst of her, she will not be moved; God will help her when morning dawns."

In heaven, the curse of our sin is gone. There will be no more pain in childbirth, no more strife between men and women. Hard and often fruitless work just to survive and, most of all, death will be gone. Heaven is full of life and healing; productive work; rest and pure, restoring water.

***Bible Reading*: Revelation 22:1–9, John 4:7–14**

Day 5

We can only imagine how awesome this revelation was to John in person. The thought of angels and their magnificent beauty and abilities is breathtaking and causes most of us to feel amazed. John wrote, "I, John, am the one who heard and saw these things. And when I heard and saw, I fell down to worship at the feet of the angel who showed me these things" (Rev. 22:8).

Revelation 20–22

When we studied Joshua, we discussed that an angel of God would never allow a person to worship them, which is proved by John's account of what happened. "But he [the angel] said to me, 'Do not do that. I am a fellow servant of yours and of your brethren the prophets and of those who heed the words of this book. Worship God'" (Rev. 22:9).

We must be careful today to not worship anyone or anything but God. No matter how magnificent the creation, it is only the Creator who is worthy of worship. There have been wonderful men and women of God who have served sacrificially, but they should never be worshiped or prayed to. Mary, Jesus's mother, and all the apostles would be most unhappy if they knew anyone worshiped them or prayed to them. This angel in Revelation said it well, "Do not do that. I, and every angel and human, am a fellow servant of yours and of your brethren the prophets and of those who heed the words of this book. Worship God."

"And he said to me, 'Do not seal up the words of the prophecy of this book, for the time is near. Let the one who does wrong, still do wrong; and the one who is filthy, still be filthy; and let the one who is righteous, still practice righteousness; and the one who is holy, still keep himself holy'" (Rev. 22:10–11). In other words, when Jesus comes, there won't be time to change your life or repent at the last minute. Read the words of this prophecy, and be warned; change now while you have the chance. Once Jesus comes again, whatever you are is how you will be for eternity.

Jesus then declared this:

> *"Behold, I am coming quickly, and My reward is with Me, to render to every man according to what he has done. I am the Alpha and the Omega, the first and the last, the beginning and the end." Blessed are those who wash their robes, so that they may have the right to the tree of life, and may enter by the gates into the city. Outside are the dogs and the sorcerers and the immoral persons and the murderers and the idolaters, and everyone who loves and practices lying. "I, Jesus, have sent My angel to testify to you these things for the churches. I am the root and the descendant of David, the bright morning star." The Spirit and the bride say, "Come." And let the one who hears say, "Come." And let the one who is thirsty come; let the one who wishes take the water of life without cost.*
>
> —Rev. 22:12–17

"Come to Me, all who are weary and heavy-laden, and I will give you rest. Take my yoke upon you and learn from me, for I am gentle and humble in heart, and YOU WILL FIND REST FOR YOUR SOULS" (Matt. 11:28–29). Jesus loves us. He loves you, and He loves me. "The Lord is not slow about His promise, as some count slowness, but is patient toward you, not wishing for any to perish but for all to come to repentance" (2 Pet. 3:9).

That is the invitation of Revelation. Come. Come now to the God who loves you and will forgive you and reconcile your relationship with Him. Come, and live with Him forever.

Bible Reading: Exodus 20:1–5, 2 Peter 3:7–18

Day 6

After these things I looked, and behold, a door standing open in heaven, and the first voice which I had heard, like the sound of a trumpet speaking with me, said, "Come up here, and I will show you what must take place after these things." Immediately I was in the Spirit; and behold, a throne was standing in heaven, and One sitting on the throne. And He who was sitting was like a jasper stone and a sardius in appearance; and there was a rainbow around the throne, like an emerald in appearance. Around the throne were twenty-four thrones; and upon the thrones I saw twenty-four elders sitting, clothed in white garments, and golden crowns on their heads.

Out from the throne come flashes of lightning and sounds and peals of thunder. And there were seven lamps of fire burning before the throne, which are the seven Spirits of God; and before the throne there was something like a sea of glass, like crystal; and in the center and around the throne, four living creatures full of eyes in front and behind. The first creature was like a lion, and the second creature like a calf, and the third creature had a face like that of a man, and the fourth creature was like a flying eagle. And the four living creatures, each one of them having six wings, are full of eyes around and within; and day and night they do not cease to say,

"HOLY, HOLY, HOLY IS THE LORD GOD, THE ALMIGHTY, WHO WAS AND WHO IS AND WHO IS TO COME."

Revelation 20–22

And when the living creatures give glory and honor and thanks to Him who sits on the throne, to Him who lives forever and ever, the twenty-four elders will fall down before Him who sits on the throne, and will worship Him who lives forever and ever, and will cast their crowns before the throne, saying,

"Worthy are You, our Lord and our God, to receive glory and honor and power; for You created all things, and because of Your will they existed, and were created."
—Rev. 4:1–11

Our awesome God is a humble God. Philippians 2:5–11 says this:

Have this attitude in yourselves which was also in Christ Jesus, who, although He existed in the form of God, did not regard equality with God a thing to be grasped, but emptied Himself, taking the form of a bond-servant, and *being made in the likeness of men. Being found in appearance as a man, He humbled Himself by becoming obedient to the point of death, even death on a cross. For this reason God highly exalted Him, and bestowed on Him the name which is above every name, so that at the name of* JESUS EVERY KNEE WILL BOW, *of those who are in heaven and on earth and under the earth, and that every tongue will confess that Jesus Christ is Lord, to the glory of God the Father.*

The God of Revelation 4 is the same God of Philippians 2. Mighty, indescribable, holy and pure—He loved us enough to empty Himself and become like one of us. Then He died on the cross to pay the penalty for our sins. He died—the ultimate consequence of sin—in order to set us free from that consequence. Jesus rose from the grave, conquering death and Satan once and for all (see Heb. 2:14–15).

Jesus said, "Behold, I stand at the door and knock; if anyone hears My voice and opens the door, I will come in to him and will dine with him, and he with Me. He who overcomes, I will grant to him to sit down with Me on My throne, as I also overcame and sat down with My Father on His throne" (Rev. 3:20–21).

Bible Reading: Revelation 22:10–21

Week 12
ARMOR OF GOD

Day 1

Throughout this year we've stepped into the lives of many people in the Bible and found they are just like us. What God has revealed is that the battles in their lives and in ours are because of the spiritual war raging between Satan and God. Satan attacks us knowing we are God's beloved. Yet we aren't hapless victims. God has not left us unaware, unprotected, or untrained. We can engage our enemy in these battles—and we can win.

Paul said this in 2 Corinthians 10:3–7:

> *For though we walk in the flesh, we do not war according to the flesh, for the weapons of our warfare are not of the flesh, but divinely powerful for the destruction of fortresses.* We are *destroying speculations and every lofty thing raised up against the knowledge of God, and we are taking every thought captive to the obedience of Christ, and we are ready to punish all disobedience, whenever your obedience is complete. You are looking at things as they are outwardly. If anyone is confident in himself that he is Christ's, let him consider this again within himself, that just as he is Christ's, so also are we.*

Defense alone will not win battles. Victory comes with the proper mix of defense and offense. The Lord has given us armor to put on for life's spiritual war, and He's given us weapons. Ephesians 6 tells us the sword of the Spirit is our weapon, and 2 Corinthians 10 says we have more than one weapon.

Armor of God

Let's consider our uniform.

> *Finally, be strong in the Lord and in the strength of His might. Put on the full armor of God, so that you will be able to stand firm against the schemes of the devil. For our struggle is not against flesh and blood, but against the rulers, against the powers, against the world forces of this darkness, against the spiritual forces of wickedness in the heavenly places. Therefore, take up the full armor of God, so that you will be able to resist in the evil day, and having done everything, to stand firm. Stand firm therefore,* HAVING GIRDED YOUR LOINS WITH TRUTH, *and* HAVING PUT ON THE BREASTPLATE OF RIGHTEOUSNESS, *and having* SHOD YOUR FEET WITH THE PREPARATION OF THE GOSPEL OF PEACE; *in addition to all, taking up the shield of faith with which you will be able to extinguish all the flaming arrows of the evil one. And take* THE HELMET OF SALVATION, *and the sword of the Spirit, which is the word of God. With all prayer and petition pray at all times in the Spirit, and with this in view, be on the alert with all perseverance and petition for all the saints.*
>
> —Eph. 6:10–18

When describing our armor, Paul used the visualization of Roman soldiers. In hand-to-hand combat most of their protective armor could and would be used as a weapon too. We should also know how to use what God has given us. The breastplate of righteousness would be like a bulletproof vest or football pads. In hand-to-hand combat, it could be used to hit and push back all the lies of the world. Righteousness is a strong weapon and defense. Our booted feet are weapons and tools as we live and spread the gospel of peace. Both the shield of faith and helmet of salvation can be used defensively and offensively, if needed. Obviously, the sword of the Spirit is our most sophisticated weapon—it is the truth, the Word of God. Additionally, our Commander in Chief has given us a sound military strategy that will defend us as well as enable us to attack with precision. Our fight is with Satan's forces, not people. So pray at all times in the Spirit, and with this in view, be on the alert with all perseverance and petition for all the saints. Gear up—the battle is on.

***Bible Reading*: Ephesians 1:13–23, Ephesians 6:10–18**

Day 2

Take up the full armor of God. There's not one item on this list of armor we can leave off and still remain safe. Each piece of armor is significant as is the order in which Paul gave them. Girding our loins is an old-fashioned way of saying fastening on the belt of truth. Roman soldiers would cinch up their toga-like clothes in order to be able to move about quickly. Their belt would also connect to their breastplate and hold their sword. It may seem more sensible to take the helmet the truth—covering our brains with accurate and credible facts. Yet we're given the belt of truth.

The loins are the place where the Hebrews thought the generative power (semen) resided. It's where life and the forming of everything starts. The picture is that God's truth encircles and holds our core, from where the beginnings of our thoughts, ideas, and beliefs are generated. If you play sports or work out, you know the importance of strengthening your core. Our stomach and back are what stabilize us and keep us balanced. Also, our core generates an explosion of strength to swing a bat, throw a ball—hold a shield and wield a sword. We use our core to reach for a glass, tie our shoes, and hold a book. Every part of daily life and every part of warfare requires a strong and secure core. So we are to put on the belt of truth.

We just learned in Revelation that Satan's chief method of attack is lies and deceit. From there, our choices domino into destructive thoughts and actions. But if we have the truth of God secured tightly around our core, we will be able to withstand the onslaught of deceit—to stand firm and not lose our balance when we're hit by lies. We will be empowered by God's truth to push forward and fight back the lies that we are unforgivable, unloved, abandoned, and rejected by God when something bad happens to us. No lie formed against us will prosper when God's truth holds us.

The breastplate of righteousness consists of two parts that protect the body on the front and back, from the neck to the middle where it connects to the belt of truth. A general meaning of righteousness is the state of a person as they ought to be—acceptable to God. God is righteous and full of integrity, virtue, purity of life, rightness, correctness of thinking, feeling, and acting. Those are the materials that make up our breastplate—or bulletproof vest. Again, we can see how that would protect us from the flaming arrows of the evil one. Satan's lies and temptations may hit us, but the truth—that we think, feel, and act correctly, that we've chosen to live with integrity, that Jesus is our righteousness and indwells and covers us—will protect us. The lies may knock us down, but they won't be able to penetrate and destroy us.

Those very things will also be a weapon we can use to strike back against our enemy. Living every day, practicing what we know to be true and righteous, allows us to understand what's going on and what our enemy is up to. We'll be able to speak out boldly that a lie is not the correct way of thinking, feeling, or acting. Because we've lived rightly, our example will push back those who would attack our reputation and the Lord's and weaken society around us.

Truth and righteousness are the first parts of the armor of the Lord. Loyalty and truth preserve the king, and he upholds his throne by righteousness (Prov. 20:28). Take up the full armor of God so that you will be able to resist in the evil day, and having done everything, to stand firm. Stand firm, having fastened on the belt of truth and having put on the breastplate of righteousness.

Bible Reading: **Isaiah 54:10–17, Colossians 1:9–14**

Day 3

It's time to get your shoes on. Shod your feet with the preparation of the gospel of peace. This part of our armor *prepares* for the spreading of the gospel. The boots of God's soldiers do a lot of walking through whatever territory God has given them, living each step for Christ. As we live each moment of each day with the fruit of the Spirit growing in us, the Light of the world shining in us, and the love of God working in us, people are being primed to hear about Jesus.

First Timothy 6:12 and 14 say, "Fight the good fight of faith; take hold of the eternal life to which you were called, and you made the good confession in the presence of many witnesses. that you keep the commandment without stain or reproach until the appearing of our Lord Jesus Christ." Our Christian walk will make people want to know how we do it. How do we feel at peace in the middle of our illness? Why would we be kind to the person who hurt us, pray for someone who lied about us, have joy when we weep for a lost loved one? Where does our hope come from when we live with constant injustice? Satan attacks through those circumstances, but how we march through them disables his arsenal of weapons.

These shoes of virtuous living are both defensive and offensive, taking us into the battle with a firm foundation and enabling us to stand firm when under attack, knowing that our best offense is a good defense, that giving our enemy nowhere to attack as we walk in truth and righteousness is a weapon in itself.

In addition to all that, we're to take up the shield of faith so we'll be able to extinguish all the flaming arrows of the evil one. The shield described here is a large, oblong shield that would protect the soldier's entire body. Thoughts, desires, feelings, imaginations, fears, lies, anger, malice, bitterness, and hatred are some of the fiery darts Satan shoots at us. Our faith in God is what will stop these missiles from penetrating our hearts and minds and extinguish the fire that could destroy us. Faith is the assurance or conviction of the truth that God is good and sovereign. It's believing that He loves us. It's knowing God is Spirit and truth even though we can't see Him or completely understand that concept. Trust comes from our confidence that Jesus Christ is who He says He is—the risen Savior and Son of God.

So how does this shield of faith work? Let's remember David. When David was just a young shepherd boy, God said he would be the next king of Israel. David killed Goliath, served King Saul, and then had to flee for his life as King Saul lied about him and tried to kill him over the next few years. And the fiery arrows were flying. *Did God really say you'd be king? How is God good if He lets you lose your family and home and reputation? You can't trust what God says to you. Saul's accusations are true—you are a glory-seeker trying to take his kingdom. No one's stronger than the king and his army. It's impossible for this to turn out well. God isn't listening. He doesn't care. You must have done something terrible to deserve this.*

The shield of faith deflects each of these accusations, fears, and lies with truth. Believe God is good. He's proven Himself in the past. You intended to harm me, but God intended it for good to accomplish what is now being done, the saving of many lives (Gen. 50:20). The Lord your God is in your midst, a victorious warrior. He will exult over you with joy, He will be quiet in His love, and He will rejoice over you with shouts of joy (Zeph. 3:17).

Bible Reading: 1 Timothy 1:15–19, Psalm 18:28–50

Day 4

Next, take the helmet of salvation and the sword of the Spirit, which is the Word of God.

> *But since we are of the day, let us be sober, having put on the breastplate of faith and love, and as a helmet, the hope of salvation. For God has not destined us for wrath, but for obtaining salvation through our* Lord *Jesus Christ, who died for us, so that whether we are awake or asleep, we will live together with Him. Therefore encourage one another and build up one another, just as you also are doing.*
> —1 Thess. 5:8–11

War is exhausting and discouraging. Days and nights of attacks and fighting flow into hours of mindless waiting. It can look as if we take two steps forward and three steps back; our efforts and sacrifices seem ineffective. The helmet of salvation seals our hope. It protects us against the desire to give up in discouragement. This hope is the knowledge that we are saved eternally and are being rescued and saved now. Discouragement can swamp us and drag us into despondency and depression when we lose track of the hope that is ours in Christ Jesus.

Paul was a man who knew warfare and discouragement, and he was a man who knew God and hope. We do not want you to be uninformed, brothers, about the hardships we suffered in the province of Asia. We were under great pressure, far beyond our ability to endure, so that we despaired even of life. Indeed, in our hearts we felt the sentence of death. But this happened that we might not rely on ourselves but on God, who raises the dead. He has delivered us from such a deadly peril, and He will deliver us. On Him we have set our hope that He will continue to deliver us (2 Cor. 1:8–10). God has saved us, God is saving us, and God will save us. That hope keeps us standing firm in the fight.

The sword of the Spirit is the Word of God secured to the belt of truth. It is not a long sword that permits us to fight at a distance. Paul was describing a small, dagger-like sword used for cutting and thrusting. Unlike modern warfare where missiles can be shot from miles away, spiritual warfare is up close and personal. If we are fighting on behalf of another person, we can now see the importance of walking in a way that prepares them for the gospel of peace. That means we have a relationship with them, a right to be close—close enough to use the sword of the Spirit accurately and precisely. We're not fighting them; we're fighting the lies and destruction Satan is firing at them. But in order to effectively wield our sword and speak God's word into their lives, they need to feel safe and trust us. Only then can we battle and instruct.

"For you have not received a spirit of slavery leading to fear again, but you have received a spirit of adoption as sons by which we cry out, 'Abba! Father!'" (Rom. 8:15). So tell God you have been living in fear and rejection; realize that's sin; turn from it, and ask for freedom from it and for His Spirit to fill you with His courage, strength, peace, love, and adoption. God will do that. Because "if we confess our sins, He is faithful and righteous to forgive us our sins and to cleanse us from all unrighteousness" (1 John 1:9). "'For I will restore you to health and I will heal you of your wounds,' declares the Lord" (Jer. 30:17).

Whatever our demons—addictions, criticalness, insecurity, bitterness, unforgiveness, anger, sensuality, timidity, lying, failure, pride, greed, doubt, envy, the occult—the sword of the Spirit is an effective weapon. Be diligent to present yourself approved to God as a workman who does not need to be ashamed, accurately handling the word of truth (2 Tim. 2:15).

Bible Reading: Exodus 15:1–6, Psalm 119:11, Matthew 4:1–11

Day 5

"With all prayer and petition pray at all times in the Spirit, and with this in view, be on the alert with all perseverance and petition for all the saints" (Eph. 6:18). What does this mean, to pray in the Spirit? If every Christian has the Holy Spirit in them and is sealed by the Spirit, why would Paul find it necessary to say "pray in the Spirit"? Prayer is about relationship with God. He can do all things and doesn't need us, but He wants our relationship to be intimate and ongoing.

Being *in* the Spirit is different from having the Spirit in us. It's being in tune with the Lord, talking with and listening to Him, letting His Spirit speak through us in tongues or a heavenly language breathed by the Holy Spirit (1 Cor. 13:1; 14:14–15). It's understanding His words and heart, praying as God leads.

Here's an example. When a dad comes home angry, oppressive, and mean, we franticly pray, "Lord, help him not to be angry. Help him not to say anything that will destroy my sister. Please don't let him be enraged at my room. Just make him happy, and help us know how to handle him. Help him to change." That's good, but it basically only addresses the outward physical aspects of a spiritual battle. It's also asking God to do what He told us to do. He told us that He gave us the power, tools, and knowledge to fight evil and release God's attributes into our life and world (Matt. 10:1–20, 16:19, Mark 3:27, Luke 10:1–20, 2 Cor. 10:3–7, Eph. 6:10–18).

Praying in the Spirit is listening as the Holy Spirit reveals the spiritual reasons behind behavior that affects us. Speaking out loud, we follow Jesus's directions: "I silence and bind the spirits of anger and oppression in Jesus's name" (Mark 3:27). "Lord, I loose Your Spirit of peace, freedom, and love in our home" (Matt. 18:18). "Father, don't let us live in fear of dad or in unforgiveness but in Your courage, power, forgiveness, and wisdom." When we can't pinpoint the exact cause for the attack (malicious or critical spirits or others), the Holy Spirit will pray for us and through us (Rom. 8:26–27, 1 Cor. 14:14–15). Our authority is the name of Jesus.

My personal testimony is that praying in the Spirit is effective and changes the whole dynamic of a home, even when some people in the home do not change. James 5:16 says, "The effective prayer of a righteous man can accomplish much." That infers a righteous person (believer in Christ) can have ineffective prayers that don't accomplish much, not because of fancy, religious words but because of our willingness to pray in the Spirit, not just the physical. God is Spirit and truth (John 16:13). It shouldn't surprise us that He can reveal the spiritual causes and pray for us and through us more effectively and differently than we can understand.

The person who prays in the Spirit never says, "Well all we can do is pray" as if that's our last resort when we're powerless to do anything else. When we pray in the Spirit, God's power and purpose are ever present, energizing us and strengthening our faith in God's plan and timing. Prayer will be the first thing we want to do as we wait to see what unexpected action God will take. We'll understand that God will use the time to refine and grow us as well as defeat Satan's plans for destruction. God's desire is to mature and strengthen us, so it is not His will to take every hardship and hurt out of our lives. He hates sin, but God will use the sinful choices in this world for the good of His children and to finish His plans, not because He needs those sinful events to happen but because He is capable of overcoming Satan's destruction and turning evil into ultimate good. Pray in the Spirit for God's good and perfect will to be done.

Bible Reading: Isaiah 55:8–13, 1 Corinthians 12:7–11, 28–31, 13:1, Colossians 1:9–20

Day 6

Ephesians 6 tells us to stand firm, put on our armor, resist, extinguish, and pray in the Spirit at all times. Second Corinthians 10 instructs us to war, destroy, take captive, and punish. First Timothy 1 and 6 say to fight. Our Father did not leave us unaware of the fact that we will be in constant war with the enemy of our soul. God said to Cain in Genesis 4:7 (NIV), "If you do what is right, will you not be accepted? But if you do not do what is right, sin is crouching at your door; it desires to have you, but you must rule over it." In 1 Peter 5:8 we're told, "Be alert and of sober mind. Your enemy the devil prowls around like a roaring lion looking for someone to devour."

It's vital that we know our enemy and his strategy. But he should not be our focus. Our strength is not in knowledge. Our strength is not in our armor or weapons or size. Our strength is not in eloquent prayers. Our strength is in the Lord. Read Ephesians 6:10–18 again.

> *Finally, be strong in the Lord and in the strength of His might. Put on the full armor of God, so that you will be able to stand firm against the schemes of the devil. For our struggle is not against flesh and blood, but against the rulers, against the powers, against the world forces of this darkness, against the spiritual forces of wickedness in the heavenly places. Therefore, take up the full armor of God, so that you will be able to resist in the evil day, and having done everything, to stand firm. Stand firm therefore, HAVING GIRDED YOUR LOINS WITH TRUTH, and HAVING PUT ON THE BREASTPLATE OF RIGHTEOUSNESS, and having SHOD YOUR FEET WITH THE PREPARATION OF THE GOSPEL OF PEACE; in addition to all, taking up the shield of faith with which you will be able to extinguish all the flaming arrows of the evil one. And take THE HELMET OF SALVATION, and the*

sword of the Spirit, which is the word of God. With all prayer and petition pray at all times in the Spirit, and with this in view, be on the alert with all perseverance and petition for all the saints.

The prophet Zechariah was given a vision. An angel said to him, "This is the word of the LORD to Zerubbabel saying, 'Not by might nor by power, but by My Spirit,' says the LORD of hosts" (Zech. 4:6). The war will be won not by human strength, might, efficiency, wealth, or an army—but by God's Spirit.

Our hearts and minds and eyes should be fastened on our Lord. God wants us to have a relationship with Him, to know Him and understand Him. His desire is for you and me to talk with Him constantly and listen to Him. Read His letters to us (the Bible), ask Him what it means and why He does things the way He does. Listen to Him as He listens to us. Abba Father wants us to walk with Him all day and all night, every step of our lives. He's given us His armor to wear, and He doesn't want us to put on something of our own—it will be inadequate. The weapons God has supplied for us are divinely powerful, and He wants to teach us how to use them.

This relationship is special, and it is sealed by God's very breath—His Holy Spirit. His breath is in us, and He wants us to walk and fight and pray in His Spirit. The Lord of all the universe has chosen to have a relationship with you and with me, and He wants us to choose to have a relationship with Him. That's one of the reasons prayer is so powerful and important. Our gentleman Father waits until we ask before He gives. He wants us engaged in this relationship, loving and trusting and participating. Be strong in the Lord and in the strength of His might. Stand firm in Jesus Christ, and follow His lead into battle, secure in His armor.

Bible Reading: Psalm 33:13–22

Week 13

ISAIAH 53–55

Day 1

Prophesying about Christ Jesus, the servant of God, Isaiah, wrote this:

> *Who has believed our message? And to whom has the arm of the Lord been revealed? For He grew up before Him like a tender shoot, and like a root out of parched ground; He has no stately form or majesty that we should look upon Him, nor appearance that we should be attracted to Him. He was despised and forsaken of men, a man of sorrows and acquainted with grief; and like one from whom men hide their face He was despised, and we did not esteem Him. Surely our griefs He Himself bore, and our sorrows He carried; yet we ourselves esteemed Him stricken, smitten of God, and afflicted. But He was pierced through for our transgressions, He was crushed for our iniquities; the chastening for our well-being fell upon Him, and by His scourging we are healed. All of us like sheep have gone astray, each of us has turned to his own way; but the Lord has caused the iniquity of us all to fall on Him.*
>
> —Isa. 53:1–6

In our last week together, we'll look one more time at the greatest gift ever given. *Seasons under the Juniper Tree* has delved into the pain and brokenness we can suffer as well as the joys and victories. Through each and every circumstance, our heavenly Father has revealed His love to us through His Son Jesus Christ.

ISAIAH 53–55

There has never been another leader with the power and charisma of Jesus guiding men and women for more than 2,000 years. He was a servant of God. You're smiling now, aren't you, because you know from Moses, Joshua, and King David that the greatest leaders are servants.

Yet Isaiah said there was nothing beautiful or majestic about His appearance, nothing to attract us to Him. He was despised and rejected, a man of sorrows, acquainted with bitterest grief. So why do so many over such a long span of time follow and love Him? We love Him because He first loved us. We love Him because He proved to be our friend. Jesus said, "Greater love has no one than this, that one lay down his life for his friends" (John 15:13).

By His own choice, the Son of God laid down His life for His friends—for you and for me. He was pierced for our transgressions, He was crushed for our iniquities; the punishment that brought us peace was upon Him, and by His wounds we are healed. Jesus paid our debt on the cross for our sins. We're at peace with God now because justice was served and completed in Jesus. The wounds inflicted on Jesus will heal our bodies, hearts, and minds, and will heal us spiritually as well. He gave Himself up for us—totally and completely. Every part of Jesus the man was grieved and wounded, and He died because sin's consequence was for every part of mankind to be broken and die. And through His death and resurrection, every part of us can now live.

> *For the grace of God has appeared, bringing salvation to all men, instructing us to deny ungodliness and worldly desires and to live sensibly, righteously and godly in the present age, looking for the blessed hope and the appearing of the glory of our great God and Savior, Christ Jesus, who gave Himself for us to redeem us from every lawless [wicked] deed, and to purify for Himself a people for His own possession, zealous [eager] for good deeds.*
>
> —Titus 2:11–14

Who has believed our message? And to whom has the arm of the Lord been revealed? Christ Jesus has been revealed to us all. Have you chosen to believe?

Bible Reading: Isaiah 53, Matthew 8:16–17, 1 Peter 2:24–25

Day 2

Isaiah 54 is a promise of salvation and restoration to a broken Israel—and to a broken world. Because of Israel's continual sin, they were taken captive by Babylon. Yet God said in Isaiah 54:7, "For a brief moment I forsook you, but with great compassion I will gather you."

Sin has broken and weakened creation. In this chapter of Isaiah, we see how Israel's—and our—sin has broken our relationship with God so that He rebuked and forsook us in anger (verses 7-9). Nature has been wrecked as evidenced in the flood and with hills and mountains shaking (verses 9-10). Our relationship with others was damaged with reproach, shame, humiliation, and disgrace. We abandon, grieve, and reject each other; we afflict, oppress, attack, condemn, and accuse (verses 4-17). Because of sin, we are also broken within ourselves. Verse 1 talks of a barren woman, which in ancient times brought shame and disgrace. Barrenness is a symbol of a person not creating life and a future, as if we'd wasted our life and failed our very purpose for being born. Personal brokenness is failure, misery, humiliation, shame, disgrace, and fear. We feel afflicted, storm-tossed, and not comforted (verses 1-15).

The consequence of sin is huge—eternal death, forever separated from God (our choice when we don't believe in Jesus) and ultimate judgment and hell. But it's also the death of life while we're living—death of relationships, peace, joy, security, contentment, and purpose. At times God lets us walk away and fester in our chosen existence. But He loves us as a perfect husband loves His beloved wife, as a devoted Father loves His adored children.

Shout for joy, you childless woman, for God will give you so many children you'll have to enlarge your tents. For those women whose husbands abandoned and rejected them, God will be your husband and redeemer. He will take the widow and care for her as well (verses 1-7). Speaking to women who at that time were completely defenseless and vulnerable without a husband, God's promise is to embrace anyone abandoned by their protector. With compassion and love, healing our broken hearts while providing for and protecting us, God will redeem us.

> *"For this is like the days of Noah to Me: as I swore that the waters of Noah would not flood the earth again; so I have sworn that I will not be angry with you nor will I rebuke you. For the mountains may be removed and the hills may shake, but My*

> *lovingkindness will not be removed from you, and My covenant of peace will not be shaken," says the Lord who has compassion on you."*
>
> —Isa. 54:9–10

If we live in rebellion, we will face the consequences, but God will not walk away from His promise. His covenant of peace will be completely fulfilled when Jesus comes again. But if Israel and you and I repent and turn back to God, we can experience His lovingkindness and peace today—in the midst of this riotous, angry world.

All your sons will be taught of the Lord; and the well-being of your sons will be great (verse 13). Our choices affect future generations, and our Father's promise and love will cover our children too. Hope and salvation extend to our children from the loving Father.

Isaiah ends this chapter by showing God's total protection, reconciliation, and restoration to His broken people. What sin destroyed, God will build up. He is our Healer and the Lover of our soul. He is our Protector, Redeemer, and Savior. He is our Husband and Father. God is love.

Bible Reading: Isaiah 54

Day 3

What God offers is excellent and free to us, but He doesn't beg us to take it. God does not tickle our ears with words we want to hear, words that will validate our choices and opinions. Honesty and truthfulness are His standards. Right and wrong are always right and wrong. Areas God leaves open for personal preference can be measured against His standard too. The Lord is upfront about the fact that life will not always be easy when we live for Him. But God's gift is abundantly good. It will prosper us, not destroy us. And it will last forever.

> *Ho! Everyone who thirsts, come to the waters; and you who have no money come, buy and eat. Come, buy wine and milk without money and without cost. Why do you spend money for what is not bread, and your wages for what does not satisfy? Listen carefully to Me, and eat what is good, and delight yourself in*

abundance. Incline your ear and come to Me. Listen, that you may live; and I will make an everlasting covenant with you, according to the faithful mercies shown to David.

—Isa. 55:1–3

The invitation is to everyone who thirsts for what God has to offer. If we aren't thirsty for what the Lord can give us, then we won't be satisfied with His waters. Jesus said, "Blessed are those who hunger and thirst for righteousness, for they shall be satisfied" (Matt. 5:6). We may have heard some people say they tried religion and it didn't do anything for them. That is because they came to God wanting something He wasn't offering. They weren't hungering and thirsting after righteousness, so they left unsatisfied and still hungry.

Without money and without cost, those who are thirsty can receive what the Lord is offering. God is not proposing a religion where we have to work or purchase His love and salvation. All who bring their trust and faith will receive what God has to give them. Paul said this:

But what does it say? "THE WORD IS NEAR YOU, IN YOUR MOUTH AND IN YOUR HEART"—that is, the word of faith that we are preaching, that if you confess with your mouth Jesus as Lord, and believe in your heart that God raised Him from the dead, you will be saved; for with the heart a person believes, resulting in righteousness, and with the mouth he confesses, resulting in salvation. For the Scripture says, "WHOEVER BELIEVES IN HIM WILL NOT BE DISAPPOINTED."

—Rom. 10:8–11

Look at what is free—water, wine, milk, and bread. Every step of faith and maturity is free of charge. We receive salvation and the living water free because Jesus paid the price on the cross. Growing spiritually mature so we can take in and understand deep biblical truths (solid food) is not just for the few who become pastors and priests. Jesus said, "But when He, the Spirit of truth, comes, He will guide you into all the truth; for He will not speak on His own initiative, but whatever He hears, He will speak; and He will disclose to you what is to come" (John 16:13).

So why spend your money on food that does not give you strength? Why pay for food that does you no good? Listen, and God will tell you where to get food that is good for the soul (Isa. 55:2). We don't need to keep searching for love and meaning, trying to find ourselves or something to fill the empty hole in us. Stop looking for fulfillment in jobs and education, in relationships and physical experiences. Don't jump from one religion to another trying to find a fit to make you comfortable. Come to Jesus. Listen so you may live, and God will make an everlasting covenant with you.

Bible Reading: Isaiah 55:1-5, John 6:31-40

Day 4

"Seek the LORD while He may be found; call upon Him while He is near. Let the wicked forsake his way and the unrighteous man his thoughts; and let him return to the LORD, and He will have compassion on him, and to our God, for He will abundantly pardon" (Isa. 55:6-7).

When we feel a thirst for God's Word, we need to go to Him for His living water. In the moment that we hunger and thirst for righteousness, we need to turn to the Lord. At the time we long for something more than what we've found in this world, we should seek God and ask Him to reveal more of Himself to us. There is an urgency to Isaiah's words. Seek God now—you don't know what the future will bring.

Here's what Jesus said in Matthew 7:6-8 and 11:

> *Do not give what is holy to dogs, and do not throw your pearls before swine, or they will trample them under their feet, and turn and tear you to pieces. Ask, and it will be given to you; seek, and you will find; knock, and it will be opened to you. For everyone who asks receives, and he who seeks finds, and to him who knocks it will be opened. If you then, being evil, know how to give good gifts to your children, how much more will your Father who is in heaven give what is good to those who ask Him!*

He was saying that God's holy Word, His truth, protection, and salvation are like precious pearls. Since pearls are beautiful and serve a special purpose, you wouldn't offer them to dogs or pigs because they wouldn't appreciate them or treat them with respect. People who don't want what God offers are like the dog and swine since they trample Jesus's costly gift and then turn on believers in Christ and tear them to pieces. But while God is near you and you can hear and feel pulled toward Him, He is offering you His pearls—so turn to Him. Ask the Lord anything you want to know or have need of, and He will give it to you when you're ready and able to handle it. Seek—search for—Jesus's gift of salvation and abundant life, and you will find it. Knock on the doors of knowledge and truth, courage and peace, forgiveness and freedom, and they will be opened to you.

If you've never accepted Jesus as Lord and Savior, now is the time He may be found. He again fixes a certain day—today—saying through David's words, "Today, if you hear His voice, do not harden your hearts" (Heb. 4:7). God the Father loves you. He reached out to you through His Son Jesus on the cross, and He's reaching out to you now. Call upon Him while He is near.

For those who are God's children but have turned away to live however they choose, the message is the same—"Today, if you hear His voice, do not harden your hearts." Let the people turn from their wicked deeds. Let them banish from their minds the very thought of doing wrong. Let them turn to the Lord that He may have mercy on them. Yes, turn to our God, for He will abundantly pardon (Isa. 55:7).

Let's not fool ourselves into thinking that because we're saved we can live any way we like. God tells us to repent—turn from sin, and walk toward Him. It's physically impossible to walk toward the east and walk toward the west at the same time. Likewise, it is impossible to walk toward the world's system of sin and toward God at the same time. While we live doing things differently than God has said, we are walking away from Him. So repent—turn around—and start walking toward God and away from the sin. In compassion He will abundantly pardon.

Bible Reading: Isaiah 55, John 16:7–15

Day 5

Why would God offer His Son Jesus's death and resurrection as payment for our sins? Why does He want a relationship with us when repeatedly we reject Him and His gifts? How do we know that God's Word is working to change us into the people we want to be? How is it that someone like me and like you can live effectively when we feel so messed up? Why does the fact that God is bigger and smarter than us give us hope and peace?

> *"For My thoughts are not your thoughts, nor are your ways My ways," declares the LORD. "For as the heavens are higher than the earth, so are My ways higher than your ways and My thoughts than your thoughts. For as the rain and the snow come down from heaven, and do not return there without watering the earth and making it bear and sprout, and furnishing seed to the sower and bread to the eater; so will My word be which goes forth from My mouth; it will not return to Me empty, without accomplishing what I desire, and without succeeding* in the matter *for which I sent it."*
>
> —Isa. 55:8–11

When our Father looks at us, He sees what we are and what we've done, and He sees the potential in us to become what He created us to be. God's perspective is so much bigger and higher than ours. It reminds us that we don't have all the answers. We may look at ourselves or others and see the mess or brokenness; we may think we could never amount to much. Or maybe we believe we or another person are perfect. Our thoughts and eyesight are not like the Lord's. He sees the truth—the good truth and the bad—and still He loves us and calls us and answers us when we seek Him. And because His ways are higher than ours, God shows compassion and mercy, love and forgiveness, when we would show the opposite.

The Lord has spoken His Word to each of us, and it is always effective. "For the word of God is living and active and sharper than any two-edged sword, and piercing as far as the division of soul and spirit, of both joints and marrow, and able to judge the thoughts and intentions of the heart" (Heb. 4:12). God's true words are like the rain and snow that fall on the earth. There are times we see those things as annoying or inconvenient, maybe even dangerous. But their purpose, like God's Word, is to water and cause development and life.

This is a guarantee and a promise. When we speak the Word of God, when we live the Word of God, our lives will be effective. We may not see it or hear the confirmation from others, but God's Word will not come back empty. It will accomplish what He desired and succeed in what God sent it to do. Again, we're reminded that God's goals and ability are bigger and higher than ours.

As a parent, my goal in living and teaching is for my children to know Jesus and live like they're loved by Him. It could be very discouraging if one of my kids chose to walk away from God. I could feel as if my hard work and prayers had been a waste of time. But if I have God's perspective, I would know that *someone* was being positively affected by my words and life. Someone will be fed and grow as they observe me living for Christ. We may not see God's Word developing in the soil of a heart, but it is.

God's perspective causes us to go out with joy and be led forth with peace (Isa. 55:12).

Bible Reading: 1 Thessalonians 2:10–13, 1 Peter 1:22–25

Day 6

*Ho! Every one who thirsts, come to the waters; and you who have no money come, buy and eat. Come, buy wine and milk without money and without cost. Why do you spend money for what is not bread, and your wages for what does not satisfy? Listen carefully to Me, and eat what is good, and delight yourself in abundance. Incline your ear and come to Me. Listen, that you may live; and I will make an everlasting covenant with you, According to the faithful mercies shown to David. Behold, I have made him a witness to the peoples, a leader and commander for the peoples. Behold, you will call a nation you do not know, and a nation which knows you not will run to you, because of the L*ORD *your God, even the Holy One of Israel; for He has glorified you. Seek the L*ORD *while He may be found; call upon Him while He is near. Let the wicked forsake his way and the unrighteous man his thoughts; and let him return to the L*ORD*, and He will have compassion on him, and to our God, for He will abundantly pardon. For My thoughts are not your thoughts, nor are your ways My ways," declares the L*ORD. *"For as the heavens are higher than the earth, so are My ways higher than your ways and My thoughts than your thoughts. For as the rain and the snow come down from heaven, and do not return there without watering the earth and making it bear and sprout, and furnishing seed to the sower and bread to the eater; so will My word be which goes forth from My mouth; it will not return to Me empty, without accomplishing what I desire, and without succeeding in the matter for which I sent it. For you will*

ISAIAH 53–55

> *go out with joy and be led forth with peace; the mountains and the hills will break forth into shouts of joy before you, and all the trees of the field will clap their hands. Instead of the thorn bush the cypress will come up, and instead of the nettle the myrtle will come up, and it will be a memorial to the Lord, for an everlasting sign which will not be cut off."*
>
> —Isa. 55:1-13

It doesn't matter where we come from. Our families may be safe and happy with both a mother and father loving and providing for our every need. Or we may come from broken families where hunger and abuse and rejection shape our home. Rich or poor, any skin color, any gender, any age—the only thing that matters is that we receive the Word of God.

Jesus Christ came as the very Word of God.

> *In Him was life, and the life was the Light of men. The Light shines in the darkness, and the darkness did not comprehend it. There was the true Light which, coming into the world, enlightens every man. But as many as received Him, to them He gave the right to become children of God, even to those who believe in His name, who were born, not of blood nor of the will of the flesh nor of the will of man, but of God. And the Word became flesh, and dwelt among us, and we saw His glory, glory as of the only begotten from the Father, full of grace and truth. For of His fullness we have all received, and grace upon grace. For the Law was given through Moses; grace and truth were realized through Jesus Christ.*
>
> —John 1:4, 9, 12-14, 16-17

Sin broke creation. Some of us have experienced obvious pain to the point where we felt completely shattered and destroyed. Others may have been blessed with kindness and ease for most of their lives. But the truth is that all of us have missed the mark of God's holiness; all of us have sinned (Rom. 3:23). And sin causes death and destruction. Each of us has faced a broken relationship with God, with other people, and within ourselves. Yet God's love gave us His only Son Jesus, and whoever believes in Him will not die but have abundant and everlasting life. Instead of a thornbush, we will have a juniper tree—evergreen through every season.

Bible Reading: Jeremiah 29:11-14, John 3:16-21

SALVATION

Salvation is really quite simple. It is not God demanding perfect behavior or even that we confess our sins. Salvation is God supplying our perfect sacrifice in payment for our sins. It's His supply of love and mercy and grace drawing us to His Son, Christ Jesus.

Therefore, let it be known to you, brethren, that through Him forgiveness of sins is proclaimed to you, and **through Him everyone who believes** is freed from all things from which you could not be freed through the Law of Moses (Acts 13:38-39). Again, in Acts 16:30-31 we're told, "And after he brought them out, he said, 'Sirs, what must I do to be saved?' They said, '**Believe in the Lord Jesus**, and you will be saved, you and your household.'"

Jesus said the same thing to Nicodemus in John 3:16. "For God so loved the world, that He gave His only begotten Son, that **whoever believes in Him** shall not perish, but have eternal life."

Paul explained it in Romans 10:8-10, 17: "But what does it say? 'THE WORD IS NEAR YOU, IN YOUR MOUTH AND IN YOUR HEART'—that is, the word of faith that we are preaching, that if **you confess with your mouth Jesus *as* Lord, and believe in your heart that God raised Him from the dead**, you will be saved; for with the heart a person believes, resulting in righteousness, and with the mouth he confesses, resulting in salvation. So, faith *comes* from hearing, and hearing [about the way to salvation] by the word of Christ."

Jesus supplied all we need to be saved. When we believe in Jesus as the Son of God who died and rose again, we are saved and sealed forever by the Holy Spirit (2 Cor. 1:22, Gal. 4:6-7). Ephesians 1:13-14 teaches, "In Him, you also, after listening to the message of truth, the gospel of your salvation—**having also believed**, you were sealed in Him with the Holy Spirit of promise, who is given as a pledge of our inheritance, with a view to the redemption of *God's own* possession, to the praise of His glory" (emphasis added on all Scripture).

So to be saved from the present and eternal penalty of our sins, we must *believe in Jesus*. That's it. This faith in Christ and the Holy Spirit in us will then supply us with the ability to respond to God's call to let go of our old, sinful way of living. We will then want to repent (turn away from sin and toward Christ) and confess our sins to Him.

God's love gives us the ability to love and respect ourselves and others. Baptism, communion, singing worship, serving, giving, obeying, changing . . . these are not demands of God on us. They are not our responsibilities. Jesus and our faith in Him give us the ability to respond to Him and His Word. He supplies us with all we need to live a regenerated, victorious life forever with God. Because of the blood of Jesus and power of the Holy Spirit, we will obey, we'll recognize our sins and repent, and we'll live a life of worship and service, looking like our Savior each step of the way. Or do you think lightly of the riches of His kindness and tolerance and patience, not knowing that the kindness of God leads you to repentance? (Rom. 2:4). The kindness of God—not the Law of God—leads us to repentance. It is His finished work.

Jesus is a giver, not a demander. He gave His life; He gives eternal life; He gives abundant life. Christ gives wisdom, knowledge, power, strength, and the ability to fight wrongs and love. Jesus gives hope and joy. He gives salvation. Open your heart and mind and arms, and receive all the Father has so lavishly given.

AUTHOR BIO

Tricia Kirchmeyer was born in Colorado and then moved to Southern California, where she raised her family. She's been married 39 years, has three children and three grandchildren, and now lives close to her grandchildren in Idaho. While raising her kids, Tricia worked in the public school system, K–12. She enjoys hiking, cooking, and reading.

Tricia has written and taught women's Bible studies, as well as written scripts for plays for vacation Bible schools and adult plays for "The Living Supper" Easter productions at her church. She has also led weekly Bible studies in the Correctional Youth Service.

NOTES

1. Charles R. Swindoll, *Esther: A Woman of Strength & Dignity* (Nashville, TN: Word Publishing, Inc., 1997), 163.

2. David Guzik, "Study Guide for 1 Samuel 14," Blue Letter Bible, accessed August 29, 2021, https://www.blueletterbible.org/Comm/guzik_david/StudyGuide2017-1Sa/1Sa-14.cfm.

3. Matthew Henry, "Commentary on Genesis 50," Blue Letter Bible, accessed August 29, 2021, https://www.blueletterbible.org/Comm/mhc/Gen/Gen_050.cfm.

4. "All Creatures of Our God and King," OpenHymnal.org, accessed August 30, 2021, http://openhymnal.org/Lyrics/All_Creatures_Of_Our_God_And_King-Lasst_Uns_Erfreuen.html.

5. "It Is Well with My Soul," OpenHymnal.org, accessed August 30, 2021, http://openhymnal.org/Lyrics/It_Is_Well_With_My_Soul-It_Is_Well-Ville_Du_Havre.html#:~:text=copyright%3A%20public%20domain.,Open%20Hymnal%20Project%2C%202010%20Revision.

6. "What a Friend We Have in Jesus," OpenHymnal.org, accessed August 30, 2021. http://openhymnal.org/Lyrics/What_A_Friend_We_Have_In_Jesus-untitled.html.

7. "Amazing Grace," OpenHymnal.org, accessed August 30, 2021, http://openhymnal.org/Lyrics/Amazing_Grace-New_Britain.html.

8. "Come Thou Fount of Every Blessing," OpenHymnal.org, accessed August 30, 2021, http://openhymnal.org/Lyrics/Come_Thou_Fount-Nettleton.html.

9. "Be Thou My Vision," OpenHymnal.org, accessed August 30, 2021, http://openhymnal.org/Lyrics/Be_Thou_My_Vision-Slane.html.

10. Phillip Keller, *A Shepherd Looks at Psalm 23* (Grand Rapids, MI: Zondervan Publishing House, 1970), 17.

11. Ibid., 55.

12. David Guzik, "Study Guide for Micah 6," Blue Letter Bible, accessed August 30, 2021, https://www.blueletterbible.org/Comm/guzik_david/StudyGuide2017-Mic/Mic-6.cfm.

13. David Guzik, "Study Guide for Philippians 4," Blue Letter Bible, accessed August 30, 2021, https://www.blueletterbible.org/Comm/guzik_david/StudyGuide2017-Phl/Phl-4.cfm.

14. Beth Moore, *Daniel: Lives of Integrity, Words of Prophecy* (Nashville, TN: Lifeway Press, 2007), 46.

15. Robert Jamieson, A. R. Fausset, and David Brown, "Commentary on Luke 15," Blue Letter Bible, accessed August 30, 2021, https://www.blueletterbible.org/Comm/jfb/Luk/Luk_015.cfm.

16. Herman Melville, "Letter to Nathaniel Hawthorne, June [1?] 1851," Melville.org, accessed August 30, 2021. http://www.melville.org/letter3.htm.

17. Rabbi Abraham B. Witty and Rachel J. Witty, *Exploring Jewish Tradition: A Transliterated Guide to Everyday Practice and Observance* (New York: Doubleday, 2001).

18. Josh McDowell and Sean McDowell, *Evidence That Demands A Verdict, Volume 1* (Nashville, TN: Thomas Nelson, 1979), 141–167.

19. David Guzik, "Study Guide for 2 Kings 5," Blue Letter Bible, accessed August 30, 2021, https://www.blueletterbible.org/Comm/archives/guzik_david/StudyGuide_2Ki/2Ki_5.cfm.